Real Enemies

Real Enemies

Conspiracy Theories
and American Democracy,
World War I to 9/11

KATHRYN S. OLMSTED

OXFORD
UNIVERSITY PRESS

2009

OXFORD
UNIVERSITY PRESS

Oxford University Press, Inc., publishes works that further
Oxford University's objective of excellence
in research, scholarship, and education.

Oxford   New York
Auckland   Cape Town   Dar es Salaam   Hong Kong   Karachi
Kuala Lumpur   Madrid   Melbourne   Mexico City   Nairobi
New Delhi   Shanghai   Taipei   Toronto

With offices in
Argentina   Austria   Brazil   Chile   Czech Republic   France   Greece
Guatemala   Hungary   Italy   Japan   Poland   Portugal   Singapore
South Korea   Switzerland   Thailand   Turkey   Ukraine   Vietnam

Published by Oxford University Press, Inc.
198 Madison Avenue, New York, New York 10016

www.oup.com

Oxford is a registered trademark of Oxford University Press

Library of Congress Cataloging-in-Publication Data
Olmsted, Kathryn S.
Real enemies : conspiracy theories and American democracy,
World War I to 9/11 / Kathryn S. Olmsted.
p.   cm.
Includes bibliographical references and index.
ISBN 978-0-19-518353-5
1. United States—Politics and government—20th century.
2. United States—Politics and government—2001–
3. Conspiracies—United States—History.
4. Deception—Political aspects—United States—History.
5. Democracy—United States—History.   I. Title.
E743.O46 2009
973.9—dc22   2008013789

1 3 5 7 9 8 6 4 2

Printed in the United States of America
on acid-free paper

For Bill
And for Julia, Sarah, and Isabella

Even paranoids have real
enemies.

—Delmore Schwartz

Acknowledgments

MY STUDENTS HAVE served as a valuable source of inspiration and suggestions for my research on conspiracy theories. I am especially grateful to my students in History 102M and 174D, who provided recommendations for new plots, theories, and Internet sites to explore.

Among the many librarians and archivists who assisted me along the way, I particularly appreciate the efforts of John Sherlock, Special Collections librarian at the University of California, Davis, whose dedication to collecting extremist literature proved invaluable to my research. I am also grateful to Jan Samet-O'Leary at Hood College, who opened the unprocessed Sylvia Meagher papers for me, and Clifford Mead at Oregon State University, who first suggested to me that Linus Pauling's papers might contain some insight into the costs of anticommunism.

The Committee on Research of the University of California, Davis, gave grants that made my trips to archives possible, and the Davis Humanities Institute provided a fellowship that gave me time off for writing. My editor at Oxford University Press, Susan Ferber, tightened and improved the manuscript considerably.

I am grateful to my friends and family members who helped me during the long process of researching and writing the book. May Liang, Jim Lintott, Karen Kwong, and Marty Schreiber provided friendly places to stay during my research trips. A long list of Davisites helped me immeasurably by transporting and entertaining my children. These generous friends include Bob Darragh and Belinda Martineau, Brad and Ann Shuman, Sherri Sandberg, Lynn Starr, Kristen Weeks-Norton, Ellen Dean and Tom Starbuck, Jen Ferrini, and Marti Schoen. My sisters, Ann Holmes and Patty Sand, provided unquestioning love and support.

Many of my colleagues listened to my ideas and shared their insights, including Alan Taylor, Clarence Walker, Andres Resendez, Lorena Oropeza, Scott Gartner, Bill Hagen, Mike Saler, Sally McKee, Omnia el-Shakry, Casey Sullivan, Lori Clune, and Beth Slutsky. Two talented journalists, Seymour Hersh and Gary Webb, provided great suggestions for my work.

I owe a special debt to the friends and colleagues who read drafts of the chapters. Katie Sibley read the chapter on anticommunism in a remarkably short time and provided great comments. Chuck Walker gave many constructive suggestions. Spring Warren read the manuscript with a novelist's eye for character and detail and shared her ideas with me during lovely runs and lunches. My colleagues Ari Kelman, Eric Rauchway, and Louis Warren read the entire manuscript and were wonderfully generous with their time, energy, and encouragement.

My children, Julia, Sarah, and Isabella, were unfailingly enthusiastic about the book and cheerfully tolerant of my frequent periods of distraction. My husband, Bill, listened to my ideas, edited my chapters, and gave endless support. I can never thank them enough.

Contents

Introduction, *1*

1   The Consent of the People: Presidential Secrecy and the
First World War, *13*

2   Lying Us into War? The Second Battle of Pearl Harbor, *45*

3   Masters of Deceit: Red Spies and Red Hunters in the McCarthy Era, *83*

4   The Dealey Plaza Irregulars: The JFK Assassination and the
Collapse of Trust in the 1960s, *111*

5   White House of Horrors: Nixon, Watergate, and the Secret
Government, *149*

6   Trust No One: Conspiracies and Conspiracy Theories from the
1970s to the 1990s, *173*

7   Cabal of Soccer Moms: 9/11 and the Culture of Deceit, *205*

Conclusion, *233*
Notes, *241*
Bibliography, *287*
Index, *309*

Real Enemies

Introduction

IF YOU SEARCH for "9/11 conspiracies" on the Google Video Web site, you can learn some shocking things. You can learn that there were no commercial airplanes involved in the September 11, 2001, terrorist attacks—just drones and cruise missiles. You can link to Web sites that claim that the World Trade Center towers fell because bombs were secretly placed in their air ducts, not because planes, commercial or military, manned or not, crashed into them. You can watch documentary films that allege that 9/11 was an "inside job" perpetrated by the George W. Bush administration to justify its invasions of Afghanistan and Iraq. If you look at the information on the most popular of these documentaries, called Loose Change, you will see that at least ten million people have already viewed it, and thirty-five thousand of them have written reviews, giving it an average rating of four and a half out of five stars.

These opinions may seem to belong on the fringe, but in fact millions of Americans hold them. Polls show that 36 percent of Americans think the Bush administration either planned the 9/11 attacks or knew that they were coming and did nothing to stop them. A majority of Americans between the ages of eighteen and twenty-nine believe these theories.[1]

In many ways, the popularity of 9/11 conspiracy theories is a mystery. What can explain this profound distrust of the U.S. government? Why, in one of the world's oldest constitutional democracies, would more than a third of the people believe that officials of their own government plotted to carry out terrorist attacks on U.S. soil to trick the people into war?

Here's one reason: it has happened before.

In March 1962, at the height of the cold war, the U.S. Joint Chiefs of Staff presented Secretary of Defense Robert McNamara with a plan to deceive Americans into supporting a war on Fidel Castro's Cuba. Their proposal: to conduct terrorist attacks in the United States and blame them on Castro in order to provide "pretexts" for "US military intervention in Cuba." They wanted to develop "the international image of the Cuban government as rash and irresponsible, and as an alarming and unpredictable threat to the peace of the Western Hemisphere."[2]

The military chiefs planned to explode bombs in U.S. cities, sink boatloads of Cuban refugees approaching U.S. shores, and gun down Cuban dissidents in the United States. They even suggested blowing up John Glenn's rocket during his historic flight as the first American in space. In each case, the chiefs proposed to plant fake evidence that would frame Castro as the guilty party.

In their most fantastical plan, they planned to shoot down a civilian airliner. The chiefs plotted to load an airplane with unsuspecting passengers and then secretly divert it to Eglin Air Force Base in Florida. Meanwhile, a drone painted to look like the civilian aircraft would fly across Cuba, where "Cubans" would shoot it down.[3] The chiefs were so eager for war with Castro's Cuba that they were willing to stage attacks on their own citizens to justify it.

There is no record of McNamara's response, but three days later President John Kennedy bluntly told the chairman of the chiefs that he did not intend to invade Cuba anytime soon.[4] "Operation Northwoods," as the military dubbed the plot to confuse anyone who stumbled across it, never made it off the drawing board.

Forty years later, the Northwoods plans, which had been declassified in the late 1990s, were featured in the opening scenes of *Loose Change*.[5] Somewhat improbably, these decades-old historical documents popped up in books, movies, and on Web sites popular with skeptical twentysomethings who were born some two decades after Kennedy rejected the chiefs' plans. After September 11, conspiracy theorists saw in Northwoods the "precise template for the remote control and plane-switching theory that is able to explain so many discrepant facts about 9/11—down to the final detail of feigned cluelessness."[6] Others believed that it proved U.S. officials' willingness to do anything to achieve their goals.[7]

In the wake of 9/11, the evidence of real government conspiracies from the past was used to support the conspiracy theories about the government of the present. To understand contemporary theories, we need to examine the history of *proven* government conspiracies, because for all their seeming outlandishness, the successive generations of antigovernment conspiracy theorists since World War I have at least one thing in common: when they charge that the government has plotted, lied, and covered up, they're often right.

A CONSPIRACY OCCURS when two or more people collude to abuse power or break the law. A *conspiracy theory* is a proposal about a conspiracy that may or may not be true; it has not yet been proven. Scholars refer to the tendency to see conspiracies everywhere as *conspiracism*, and this tendency long ago spread from the margins into the main body of American political culture. Government officials, even presidents, sometimes propose conspiracy theories, giving official sanction to the paranoid interpretation of history.

Americans have a special relationship to conspiracy theory. Because immigrants bring a new mix of religions and ethnicities and histories to their land, Americans have worried that their country is especially open— and vulnerable—to alien subversion.[8] Over the past two hundred years, frightened Americans have targeted Catholics, Masons, Mormons, and Jews because these native groups were allegedly guided by the instructions of an alien power. The historian Richard Hofstadter argued that there was a "paranoid style" in American politics, prompted in part by Americans' need to define themselves by casting out the "un-Americans."[9]

Throughout the nation's history, many Americans have particularly feared that their federal government would fall victim to one of these conspiracies—or become a tool of conspirators. As the historian David Brion Davis has said, "Americans have been curiously obsessed with the contingency of their experiment with freedom."[10] Ever since the nation's founding, they have worried that the great instrument of the people's will would be turned against them. The philosophers of early America knew their ancient history and their Shakespeare, and they were always looking over their shoulder for potential Caesars. From the Illuminati scare of the late eighteenth century to rumors of a Catholic revolution in the nineteenth century, Americans feared that alien forces aimed to take over their government.

This book argues that American conspiracy theories underwent a fundamental transformation in the twentieth century. No longer were conspiracy theorists chiefly concerned that alien forces were plotting to capture the federal government; instead, they proposed that the federal government itself *was* the conspirator. They feared the subversive potential of the swelling, secretive bureaucracies of the proto–national security state. In effect, the institutionalized secrecy of the modern U.S. government inspired a new type of conspiracy theories. These theories argued that government officials lied to citizens, dragged the peaceable American people into foolish wars, and then spied on and oppressed the opponents of war.

Such portrayals were born out of a time when the federal government first grew powerful enough to accomplish these nefarious goals. This book, therefore, traces the fear of conspiracies within the U.S. federal government from the birth of the modern state in World War I to the current war on terror.

World War I was a watershed in the development of the U.S. government: it marked the moment when the government gained the power to carry out real conspiracies against its citizens—and when it began to use that power. During the conflict, the U.S. federal government drafted millions of its citizens, commandeered factories and railroads, and spied on and imprisoned dissidents. Through the newly established central bank, the president could control the ebb and flow of American money across the oceans to belligerent countries. The government criminalized dissent with the Espionage and Sedition Acts and encouraged Justice Department agents such as the young J. Edgar Hoover to hound antiwar radicals.[11] Sinister forces in charge of the government could do a lot more damage in 1918 than they could have done just a few years earlier; in fact, in the view of some conspiracists, the state *was* the sinister force.

The powers of the state continued to grow throughout the twentieth century, especially after the cold war began. The fear of communist plots inspired the U.S. government to adopt the conspiratorial tactics of its enemy. Determined to combat this international communist conspiracy, the CIA teamed up with the mafia on murder plots, the FBI spied on civil rights leaders who it feared were secret communists, and President Richard Nixon took governing conspiracies to a new level by conspiring to use state power to punish his personal enemies, whom he saw as the nation's enemies. Paradoxically, the end of the cold war did not ease these worries but instead prompted many Americans to redirect their fears from the Soviets to their own government. This suspicion of the government continued to climb after 9/11, as President Bush's attempts to centralize power in the presidency and his administration's deceptions about the Iraq war led many Americans to believe him capable of the worst crimes imaginable.

Most conspiracy theories about the U.S. government focus on wartime decision making or tragic national events. Theorists have tried to explain what they saw as the inexplicable: why the U.S. started or joined a war, or why it suffered a catastrophe or sudden reversal. They saw the war decisions as historical mysteries that American citizens needed to solve. Why, they wondered, did the United States join the Great War in 1917, after a majority of voters had reelected President Woodrow Wilson partly because he kept the country out of war? Why, in 1941, was the nation so woefully unprepared for the Japanese attack on Pearl Harbor? Could the president have known the attack was coming—and decided to allow it to take place for his own diabolical reasons? Why did the United States, for a brief time the world's only nuclear superpower, win World War II but then lose its atomic monopoly? Why, in 1963, could an American communist gun down the president in the middle of a major city in broad daylight? And, more recently, how could a handful of Arabs destroy the World Trade Center towers and crash a plane into the Pentagon?

In all of these cases, government officials took the conspiracy theory seriously enough to investigate it. Sometimes the official storytellers rejected a conspiracy, as they did in the Kennedy assassination; sometimes they suggested a conspiracy, as when Bush administration officials implied that Iraq secretly gave the 9/11 terrorists the help they needed to carry out their attacks. When government officials proposed a conspiracy, they became conspiracy theorists.

The officials also became storytellers. Social scientists argue that by constructing narratives, we make sense of other people's motives and behaviors; we can also begin to understand and cope with our own feelings and actions.[12] "We tell ourselves stories in order to live," the essayist Joan

Didion has said.[13] Conspiracy theories are easy ways of telling complicated stories. Official conspiracy theorists tell one story about an event; alternative conspiracy theorists doubt the stories told by public officials, and then, to make sense of the world, they tell their own.

The history of conspiracy theories is often the story of the struggle over the power to control the public's perception of an event. Government officials try to control this narrative. President Wilson proclaimed that he was fighting a war to make the world safe for democracy; President Franklin Roosevelt insisted that the U.S. government had received no warning of an imminent Japanese attack on December 7, 1941. Conspiracy theorists challenge this official story, proposing counternarratives to the government's history of an event.

Early in the twentieth century, ordinary citizens found it difficult to distribute their alternative histories to a wide audience. Jacob Abrams, an anarchist who believed in a capitalists' conspiracy behind U.S. intervention in the Russian revolution, used a small printing press to publish his own antiwar leaflets and urged his friends to toss them from the third floor of a Manhattan building onto the heads of surprised pedestrians. The government found the pamphlets to be seditious and put Abrams and his comrades in prison for their efforts.[14]

In the first half of the twentieth century, American elites—men with cultural authority and access to the media—had more success in spreading their theories. Skeptical reporters wrote stories in newspapers opposed to the administration in power; revisionist historians found small presses willing to publish their work. Most significantly, members of Congress could launch an official investigation of a conspiracy theory, usually when different parties controlled Congress and the presidency. Republican Senator Joseph McCarthy squared off against Democratic President Harry Truman; Democratic Senator Frank Church challenged Republican President Gerald Ford. Congressional investigators used their subpoena power to pry loose documents from a secretive White House. In these and other cases, members of Congress investigated the alleged misdeeds of the president, while the president countered that the investigators were endangering the nation's security by revealing its secrets. The two-party system, combined with the democratic checks and balances created by the Constitution, produced a dynamic that fed the conspiracist imagination, which sought to explain real or purported failures of American democracy.

Although elites continued to confront the president throughout the twentieth century, by the 1960s ordinary citizens gained more power to challenge the secret actions of the national security state. With the passage of the Freedom of Information Act in 1966, all Americans were now empowered to examine previously classified government documents—the raw materials of history—and construct their own alternative stories of events. In effect, information became more democratized, though officials still blacked out huge sections of documents and refused to let go of others altogether. This governmental ambivalence about freedom of information—releasing, say, a Northwoods memo, but keeping other documents secret—sometimes had the effect of frightening citizens rather than reassuring them.

Changes in the media also led to the dispersion of cultural authority to challenge the government's narrative. Though fewer owners controlled newspapers and radio and television networks, conspiracy theorists found other media to spread their theories. Researchers of the John F. Kennedy assassination, for example, used grassroots citizen groups, guerrilla theater troupes, and even pornographic magazines to tell other Americans about their theory that U.S. government officials—perhaps even the current president—had conspired to kill President Kennedy. Hollywood was a powerful disseminator of conspiracy theories. Its community included *JFK* director Oliver Stone and *X-Files* writer/producer Chris Carter, who could construct powerful visual arguments and expose millions to their counter-narratives. The Internet further leveled the playing field for proponents of alternative conspiracy theories. Anyone in the world could broadcast a personal theory to a potential audience of billions and form a virtual community with fellow skeptics. The Internet provided the Jacob Abramses of the twenty-first century with the tallest building in the world.

This book traces successive generations of these modern skeptics of the government. It introduces senators from the heartland who believed that Wall Street financiers had connived with treacherous agents in the White House to push an unwilling country into World War I. It recovers the story of the World War II admiral who believed that he had been scapegoated by an interventionist president who knew much more about the Japanese attack at Pearl Harbor than he was willing to say. It reconstructs the atmosphere of fear in the country after the United States won World War II but lost its monopoly on the bomb.

These stories of conspiracy often had surprising consequences. A Nobel Prize–winning scientist may have missed out on making his most important discovery because the conspiracy theorists at the FBI believed he threatened national security. This scientist then turned his genius to proving that other secret government agents had conspired to kill the president he believed was working for peace. A senator from the rural West, outraged over CIA domestic spying, was driven to try to expose the government's lies of the past. This senator was the ultimate liberal—a proud believer in the tenet that a strong government could help its least advantaged citizens—yet his investigations inadvertently fueled antigovernment anger by teaching millions of Americans to despise and distrust their elected officials.

The last two chapters introduce the swashbuckling journalist who dared to charge that the CIA allowed some of its anticommunist allies to bring drugs into the United States—and his dismissive colleagues in the press who forced him to pay a stiff price. Finally, these chapters link this history to the citizens of today who are trying to make sense of the war in Iraq, sometimes by discerning a pattern of treason behind official failures and deceptions.

My goal is not to try to prove or disprove the conspiracy theories discussed in this book. Some are impossible to prove; others have been effectively rebutted by experts.[15] Instead, I examine why so many Americans believe that their government conspires against them, why more people believe this over time, and how real conspiracies by government officials have sparked these conspiracy theories about the government.

REAL ENEMIES MAKES three arguments about why modern Americans began to suspect their government of plotting against them. First, as the government grew, it gained the power to conspire against its citizens, and it soon began exercising that power. By the height of the cold war, government agents had consorted with mobsters to kill a foreign leader, dropped hallucinogenic drugs into the drinks of unsuspecting Americans in random bars, and considered launching fake terrorist attacks on Americans in the United States. Public officials had denied potentially life-saving treatment to African American men in medical experiments, sold arms to terrorists in return for American hostages, and faked documents to frame past presidents for crimes they had not committed. These officials justified their conspiracies as a response to conspiracies supposedly plotted by un-American forces. "We're up against an enemy, a conspiracy," Richard Nixon told his aides once, as he devised one of his own plots.[16] Later, as industrious congressmen and journalists revealed these actual conspiracies by the government, many Americans came to believe that the most outrageous conspiracy theories about the government could be plausible.

Second, many Americans developed alternative conspiracy theories in response to the official conspiracy theories proposed by the government. Government agents in the modern era often found it convenient to promote some officially sanctioned conspiracy theories. They said that un-American forces were working with the Germans (or the communists, or the terrorists) and that the U.S. government needed to take on more powers to control these domestic enemies.

In other words, government officials promoted a certain conspiracist style—a deep, pervasive fear of hidden plotters—but they wanted to maintain the power to construct these conspiracy theories themselves and quash those that did not serve official interests. "Let us never tolerate outrageous conspiracy theories concerning the attacks of September the 11th," President Bush said on November 10, 2001, shortly before his own administration began spreading outrageous conspiracy theories concerning September 11 and Saddam Hussein.[17] This book examines the relationship between official conspiracy theories (bin Laden plotted with Saddam) and unofficial or alternative conspiracy theories (bin Laden plotted with, say, Dick Cheney).

Finally, the government's efforts to spy on and harass dissenters convinced many Americans that the government was out to get them. There were so many U.S. agents charged with stopping "sedition" in 1918 that they tripped over one another during their investigations. One former agent recalled that he would sometimes interview a suspect in a sedition case during World War I only to find that "six or seven other government agencies had [already] been around to interview the party about the same matter."[18] In 1936, President Roosevelt formally gave the Federal Bureau of Investigation the power to monitor "subversive activities" in the United States in peacetime, and the FBI began to add agents and new powers. During the Roosevelt years, from 1933 to 1945, the FBI's budget grew from $2.7 million to $45 million, and the number of special agents jumped from 266 to some 5,000.[19]

During the cold war, the FBI started its domestic covert action programs, known by the acronym COINTELPRO, in which agents infiltrated dissident groups and eventually tried to "expose, disrupt, misdirect, discredit, or otherwise neutralize" them.[20] The FBI did not just monitor these individuals, but tried to break up their marriages, "seed mistrust, sow misinformation," and provoke them to commit crimes so that they could be arrested.[21] The FBI originally directed this program at American communists, but it soon expanded its definition of communism. By 1960, when the Communist Party counted about five thousand members in the United States, the bureau maintained more than eighty times that number of files on "subversive" Americans at its headquarters, and FBI field offices around the country collected even more.[22]

Not surprisingly, these surveillance and harassment programs aggravated the antigovernment fears of many Americans. Strangely enough, these fears also served the bureau's purposes. One purpose of COINTELPRO, according to an official memo, was to "enhance the paranoia endemic in [dissident] circles" and convince activists that "there is an FBI agent behind every mailbox."[23] The agents believed that paranoid, divided dissident groups were easier to handle than purposeful, united dissident groups. In other words, the FBI conspired to create fear of conspiracy. And it succeeded. When the dissenters learned of these official government programs to deny them their First Amendment rights, they felt that their long-time fears had been vindicated. As the poet Delmore Schwartz has said, even paranoids have real enemies.[24]

These government actions—the official conspiracies, the official conspiracy theories, and the attempts to quash alternative conspiracy theories—fueled the fears of dissenters. Government officials tried to control how the public interpreted events, sometimes lied about these events, and spied on and harassed those citizens who suggested different interpretations. Because of the countervailing tradition of openness in the U.S. government, some reporters and whistleblowers eventually revealed these conspiracies and domestic spying programs for all to see. But instead of being reassured by the process of revelation, skeptics were outraged—and afraid of what could come. They charged that other, as yet undiscovered secrets lay within the government's darkest vaults.

Over four decades ago, Richard Hofstadter noted that conspiracy theorists seem to follow the rules of logic until they suddenly make the "big leap from the undeniable to the unbelievable."[25] Writing in the 1960s, he never could have imagined how the revelation of the real government conspiracies after Watergate and Iran-contra could terrify so many Americans into making that jump. Once they learned bizarre details of real government conspiracies in the 1970s and 1980s, the critics leaped over the last remaining limits on their imaginations. By the dawn of the new millennium, some believed that the government encouraged aliens to abduct and molest them, or that it was responsible for the spread of illegal drugs, or that government officials blew up the World Trade Center towers. And some of them believed all of those things at once.

WHO BELIEVES THESE alternative conspiracy theories? The tendency to believe in conspiracy theories transcends race, class, and even political ideology. Black separatists often embrace conspiracy theories, and so do white supremacists. Right-wingers are receptive to conspiracy theories, but so, too, are leftists.[26] Men love conspiracy theories, but women aren't immune to their charms. Before the 1960s, most leading conspiracy theorists were men, but women began to play significant roles as conspiracism became democratized with the John Kennedy assassination. Yet no one admits to being a conspiracy theorist. As the filmmaker Michael Moore has said, "I'm not into conspiracy theories, except the ones that are true or involve dentists."[27]

Unlike Hofstadter, I do not try to psychoanalyze these theorists and determine which elements in American culture and history led them to become "paranoid." I see these antigovernment conspiracy theories as an impulse, as an understandable response to conspiratorial government rhetoric and actions. But though the impulse behind conspiracy theories is often understandable, that does not mean that the conspiracy theories themselves are logical or free from internal contradictions. Conspiracists come to believe in their theories the way zealots believe in their religion: nothing can change their mind. When new evidence surfaces, or when experts insist that, say, towers *can* collapse if airplanes hit them and fires burn hot enough, the conspiracy theorists dismiss the experts as blinded by their own preconceptions at best, or part of the conspiracy at worst.

Conspiracy theorists are not only rigid, but are also at times susceptible to the arguments of charlatans who sense an opportunity to profit from fear of conspiracy. A Jim Garrison, the New Orleans district attorney who prosecuted a Louisiana businessman for plotting to kill John Kennedy, or a Joseph McCarthy, the demagogue who gave his name to an era, can sometimes manipulate their fears with surprising effectiveness and tragic results.

But most of the ordinary conspiracy theorists in these pages were not motivated by personal gain. On the contrary, most of them believed, in all sincerity, that their country faced an imminent and existential threat. They believed that they needed to act, and act quickly, to save America. The republic was always in peril, and they, personally, were the ones to save it.

These conspiracy theorists were authentic patriots, convinced that they needed to do what they did for the sake of the country. The official conspiracy theorists always justified their surveillance by linking domestic dissidents with foreign plotters. They said that they needed to spy on these citizens because these Americans took their orders from the nation's enemies. The dissidents were *un-American.*

The dissidents, on the other hand, maintained that *they* were the true patriots who were defending their country from un-American forces. From those who decried a war fought on the "command of gold" in 1917 to the anti-Bush activists of the twenty-first century, they believed that their country would perish without their efforts to find the Truth. "I wouldn't be a patriot if I didn't try to prove the government's story is preposterous," said Barbara Honegger, a former Reagan administration official and a member of the 9/11 Truth movement.[28] This is the story of the patriots in the government and the patriots who distrust the government, and how they have combined to create an escalating spiral of fear.

1

The Consent of the People:
Presidential Secrecy and the
First World War

IN JUNE 1918, federal agents invaded the plant of a small Washington, D.C., publisher, searching for the printing plates for a book that promoted "seditious" ideas. *Why Your Country Is at War and What Happens to You After the War* charged that a cabal of bankers and public officials had manipulated the country into joining the Great War in Europe. The author, a former Congressman from Minnesota named Charles A. Lindbergh Sr., claimed that he had discovered the real truth about the war. "I believe that I have proved," he argued, "that a certain 'inner circle,' without official authority and for selfish purposes, adroitly maneuvered things to ... make it practically certain that some of the belligerents would violate our international rights and bring us to war with them."[1]

In the federal government's view, those words endangered the republic. On the orders of the attorney general of the United States, A. Mitchell Palmer, the government agents found the plates and smashed them. For good measure, they also destroyed the plates for Lindbergh's earlier book, published in 1913, which decried the subversion of the republic by the "money trust."[2]

While the content of Lindbergh's books reflected the demonology of the nineteenth century—the "money sharks" and the Catholics—the treatment they received foreshadowed the defining villain of the twentieth. The destruction of Congressman Lindbergh's books marked a turning point in the development of the U.S. federal government and of conspiracy theories about the government. When Lindbergh published his first book about the "money power" conspiracy that supposedly controlled the country, the federal government had neither the budget nor the inclination to view him as anything but a crank. The total federal budget was less than $1 billion. The fledgling federal police force, the Bureau of Investigation, had fewer than one hundred agents and no responsibility for suppressing dissent. And most American conspiracy theorists did not concern themselves with government crimes. Like Lindbergh, they worried about the money power or the Jews or the Catholics or the Masons, but not the government. It simply was not big or strong enough to merit their fear.

But just five years later, in 1918, the federal government controlled an almost $13 billion budget, employed more than eight hundred thousand civilian workers, and included several agencies charged with countering subversion.[3] Under the Sedition Act of 1918, public officials gained the power to arrest anyone who uttered or printed any "disloyal, profane, scurrilous, contemptuous, or abusive language" about the government—anyone who dissented, in other words, from the war effort. Empowered by the Sedition Act and its predecessor, the Espionage Act, government officials also destroyed books that challenged the official explanations for entering the war. In the process, these federal agents elevated Charles Lindbergh from harmless critic to Enemy of the State.

As the government defined conspiracy theorists like Lindbergh as the enemy, conspiracy theorists responded by redefining their enemy. Some Americans had worried for decades that malign forces might take over the government. Now, with the birth of the modern state, they worried that the government itself might be the most dangerous force of all.

The government could draft men to fight an unpopular war, imprison its most vocal opponents, and suppress the writings of dissidents. The locus of power had begun to shift, and American fears shifted along with it. Conspiracy theorists like Lindbergh now had some real enemies to worry about.

For the next twenty years, Americans would continue to debate the reasons for their nation's participation in the Great War and argue over whether it was fought for freedom or gold, for self-determination or England, for democracy or the narrow interests of a selfish inner circle.

For the rest of the twentieth century and into the next, they would continue to challenge, and to fear, the proto–national security state born of the war. In the end, World War I skeptics came to believe that it was the U.S. state itself—the expansive, militarized, twentieth-century state that emerged from the war—that truly imperiled the American republic.

WHEN THEY BEGAN examining the official government explanations of the Great War, many conspiracy theorists found it strange that Americans had marched off to join a European war in 1917. After all, when the war exploded across Europe back in 1914, almost no one, not even the bellicose Theodore Roosevelt, thought that the United States should fight.[4] President Woodrow Wilson proclaimed that the conflict was "one with which we have nothing to do, whose causes cannot touch us."[5] To many Americans at the time, the war seemed to provide proof of the folly and destructiveness of the Old World and the superiority of the New. As the president explained, future generations would see the United States as "blessed among the nations" because it worked for peace and stayed above the fray.[6] In his ideal world, Americans were "too proud to fight" the wars of Europe.[7]

But if the United States was too proud to fight in the war, it was not too proud to trade with both sides. Indeed, in the newly globalized world of the early twentieth century, the U.S. economy depended on trade with other industrialized nations for continued growth. The world had become so interconnected that "there was hardly a village or town anywhere on the globe whose prices were not influenced by distant foreign markets," according to historians of globalization. In this era of the "first great globalization boom," American wages, commodity prices, and infrastructure expansion—in sum, the health of the economy as a whole—were determined by the influx of foreign labor and capital.[8]

In theory, U.S. policy allowed both sides in the war to buy arms and food and manufactured goods from American companies. But the British blockade of Germany prevented American ships from trading with the Central Powers, and soon the "neutral" United States found itself effectively aligned with the Triple Entente of Britain, France, and Russia. This was especially true after late summer 1915, when Wilson quietly lifted restrictions on loaning money to countries at war. From 1915 to 1917, U.S. banks loaned $2.5 billion to the Entente, but less than one-tenth that amount to the Central Powers. By 1916, the United States was selling more than $3 billion in goods every year to Britain and France, but doing only $1 million a year in business with Austria-Hungary and Germany.[9]

This growing economic interest in an Allied victory was reinforced by a sentimental one: many American elites greatly admired the English. Top government officials, key bankers in New York, and even the president himself seemed from the start to hope secretly for a British victory, despite their officially neutral rhetoric.[10] The British claims of German atrocities in Belgium, later shown to be greatly exaggerated, deeply affected the president, whose eyes filled with tears when he discussed them with the British ambassador.[11] Most Wall Street banks, including the House of Morgan, which served as the British purchasing agent during the war, desperately wanted the Allies to win. "Our firm had never for one moment been neutral; we didn't know how to be," said Morgan's Thomas Lamont after the war. "From the very start we did everything we could to contribute to the cause of the Allies."[12]

As American ships transported arms and goods to the Allies, the United States was sucked into the vortex of the conflict. To combat the blockade, the Germans began to sink ships headed to the ports of their enemies, including passenger liners that might be carrying weapons. In 1915, a German submarine sank the luxury liner *Lusitania*, killing more than one thousand passengers, including 128 Americans. The United States vigorously protested the sinking—too vigorously for Secretary of State William Jennings Bryan, who quit over what he regarded as President Wilson's provocative policies. The Germans ultimately promised to be more judicious about their targets, and the United States avoided joining the war for two more years. In 1916, Wilson ran for reelection with the slogan "He Kept Us Out of War."

But in the winter of 1917, as the Germans made an all-out push for victory, the U-boats renewed their program of unrestricted submarine warfare. While the Wilson administration struggled to decide how to respond to the attacks on American ships, German Foreign Minister Alfred Zimmermann sent a coded telegram to Mexico urging the revolutionary government there to consider an alliance with Germany in exchange for a huge chunk of the southwestern United States. When the British intercepted and decrypted the Zimmermann telegram and triumphantly presented it to U.S. officials, Wilson decided that the time had come for the United States to enter the conflict.

But many Americans still agreed with the president's original view, that the United States should never descend to the European level of barbarism.

When the president asked Congress to pass a law giving him the power to arm American merchant ships against submarines, a group of eight senators filibustered the bill to death in a marathon twenty-six-hour floor session. Wilson remarked angrily that a "little group of willful men" had hijacked U.S. foreign policy.[13] The senators argued that they were defending the Constitution against executive tyranny. "Under this bill the President can do anything; his power is absolutely limitless," said Senator George Norris of Nebraska. "This, in effect, is an amendment of the Constitution, an illegal amendment. We are abdicating, we are surrendering our authority."[14] Norris refused to surrender his authority, but Wilson took it anyway. The president declared that the Constitution already gave him the power to arm the ships, and he quickly issued orders allowing American gun crews to shoot German submarines on sight in war zones.[15]

In April 1917, Wilson took the next step and asked Congress to declare war. Some antiwar senators continued to insist that bankers and industrialists with investments in Britain were forcing the United States into a pointless bloodbath. Using a phrase that later became famous, Senator Norris eloquently explained his vote against intervention. "We are going into war upon the command of gold," he said. "I feel that we are about to put the dollar sign upon the American flag."[16] Norris lost his battle in 1917, but his words would be revived and revered two decades later.

The six senators and fifty representatives who voted against the war represented a substantial minority of Americans who opposed intervention and distrusted the Wilson administration from the start. Some of these Americans opposed the war because they had relatives in Germany or their ancestors had come from Germany, or because they deplored the brutality of the British suppression of the Irish revolution.

Many antiwar Americans, though, saw the conflict through the lens of populism. The People's Party of the 1890s had mobilized the farmers of the South and Midwest to fight the predatory practices of eastern and British railroads and banks. At times, the Populists had used conspiracist language—sometimes overtly anti-Semitic or Anglophobic—to attack the "secret cabals of the international gold ring."[17] Many midwesterners and southerners saw U.S. military intervention as yet another case where the government listened to the command of gold, not the needs of the people.[18]

Once the United States entered the war, the government embarked on a massive campaign to manufacture support and eradicate dissent. Just as Senator Norris had feared, the presidency took on expansive powers as executive agencies proliferated. The executive branch gained the authority to control the newspapers, take over the railroads, set wages, and even move the hands of the clock with the beginning of Daylight Saving Time. Above all, with the first comprehensive draft in U.S. history, the government secured the power to pluck reluctant farmers out of their cornfields and dispatch them to the killing fields of France. No wonder the antiwar senators trembled: the traditionally small federal government was extending its reach into the lives of every American.

President Wilson assured Americans that the war was worth all their sacrifices: it was no mean struggle for "conquest and domination," but a crusade to "make the world safe for democracy." In his Fourteen Points he laid out the principled aims for this "culminating and final war for human liberty," including self-determination and the end of secret deals between imperialistic nations. In the postwar world, there would be "open covenants of peace, openly arrived at," which guaranteed all people justice, equality, liberty, and safety. "The day of conquest and aggrandizement is gone by; so is also the day of secret covenants entered into in the interest of particular governments," he pledged. He would not ask Americans "to continue this tragical and appalling outpouring of blood and treasure" for anything less.[19]

For the Americans who questioned the president's idealistic rhetoric, the Wilson administration launched an unprecedented propaganda effort to convince them of the justice of the Allied cause and of the evils of both the "Hun" abroad and war resisters at home. The director of the propaganda campaign, George Creel, saw it as his duty to "bring home the truths of this great war to every man, woman, and child in the United States, so that they might understand that it was a just war, a holy war, and a war in self-defense."[20] Americans encountered government posters in subways and on street corners, government advertisements in their magazines, and government pamphlets in their post offices and schools.

These posters and pamphlets had one purpose: to spread the official conspiracy theory set forth by the Wilson administration. According to this theory, the Germans started the war as part of a plot to conquer innocent nations. The "military masters" of Germany, Wilson said, planned to "throw a belt of German military power and political control across the very center of Europe and beyond the Mediterranean into the heart of

Asia." The German Empire was a "sinister power" that had "stretched its ugly talons out and drawn blood from us."[21]

Even worse, this "sinister power" received help from people within the United States, according to the official conspiracy theorists. Wilson proclaimed that Germany "filled our unsuspecting communities and even our offices of government with spies and set criminal intrigues everywhere afoot against our national unity of counsel, our peace within and without, our industries and our commerce."[22] In Wilson's view, some naturalized Americans had poured the "poison of disloyalty" into the nation's arteries.[23] The administration knew how to respond to these traitors. "If there should be disloyalty," the president said as the nation entered the war, "it will be dealt with with a firm hand of stern repression."[24]

This hand of repression came down hard on American dissidents. With the Espionage and Sedition Acts, the U.S. government outlawed criticism of the government, the president, and the war effort, thus effectively criminalizing opposition to the war. When Jacob Abrams printed antiwar leaflets and his friends tossed them from a Manhattan building, government officials arrested them for sedition. In their pamphlets, the radicals charged that President Wilson had "hypnotized the people of America to such an extent that they do not see his hypocrisy."[25] For their criticism of their government, they received prison terms and a place in history as defendants in a famous Supreme Court case, *Abrams v. United States*. Despite an eloquent dissent by Justice Oliver Wendell Holmes, the Court upheld their convictions in 1919. The government also charged hundreds of other war opponents with sedition: the socialist leader Eugene V. Debs went to jail for saying the war was being fought by the poor for the rich; another man was indicted for proclaiming that the war was "a Morgan war and not a war of the people."[26] Twenty years later, millions of Americans would agree with that statement, but in 1918 public support for it could land one in prison.

At the Department of Justice, a young former librarian named J. Edgar Hoover began tracking enemy aliens and dissenters. Hoover started by targeting German Americans but moved smoothly to surveillance and harassment of communists after the war. In 1919, he would set up an index card system that catalogued every suspected subversive person, group, and publication in the country; by 1921, he had 450,000 cards.[27] Hoover and his domestic surveillance system would continue to haunt American dissidents for over five decades.

The expanding security state worked in tandem with extralegal societies of superpatriots to keep dissenters in line. As Attorney General Thomas W. Gregory explained, antiwar Americans should ask God for mercy, "for they need expect none from an outraged people and an avenging Government."[28] Taught by their government that opposition to the war was both illegal and immoral, many pro-war Americans turned with fury on dissenters.

Two of the most extreme examples of vigilantism occurred in Minnesota and Montana. When former congressman Charles Lindbergh ran for governor of Minnesota in 1918, his supporters were shocked by the vehemence and the violence of the campaign against him. During his repeated attempts to deliver an antiwar message to throngs of potential voters, frenzied mobs pelted him with eggs and vegetables and drowned his speeches in boos and jeers. As his teenage son, also named Charles, waited anxiously by the family car to drive his father to the next campaign stop, vigilantes hanged the candidate in effigy, turned fire hoses on his supporters, and shot at him as he leaped into his car and sped away. On one occasion, his campaign was forced to retreat to Iowa, which, Congressman Lindbergh said, "is still part of the United States and where free speech still prevails."[29]

Lindbergh lost the election, but at least he escaped with his life. Other opponents of the war were not so lucky. In wartime Montana, some citizens were infuriated when the federal prosecutor there refused to bring charges of espionage against the anarchist leader Frank Little, who had criticized the government and the war effort. The prosecutor, a young lawyer named Burton K. Wheeler, insisted that Little's antiwar speeches were not against the law, however objectionable the local community found them.

Montanans were even more anxious, intolerant, and polarized than Minnesotans. The powerful mining companies that controlled politics in the state supported the war, but thousands of local immigrant workers, who were subject to the draft even though they were not yet citizens, opposed both the war and the copper companies' brutal union busting. The strength of opposition to the war caused some citizens to imagine German conspiracies in Montana, six thousand miles from the fighting. Residents reported seeing German spies on the streets of Helena, bomb-toting German saboteurs deep in the mines, German wireless communication stations high in the Bitterroot Mountains, and spectral German "airships" in the big Montana sky.[30]

After draft riots rocked Butte, pro-war Montanans organized vigilante groups to force dissenters to buy war bonds and perform public acts of patriotism such as kissing the flag. Resisters were tarred and feathered, beaten, and lynched. The day after Wheeler's decision not to bring charges against Frank Little, six men dragged the union leader from his bed and hanged him from a railroad trestle.[31]

The vice president of the United States praised the lynch mob—the hanging had a "salutary effect," Thomas Marshall proclaimed—but Wheeler learned a different lesson. Like Congressman Lindbergh and his son, Wheeler had seen firsthand that war hysteria could cause Americans to become "unpatriotic, lawless, and inhuman."[32] Fearing a repeat of the wartime hysteria, Wheeler and Charles Lindbergh Jr. would fight bitterly against U.S. intervention in the next world war.

The opponents of vigilantism during the Great War were shocked to discover that Americans were capable of perpetrating these outrages against civil liberties and human life. But one aspect of the vigilantism outraged these nascent civil libertarians more than anything else: the federal government itself, they believed, had deliberately fanned the flames of irrational fear and thereby encouraged the violence.

The government's responsibility for this assault on constitutional rights was horrifying to many Americans. As the historian Charles Beard later wrote, "Never before had American citizens realized how thoroughly, how irresistibly a modern government could impose its ideas upon the whole nation and, under a barrage of publicity, stifle dissent with declarations, assertions, official versions, and reiteration."[33] Americans realized that their government could not only suppress dissent: it could also control the terms of debate.

The Wilson administration had set forth a narrative of the war, featuring sinister Germans, democratic war aims, and noble allies. It had suppressed, censored, spied on, and jailed anyone who attempted to present a different story about the war. Over the next decade, some citizens' anger at the government's manipulation of public opinion slowly evolved into profound doubt about the government's truthfulness and trustworthiness. As more Americans grew suspicious of the government's official history of the conflict, they resolved to find the "real reasons" for U.S. intervention and to expose the lies and evasions of wartime leaders.

LIKE MANY OF HIS generation of historians, the leading historical revisionist of the Great War began his career as a propagandist for the U.S. government. Harry Elmer Barnes, who received his Ph.D. from Columbia University in 1918, had been among the many scholars who volunteered to write anti-German propaganda for the government and for pro-war organizations.[34] These historians produced syllabi for schools, explanatory pamphlets, and a "war cyclopedia" that contained cross-referenced entries such as "rumors, malicious and disloyal" and "German government, bad faith of."[35] Barnes was among the most enthusiastic of these propagandists, searching German history for examples of the evils of German society and the virtues of the Allied cause.[36]

Two years after the end of the war, Barnes read a disturbing article in the *American Historical Review* by Professor Sidney Fay. The essay, titled "New Light on the Origins of the World War," questioned whether the Germans deserved the blame for the war. As he devoured Fay's article, Barnes discovered that his propaganda articles had been wrong. He learned that the Germans were not directly responsible for "all the loss and damage" of the war, as the Versailles Treaty had claimed. The German leaders were at times clumsy or stupid, but they were not the insidious Huns of Allied propaganda.[37]

Barnes soon exchanged one set of villains for another. If the Germans were not criminals plotting war, then perhaps the *real* criminals had escaped detection. Determined to find the true conspirators behind U.S. entry into what he saw as a pointless war, Barnes sparked a wave of revisionism on the causes of U.S. intervention. Reviving the arguments of the peace movement of 1917, he helped to mold a generation of alienated intellectuals and activists who found deception, incompetence, and conspiracy in the foreign policy of Woodrow Wilson's administration.

Revisionist historians like Barnes were able to write their alternative histories of the war thanks to the revolutionaries in Russia, who had thrown open the doors of the czar's secret archives. Giddy with power and determined to prove Lenin right, the triumphant revolutionaries allowed Western scholars to mine their archives for copies of the secret treaties of the Allies. These treaties outlined the Allies' plans for gobbling up parts of Eastern Europe after the war. The Moscow papers showed that the British and French were at least partly guilty of the charge that their war aims were based on selfishness and greed.

Yet Wilson had claimed that the war was fought for democracy, self-determination, and open covenants. To Barnes, Wilson's grand statements were "the grossest form of compensatory, if partially sub-conscious, hypocrisy to assuage him for his unpleasant knowledge of the Secret Treaties."[38] The president had lied to him, Barnes believed, and had manipulated him and his fellow historians into producing provably false and misleading propaganda.

Regretting his part in helping the government create the myth of the "black devilishness of the Central Powers and the lamb-like innocence of the Entente," Barnes and other disillusioned propagandists set out to revise the world's understanding of the causes of the war.[39] A torrent of books and articles challenged earlier interpretations.[40] Every year, new books expanded on the revisionists' arguments: Austria-Hungary was justified in declaring war on Serbia; the Germans had not committed atrocities in Belgium; if any one nation deserved blame for the war, it was Russia, not Germany or Austria-Hungary.

As the revisionists examined German guilt, they began to question the truthfulness of the U.S. government. If in fact the Germans had not started the war and committed war crimes, they reasoned, then the United States had no reason to wage war against them. By the mid-1920s, Americans were publishing a flood of revisionist writings on U.S. entry into the war. Barnes's *Genesis of the World War* and *In Quest of Truth and Justice*, Frederick Bausman's *Facing Europe*, and C. Hartley Grattan's *Why We Fought* sought to discover why the United States had made what these writers saw as a colossal mistake. These historians all posed the same question: Why, given initial resistance to joining the war, had the people of the United States been pushed into what Barnes called an "unmitigated disaster"?[41]

The earliest revisionist works posited three answers, all of which emphasized the power of wicked individuals. First, they revived the arguments of Norris, Lindbergh, and the Populists to decry the influence of a few powerful bankers and industrialists over U.S. policy. Norris, they decided, was right: the war *had* been fought on the "command of gold." Barnes summed up this view in 1924: "We did not actually go into the World War to protect ourselves from imminent German invasion, or to make the world safe for democracy, but to protect our investment in Allied bonds."[42] The United States, wrote John Kenneth Turner in his 1922 book *Shall It Be Again?*

"is a financial oligarchy," with the president a mere servant of the money power.[43] The "money power," of course, referred to bankers, but sometimes the revisionists conflated "the bankers" with "big business." According to this argument, the arms makers, particularly the Du Pont family, and the big bankers, particularly the House of Morgan, worked together to ensure that their demand for profits trumped the American people's innate desire for peace.

Second, the revisionists blamed a handful of English officials for "poisoning" American public opinion. In their view, some wily English propagandists had cleverly prepared the United States for the war by spreading a distorted view of German actions. The propagandists themselves provided evidence for this argument by bragging about their enormous influence. Sir Gilbert Parker, the chief British propagandist in the United States, boasted in a *Harper's* article in 1918 that his prewar activities had been "very extensive" and hugely successful.[44] In singling out men like Parker for calumny, the revisionists drew on a strong tradition of American Anglophobia. Many working-class and rural Americans had a long list of grievances against the English: they were snooty; they were imperialistic; and, before the war at least, they owned a lot of the loans held by Americans. In the Midwest, where admiration for England smacked of elitism and pretension and just plain un-Americanism, many residents found it easy to believe that Englishmen had stacked the deck against them.

Finally, the revisionists blamed the evil individuals who worked in the executive branch and exercised power over the president. Just who, they wanted to know, had convinced President Wilson to abandon his earlier, wiser policy of neutrality? Which individuals had colluded with the economic royalists to change his weak mind? Increasingly, they pointed the finger of blame at two Wilson aides who, the revisionists believed, had an unusual and ultimately un-American affection for British aristocrats. In the revisionists' view, these two men had singlehandedly changed the course of history.

THE PRIMARY "ANGLOMANIACS" in the Wilson administration, in the view of Barnes and other critics, were the president's closest friend and adviser, Col. Edward House, and his ambassador to Great Britain, Walter Hines Page. The revisionists had some difficulty deciding which man was more diabolical. Page was clearly more biased than House toward Britain, but House had more influence over the president, at least for a time. Both men had been seen as pro-English during the war, but their attempts to aid Britain were not fully exposed until they began to boast of them in their memoirs. The first volume of Page's autobiography was released in 1922, and House's own multivolume account reached the public beginning in 1926. These self-serving memoirs ironically became the primary source material for the two men's harshest critics.

Colonel House was a natural villain for conspiracy theorists. The "colonel" had never actually seen battle or served in the military, but had received his honorary title from one of the many grateful Texas politicians he had helped to put into power. He never held political office, or ran for office, or even held any official governmental post. He wrote a utopian novel in which a hero suspiciously similar to himself overthrew the U.S. government and appointed himself dictator. Yet this shadowy man of apparent authoritarian proclivities became one of President Wilson's most important advisers.[45]

When the colonel first met Wilson in 1911, he was already known as the political mastermind behind four successive governors in his home state of Texas. House was a Democrat, as were all politically ambitious Texans in the early twentieth century, and eager to find a candidate for president who was deserving of his support and capable of winning. A sickly man with no identifiable illness, House liked to hover in the background and exercise power through other men. He arranged to meet the rising star from New Jersey who had the best chance of winning the White House for the Democrats. For his part, Wilson was pleased to win the support of the fabulously wealthy donor who had a reputation as a political fixer. The men liked each other from the start. "We found ourselves in such complete sympathy, in so many ways," the colonel remembered later, "that we soon learned to know what each was thinking without either having expressed himself."[46]

Once Wilson took office in 1913, House became his top adviser and controlled access to him. He decided who could see the president, whose requests were passed along to him, and who received jobs in the administration. The colonel believed that it was his duty to "offset the criticism and lighten the burden of detail that weighs upon every President."[47] Yet he refused to take a formal post or draw a government salary. The lack of an official title only added to House's air of mystery.

Although he advised Wilson on virtually every issue, his main responsibility lay in foreign policy. Beginning in 1913, the president directed House to make several peacemaking trips to Europe. During his sojourns in England and Germany, House grew convinced that the United States needed to enter the war and ensure victory for the Allies. In one of his most deceptive and convoluted maneuvers, he tried to persuade Wilson to offer an ultimatum to the kaiser in 1916. Either the Germans agreed to attend a peace conference, House suggested, or the United States would join the war. But Wilson insisted on softening the ultimatum's language, and the British lost interest in the proposal.[48] House's influence with the president was clearly on the wane.[49]

But House *thought* that he had tremendous power. At times, he seemed to claim an almost demonic influence over the president. "I was like a disembodied spirit seeking a corporeal form," he wrote in his memoirs. "I found my opportunity in Woodrow Wilson."[50]

Reviewers of his memoirs accepted at face value House's claims of omnipotence. "Wilson relied on House alone, and in everything," declared a writer for the *Saturday Evening Post*, an admirer and defender of the colonel.[51] House's critics also emphasized his power over Wilson, but they cast him more as Rasputin than Talleyrand. Oswald Garrison Villard, the publisher of the *Nation*, read House's memoirs with increasing amazement. He was appalled by "the trickery, the insincerity, the double-dealing, the hypocrisy" displayed by the colonel, not to mention his "supernatural, not to say diabolical, cleverness."[52] House's belated claim of authorship of his 1913 novel, *Philip Dru: Administrator*, which had been credited to "anonymous," only confirmed his critics' suspicions. In its endorsement of a military coup by a benevolent dictator, House's book did not reassure those who were concerned about his possible subversion of democracy.

Hatred of Colonel House performed a useful function for the war's opponents. If he was to blame for the war, then the way to avoid future wars was simple: expose and remove wicked advisers like the colonel. When he died in 1938, some anti-interventionists seemed to hold him personally responsible for all the American lives lost in 1917 and 1918. "The American people to the last man and woman," wrote Villard in the *Nation*, "ought to be told again how Colonel House's activities helped to bring on war in 1917 and how the fate of their children may still be settled by two or three men in and out of office."[53] Villard neatly triggered historical American anxieties—an inner circle was trying to subvert the republic and institute dictatorship—and provided a solution to them at the same time. By blaming these "two or three men," Villard granted himself more control over an increasingly frightening world situation. Expose the handful of evil men in Washington, he implied, and we can avoid a second great war.

The only man in the Wilson administration more odious than House, in the view of the revisionists, was the American ambassador to Britain, Walter Page. Like House, Page used his memoirs to reveal the extent of his influence on Wilson's decision to go to war. In Page's telling, Wilson's State Department had been willfully blind to the clear moral superiority of the "sacred cause" of the Allies in the early years of the war. As Wilson's representative in London, Page had worked to moderate what he saw as his government's unnecessarily hostile stance toward the British, who, he believed, should be supported because they were democratic and racially pure. In one case, a State Department missive protesting British violations of American rights had lacked the tenor that he thought Anglo-Saxons should use when communicating with their equals. "There is nothing in its tone," he complained to Colonel House, proving "that it came from an American to an Englishman: it might have been from a Hottentot to a Fiji Islander."[54]

Outraged by this disrespect toward fellow Anglo-Saxons, Page worked assiduously to signal to the British that the State Department did not represent real U.S. interests. The most flagrant example of Page's preference for the English appeared in the memoirs of his close friend, British Foreign Secretary Sir Edward Grey. In Grey's account, Page came to him one day with a State Department demand that the British stop seizing American ships. "I am instructed to read this dispatch to you," Page explained. After performing his official duty, Page then said, "I have now read the dispatch, but I do not agree with it; let us consider how it should be answered." When the story became public in 1925, the *New York Times* editorialized that Page's decision to undermine his own government set a "demoralizing and disastrous" precedent.[55] Revisionists went further. Page, wrote C. Hartley Grattan, was a latter-day Benedict Arnold.[56]

According to his critics, Page had subverted the peaceable members of the Wilson administration—and the will of the American public—by manipulating the president into war. Without Page and his "virulent pro-English attitude," Harry Barnes contended, "the story of American foreign policy from 1914–1919 would have been far different from what it was."[57]

In Barnes's view, Page was an unelected figure whose access to power had world-changing consequences. Barnes was propagating a classic conspiracist view of historical causation. In a mirror image of Wilson's denunciation of antiwar senators as "a little group of willful men," Barnes believed that a different but equally insidious group had dragged a reluctant country into an unnecessary war.

By the end of the 1920s, the skeptics' theory of the reasons for U.S. entry had assumed its broad outlines. They believed that they had uncovered several "truths": the American people had not wanted to enter the war; certain "interests" had subverted their democratic preferences; and these interests included bankers and Anglophile presidential aides. At this point, these theories were standard fare for American conspiracists. The theories about House and Page were reminiscent of earlier fears of evil advisers like the Illuminati, or the secret brotherhood that allegedly controlled the world, insinuating themselves into the president's inner circle. In fact, some later theorists would charge that House was a key agent of the Illuminati conspiracy.[58]

In the 1930s, though, as the size of the government mushroomed during the New Deal and as another world war loomed, American conspiracy theorists would shift their sights from individual targets to more systemic and institutional ones. Domestic and international crises suddenly provided the opportunity for one of the most radical and extensive investigations of a war decision in the nation's history. In 1934, the Senate voted to begin a probe that would raise searching questions about the reasons for intervention in the previous war. With the Senate Munitions Inquiry, the skeptics of the Great War would eventually focus on a modern enemy: the expanding powers of the presidency.

FOR YEARS PACIFISTS and socialists had been calling without success for an investigation of war and war profits. But as the world lurched toward war in the 1930s, the question of U.S. involvement in a foreign war suddenly seemed urgent to many Americans. Japan invaded Manchuria in 1931, Hitler became chancellor of Germany in 1933, and Mussolini prepared to invade Ethiopia. A world conflagration was on the horizon, and most Americans wanted no part of it.

Americans worried even more about the collapse of their own economy. During the Great Depression, the years of spiraling unemployment and poverty eroded the nation's faith in businessmen and in an unregulated market. In this climate, many citizens supported public officials who attacked corporate and financial titans.

As the Great Depression continued and the world crisis escalated, many Americans came to agree with the revisionists that the war had been a waste of lives and money. More than a hundred thousand Americans had died in the war, but for what? To make the world safe for Hitler, Stalin, and Mussolini?

The popular culture of the 1930s reflected this revulsion against war. Scholars began questioning the wisdom of U.S. participation in just about every war. Walter Millis exposed the ignorance and deceit behind the Spanish-American War in *The Martial Spirit*, and historians argued that the Civil War had been the product of a "blundering generation." Even the kaiser's soldiers—rapacious brutes of government propaganda just fifteen years earlier—became heroes in popular culture. The German antiwar novel *All Quiet on the Western Front* humanized the German soldiers and caused more Americans to question the official history of the war. Young Americans were particularly moved by the books and movies about the mistakes of the previous war. As the journalist Eric Sevareid remembered, the students of the 1930s were "revolted by the stories of the mass hysteria of 1917, the beating of German saloon keepers, the weird spy hunts, the stoning of pacifists, the arrests of conscientious objectors."[59]

When the Democrats recaptured the White House and Congress in the election of 1932, they seemed eager to rethink and reexamine established policies. Franklin Roosevelt's New Deal for the American people had not been clearly defined during the campaign, but the new president quickly indicated his intention to use government to solve the economic crisis. He was particularly receptive to attacks on the corporate leaders who opposed his expansion of the federal government.

The economic, diplomatic, and political shocks of the 1930s, in short, gave pacifists a chance to teach Americans about the futility of war. One veteran peace activist seized this opportunity and pushed her advantage to secure a congressional inquiry into the causes of wars. Dorothy Detzer, one of the most influential female lobbyists of the interwar years, had been representing the Women's International League for Peace and Freedom (WILPF) on Capitol Hill since the 1920s.[60] She had nursed casualties of war with Quaker relief societies in postwar Europe for three years, before returning home to find her beloved twin brother, Don, suffering the corrosive effects of mustard gas from his wartime service.[61] As she watched him die, she resolved to do everything she could to make sure that other men would not have to fight and suffer.

As the national secretary of the WILPF in the early 1930s, Detzer buttonholed members of Congress and urged them to launch a massive investigation of the arms makers, who, she argued, tried to foment wars in their quest to make more money. In her view, if Congress took the profits out of war, peace would follow.[62]

By stressing the role of the arms dealers, Detzer and other pacifists departed from the arguments of most revisionist historians. In the view of the scholarly skeptics of the war, the bankers had played a much more pivotal role than the munitions makers in influencing the Wilson administration. As Barnes wrote in 1934, arms manufacturers "never exerted so terrible an influence upon the promotion of warfare as did our American bankers between 1914 and 1917."[63]

But in the mid-1930s, a series of journalistic exposés suddenly pushed the arms makers to the forefront of the public debate. In March 1934 the business magazine *Fortune* published "Arms and the Men," charging that the privately owned, profit-motivated arms industry helped to foment wars. At the same time, George Seldes's *Iron, Blood, and Profits* exposed the international "munitions racket," and Helmuth Engelbrecht and Frank C. Hanighen took aim at the "merchants of death" in their best-selling book. Both books argued that wars would continue to ravage the world unless governments investigated and tamed the arms makers.

In contrast to the conspiracy theorists later in the century, these World War I skeptics were elites who used the traditional print media to bring their ideas to the public. These journalists and historians wrote books, magazine articles, and newspaper columns disputing the Wilson administration's history of the Great War. With Detzer's help, they were hoping to use another traditional means—the congressional investigation—to promote their ideas.

The popularity of the books on the death merchants helped Detzer to build a broad coalition of unlikely allies. Detzer was an internationalist and a leftist, yet she drew support from conservative and nationalist groups and individuals. The American Legion, for example, worked against her on almost every other issue, but in this case its members shared her concern that arms merchants' desire for profits might lead to unnecessary wars.[64]

Henry Ford, the auto magnate and noted isolationist, also endorsed an investigation. If the world could rid itself of "scheming munition makers looking for enormous profits," Ford proclaimed, then "the people would enjoy peace."[65]

President Roosevelt decided to support the investigation as well. Besides his general approval of greater government oversight of the arms industry, Roosevelt saw potential political benefits in an inquiry. A high-profile Senate investigation of the arms makers would inevitably target Pierre Du Pont, the wealthy arms manufacturer who was pouring millions into the effort to defeat Roosevelt's reelection bid in 1936. As Roosevelt nurtured America's infant welfare state and called for more government involvement in the economy, Du Pont organized his fellow industrialists into the Liberty League, a group dedicated to the defeat of the New Deal. In Roosevelt's view, a high-profile investigation of the merchants of death seemed politically advantageous: it would annoy Du Pont, confirm the selfishness of Roosevelt's most determined opponents, and please the eight hundred thousand members of the American Legion.[66] Once the president gave his approval, the Senate quickly passed the resolution and set up a select committee to investigate the arms industry.

The members of the committee and its staff represented the breadth of the coalition supporting the munitions investigation. Populist Republicans, conservative Democrats, democratic socialists, and even secret communists hoped to use the committee to demonstrate the dangers of a privately owned munitions industry. The committee's chairman, Gerald Nye of North Dakota, was an agrarian Republican whose state had strongly supported the People's Party in the 1890s and still retained a popular fear of banks and eastern "interests." After Nye, the most important committee member was Missouri Senator Bennett Clark, a Democrat and son of the legendary speaker of the House, Champ Clark. One of the founders of the American Legion, Clark was at once populist, conservative, anti–big business, and anti–New Deal.

The committee's staff also included some energetic socialists, including Stephen Raushenbush, the chief of staff. Raushenbush, who had simplified the spelling of his name, was the son of Social Gospel minister Walter Rauschenbusch, who, as early as 1907, had blamed arms makers for starting wars. During the investigation, conservatives attacked Raushenbush and other leftist staffers as Marxists who were conspiring to destroy republicanism and promote "socialistic control of all American private enterprise."[67] Indeed, though no one knew it at the time, the committee's counsel, Alger Hiss, was a Soviet spy who had been ordered to infiltrate the committee to obtain secret military documents for the communists.[68] Finally, the committee employed as consultants several well-known critics of the arms industry, including *Merchants of Death* coauthor Engelbrecht and the journalist John T. Flynn, the author of a *New Republic* column titled "Other People's Money" and a forceful conspiracist in the next war.

The Nye Committee, in short, was nothing if not eclectic in its composition. However, its conservative Democrats, progressive Republicans, and avowed socialists all shared a passion to challenge the established "interests," whether they resided on Wall Street or in the White House. They may have argued vehemently about the merits of the expansion of the welfare state, but they all agreed that the warfare state threatened American democracy.

The Senate charged the committee with investigating the arms trade and recommending new laws to regulate it. At first, this seemed a question of current policy, but the committee discovered that it could not recommend future laws to regulate the arms makers unless it fully understood their role in the previous war. Over the next two years, the committee's task evolved from a simple exposé of war profiteers into a historical investigation of the government's mistakes and lies from two decades earlier.

The committee initially targeted the group of men vilified by Detzer, Walter Rauschenbusch, and the recent best-selling books: the merchants of death. Throughout the committee's first set of hearings, Senator Nye tried to find proof for his conviction that greed led arms traders to promote wars. His investigators did discover internal industry documents that proved highly embarrassing to the arms merchants, including memos denouncing the State Department's peacemaking efforts as "pernicious" and deriding U.S. diplomats as effeminate "cooky pushers."[69] Some individuals, such as Sir Basil Zaharoff, the "munitions king" of Switzerland, had amassed fortunes from war; other arms merchants had tried to start wars in South America. The Du Ponts came across as mustache-twirling villains. Lammot, Pierre, and Irenée Du Pont, clad in dark suits and protected by a phalanx of lawyers, smugly insisted that they had never profited from the war, despite their company's $1.25 billion in sales and their personal annual incomes of more than $1 million during the years of the Great War.

The Nye Committee's investigation of the arms makers succeeded in convincing the public that the "death merchants" had played a role in causing the war. As a result of the investigation, Americans became even more determined to avoid future wars. In 1936, as part of the largest mass student movement in U.S. history up to that point, half a million college students marched out of class to protest war.[70] The same year, Robert Sherwood won the Pulitzer Prize for his play criticizing European arms merchants, *Idiot's Delight*. In 1939, 68 percent of Americans agreed that the United States should not have joined the Great War, and 34 percent said that "propaganda and selfish interests" were to blame for this mistake.[71]

Yet despite its success in helping to influence the public's memory of the war, the Nye Committee could not prove that the merchants of death had any direct influence on policy makers. The committee could discover no documents or witnesses to show that the Du Ponts and their fellow munitions makers had any sway over the president. At the same time, a staff investigation into the role of British propaganda also ended in failure. Investigators spent months trying to prove that "London gold" had financed the purchase of key newspapers and then planted pro-British stories in them.[72] But the detectives never found enough evidence to justify public hearings on that subject.

After failing to prove that arms makers or British bribes played any meaningful role in the intervention drama, the committee at last turned to more promising lines of inquiry. Eighteen months into the investigation, the senators began to focus their public hearings on the men the revisionists had always viewed as the real problem: the classic villains of the Populists, the bankers.

By following the money, the committee hoped to discover if, as George Norris had charged back in 1917, the United States had gone to war on the command of gold. This investigation had the potential to produce real evidence of official blunders and crimes. After the war began in Europe, the Wilson administration had changed its policy on loans to allow bankers to send more money to the Allies. Some committee members believed that these loans had tied the United States to one side and effectively forced U.S. intervention in the war. If the committee could show that bankers had *pressured* Wilson to loosen credit, they could prove the bankers' responsibility for America's decision to join the war.

When the committee talked about "the bankers," they really meant the House of Morgan. The Morgan bank had handled more than $3 billion in British money as the sole purchasing agent for the British government from 1915 to 1917. Through its Export Department, it had bought the British war supplies in the United States—horses, airplane engines, machine guns, corned beef, bugles, and TNT—and arranged for their shipment across the submarine-infested Atlantic. Eighty-four percent of the munitions bought in the United States by the Allies from 1915 to 1917 passed through Morgan hands.[73] When the British could no longer pay for their purchases, the Morgans arranged to loan the Allies hundreds of millions of dollars. During the war, anti-interventionists had pointed to the House of Morgan as the most powerful symbol of the commanding power of gold. Now, in the depths of the Great Depression, the white-haired Morgan executives who represented the "money power" were obvious targets for the committee's wrath.

The Morgan executives rolled into the capitol ready to do battle. Outside their post at the Shoreham Hotel, where they occupied an entire wing, the bankers stationed plainclothes security guards to keep pesky reporters and curiosity seekers at bay. Photographers were allowed in their rooms in the evening to take reassuring pictures of the avuncular officials donning their dinner jackets and reading the newspapers. Messengers dashed about the bank's forty hotel rooms with dispatches from New York, and aides consulted the voluminous files and ledgers from the Great War that overflowed into the bankers' main living room.[74] The documents refreshed the memory of the two most important witnesses before the committee: Thomas Lamont, the former executive who had helped set Morgan policy twenty years earlier, and John Pierpont "Jack" Morgan Jr., the heir to the Morgan empire.

The head of his family business since his father's death in 1913, Jack Morgan was less ambitious and more casual than his legendary father. But he was equally determined to protect the House of Morgan from what he saw as the probes of impudent, provincial congressmen. Though he was approaching seventy, Jack Morgan was still a tough businessman and a formidable opponent in the boardroom and the hearing room. He had survived three assassination attempts, including one in 1915 by a pro-German gunman who invaded his home, and a prolonged congressional investigation of Wall Street investment bankers in 1932, which revealed the very unpopular fact that he had paid no income taxes for two years. Morgan had come off poorly in that previous investigation, which had been chaired by a feisty Sicilian immigrant, New York's Ferdinand Pecora. Reporters waited eagerly to see how the blue-blooded Anglophile would handle the folksy but determined investigators from the Midwest in this latest probe.[75]

The Nye Committee members aimed to answer one question that they deemed essential to proving a conspiracy behind intervention: Why did the U.S. government decide, once in October 1914 and again in August 1915, to loosen American regulations to allow more loans to the Allies? At the start of the war, the United States had maintained a "money embargo" and prohibited loans to both sides. Secretary of State William Jennings Bryan, whose suspicion of banks stretched back to his denunciation of the international gold ring in his "Cross of Gold" speech in 1896, urged the embargo on Wilson. "Money is the worst of all contrabands because it commands everything else," Bryan warned the president prophetically in August 1914.[76] Yet just two months later, the president, on the advice of State Department counselor Robert Lansing, decided that American banks could offer some short-term "credits" to Allied countries when they could not pay for their purchases. Wilson had reasoned that credits were quite different from loans. Yet at the Nye Committee hearings, even Jack Morgan had to admit that credits and loans were basically the same. He insisted, however, that his bankers "never had anything to do with any effort, if one was made, to get President Wilson to change his mind."[77] Indeed, the committee could find no evidence that they did.

However, the committee did find a more promising paper trail related to the second presidential decision to allow more loans. The committee investigators grew convinced that a key event had occurred in August 1915. That summer, after months of buying American goods, the British began to run an enormous trade imbalance with the United States. The value of the pound started to drop against the dollar, and officials in both countries believed that the dollar was so overvalued that the British would have to halt their American purchases immediately.

Indeed, the drop in the value of the pound could bring about a U.S. economic collapse, argued the U.S. treasury secretary, William McAdoo, and Robert Lansing, secretary of state following Bryan's resignation. "Our prosperity is dependent on our continued and enlarged foreign trade," McAdoo wrote the president. "To preserve that we must do everything we can to assist our customers to buy." Great Britain, he said, "is and always has been our best customer."[78] Lansing went even further and predicted "industrial depression, idle capital and idle labor, numerous failures, financial demoralization, and general unrest and suffering among the laboring classes" unless the U.S. government did something to increase British purchasing power.[79]

To avert this disaster, Lansing and McAdoo persuaded the Federal Reserve Board to relax its regulations on loans, which would allow the British to buy more arms. They also urged the president to encourage banks to make large loans to nations at war. In the view of some Nye Committee members and staff, these two cabinet members served as agents of the bankers. "I think it is highly significant," wrote one staff member to Raushenbush, "to show that the line of reasoning which Lansing presented to the President…was a line developed by [Federal Reserve] Governor Strong *at the instigation of the Morgans*."[80] The investigators were growing convinced that the bankers had secretly manipulated U.S. policy to bring America closer to war.

Two Federal Reserve board members adamantly resisted the change in regulations at the time. Paul Warburg and Adolph Miller, both of German descent, strongly believed that the government should continue to oppose unlimited loans. Warburg angrily told the governor of the Federal Reserve Bank that the U.S. plans to ease credit for the British were nothing short of immoral. "To think that this war must go on to keep our trade going is an abomination," he wrote.[81] But McAdoo told the president to disregard the two bankers because their objections were based on their sympathy for their ancestral nation. "If they were thinking of our interests instead of Germany's, they would not [object]," he wrote.[82]

The Nye Committee saw Warburg as something of a hero, and here they departed from one aspect of the American conspiracist tradition. In contrast to many Populists, the Great War investigators believed that the Jews were on their side. The most vociferous opponents of American aid to the Allies had been Paul Warburg, a Jew, and his German Jewish American firm, Kuhn-Loeb. During the war, in fact, some British officials blamed "the Jews" for the U.S. government's reluctance to help London.[83] Twenty years later, the Nye Committee members viewed Warburg as an ally, and Protestant Anglophiles like Jack Morgan and Thomas Lamont as the enemy. As a result, in all of their attacks on "the bankers," the Nye Committee members never stooped to anti-Semitism.[84]

Though Warburg's angry dissents impressed some Nye Committee members in 1935, they had no effect on policy in 1915 and 1916. The Federal Reserve Board relaxed its credit regulations—though without a strong public statement of support from the president—and the House of Morgan quickly arranged a massive loan to the English and the French.[85] Morgan money bought more dynamite and mules and wheat for the Allies, which enabled them to win the war. It also brought more American ships into the sights of German submarines and, thus, American boys to the trenches of France.

Senator Bennett Clark believed that he could identify the moment when the Morgans forced the United States to abandon neutrality. The key issue, he decided, was the drop in the value of the pound. The ensuing exchange crisis had caused the U.S. government to allow the Anglo-French loan, and the loan had led the United States into war. So why, he wondered, did the exchange crisis occur? It was obvious: the House of Morgan, as the chief holder of British securities in the United States, created the crisis, and thus brought on the war. The Morgan bank, he charged, "stepped out from under and permitted the sterling exchange to flop," and then pressured McAdoo to facilitate the huge loan. "The question of exchange," Clark charged, "was used as a lever to bring about a complete change in our neutrality policy."[86]

The bankers could barely conceal their fury at this interpretation. Thomas Lamont disputed the committee's allegation that the "money power" ever influenced U.S. governmental policy. "Bankers do not bring leverage on governmental Departments over here, and if they attempted to do it they would be very badly rebuffed," he said huffily. The committee members could not contain their disbelief. "Do you mean they do not do it, or that they do not admit that they do it?" Nye sneered in response.[87] Jack Morgan chose a more limited, and effective, defense: he categorically denied that he or his firm had helped to cause the exchange crisis. "That is one of the most discreditable actions which is foreign to our history and it is foreign to our tradition, and we never did such a thing in our lives," he said.[88]

To prove his case, Morgan dramatically produced a cable proving that his bank had offered to lend the British $100 million as the pound began to slip. The British had declined the offer. In other words, Morgan had tried to *prevent* the exchange crisis, not create it. But Clark refused to allow the facts to get in the way of a good theory. It did not matter "whether the British Government was responsible for pulling the props out from under the exchange market," he explained, "or whether Morgan & Co. was responsible for it." The point, he said, was that the British wanted to "use our money" to fight the war.[89] British bureaucrats, American bankers—what difference did it make? Rich, deceitful, and un-American, they had all conspired to send American boys to die for foreign capital.

Although Clark could not prove that the House of Morgan forced U.S. intervention, he did have documents showing that the bank had bullied American companies and forced them to support the British loans. Back in 1915, once the bank received government permission for the Anglo-French loan, the Morgans needed to find companies to underwrite it. For this, they turned to American munitions manufacturers. The Morgan bankers wrote letters to arms makers suggesting, in language Clark found overtly threatening, that these companies would not get any more orders from the English unless they subscribed to the loan. The Missouri senator managed to make Wall Street sound like a mafia operation. "In the parlance of the street, that was 'putting the heat' on those people?" Clark asked the bankers. Lamont reacted angrily. "We do not use that parlance," he retorted.[90]

Some committee and staff members believed that the bankers were not only gangsters but also liars. They were convinced that the full truth of the exchange crisis and the Anglo-French loan had disappeared along with crucial Morgan documents. "Confidentially," Stephen Raushenbush wrote to one committee member, "we think that they have cleaned out their files and have lied to us at length."[91] But the committee could not prove this. As Morgan effectively parried Clark's attacks, the Missouri senator and his colleagues began to lose the support of much of the press.

Up to this point, the Nye Committee was attacking the standard villains of American conspiracy theories. Congressman Charles Lindbergh and even the writers of the Populist movement would have felt at home in a hearing room in which Morgans and Du Ponts were assailed as greedy speculators intent on thwarting the will of the people. But near the end of the investigation, Nye, Clark, and the other investigators came to focus on a much more elusive and nebulous target. Though the committee failed to find proof that individual bankers had manipulated the international monetary system to force intervention, it did make another discovery that some members found even more disturbing: the lack of transparency and democracy in the U.S. government.

The intense debate over loans and credits took place not in Congress, but in secret meetings of the Federal Reserve. For Americans in the mid-1930s, it was surprising and frightening to find out how little they had known about their nation's policies during the war. The Nye Committee members raised "the dark velvet curtain of history" on the shadowy actors in the drama, the historian Charles Beard wrote in 1936. "They disclose[d]," he continued, "the starkness of the ignorance that passed for knowledge and wisdom in those fateful days."[92]

Most explosively, the Nye Committee learned that the president had actively fostered this ignorance: he had lied to Americans and to Congress about the Allies' real aims in the war. Near the end of the inquiry, the Nye Committee staff learned from secret documents that Wilson and Secretary of State Lansing had known soon after intervention in April 1917 that the Allies had written secret treaties divvying up territory in the event of their victory, though Wilson had stated categorically during the war that the "processes of peace" would be "absolutely open" and would involve "no secret understandings of any kind."[93]

After the war, Wilson explained that he had believed these statements to be true at the time that he made them. In a meeting with the Senate Foreign Relations Committee in August 1919, he answered definitively—and inaccurately—a direct question from Senator William Borah of Idaho about his knowledge of the treaties. Earlier in 1919, he said, the "whole series of understandings were disclosed to me for the first time."[94]

The Nye Committee proved what Harry Barnes and others had claimed in the 1920s: the president had not told the truth. Secretary of State Lansing's diary and other formerly secret papers showed that Wilson had indeed known of the treaties in 1917. When Senator Clark produced the papers at a hearing, Nye proclaimed that Wilson had lied to the nation.[95] Moreover, he alleged, the Wilson administration had misled the nation throughout 1915 and 1916. Before intervention, the Wilson administration was just "pretending neutrality" while "actually hoping for a break with Germany, inviting that sort of break," he concluded.[96]

Nye's accusations against Wilson provoked a furious reaction from the president's defenders. The Republican senator's charge against "a dead man, a great man, a good man," as Democratic Senator Tom Connally of Texas put it, outraged many Democrats in Congress. The Senate had not charged the committee with rewriting history, Connally contended. Yet now the Munitions Committee, "out of the depths of its wisdom, out of its occult powers, out of its marvelous connection with the stars of the heavens which we ordinary mortals never understand," presumed to tell the majority of Americans that they were wrong in 1917.[97] Connally was so furious that he pounded his Senate desk until the first knuckle on his left hand became permanently misshapen. The next day, Senator Carter Glass of Georgia banged his desk so hard as he denounced Nye's "miserable and mendacious suggestion" that his knuckles bled.[98]

At first, Senator Nye did not appear in the Senate to defend himself, apparently believing that it would be better to leave the explanation to a Democrat. Senator Clark gamely tried to defend the committee from the attacks of his fellow Democrats, arguing that Nye had said Wilson "falsified" rather than "lied." Clark insisted that the committee had no partisan motives. The historical inquiry, he explained, was necessary so that the committee could prevent such mistakes in the future.[99]

But Clark's defense was swept away in the flood of angry press coverage. Journalists and public officials rushed to defend the late president. "There are lies forced upon statesmen by patriotic duty," wrote Arthur Krock in the *New York Times*, "which are writ in letters of gold in the books of the Recording Angel."[100] Krock claimed that Senator Clark's attack on the late president was motivated by his desire to avenge his father, who had lost the Democratic presidential nomination in 1912 to Wilson. Another Wilson supporter, Joseph Tumulty, one of his closest confidantes, proclaimed that "envy" had motivated the committee to attack Wilson's "genius and statesmanship."[101] Two Democrats on the committee, Walter George and James Pope, angrily distanced themselves from the chairman and repudiated "any effort to impugn the motives of Woodrow Wilson and to discredit his great character."[102]

To the skeptics, though, Nye's charge revealed a startling truth: Wilson had systematically misled U.S. citizens about the war. In the revisionists' view, Wilson knew that the United States had abandoned neutrality with the Anglo-French loan of 1915, yet he bragged in 1916 that he had kept the country out of war. He also knew that the Allies were not fighting a war to make the world safe for democracy, but to grab lands controlled by Germany. To his critics, it was clear that Wilson thought that Americans would never support the war if they knew its real aims. So instead he had crafted a fiction for them, a story about sinister empires with sharp talons and a lovely postwar world without victors or vengeance. Then he had imprisoned anyone who dared to tell the truth.

What could they do to stop this from happening again? They could not turn the clock back and strip the executive branch of its current powers; President Roosevelt was far too popular for them even to attempt this. So they decided to limit the president's opportunities to misuse his powers—to draw an unwilling nation into a foreign war—by restricting profits and trade during wars.

First, the committee wanted to confiscate war profits and nationalize the munitions industry. If no one made money from war, they believed, then no "interests" could manipulate the country into war. But the Roosevelt administration's opposition helped to doom these efforts. The president lost patience with the committee once it stopped attacking the Du Ponts and began championing open government and limits on presidential power. Privately, the Nye Committee staff members believed that the president did not want them to propose any legislation "with real teeth in it."[103] But even if Roosevelt had endorsed these radical reforms, they would not have saved the United States from the horrors of the war to come.

The other solution was to limit international trade during wars. Members of the Nye Committee realized that Wilson had made his decision to abandon neutrality because the U.S. economy was increasingly dependent on transatlantic trade. Nye began groping toward an understanding of this issue near the end of the hearings. "It was commercial activity as a whole, in which the bankers had a hand," he explained to Jack Morgan in 1936, "which did finally break down completely our neutrality." Morgan agreed with him, but disputed his assertion that the bankers played a prime role. Everyone, he retorted, had a hand in the trade that led to intervention.[104]

If the United States had been drawn into war by "commercial activity as a whole," then the revisionists believed the country must isolate itself from future conflicts. Charles Beard suggested that the United States needed to till its own garden and cut off loans and the munitions trade to belligerents in times of crisis.[105] Some senators agreed. "I would rather temporarily abandon all our world commerce," said Nye Committee member Homer T. Bone, "than to have this Republic, which my father fought to preserve, destroyed or irreparably injured by another great war."[106]

With this goal in mind, Nye succeeded in persuading Congress to approve the Neutrality Acts of 1935 and 1936, which prohibited Americans from loaning money and selling arms to countries at war. Nye and other anti-interventionists wanted to ban all trade with belligerent nations during wars, but here he was not successful. A 1937 law allowed countries at war to buy nonlethal supplies from the United States as long as they paid cash for them and carried them away in their own ships. The Nye investigators hoped that these laws would tie the hands of future would-be conspirators in the White House. The acts, Raushenbush wrote, "will make it far less likely that a President will dare to involve us in a foreign war through misuse of his great powers."[107]

Years later, with the experience of World War II behind them, many historians came to see the Neutrality Acts as terribly misguided.[108] Scholars agreed with Franklin Roosevelt, who wrote to Colonel House in exasperation that the anti-interventionists seemed to reduce the whole war to a few acts of individual "skullduggery" by House, Lansing, and Page.[109]

The Nye Committee was certainly guilty at times of blaming a few conspirators for complicated events. The members became distracted by their outrage over the manifest immorality of "merchants of death," the enormity of the Morgan profits, and the curtain of secrecy concealing the changes in loan policy. But they also proved willing to wrestle with disturbing questions about the growing militarization of the American state and society.[110] They were outraged by what they saw as the imbalance between Americans' heroic sacrifice in the war and the petty, vengeful results, by the disjuncture between the president's idealistic rhetoric and the despair of the postwar world.

By the end, the investigators believed that the dangers to the republic were much greater than a few individuals. The growing secrecy and power of the presidency was the real problem. "I am enough of a democrat to want more than one man to pass on the war decisions and the major pre-war policies," Raushenbush wrote in a private letter. Mocking Wilson's rhetoric about open covenants of peace, he continued: "If there are going to be wars, let them be open wars openly arrived at with the consent of the people."[111]

This fear of the president abusing his powers and deceiving the country into war would resonate with many Americans for the next century. The Nye Committee had discovered the taproot of modern conspiracism.

AS THE NYE COMMITTEE wound up its work, it struggled to explain the meaning of its investigation for future government policy. For many of the investigators, the inquiry showed that modern presidents could make decisions about war and peace in complete secrecy. And as they contemplated the implications of this growing presidential power in the current world climate, they became alarmed.

President Roosevelt first troubled the investigators and Great War revisionists when he tried to stymie any real reforms the munitions inquiry might propose. A former assistant Navy secretary who had focused on domestic problems in his first term, Roosevelt seemed to become more internationalist, and perhaps more interventionist, in his second. When the Nye Committee investigators compared the current president to the one they had just investigated, they grew worried. As Raushenbush explained, Woodrow Wilson was "never a big-Navy, four-Army man." Furthermore, he presided over "the most idealistic administration this country has ever had." Yet he made secret decisions that led to war, and then lied about them. What could Americans now expect from the big-Navy, four-Army man in the White House, a man whom even his most ardent supporters would never describe as idealistic?[112]

As the world slid toward crisis in the late 1930s, many anti-interventionists awoke to the terrifying realization that the brilliant politician in the White House could be their greatest enemy of all. Shrewder than Colonel House and more powerful than Jack Morgan, the president might be even more dangerous to U.S. democracy than the plotters of the previous war. Perhaps, they worried in their darkest moments, he might even create an "incident" to force the country into another unwanted war.

2

Lying Us into War? The Second Battle of Pearl Harbor

PRESIDENT FRANKLIN ROOSEVELT gripped the podium and stared with determination at the entire leadership of the U.S. federal government—the House, the Senate, and the Supreme Court—arrayed before him. In the glare of floodlights for newsreel cameras, interrupted by roars from the audience, he spoke of the Japanese attack on Pearl Harbor the previous day, December 7, 1941, a "date which will live in infamy." To the cheers of the crowd, he asked Congress to declare a state of war between the United States and Japan. The American people, he said, would fight to victory and make certain that "this form of treachery" would never endanger the country again.[1]

But even before Roosevelt delivered his speech, some Americans began to suspect treachery of a different kind. In the view of some anti-interventionists, the Japanese assault was the event they had long feared, the "incident" that would allow Roosevelt to drag an unwilling country into war. On the night of the attack, Senator Gerald Nye proclaimed that the president had "maneuvered" the country into war, and the next day Col. Charles Lindbergh Jr. agreed with a friend who muttered that Roosevelt had gotten the United States into the European conflict through the Asian "back door."[2] Later, Congresswoman Clare Boothe Luce would voice the definitive phrase of the Roosevelt critics. The president, she said, "lied us into a war because he did not have the political courage to lead us into it."[3]

These Roosevelt critics made some valid points. The president's foreign policy in Asia had been quite secretive. He had indeed made decisions that he knew might provoke the Japanese into an attack, and he made these decisions in response to events in Europe. After the raid, he pretended that he was as shocked by it as other Americans. Finally, he tried to bury key documents and to force the Pearl Harbor commanders to assume full responsibility for the disaster.

To this brew of governmental secrecy and lies, the anti-interventionists added their long-standing hatred of the president. They fumed at his official conspiracy theories about "enemies within our gates"; they suspected that he was using the newly expanded Federal Bureau of Investigation to spy on and intimidate loyal Americans who opposed his internationalist foreign policy. They believed that he wanted to enter the Second World War to sate his voracious appetite for power and create an American form of dictatorship. As they uncovered more examples of Roosevelt's deceit, their loathing for him grew, until they saw him as a murderer, a proto-fascist, and, at the same time, an unwitting agent for international communism. The Roosevelt critics would later spread the theory that the president provoked the Japanese into attacking Pearl Harbor, deliberately failed to warn the Hawaiian commanders that the raid was coming, and was relieved and even pleased when it occurred.

Roosevelt's disingenuousness, his cover-ups, and his sometimes secret, sometimes public expansion of presidential powers triggered a kind of mania in his enemies. Ultimately, they came to see him as a graver threat to the republic than the Japanese.

THE FEDERAL REPRESENTATIVES assembled before Franklin Roosevelt for his Pearl Harbor speech wielded a lot more power—and shouldered many more responsibilities—than had their counterparts in the previous war. During the New Deal, the government's share of GNP roughly doubled, as did the number of government workers. All levels of government increased their expenditures to meet the crisis of the Great Depression, but the federal government grew proportionately faster than state and local governments. Meanwhile, Congress reduced exemptions for the working poor and raised tax rates for everyone, so more Americans paid taxes to support this burgeoning central government. As the federal budget grew from $4.6 billion in 1932 to $9 billion in 1940, the number of Americans filing income tax returns more than tripled, from 3.9 million to 14.6 million.[4]

Americans received an increasing number of benefits from the government in return for these taxes. Under Roosevelt's New Deal, the federal government took on unprecedented responsibilities for economic and social security. Through the creation of an "alphabet soup" of federal agencies, the government provided jobs to the unemployed, welfare and pensions to the unemployable, and protection for workers who wanted to use their collective power to demand better wages and conditions. The New Deal, as the historian David Kennedy has said, "gave to countless Americans who had never had much of it a sense of security, and with it a sense of having a stake in their country."[5] Roosevelt's policies and personal style were phenomenally popular, with about 60 percent of voters consistently approving of his performance.[6]

Yet some Americans still despised Roosevelt. Conservatives never forgave him for signing the National Labor Relations Act, which gave government protection to unions. Some leftists, on the other hand, thought that Roosevelt should have made more radical changes, such as nationalizing the banks. Yet although progressives and conservatives disagreed on whether Roosevelt had done too much or too little, they all agreed on one point: the president seemed to have an ominous lust for power.

One-time liberals such as the journalist John T. Flynn, the historian Harry Elmer Barnes, and Senator Burton Wheeler, a Montana Democrat who had been one of the New Deal's most enthusiastic supporters in Congress, were horrified by Roosevelt's 1937 attempt to enlarge the Supreme Court. Flynn called the court-packing plan "the great massacre of the six old men," and Wheeler wrote in his memoirs that FDR's "unsubtle and anti-Constitution grab for power" reminded him of totalitarian dictators.[7] They saw the president as a menace to the delicate checks and balances written into the supreme law of the land by the nation's founders.

Roosevelt's critics were also outraged by his efforts to retool the executive branch beginning in 1937. Branding his reorganization proposal the "dictator bill," Roosevelt's opponents claimed the bill would, as Representative Hamilton Fish said, "concentrate power in the hands of the President and set up a species of fascism or nazi-ism or an American form of dictatorship, far from the ideals of Jefferson and Lincoln." Another representative fulminated that the bill would pave the way for a "demagogue with personal power madness" to "assassinate the American Republic."[8] In 1939, a majority of Congress disagreed with these critics and passed the

Reorganization Act, which allowed Roosevelt to create the Executive Office of the President and gave the chief executive more authority and staff.[9]

The opponents of the Reorganization Act worried about any president getting too much power, but they were particularly anxious about this president. Roosevelt's critics quite simply distrusted everything he said. He did seem to have a talent for genial deception; many people would leave an interview with him convinced that he supported them, only to feel betrayed later. Eleanor Roosevelt described this delicately as her husband's ability to take "color from whomever he was with, giving to each one something different of himself." She insisted that he did not intend to mislead anyone, but that he simply "disliked being disagreeable."[10] The president himself admitted that he was a "juggler": "I never let my right hand know what my left hand does."[11]

Roosevelt's critics, though, believed there was a simpler term for this: lying. He was, John T. Flynn wrote, a "thoroughly unscrupulous" man who would "ditch" allies and principles "with as little conscience as he ditched all his party platforms."[12] Charles Lindbergh Jr. later described him as "a man of great cleverness and little wisdom, personally vindictive, and politically immoral."[13]

In his critics' eyes, there was no lie Roosevelt would not tell, no means he would forswear, if it would help him to achieve his objectives. By the end of his second term, the president's enemies were most concerned about what they saw as his efforts to draw the United States into another war.

IN THE LATE 1930s, as the Japanese rampaged through China, Mussolini conquered Ethiopia, and Hitler took Czechoslovakia, Americans consistently told pollsters that they wanted nothing to do with these conflicts. Like Harry Barnes, Gerald Nye, and the other Great War revisionists, most Americans believed that the previous war had been a terrible mistake that should not be repeated. In the spring of 1941, when Britain stood alone against the Nazis, 81 percent of Americans said they wanted to stay out of war.[14] Most Americans did put some limits on their isolationism: 62 percent said they would be willing to join the war if Britain would fall to the Nazis without U.S. intervention.[15] But as late as November 1941, 31 percent opposed even providing more help to Britain and the Soviet Union by revising the Neutrality Acts. Until the very eve of the Pearl Harbor attack, one-third of the public was determined to do everything possible to avoid joining the war.[16]

The president was equally determined to do everything he could to help the British. A dedicated antifascist, Roosevelt had been suspicious of the Nazis from the moment they took power in 1933.[17] He grew more uneasy and angry about Hitler's policies throughout the 1930s, but he was reluctant to challenge American public opinion. In 1938, the British ambassador to the United States explained that Roosevelt "is strongly anti-German and is revolted at what the German Government are doing but...at the same time he fully appreciated limitations which public opinion places on his policies and actions."[18]

When Germany invaded Poland in September 1939, Roosevelt responded definitively to a reporter's question about whether the United States could avoid involvement. "I not only sincerely hope so, but I believe we can," he said, "and that every effort will be made by the Administration so to do."[19] Before the 1940 election, he publicly maintained that he would not send American boys to die overseas, even as he grew privately convinced that U.S. security depended on British survival. "I have said this before, but I shall say it again and again and again," he proclaimed. "Your boys are not going to be sent into any foreign wars."[20] Roosevelt's enemies recalled this statement frequently, and with great bitterness, after Pearl Harbor. Even historians who sympathize with Roosevelt's internationalist views have characterized his pre-intervention public pronouncements as misleading and "deliberately disingenuous."[21]

The anti-interventionists were not surprised by Roosevelt's deceptions: they saw them as part of his campaign to expand the powers of the presidency. He had no sincere love for Chinese freedom or British democracy, they believed. In their view, he pretended to have these values only as a means to an end: to persuade the American people to support his drive for big government and total personal power. Roosevelt, Flynn wrote to Robert E. Wood, "will break his promises to England as quickly as he breaks them to the American people."[22] Both Flynn and Harry Elmer Barnes, leading promoters of Pearl Harbor conspiracy theories in later years, firmly believed that Roosevelt planned to use the war to bring fascism to America.[23] To his critics, Roosevelt was starting a war scare as part of his plan to grab power at home. He wanted, Senator Hiram Johnson said, "to knock down two dictators in Europe, so that one may be firmly implanted in America."[24]

A massive rearmament program fulfilled many of Roosevelt's nefarious goals, the critics believed: it camouflaged what they saw as the failure of his economic policies; it satisfied his lust for a strong Navy, which was essential for overseas adventures; and it fed his appetite for power. In their view, it was not the "merchants of death" who promoted a dangerous arms race, but a power-mad president who wanted to set the United States "on the road to dictatorship," as Senator Johnson said.[25] In his opponents' eyes, the very act of opposing Hitler transformed Roosevelt into an American Hitler.

As the real Hitler advanced in Europe, the anti-interventionists moved from dread to outright panic. Many had been counting the days until the end of Roosevelt's second term, only to be thrown into despondency after the Democratic convention of 1940 in Chicago. There, with the party bosses in control, the chief of the city's sewer system linked the amplifiers at the convention to a microphone in a room below the Chicago Stadium. At the crucial time, he began chanting, "We want Roosevelt!"—a cry that reverberated through the stadium. The "voice from the sewer," as it became known, led the delegates in drafting the president for an unprecedented third term.[26] Disgusted by the convention's "sham draft," FDR's critics continued to compare him to European dictators. During the campaign, some Republicans sported buttons that read "Third Reich. Third International. Third Term."[27]

In the eyes of the anti-interventionists, the president showed more evidence of his contempt for democracy in September 1940. That month, as Hitler's bombs pounded London, Roosevelt announced that he had unilaterally and secretly reached an agreement with Prime Minister Winston Churchill to trade U.S. destroyers for British bases in the Western hemisphere. The president negotiated the deal on his own authority after his attorney general advised him that he had the constitutional authority to do so. The anti-interventionists disagreed, with Senator Nye calling the deal a "dictatorial step."[28] Many historians have viewed the deal as an essential effort to preserve national security at a time of crisis, but his opponents at the time feared that it was part of his plan to destroy the checks-and-balances system.[29] As Senator Henry Cabot Lodge Jr. explained, "If the Executive can do these things without action by Congress, can he not also declare war without Congress?"[30]

The day after Roosevelt announced the bases-destroyers deal, leading opponents of war formed the America First Committee, which would become the most significant group against intervention. Several activists who would later promote World War II conspiracy theories, including John T. Flynn, joined the organization. The historians Charles Beard and Harry Elmer Barnes offered their support. America First attracted populists and conservatives, pacifists and extreme nationalists, millionaire businessmen and socialists.[31]

Colonel Charles A. Lindbergh Jr. was America First's most important spokesman. Dubbed the "Lone Eagle" by the newspapers after becoming the first person to fly alone across the Atlantic, he was one of the most recognized men in the world at the time. While visiting fascist Germany, Lindbergh was impressed by the Nazis' skill in aviation, their energy and efficiency, and their determination to stop communism. He heralded the Germans' technical achievements while ignoring the Nazis' crimes, especially their brutal treatment of the Jews. The German government rewarded him with the Service Cross of the German Eagle, the highest award given to a non-German.

Some America First members shared Lindbergh's admiration for the Nazis, but others despised them. The anti-interventionists were united, though, in their conviction that American intervention abroad would endanger democracy at home. A war with Germany would strengthen the U.S. presidency and weaken the strongest bulwark against Stalin in Europe. When measured against these dangers, Hitler's crimes against human beings thousands of miles from U.S. shores seemed slight to the anti-interventionists. And they were determined to thwart what they saw as Roosevelt's plan to pull them into the war.

After he won his third term, Roosevelt took his biggest step toward aiding Great Britain: he asked Congress to pass the Lend-Lease bill, which gave him the power to "lend, lease, or otherwise dispose of" supplies to any country he deemed essential to the defense of the United States.[32] No longer would the British need to pay cash for their goods; the U.S. government would loan them whatever they needed. Despite Roosevelt's insistence that the law would help the country avoid war, the anti-interventionists knew that Lend-Lease signaled a turning point in U.S. foreign policy, and they put up a tremendous fight against it. They repeatedly invoked the "lessons of history" taught by the revisionists and the Nye Committee. Senator Wheeler, the leader of congressional forces against Lend-Lease, used arguments similar to those George Norris had made in 1917.[33] The "interests" were once again foisting "one war measure after another on you, a peace-loving and unsuspecting people," he told Congress. The people should respond by refusing to play the game of the Morgans and the Rockefellers.[34] "Remember," Wheeler told his supporters, "the interventionists control the money bags, but you control the votes."[35]

The anti-interventionists also stressed the dangers of a leviathan government in wartime, particularly the dangers of an imperial presidency. The peril to the republic, Lindbergh testified to a congressional committee, "lies not in an invasion from abroad. I believe it lies here at home in our own midst."[36] In other words, the real enemy was not the Nazis; it was the specter of the mobs that had terrorized his late father and of an American Hitler trying to impose fascism in the name of antifascism. Senator Nye decried Congress's willingness to surrender its constitutional purview to a "power-hungry executive" and reduce itself "to the impotence of another Reichstag."[37] If Congress was another Reichstag, then Roosevelt, by extension, must be another Hitler. The America First leaders maintained that the New Deal's centralizing bureaucrats wanted, as Senator Wheeler said, to "establish fascism in the United States."[38]

The opponents of intervention saw the Second World War as a replay of the First, with both sides motivated by selfishness and greed.[39] Once again, British imperialists were tricking the peace-loving United States into sacrificing American lives so that the British could continue to rule "conquered and subject peoples in three continents," as Gen. Hugh Johnson said.[40] In June 1941, when Hitler invaded the Soviet Union, the anti-interventionists saw even less reason for their nation to ally itself with Germany's enemies.

When they insisted that neither side in the war had a righteous cause, the anti-interventionists downplayed Hitler's brutal and increasingly genocidal policies against the Jews. Indeed, anti-Semitism was the elephant in the room that the more "responsible" anti-interventionists tried to ignore. Some, like John T. Flynn, tried to keep the most vehement anti-Semites out of America First. They also tried to persuade prominent Jews to join the organization.[41] But Lindbergh laid bare the anti-Semitic core of anti-interventionism when he gave a speech in Des Moines in September 1941 that identified the three forces leading the country to war: the Roosevelt administration, the British, and the Jews. Lindbergh singled out the Jews for special criticism: "Their greatest danger to this country lies in their large ownership and influence in our motion pictures, our press, our radio and our Government."[42]

Most newspapers and public officials condemned Lindbergh's speech—Wendell Willkie, the 1940 Republican nominee for president, called it "the most un-American talk made in my time by any person of national reputation"—and Flynn and some America First leaders were distressed by it.[43] But many anti-interventionists believed that Lindbergh had simply told the "truth," that, as the lawyer Amos Pinchot explained, "as a group, the Jews of America are for intervention."[44] These anti-interventionists shared Lindbergh's conviction that Americans would never willingly join a war against Germany; instead, they were being forced into it by selfish Brits, a lying executive, and Jewish warmongers. Though they insisted that these beliefs were not anti-Semitic, they ignored the long history of American anti-Semitism that lay behind Lindbergh's accusation.[45]

In many ways, the anti-interventionists were, as the historian Manfred Jonas has said, "moving further and further away from reality."[46] They refused to see the differences between the First World War and the Second, between the British and the Nazis. They did, however, understand that the U.S. government was changing in immense—and, they believed, frightening—ways. Senator Robert Taft, the dean of anti-interventionist conservatives, argued that support for Britain would be the first step down a slippery slope to a national security state. "If we admit at all that we should take an active interest," he said in 1939, "we will be involved in perpetual war."[47] The United States would become more like European countries, with a powerful, centralized government launching wars around the globe. The increase in the coercive power of the government—to draft men, to commandeer resources, to suppress dissent—would imperil Americans' historic independence and autonomy. It would provoke the hysteria and mob violence that Wheeler and Lindbergh had witnessed firsthand in the previous war, while concentrating frightening powers in the president's hands. It would, as Wheeler said, "slit the throat of the last Democracy still living."[48]

Roosevelt responded with some heated rhetoric of his own. Drawing on Woodrow Wilson's petulant description of the "little group of willful men" who opposed war, he called the America First leaders a "small group of selfish men who would clip the wings of the American eagle in order to feather their own nests."[49] He compared "Lone Eagle" Lindbergh to the Copperheads, the Confederate sympathizers in the North during the Civil War. In another speech, he proclaimed that "evil forces" were "already within our own gates."[50] Like the attorneys general in the previous war, Thomas Gregory and A. Mitchell Palmer, he pledged that the government would wreak vengeance on those who would destroy it. Sometimes, he told the American people on the radio, the president needed to "use the sovereignty of Government to save Government."[51]

Radio was a new medium for spreading official theories about conspiracies, and FDR was the master of it. From his first Fireside Chat in 1933, Roosevelt realized that he could use radio to disseminate an unmediated message to Americans in their homes. Through his radio addresses, Roosevelt told Americans that their banks were safe, that the New Deal was working, and that the United States was not going to join the European war. He also used radio to attack the men he sincerely believed were part of a fifth column in America, an "unholy alliance" between the "extreme reactionary and the extreme radical elements of this country."[52] Roosevelt's opponents also used the radio to spread their conspiracy theories; Father Charles Coughlin, for example, put together a network of stations to amplify his message that Jews were ruining the economy and dragging the country into war. But before he soured on the president and his "Jew Deal," Coughlin praised Roosevelt as a "natural born artist" with the radio.[53] The anti-interventionists worried that the charismatic president would exploit radio to convince Americans that his opponents were traitors and that he was justified in sending U.S. troops into the Nazis' line of fire.

By the fall of 1941, the president had unilaterally stationed U.S. troops in Greenland and Iceland and ordered Navy convoys to patrol the oceans near the Lend-Lease ships. As in the previous war, German U-Boats began firing on the U.S. ships that were helping the British. They also attacked the U.S. Navy convoys. On October 17, eleven sailors died when the Nazis torpedoed the *Kearny*, a U.S. destroyer. Two weeks later, the Germans sank the USS *Reuben James*, killing 115 sailors. Although Americans were now dying in the North Atlantic, Roosevelt still did not ask Congress for a declaration of war, for the good reason that he would not get it. A majority of Congress still opposed entering the war.

The president's critics seemed to be living in an alternate universe. Leaping from the undeniable (Roosevelt lied) to the unbelievable (he was a fascist), they were convinced that he and his warmongering supporters had no desire to save democracy. "What hypocrisy! What sham!" Burton Wheeler exclaimed. "Are you going to listen to these political and economic royalists or will you heed those Americans who stand for peace?"[54] Nor, in their opinion, was Roosevelt sincere in his hatred of fascism; instead, he wanted to bring a brand of fascism to the United States and install himself as führer.

In Wheeler's view, the president had his knife at the throat of American democracy. Roosevelt was just waiting for an incident that would give him the opportunity to plunge it in.

MOST ANTI-INTERVENTIONISTS assumed that this incident would occur in the Atlantic, where Germans were already shooting at and killing Americans. But there were some opponents of war, including John T. Flynn and former President Herbert Hoover, who worried even at the time that Roosevelt would enter the European war through the back door in Asia.

Tensions between the United States and Japan had been building since the Japanese occupation of Manchuria in 1931. In 1937, when Japan launched a full-scale invasion of China, most Americans sympathized with the Chinese Nationalist government of Chiang Kai-shek. Americans knew the Chinese from the popular Pearl S. Buck novel about noble peasants, *The Good Earth*, from reports by enthusiastic Christian missionaries, and from Henry Luce's *Time*, which celebrated Chiang's brave fighters against the ruthless invaders.[55] When the Japanese military bombed civilians in Shanghai and butchered an estimated two hundred thousand people in Nanking, Americans saw the images on their local movie screens, as reporters and newsreel cameramen risked their lives to document the Japanese atrocities.[56]

To demonstrate American resolve against Japanese expansionism, Roosevelt moved the headquarters of the Pacific fleet from San Diego to Pearl Harbor, Hawaii, in May 1940. Over the next year and a half, the level of hostility between the two countries steadily increased: the Japanese conquered more territory and people, while President Roosevelt embargoed the sale of defense-related items to Japan. In the summer of 1941, the United States stopped selling oil to the Japanese, despite some American policy makers' concerns that such an embargo could provoke Japan to attack the oil-rich East Indies.[57]

These concerns were compelling. The Japanese viewed the U.S. oil embargo as an act of war. If the Americans did not restore the flow of oil soon, the Japanese military planned to grab the Dutch East Indies and achieve independence from American oil. But to take and control the East

Indies, they believed that they needed to knock out British and U.S. bases in the Pacific. As the military secretly prepared for this strike, Japanese diplomats in Washington made one last attempt to persuade the Americans to restore trade.[58]

U.S. military leaders told the president that they needed more time to prepare for a war in the Pacific and urged him to follow a more conciliatory policy. But Roosevelt sided with the hard-liners in his cabinet who contended that the United States could not compromise on China. In part, the president felt morally compelled to help the Chinese; in part, he feared that a Chinese collapse would allow Japan to join Hitler's attack on the Soviet Union. And if the Soviet Union fell to fascism, Britain might follow.[59]

While Germans and Americans moved toward war in the North Atlantic, negotiations with Japan reached an impasse. On November 26, Secretary of State Cordell Hull sent a ten-point note that Pearl Harbor conspiracists would later call the "Hull ultimatum." In it, Hull restated the American demand that the Japanese must get out of China and Southeast Asia if they wanted to restore the flow of imports from America. All of Roosevelt's advisers understood the consequences of this message. After a glum cabinet agreed to the wording, Henry Stimson, the secretary of war, made an entry in his diary that would become notorious. "The question was," he wrote, "how we should maneuver them into the position of firing the first shot without allowing too much danger to ourselves."[60]

The Japanese did not need to be maneuvered; they were planning to fire the first shot. For months, Japanese military leaders had been preparing an intricate, multipronged attack. They would strike at Dutch oil fields in the East Indies, British forces in Malaya and Singapore, and U.S. air forces in the Philippines. The centerpiece of the plan was tactically bold and, if it worked, brilliant: a surprise assault on the U.S. fleet in Hawaii. Success depended on overcoming numerous technical problems: crossing thousands of miles of ocean undetected, launching airplanes hundreds of miles from their target, and dropping torpedoes from the air into a relatively shallow bay.

In late November, convinced that they could never reach agreement with the United States, Japanese military leaders ordered the commander of a strike force in the Kurile Islands to begin sailing east. The vessels set out on their 3,500-mile mission in total radio silence. The Japanese Navy took no chances that a panicked sailor might break the silence: officers removed the radio transmission keys and took out some of the fuses. As the task force sailed for Pearl Harbor, the Imperial Navy started a "radio deception" program so that eavesdroppers from the U.S. Navy would think that the ships were actually in Japanese home waters.[61]

American naval officers did not know about the strike force, but they did know that the Japanese were preparing for war. Thanks to a stunning cryptological breakthrough, appropriately code-named "Magic," American code breakers had been reading Japanese diplomatic messages since the fall of 1940. Shortly before Pearl Harbor, Army cryptographers were reading between fifty and seventy-five cables a day from Tokyo. To keep the Japanese from learning that their codes had been broken, the U.S. government closely guarded the secret of Magic. The translators put the messages into locked briefcases and delivered them to a handful of top military and civilian officials.[62] The Pearl Harbor commanders did not receive copies.

On November 27, because the Magic intercepts showed that Japanese diplomats expected war with America soon, the U.S. Army and Navy sent cautionary telegrams to U.S. military bases all over the world. "Negotiations with Japan appear to be terminated to all practical purposes with only the barest possibilities that the Japanese Government might come back and offer to continue," wrote Gen. George Marshall in the Army's message. "Japanese future action unpredictable but hostile action possible at any moment." The Navy's telegram was even more blunt. "This despatch is to be considered a war warning," it announced in its first sentence.[63]

In Hawaii, the top officers in both services, Gen. Walter Short and Adm. Husband E. Kimmel, received the messages but took little action. The two commanders were not on the Magic distribution list, so they did not understand the context of the message from Washington. Short thought that there was little chance of an attack on Hawaii and presumed that the message was intended primarily for Gen. Douglas MacArthur in the Philippines. Kimmel also thought that the Navy was warning him that Japan was going to "attack some place," but not Hawaii.[64] Indeed, the top Army and Navy officers anticipated a strike on British possessions or on the Philippines. No one from Washington called Hawaii to follow up on the telegrams.

On the evening of December 6, a Navy lieutenant carried a copy of the most significant Magic telegram to the president, who was working in his study with his aide Harry Hopkins. In the first thirteen parts of its fourteen-part message, Japan signaled its intention to reject U.S. demands that it leave China. Roosevelt took about ten minutes to read the sheaf of fifteen typed pages and then turned to Hopkins. This means war, the president said, essentially, and Hopkins agreed.[65]

U.S. cryptographers never decoded a Japanese message saying "We will attack Pearl Harbor." In fact, the United States could not have intercepted such a message because Japanese diplomats never knew about the Imperial Navy's Pearl Harbor plans. If the United States had broken the Japanese naval code, then it might have been able to anticipate the attack (though some historians argue that even the naval messages did not provide enough information). But U.S. military leaders had devoted most of their cryptological resources to decoding the high-level diplomatic cables. As a result, American leaders knew only that war was coming somewhere, sometime soon.[66]

Furthermore, all of the American leaders expected an attack on the Philippines, not Oahu. Several top officials began nonstop meetings on Sunday morning, December 7, as they figured out how to respond to a Japanese assault—an assault that seemed virtually certain once the fourteenth part of the Magic message to the Japanese diplomats in Washington was received and decoded that morning. The last part of this message stated that it was impossible for the United States and Japan to reach an agreement. Subsequent cables told them to deliver this message at 1 p.m. Washington time and to destroy their remaining code machine and ciphers.[67] If anyone questioned that the Japanese meant war, these last secret messages, snatched from the air by an intercept station in Seattle and swiftly decoded by panicked Americans in Washington, resolved those doubts. But no one tried to alert the Pearl commanders until less than an hour before the ominous 1 p.m. Eastern time deadline, or dawn in Hawaii, when General Marshall shunned the insecure telephone in favor of the radio.[68] A messenger delivered the crucial warning to General Short's office after the battle was over.

The results of the intelligence failure were catastrophic. The Japanese sank or disabled eighteen U.S. ships and destroyed almost two hundred U.S. airplanes. More than twenty-four hundred Americans were killed.

IMMEDIATELY AFTER THE ATTACK, some public officials demanded to know how such a disaster could have occurred. As the president briefed top congressional leaders in the White House, Democratic Senator Tom

Connally became apoplectic. "Hell's fire, didn't we do anything?" he demanded of the president. He said he was astounded "at what happened to our Navy. They were all asleep."[69] Other members of Congress shared his anger. "There will have to be an explanation—sooner or later—and it had better be good," Congressman Roy Woodruff, a Republican from Michigan, told Congress the next day.[70]

Caucasian Americans were especially shocked that Asians had successfully planned and executed the raid. British and U.S. military officers believed that the Japanese could never become skilled pilots because they lacked good eyesight and balance. Some U.S. officers initially thought that the Germans had planned the attack. When Japanese planes flew over the Philippines and destroyed U.S. planes still sitting on the tarmac, General MacArthur insisted that Japanese could not have been at the controls. It must have been white mercenaries, he concluded.[71] Years later, when Congress investigated Pearl Harbor, some citizens continued to find it hard to believe that the "dumb Japs" could by themselves win such a stunning military victory.[72]

But Americans did not have the luxury of dwelling on doubts or questions at the time. On December 8, the president rallied the nation to war with his eloquent speech before Congress. As the historian Emily Rosenberg has shown, he portrayed Pearl Harbor as an outrage against civilization by a barbaric foe, a modern Alamo or Custer's Last Stand.[73] By framing the attack as a stab in the back, Roosevelt hoped to unite the nation behind him.

Supporters of the administration acted swiftly to quash any discussion of incompetence or conspiracy. The chairman of the Naval Affairs Committee, Senator David I. Walsh of Massachusetts, told his colleagues that they must trust the president. "My God!" he exclaimed. "We have no other course but to throw ourselves and all that we have—heart, soul, body, mind, and all our possessions, into his hands, for him to use as our war President."[74] Americans agreed that the nation needed to have confidence in the executive. For more than a week, the Navy did not announce how many ships had been sunk at Pearl Harbor, and a vast majority of citizens told pollsters that they believed that this secrecy was necessary.[75]

But even at this early hour, the Roosevelt administration realized that calls to patriotism and unity were not enough. If the president hoped to avoid a congressional investigation of the Pearl Harbor disaster, he would have to start an inquiry of his own. After a brief Navy probe, the president announced on December 16 that he had appointed a five-man commission to investigate Pearl Harbor. Supreme Court Justice Owen Roberts, a Republican, chaired the review. In proposing this inquiry, President Roosevelt set a precedent that would inspire his successors to appoint the Warren Commission, the Rockefeller Commission, the 9/11 Commission, and other, lesser panels of elder statesmen to investigate national disasters—and to avert investigations by Congress. All these commissions were designed to prevent the emergence of conspiracy theories, but their apparent role as official whitewashes often provoked even greater skepticism.[76]

The Roberts Commission had a very narrowly defined mission: to determine if any errors by U.S. military officials contributed to the disaster. The commissioners were not asked to investigate the possible mistakes by civilian leaders in Washington, nor were they told of Magic. This approach was convenient for Washington officials, but it was also essential for the war effort: the Japanese were still sending their diplomatic messages in the same, compromised code, and any revelation of the prewar decryptions could jeopardize wartime intelligence collection. Moreover, the Japanese naval code was beginning to yield its secrets to U.S. cryptographers, whose efforts would prove invaluable to the U.S. Navy in later battles. The concealment of Magic not only saved the Roosevelt administration from embarrassment; it also saved American lives. After five weeks of investigation, the commission issued a report that predictably blamed the two Hawaii commanders for errors of judgment.[77]

Most members of Congress and the media accepted the Roberts report. But there were some Americans who remained skeptical of the official story and were determined to prove it false.

HARRY ELMER BARNES and John T. Flynn were the natural leaders of the World War II conspiracist community. Because they had vociferously opposed U.S. intervention in the war until the day of the attack, they saw Pearl Harbor as a personal humiliation as well as a national tragedy. Moreover, they shared another characteristic of early Pearl conspiracists: a deep, visceral hatred of Franklin Roosevelt and a belief that he would use any means necessary—even murder—to achieve his goals.

The revisionist community of the Second World War rested on the shoulders of Barnes, the " 'Atlas' of Revisionism," as he proudly called himself in his later years.[78] Barnes's strident anti-interventionism had caused the *New York World-Telegram* to drop his column in 1940 in response to what Barnes believed was pressure from "the war-mongers," British intelligence, and the Morgan bank. He bitterly reflected that if the United States entered the war, "there will be no need of columnists in a few years. The columns will be furnished by the Department of Propaganda."[79]

In the first year and a half of the war, Barnes had to mute his suspicions about the president and the war as the country rallied round the troops. Even the publishers of his textbooks asked him to rewrite certain sections to make them more patriotic.[80] But by 1943, as the military tide turned and an eventual U.S. victory seemed likely, some Roosevelt opponents began encouraging Barnes to turn his skeptical eye to the current war. Charles Tansill, a conservative historian and later Pearl Harbor conspiracist, urged Barnes to write a revisionist work, as did William Neumann, a young pacifist historian who had been inspired by Barnes's earlier books. "I had thought that the work that you and others did in the '20s and '30s might forestall a reoccurrence," wrote Neumann, "but the comedy begins anew."[81]

Barnes quickly set to work assembling a community of scholars and journalists who were skeptical about the official version of U.S. entry into the war. He corresponded with several like-minded historians, all of them prewar anti-interventionists, and provided them with encouragement, information, and connections. As he networked with prominent scholars and novices alike, Barnes also trolled for money for his project from Robert E. Wood, the Sears, Roebuck CEO who had led and helped to bankroll the America First movement.[82] Ultimately, Barnes's friends and colleagues would write some of the most influential early Pearl Harbor revisionist works.[83] His goal was stunningly ambitious: in the midst of total war, he hoped to persuade the American people that their commander-in-chief was a would-be dictator who had ruthlessly allowed twenty-four hundred Americans to be murdered so that he could pursue his imperial ambitions.

One of Barnes's most significant correspondents was his comrade in the lost cause of isolationism, John T. Flynn.[84] Like Barnes, Flynn had a personal stake in showing that the war he had so fervently resisted was based on a lie. Also like Barnes, Flynn had paid a professional price for his unyielding isolationism in 1940, when the *New Republic* "liquidated" his column.[85] Undaunted, he continued to criticize the Roosevelt administration. In 1943, he succeeded in finding a publisher for *As We Go Marching*, a book-length polemic on the alleged fascist tendencies of the New Deal. Flynn sent his manuscript to Barnes, who responded with four type-written, single-spaced pages of suggestions and praise. The book did not mention Pearl Harbor, as Flynn had no evidence yet to confirm his deep suspicions of conspiracy. Barnes had no evidence, either, but he did urge Flynn to stress "FDR's indomitable and boundless will to power, and his utter opportunism."[86]

While Barnes and Flynn nursed their grievances and suspicions in the early years of the war, another man with a strong personal interest in Pearl Harbor began preparing his plans to refute the official story. Up until the early morning hours of December 7, 1941, Adm. Husband E. Kimmel had enjoyed a sterling career. The son of a Confederate officer, he had served with distinction in World War I and worked briefly as an aide to Assistant Navy Secretary Franklin Roosevelt. In February 1941, he assumed command of the U.S. Pacific Fleet.[87] At the time of the Japanese attack, Kimmel seemed destined for even greater glory.

Yet along with General Short, Kimmel found himself sharing the blame for the military's lack of preparedness at Pearl Harbor. At first, Kimmel believed it was his patriotic duty to accept responsibility. Like Short, he reluctantly submitted his resignation after the Roberts report, thinking that his early retirement would bring his period of disgrace to an end.

He was wrong. In an uncharacteristic display of political ineptitude, President Roosevelt startled his war and Navy secretaries in late February 1942 by deciding that the Hawaiian commanders should be court-martialed. The trials would be held after the war.[88] Roosevelt apparently believed strongly that Kimmel and Short were responsible for the large number of casualties and wanted them punished. But Kimmel's continued willing-ness to accept blame with silence and grace was dependent on the Navy's willingness to limit his punishment. Now he felt betrayed. "I do not wish to embarrass the government in the conduct of the war," he wrote. "I do feel, however, that my crucifixion before the public has about reached the limit."[89]

Kimmel argued that it was only fair for the Navy to hold his court martial immediately. That way, he could face his accusers and clear his name. But the Roosevelt administration insisted that wartime trials would endanger national secrets. Starting in the fall of 1943, Congress revis-ited the Pearl Harbor court martial issue every six months, as it debated whether to keep extending the statute of limitations for prosecution of the two commanders. Each time, the debates provided opportunities for the president's critics to discuss the broader issue of whom to blame for the disaster.[90] In June 1944, amid the partisan rancor of an election year, Congress agreed to delay the trials once again, but only if the Army and Navy launched new Pearl Harbor investigations. To avoid the appearance of a cover-up, Roosevelt reluctantly agreed to the new inquiries. By this time, Kimmel was so enraged that he refused to accept any responsibility at all for the catastrophe.[91]

As the first post–Pearl Harbor presidential election approached in 1944, Kimmel discovered that he might use partisan politics to help his cause. It was a difficult election for the Republicans because any attacks on the president's current war policy seemed unpatriotic, while criticism of domestic policies seemed irrelevant. The solution, some activists urged, was to assail Roosevelt's *prewar* foreign policy and suggest that a different president might have kept the country out of war, or, at the least, been better prepared at its start. In the spring, as the party united behind New York governor Thomas Dewey, Republican leaders began exploring the possibility of using Pearl Harbor as a campaign issue.

Knowing of Kimmel's anger, a Republican Party staffer, George H. E. Smith, approached the admiral's lawyer and began working closely with him to prepare a precise chronology of what key officials knew and when they knew it.[92] Excited by the partisan possibilities, Smith reported back to his party's bosses that the catastrophe could be portrayed as a lethal example of New Deal incompetence. "It can be shown with telling documentation," he wrote, "that the Roosevelt pre-war approach to foreign policy was so stupid and inept that it constituted a danger to American interests and to world peace which contributed to the ultimate outbreak of war."[93]

Meanwhile, Flynn and Barnes also contacted the Republicans. Flynn worked as a consultant for the GOP, giving speeches and writing essays that amplified his argument that the New Deal was essentially fascistic. He proclaimed that Roosevelt's reelection would mean the triumph of the "unholy alliance of corrupt politicians interested in jobs and reckless radical zealots interested in revolution."[94] Yet Flynn's arguments were tame compared to Barnes's polemics. In a letter to Bruce Barton, a party official and advertising executive, Barnes told the Republicans it was time for them to stop acting like a "Quaker deaconness" and start telling the truth about the president. Roosevelt had, in fact, caused "the murder and maiming of thousands—perhaps millions—of American boys in a deliberately-provoked and futile war."[95] Barton responded calmly that Dewey could not attack the commander in chief on war policy. With ten million men in the armed services, he said, Americans "do not want to hear anything about the war except that it is being won and that their boys therefore are each day nearer home."[96]

Despite the universal desire to support the troops, the drumbeat of accusations about a possible White House conspiracy continued. With two months left to go in the campaign, Senators Burton Wheeler and Henrik Shipstead proposed a Senate investigation of allegations that Roosevelt had ordered the imprisonment of a U.S. code clerk who could prove that the president was lying about prewar aid to Britain. Tyler Kent, a former employee of the U.S. embassy in London, had been convicted in Britain of spying for the Nazis. But Kent's mother insisted that his real crime was his knowledge of secret messages exchanged between Roosevelt and Winston Churchill.[97] The Senate declined to investigate Kent's patently self-serving and false defense.[98]

Meanwhile, in the House, Republican congressmen began demanding answers from the White House on Pearl Harbor. In a speech clearly influenced by Smith's research, Representative Hugh Scott posed twenty-four troubling questions about intelligence failures before the war. Scott used awkward, tentative phrasing, but behind his use of the passive voice lurked unmistakably aggressive intentions. There were reports, he said, that the U.S. government had received warnings of the Pearl Harbor attack from the Korean underground, Australian intelligence, and a U.S. naval officer. And yet the government had done nothing.[99] Implicitly, Scott was raising the big question: Was the president so willfully blind to all signs of a Japanese conspiracy because he was remarkably stupid, or, indeed, was he the most diabolical conspirator of them all?

Flynn also struggled with this question. He and other Roosevelt critics feared that a fourth term for Roosevelt might mean the end of American democracy. Charles Lindbergh even worried that the president might cancel the election and appoint himself dictator. Deeply fearful of the consequences of a Democratic victory, Flynn decided it was time to write what he and other Pearl Harbor critics knew about the background to the attack. With just weeks to go before the election, he convinced the archconservative, formerly isolationist *Chicago Tribune* to publish the first revisionist account of the origins of World War II.

"The Truth about Pearl Harbor" contained the essential outlines of later Pearl Harbor conspiracy theories. According to Flynn, Roosevelt had goaded the Japanese into attacking—and had indeed known that an attack was imminent—but had done nothing to warn the commanders at Pearl. Afterward, he and his secretary of state proceeded to cover up their ineptitude and impose on "two helpless officers the odium of their guilt."[100] The *Tribune* called it an "overpowering" exposé of "a governing clique seeking to save itself from disgrace by damning innocent men."[101] Flynn printed thirty thousand copies of the article and sent one "to every publisher and every editor in [the] country, to every commentator, columnist and news service," along with every congressman and senator and "large numbers of influential private persons." He hoped to force a congressional inquiry.[102]

Although Flynn accused Roosevelt of needlessly provoking war, he did not think that the president knew when and where the attack would come. Indeed, there was no evidence that he did. But as Flynn composed his article, Republican leaders were learning a national secret, a secret that potentially could lead to credible evidence of a deeper conspiracy. Someone privy to the military inquiries told them about Magic.

THE MAGIC CABLES would provide tantalizing evidence to Pearl Harbor conspiracists that the government was covering up the truth. The president's critics were looking for evidence of conspiracy before they ever heard of Magic. Its revelation just confirmed their beliefs.

For much of the war, only a few top officials and intelligence analysts knew about Magic. But bits of information about the program began to leak in the summer of 1944 as the Army and Navy continued their congressionally mandated inquiries.[103] The Army Board was particularly interested in reading the Magic cables, but the White House refused to give the investigators the most important decrypts. The Army investigators were intrigued; they knew that these potentially explosive documents existed, but they did not know exactly what they said.

With the investigations continuing and the presidential election heating up, a partisan leak was inevitable. In late September, six weeks before the election, Governor Dewey heard about Magic. He later said that a "number of individuals" had leaked him the information and told him it was his "duty to expose the facts so that the people might make their choice in the election on the basis of full knowledge of the dreadful incompetence or misconduct of the national administration."[104]

The leak put Dewey in a bind. He wanted to persuade the voters that Roosevelt had been incompetent or worse before Pearl Harbor. But he did not want to appear to be leaking national secrets in the midst of war. When he launched a slashing but somewhat vague attack on Roosevelt's "desperately bad" prewar foreign policy, the president and his advisers moved swiftly to shut him up.[105]

On September 26, an aide to Gen. George Marshall flew from Washington to Oklahoma to deliver a sealed letter to the candidate from the supreme Army commander of America's war. Marshall's letter began by ordering Dewey to stop reading unless he was prepared to keep the secrets about to be revealed to him. A smart man, Dewey sensed a trap: What if the letter "revealed" what he already knew? By consenting to the conditions, he would agree to muzzle himself. Handing the letter back, he told the aide that he would be "happy to talk to General Marshall on any matter if he so desired" but that he was not prepared to make "blind commitments."[106]

Two days later, Marshall's aide visited Dewey again, this time at the governor's mansion in Albany. The general had written another letter, this time acknowledging that Dewey had the right to disclose any information he already knew. Despite grave misgivings, Dewey finally agreed to read the letter and learn the administration's arguments against telling the public what he had learned about Pearl Harbor.

In the letter, Marshall revealed the U.S. government's success in breaking the Japanese code. The Magic intercepts had been extremely significant, he said, but had not told the government that an attack would come in Hawaii. The whole Magic story was thus irrelevant to understanding Pearl Harbor. Moreover, it could not be made public. The Japanese, the general explained, had no idea that the United States had broken the code, and *they were still using it*. As a true patriot, Dewey was honor-bound to keep the secret for the good of the country.[107]

Dewey found this hard to believe. The Japanese had not changed their codes in three years? Actually, Marshall was telling the truth: Japanese diplomats did continue to send significant messages in the prewar code, and much of the U.S. military's knowledge of Hitler's plans in Europe came from the dispatches of the Japanese ambassador in Berlin.[108] Even more important, U.S.

code breakers worried that the disclosure of the Magic deciphering machine would alert the Japanese that the United States had broken their naval codes after Pearl Harbor. The United States had won the Battle of Midway because of this intelligence coup, which provided a window on Japanese planning.[109] But Dewey did not entirely believe Marshall on this point. Convinced that Roosevelt was a "traitor" who deserved impeachment because of Pearl Harbor, he felt justified in doing all he could to force the man from office.[110] He knew, though, that he had no choice but to abandon this line of attack. If he kept quiet, he lost a valuable campaign issue, but if he revealed the information, the administration could justifiably accuse him of treason.

The Pearl Harbor critics were stunned in November 1944 when Roosevelt won another vote of confidence from the American people, defeating Dewey 53 to 46 percent in the popular vote. As the president's party won its seventh straight national election, Roosevelt's critics remained shut out of power. They were marginalized; and people on the margins are most inclined to see conspiracies against them.

THE PRESIDENT'S CONTINUED popularity mystified his critics. Why were the American people so resistant to their message? The obvious answer, of course, was that they were attacking a popular president during a necessary war. But FDR's critics saw their failure differently. It was the result of a plot—a plot against America. In their mind, a cabal of government agents, media provocateurs, and antifascist activists were part of the plot. It was the critics' task to unmask these conspirators. In this way, they—the unfairly maligned opponents—could regain control. But they had to be careful in their quest to expose the true story of the Roosevelt administration. "Any discussion of this enterprise should be highly confidential," Barnes told Robert Wood, "for if there is anything the powers that be fear it is a calm exposition of the facts."[111] The truth could set them free. It could also prompt the FBI to start a file on them.

The Pearl Harbor skeptics had good reason to believe the government was out to get them, for indeed it was. After the excesses of World War I and the early postwar years, Attorney General Harlan Fiske Stone in 1924 had appointed young J. Edgar Hoover to head the Bureau of Investigation and strictly limited it to "investigations of violations of law." But during the New Deal, Hoover's newly expanded Federal Bureau of Investigation moved back into the business of spying on the "ideas and associations" of potential dissenters.[112]

Roosevelt first directed the bureau to begin systematically collecting intelligence on "subversive activities in the United States" in 1936. As a U.S. Senate committee later noted, Roosevelt's failure to define "subversive activities" for the bureau laid the groundwork for decades of "excessive intelligence gathering about Americans."[113] The president made this decision unilaterally and secretly, at Hoover's suggestion. Indeed, as Hoover explained in a memo in 1938, it was "imperative" to keep the domestic spying program secret, not to thwart foreign spies, who undoubtedly knew they were being followed, but "to avoid criticism or objections which might be raised to such an expansion by either ill-informed persons or individuals having some ulterior motive."[114] These "ill-informed persons" were apparently members of Congress.

Once the war began in Europe in 1939, Roosevelt and Hoover shared an obsession with identifying potential subversives. As the director of the agency charged with stopping subversion, Hoover took responsibility for spreading public fear and offering his bureau as an antidote to that fear. "It is known," Hoover told Congress five days after the war began, "that many foreign agents roam at will in a nation which loves peace and hates war. At this moment lecherous enemies of American society are seeking to pollute our atmosphere of freedom and liberty."[115] He then asked for, and received, more money from Congress to fight these enemies. In effect, as the civil liberties activist Frank Donner has noted, Hoover was making himself into the U.S. minister of internal security.[116]

The president saw potential benefits in expanding Hoover's budget and authority. In 1940, as the war raged in Europe and the "Great Debate" over intervention raged at home, Roosevelt broadened the definition of "subversive activities" to include sending hostile telegrams to the president. "As the telegrams all were more or less in opposition to national defense," his press secretary, Steve Early, wrote to Hoover, "the President thought you might like to look them over, noting the names and addresses of the senders."[117] Hoover obliged, and Roosevelt thanked him for the "interesting and valuable" reports.[118] The president also ordered the FBI to tap the phones of people who might later engage in subversive activities.[119] Congress had explicitly prohibited wiretapping, but Roosevelt's attorney general at the time approved the FBI's wiretap program. The law, he said, made it illegal to "intercept and divulge" communication, and the government had no intention of *divulging* the information—except, of course, to other parts of the government.[120]

Roosevelt ordered Hoover to wiretap, bug, and physically spy on his anti-interventionist opponents during the Lend-Lease debate of early 1941.[121] He contended that they must be getting money from the nation's enemies. Hoover complied with reports on Senator Nye, Senator Wheeler, Colonel Lindbergh, and the America First Committee, among others. In a clear case of harassment, the Internal Revenue Bureau also investigated the finances of America First without giving a reason for the inquiry.[122]

The FBI's reports on the anti-interventionists were filled with gossip about the president's political opponents but contained no evidence of illegal activity or foreign connections. The surveillance did, however, help the government collect political intelligence. Ironically, considering Hoover's diligence, Roosevelt was not content with the FBI reports alone, and soon hired his own personal spy, the former journalist John Franklin Carter, and attached him to the State Department. Paid with "special emergency" funds, Carter amassed a staff of eleven men charged with spying on the president's enemies. Hoover was furious and began spying on FDR's spy.[123]

With Hoover's assistance, Roosevelt used taxpayer money and federal bureaucrats to investigate and harass his political enemies. To Flynn, the president's expansion of the FBI was part of his plan to establish a police state and drag the country into war. "You have to terrify the people before they will authorize military expenditures," he wrote to Senator Bennett Clark in 1940. "This is part of that program."[124] Roosevelt may have sincerely believed—or else convinced himself that he believed—that he needed to monitor and suppress his enemies at a time of national emergency. In his opponents' eyes, though, he was concocting a phony emergency to expand his power.

At the same time the FBI expanded its secret surveillance of dissidents, the Justice Department publicly pursued opponents of war by prosecuting thirty right-wing leaders for wartime conspiracy. In *U.S. v. McWilliams*, the government charged a motley collection of fascist intellectuals and Hitler sympathizers with spreading propaganda to further the international Nazi conspiracy. The indictment was clearly an abuse of prosecutorial authority. Though most of the defendants were anti-Semites, the government could not prove that they had received money or instructions from abroad. Most of the alleged "conspirators" had never even met before the trial. In a brazen act of intimidation, the special prosecutor darkly hinted that he might add Senator Burton Wheeler to the list of alleged seditionists. The case quickly descended into farce as the defendants made a mockery of the proceedings. After seven months of trying to control the shouted objections, befuddled witnesses, and ad hominem attacks, the trial judge dropped dead of a heart attack. His successor declared a mistrial, and the Justice Department ultimately abandoned the case.[125]

In retrospect, the Roosevelt administration's bumbling attempts to prosecute American fascists seems to prove its ineptitude at conspiring against its most extreme opponents. But former anti-interventionists viewed the case as yet another confirmation of the New Deal's totalitarian tendencies. As Harry Elmer Barnes wrote to Roger Baldwin of the American Civil Liberties Union, this "frame-up makes the Reichstag Fire Trials seem fairly respectable jurisprudence and equitable criminal procedure by comparison."[126]

While the government tried to criminalize their dissent, the Pearl Harbor critics believed, the Jewish-owned media prevented them from publishing their criticism of the president. Ignoring the enormous power of the Hearst and Patterson-McCormick press, the anti-interventionists believed that Jewish-controlled newspapers, magazines, and commentators defined the public debate and managed everything that Americans saw, heard, and read about Roosevelt. This helped to explain why FDR, the enemy of America, had been elected president four times.

In the view of the anti-interventionists, the Jews' most important weapon in the propaganda wars was their control of Hollywood. Before Pearl Harbor, prominent anti-interventionists believed that Jewish movie moguls tried to manipulate the public by making pro-British and anti-Nazi movies. Flynn helped Senators Wheeler and Nye to launch an investigation of alleged Hollywood pro-war propaganda just months before the United States entered the war. The anti-interventionists feared that their opponents would use this tool of mass persuasion to push their own un-American agenda.[127] Flynn believed that antifascist movie producers were "the most potent and dangerous fifth column in America."[128]

Flynn and other mainstream Pearl Harbor conspiracists had a complicated relationship to anti-Semitism. They repeatedly and publicly disavowed any prejudice against Jews. Flynn in particular repudiated American Nazis, worrying that the public would associate him with them. Yet his declarations of concern for American Jews always had a menacing undertone. If the Jews knew what was good for them, he often said, they would stop provoking the rest of us. Otherwise, the victimized conservatives would rise up against "minority groups," and Jews would find that their paranoid fantasies had become reality.[129]

Flynn nursed such intense hatred of "Jewish Hollywood" because he believed that his political enemies controlled the modern media, and thus controlled the public's understanding of the war. Flynn and his friends still had access to the print media; even after the *New Republic* cancelled his column, he could publish in the *Chicago Tribune* and with right-wing publishing houses. But his opponents seemed to command the attention of the new media, radio and motion pictures. "The moving picture industry," wrote Flynn in a confidential memo to the America First Executive Committee just months before Pearl Harbor, "went out 100 per cent for war propaganda pictures. The radio gave time to some of our speakers but filled in the space between with a ceaseless flow of propaganda."[130] In his view, FDR and the Jews of Hollywood had the unchallenged authority to tell the story of the war—and the story of its supposedly un-American opponents.

As if persecution by the Jews and the government were not enough, the old anti-interventionists also felt besieged by antifascist activists. These American opponents of Hitler had organized in pro-intervention groups in the late 1930s as the crisis in Europe escalated. One of the loudest voices for intervention was the Friends of Democracy, whose national committee included such luminaries as the German-born writer Thomas Mann and the philosopher John Dewey. L. M. Birkhead, a former minister who served as national director, accused America First of harboring Nazis and giving "aid and comfort" to Hitler.[131]

Once the war started, the antifascists intensified their attacks. Several wrote salacious exposés that accused prewar anti-interventionists of promoting un-American ideas. Although anti-interventionists claimed that they wanted to save the republic, the authors argued, in fact they were engaged in a "plot against America." In *Sabotage! The Secret War against America*, Albert E. Kahn and Michael Sayers alleged that Nazis secretly controlled America First and manipulated anti-interventionist congressmen. Other anti-isolationist books took the classic form of the diary of an undercover agent. Richard Rollins's *I Find Treason*, for example, told the story of his infiltration of the American Nazis. The most popular book-length exposé was *Under Cover: My Four Years in the Nazi Underworld of America—The Amazing Revelation of How Axis Agents and Our Enemies Within Are Now Plotting to Destroy the United States,* by the antifascist activist Avedis Derounian, writing under the name John Roy Carlson. A gripping tale of the author's secret involvement in America First and other right-wing organizations, *Under Cover* sold more than a million copies and became the best-selling nonfiction book of 1944.[132]

Under Cover infuriated the former anti-interventionists. They believed that they represented the only citizens who truly put America first, yet now their enemies were calling *them* unpatriotic. The former America First members mobilized to prevent the antifascist activists from maligning the true Americans. "We must say to the bureaucrats and the crackpots and the Communists and all of the disciples of totalitarianism," said Texas Congressman Martin Dies, "Americanism must live, America shall live." Behind the antifascist exposés, Dies saw a "well-organized and highly financed conspiracy."[133]

Flynn responded with a well-organized and highly financed conspiracy to discredit the antifascists. He secretly raised money from rich industrialists to hire investigators to dig up dirt on *Under Cover*'s author, the "alien-born" Derounian.[134] He hoped to raise $50,000 to turn the public against the antifascists. Flynn also published numerous articles and two long pamphlets on Derounian and his "smear terror." In a mirror image of Derounian's technique, Flynn portrayed the "smear conspiracy" as an un-American attempt to divide the country.[135] He encouraged Senator Wheeler to fight for a congressional investigation of the antifascists, "pitched on the theory, which is true, that there is some power, cloaked in secrecy and financed in some secret way, which is carrying on a campaign of slander and traduction against American citizens in positions of leadership."[136] Congress declined to fund Wheeler's request.

Flynn apparently saw no irony in demanding a congressional investigation of antifascists as America fought a war against fascism. In his Alice-in-Wonderland view of the war, the American fascist sympathizers on trial in *U.S. v. McWilliams* were the victims of a government run amok. The real villains of the war were the Americans who were *excessively anti-Hitler.*

Why were these antifascists such a danger to a country fighting a total war against fascism? Beyond their anger at being called traitors to a country they loved, the conservatives saw a conspiracy of various un-American forces behind the antifascist crusade. There were three main groups backing the anti-isolationist books, Flynn believed: the Jews, the Roosevelt administration, and the communists.[137]

And here he marked a seemingly small but very important development in twentieth-century conspiracy theories. In his famous Des Moines speech, Lindbergh had railed against the Jews and Roosevelt, but the British had been the third member of his unholy trinity. Flynn's substitution of the Red menace for the British one showed the increasing importance of anticommunism among the Pearl Harbor conspiracists. Indeed, as the war continued, he saw little reason to distinguish between the communists and the New Dealers. They were all pursuing the same goal: subversion, totalitarianism, and the demonization of the few good men who opposed their plot.

Those who saw the hand of Stalin at work in America were voices in the wilderness during the war. They had high hopes, though, for the new world that would be born when the shooting stopped. "No matter in what direction the election goes," wrote Flynn to the conservative publisher DeWitt Wallace in October 1944, "the atmosphere is going to change. I am as sure of that as I have ever been of anything in my life."[138] Flynn and his friends would be back on top, and the real un-Americans would come to regret it.

THOUGH THEY WERE despondent about its results, the election did provide Roosevelt's critics with one consolation. Once FDR won his fourth term, the administration agreed to release the summaries of the Army and Navy inquiries into Pearl Harbor. The summaries made it clear why the administration wanted to keep the full reports secret. In contrast to the White House–controlled Roberts Commission, the Army and Navy both placed much of the blame on Washington. The Navy virtually exonerated Admiral Kimmel, and the Army Board sharply criticized both General Short and his superiors in Washington.[139] Secretary of War Henry Stimson and Navy Secretary James Forrestal ordered yet more investigations to counter the embarrassing summaries.[140]

Then, on April 12, 1945, the man so hated by the Pearl Harbor revisionists, the president with a "boundless will to power," suddenly passed from the scene. Hundreds of thousands of people gathered the next day to watch the presidential train carry Roosevelt's casket from Warm Springs, Georgia, to Washington. Many of the mourners wept openly.[141]

Those who believed him guilty of conspiracy greeted Franklin Roosevelt's death with relief and even celebration. Harry Elmer Barnes and his friends, for example, rejoiced in the "liberation" of America.[142] In the short term, the revisionists needed to remain quiet as most Americans mourned the loss of their beloved president. But Roosevelt's death emboldened his critics; at long last, they might be able to get a thorough investigation of what they saw as his greatest crime.

The new president bore no personal responsibility for the disaster at Pearl Harbor and was less concerned with avoiding charges of intelligence failures or conspiracy. Still, Harry Truman was a loyal Democrat who wanted to protect the memory of the man who had chosen him to be vice president. During his first few months as president, Truman focused on ending the war, not investigating its origins. Once the war concluded in August, though, the new president had to balance his loyalty to Roosevelt against the political liability of appearing to endorse a cover-up.

These concerns became urgent just two weeks after the atomic bombs ended the war. A naval officer in the White House learned that military officials had apparently leaked top-secret documents to Flynn, who was using them to write a new exposé on Pearl Harbor for the *Chicago Tribune*. The president and his advisers decided they needed to preempt Flynn by releasing the Army and Navy reports on Pearl Harbor.[143] Before the release, though, military officers censored the reports and took out all references to Magic, which had revealed the Japanese determination for war in the fall of 1941. The blistering Army Board report said that Washington officials had learned that a Japanese attack was imminent "from informers and *other sources*." But just who or what were these "other sources"? The censored report was deliberately vague.[144]

Truman had tried to keep the truth about Magic from reaching the public, but it was impossible for him to stop all the leaks. As a result of the investigations, many Army and Navy officers knew about Magic, and they were furious with Roosevelt for pursuing Kimmel and Short. One of them apparently leaked the story of the code breaking to Flynn. Within days of the release of the military reports, Flynn published the first public account of Magic.[145]

In "The Final Secret of Pearl Harbor," published in the *Tribune* and reprinted as a pamphlet, Flynn charged that British and American officers had broken the Japanese code in 1941 and knew that the Japanese were poised to attack. Although Flynn did not publicly accuse the president of knowing *where* the attack would come, Roosevelt was clearly the villain of the piece. Flynn charged him with "doing everything except swimming under water with the bombs in his teeth," the *New Republic*'s columnist TRB snidely noted.[146] Privately, Flynn and *Tribune* publisher Robert McCormick told each other that they suspected the real truth of Pearl Harbor was still to be revealed. In their view, Pearl Harbor was not the result of incompetence; it was a conspiracy.[147]

The revelation of Magic was so explosive that the president and his party could no longer avoid a congressional investigation. To preempt the Republicans, the Democratic leadership of the House and Senate called for an immediate joint congressional inquiry. Senate Majority Leader Alben Barkley appointed himself chairman. The committee included six Democrats and four Republicans, a division reflecting the Democrats' numerical edge in Congress.[148] The Democrats had agreed to an inquiry, but they were determined to hire the staff and control the direction of the probe.

The Republicans were equally determined to be heard. To foil the Democrats' control of the staff, they raised private funds to hire a GOP activist as their own "chief research expert."[149] The stakes were high: Senator Homer Ferguson of Michigan, one of two Republican senators on the panel, proclaimed that nothing less than the survival of American democracy depended on "ascertaining the truth" about Pearl Harbor.[150] The Republicans speculated darkly that the Truman administration was trying to bury this truth. Rumors circulated throughout Washington that some of Roosevelt's most damning papers had suddenly disappeared.[151] The journalist John Chamberlain predicted that the investigation would make the rancorous debates over entry into World War I "look like a polite exchange at a garden party."[152]

The congressional hearings opened in November 1945 with all of the media attention one would expect for a major investigation of the possible subversion of American democracy. Four hundred fifty spectators and five newsreel cameras crowded into the Senate Office Building's caucus room to observe the proceedings. Under the intense lights installed for the cameras, the five senators and five congressmen sat sweating at long tables facing their witnesses. The committee members struggled to make their voices heard over the whirring of motion picture cameras and the popping of flashbulbs. On the walls, brightly colored maps told the story of the battle. Senator Ferguson brought his own prop: a whitewash brush he ostentatiously placed on the desk in front of him.[153]

The first two witnesses, the chief of naval intelligence and a colonel on the general staff, confirmed what Flynn had revealed. As *Newsweek* writers reported in italics for emphasis: "*The Government of the United States was in full possession of advance information that Japan intended to strike within a matter of days, and the knowledge came from a source beyond dispute—Japan itself.*"[154] Washington was reading most of Japan's secret messages for months before the attack, the witnesses testified, and by December 3 top officials knew that the war could begin at any moment.

For the next six months, the committee members tried to tease out the implications of this disclosure. Because they knew that the Japanese were planning to attack, did Washington officials do all that they could to alert the Hawaii commanders? General Marshall insisted that they had.[155] Admiral Kimmel and General Short insisted just as emphatically that "vital information" had been withheld from them. "Had this information been furnished to me," Short testified, "I am sure that I would have arrived at the conclusion that Hawaii would be attacked and would have gone on an all-out alert."[156]

The committee spent much time investigating whether the Japanese had sent a message before the assault known as the "winds code." Thanks to an earlier intercepted message, U.S. intelligence knew that the Japanese had told their agents to listen for a secret message in the middle of their propaganda radio broadcasts. If all other means of communication failed, then the weather report would transmit the message that war was imminent. "East wind, rain" would alert Japan's spies that relations with the United States had turned stormy.[157]

The winds code greatly appealed to the media: it conjured up B-movie images of Japanese secret agents huddled around their radio receivers, straining to hear the sinister message from their commanders. But did the Japanese government ever send the message? One witness, Capt. Laurance Safford of the Office of Naval Communications, testified that he had seen a version of the "winds message" on December 4, 1941. A naval translator had scribbled the message—"war with U.S.; war with England; peace with Russia"—in colored crayon on yellow teletype paper, Safford said. Yet no one could find this piece of paper. Members of the investigating committee searched desperately for it, but, John T. Flynn wrote, "always there was a mysterious hand somewhere to frustrate them." Flynn further charged that Navy officials had traveled around the world to destroy all evidence of every single intercept of the winds message. Then they had threatened and browbeaten witnesses and forced them to repudiate Safford's charges.[158]

To the committee's chief counsel, a seventy-one-year-old conservative Democratic lawyer named William Mitchell, the fuss over the winds code was emblematic of the blind hatred of the Roosevelt opponents. First, not one other witness ultimately supported Safford's testimony. This meant that Captain Safford himself was either a lone fighter for truth or, as Mitchell and others believed, a bit of a nut. Safford had spent years struggling to prove that the Navy and the administration had "framed" Admiral Kimmel, and he was convinced that his enemies were engaged in a conspiracy to discredit him.[159] Mitchell found such a conspiracy incredible. Even more important, the counsel insisted again and again, it did not matter whether or not the winds code had been transmitted and intercepted. The Roosevelt administration already *knew* that Japan was preparing for war in early December. So why did Pearl Harbor revisionists such as Flynn call the alleged disappearance of the winds message a "bombshell"? Mitchell became so angry over what he saw as the Republicans' grandstanding that he and his staff quit in protest just one month into the investigation.[160]

Pearl Harbor, once a unifying symbol for the country, had now become a symbol of partisan discord, the *New Republic* noted.[161] The Republicans tried to use every witness and document to prove that evil forces were at work in the prewar White House. "It is possible that Hull pulled the trigger," said Senator Owen Brewster at one point, thus neatly shifting blame from the Japanese to America's own secretary of state.[162] Republicans who were not on the committee were even less restrained in their accusations. On the floor of the House, Congressman Dewey Short expressed shock that one witness was still alive to tell his story. "I'm surprised he has not been liquidated," Short said.[163]

Despite their claims, neither side really wanted to discover "the truth" about Pearl Harbor, but to use the Japanese attack to further their own interests.[164] For their part, the Democrats believed that Pearl Harbor showed the folly of isolationism. There was no point in trying to assign individual blame for a tragedy that stemmed from America's collective unwillingness to confront the dangers of a changing world. The whole country, President Truman said, had failed to foresee the menace posed by its enemies.[165]

The Republicans were furious at the president's attempt to blame the country for Pearl Harbor. For them, the tragedy demonstrated the evils of the man who had overseen the expansion of America's bumbling yet malevolent government. They had no trouble pinning the blame on one person. "Make no doubt of it," the *New Republic* columnist TRB claimed at the height of the congressional investigation, "this is a trial of Roosevelt."[166]

In part, the Republicans wanted to blame FDR for opportunistic reasons. "Republicans have long been clamoring for an *issue*," wrote party operative George H. E. Smith to several GOP leaders. "Pearl Harbor is ready-made for them on the highest emotional plane." If the party fumbled this chance, he warned, it should give up hope of ever regaining power. The Democrats, he said, would feel emboldened to change "the entire political and economic system of this country."[167]

But Republican leaders were exploiting Pearl Harbor not just for political gain. Many of them genuinely believed that the government was covering up evidence of a conspiracy. This was partly because the Roosevelt and Truman administrations had, indeed, tried to cover up "the truth" about Pearl Harbor. The government had authorized several investigations of the tragedy since 1941, but had always released information piecemeal and out of context. As the operative Smith noted, the government's constant problem was "how to get the Pearl Harbor skeleton out of the closet" without harming the Democratic Party.[168] Its uneasy and unconvincing solution was to reveal the skeleton one bone at a time, "now a femur, now a jawbone," as the journalist John Chamberlain put it.[169] Republicans responded by wondering if a murder had been committed.

The Democrats and Republicans could not even agree on their conclusions. The committee issued two reports that were antithetical in tone and content. The majority report was signed by all six Democrats and, in a move bitterly resented by revisionists, by the two Republican House members. In its most important passage, the majority report proclaimed that the committee had found no evidence that Roosevelt or his cabinet "tricked, provoked, incited, cajoled, or coerced Japan into attacking this Nation in order that a declaration of war might be more easily obtained from the Congress."[170]

But the two Republican senators told a much different story, one filled with manipulation, cover-ups, and deceit. Although they stopped short of contending that he intentionally exposed the fleet to attack, Ferguson and Brewster accused Roosevelt of provoking the Japanese, and then failing to put the Hawaiian commanders on full alert. These dissenters did not believe that the president withheld information because he wanted to protect the nation's code-breaking secrets; instead, they argued that he deliberately deceived the public for his own sinister purposes. "Indeed, the high authorities in Washington seemed to be acting upon some long-range plan which was never disclosed to Congress or the American people."[171] Throughout their quest to reveal this long-range plan, the investigators found that "there was a deliberate design to block the search for the truth."[172] In their view, it was their own government, not that of the enemy, that was guilty of infamy on December 7.

IN THE YEARS TO COME, many authors continued to search for the elusive, absolute "truth" about Pearl Harbor. The *Chicago Tribune* reporter George Morgenstern and the historian Charles Beard built on Flynn's work in the late 1940s; Charles Tansill, the conservative historian who had urged Barnes to examine the war's origins back in 1943, published his own revisionist work in 1952.[173] Flynn persevered with his quest to prove the plot at Pearl until he became too old and ill to work.[174] Harry Barnes also kept up the crusade by inspiring, editing, reviewing, and promoting books that argued for a conspiracy. "If I dropped Revisionism," he wrote in 1958, "it would stop as suddenly all over the world as the bloodstream of Marie Antoinette stopped when the guillotine blade dropped on her neck."[175] Although Barnes found a ready market for his work with right-wing publishers, he grew infuriated by the "mythmongers" and the "court historians" and became obsessed with proving that U.S. entry into World War II was "the most lethal and complicated public crime of modern times." Unhinged by the continued resistance to his arguments, the legendary revisionist of the First World War refused to believe the grisly evidence of Hitler's Final Solution. Once the patron saint of independent thinkers, Harry Barnes became a hero to Holocaust deniers.[176]

Admiral Kimmel and his admirers formed a different, intersecting circle of men who spent years trying to prove that the admiral had been the American Dreyfus, scapegoated by selfish politicians. Kimmel's cause was taken up by Adm. Robert Theobald, who worked with Barnes and Flynn to produce a major revisionist work in 1954.[177] These conspiracists created a community: they shared their research, helped secure funds and publishers, and reassured one another that the truth would ultimately prevail. But they could not prove that Roosevelt knew when or where the assault was coming, or that he deliberately provoked the Japanese into attacking.

In the 1970s and 1980s, the collapse of faith in the government after Vietnam and Watergate inspired a new generation of Pearl Harbor conspiracy books. Unlike earlier books, these new works did not suggest that the United States should never have entered World War II. To these authors, the broader issue was not isolationism versus interventionism but the consistent pattern of deceit by the federal government. However, none of these books ever proved the central allegation of Pearl Harbor conspiracy theories: that Roosevelt had known in advance of the specific location of the Japanese attack.[178]

The Pearl Harbor theories of the 1940s pointed both to the past and to the future. In many ways, these theories were the last gasp of isolationism. Opponents of intervention had worried that joining the war would mark the beginning of an American empire. The militarization of society, John T. Flynn worried, could herald the death of the republic. "We will not be able to stop it," he wrote in 1938 to the anti-interventionist senator William Borah, "it will get all mixed up with our thinking; it will thrust forward into the solution of our domestic problems foreign quarrels with which we should have nothing to do."[179] The Pearl Harbor conspiracists looked back with longing to the period before the United States had joined the perpetual war for perpetual peace.

Yet the early Pearl Harbor theories were not merely nostalgic. They also helped to construct a foundational myth of modern conservatism. In the mind of the conspiracists, Pearl Harbor demonstrated everything that was wrong with the New Deal: the "confusion, incompetence, wasteful extravagance, double-dealing and double-talking" of the expansive federal government, the GOP activist George Smith contended.[180] Franklin D. Roosevelt, the double-dealing and double-talking architect of this oppressive government, had "lied" the nation into war. This is what happened, the conservatives believed, when the government gained too much power at the expense of the people. As Representative Martin Dies told Congress, "When any group of supermen or social planners get control of government and impose their fanatical beliefs, they become avaricious for power and they subjugate the whole body politic."[181]

But were these planners really supermen, or were they just incompetent bureaucrats? The Pearl Harbor conspiracists could not seem to make up their minds on this point. The *Chicago Tribune* argued that Pearl Harbor showed Roosevelt's "insouciant stupidity or worse."[182] Yet how could an insouciantly stupid administration pull off such a grand conspiracy? The expanding government, these antistatists argued, could do nothing right—except when it enslaved its citizens. This inconsistency in logic would plague many antigovernment conspiracy theories for the rest of the twentieth century.

The Pearl Harbor critics also expected this conspiratorial organization called a government to leave clues for its enemies to prove its perfidy. Their reliance on the documents of the centralized state to prove their case against the state showed the increasing irrelevance of antistatist ideology. Roosevelt's opponents firmly believed that government investigations would prove the existence of a government conspiracy. Roosevelt, they seemed to think, was capable of provoking a Japanese attack, scapegoating the local commanders, and then wiping out all evidence of a conspiracy—except for a few documents he carelessly left behind for future anti-Roosevelt investigators.

But for all their hatred of the expansive, incompetent, yet malevolent federal government, the Pearl Harbor conspiracists began to see some virtues in one of the official agencies they used to fear. Back in 1940, Flynn had regarded the FBI as a part of President Roosevelt's plan to frighten the American people into granting more power to the presidency. In his view, J. Edgar Hoover, the man responsible for many of Attorney General Palmer's "atrocities after the last war," helped to persuade Americans that they needed to surrender some of their liberties to the government so that the government could protect them.[183]

But Flynn came to discover that Hoover shared some of his concerns and philosophies. Like Flynn, Hoover worried about the men and women they called "antifascists" during the war and "Reds" afterward. Throughout the war, Hoover's FBI leaked derogatory information about the anti-anti-interventionists to Flynn and his friends.[184] Hoover also shared their tendency to demonize their opponents as enemies of the republic.

Now that the war was over, the Roosevelt critics saw the glimmerings of a new dawn. "Their smearing days are over, John," Burton Wheeler had written Flynn in the midst of the war, "and the more they try to smear people now, the more it is going to react against them when this war is over."[185] It was time to expose the real plot against America, and this time the FBI was going to help them do it.

3

Masters of Deceit: Red Spies and Red Hunters in the McCarthy Era

IN THE EARLY YEARS of the cold war, when teams of scientists around the world were racing to discover the structure of DNA, an American chemist stood out among the contenders as the individual most likely to answer the fundamental question about the nature of life. One of the most brilliant scientists of the century, Linus Pauling was the leader of revolutions in quantum chemistry and molecular biology. The California professor had written several seminal works in chemistry, including his groundbreaking *Nature of the Chemical Bond*, and he published forty-three scientific papers from 1950 to 1952 alone.[1] European scientists, excited by Pauling's latest research, organized a meeting in London in May 1952 to discuss his recent discoveries.

There was only one problem: the U.S. government would not allow the guest of honor to leave the country. The State Department's passport office decided that permitting Pauling to attend the conference would not be in the "best interests of the United States."[2] According to the government, the famous professor and antinuclear activist might be a communist.

Pauling's outspoken leftist politics had first attracted the attention of the FBI in 1947.[3] At the start of the cold war, he had begun to associate himself "in a smaller or larger way with every peace movement that has come to my attention," he proudly recalled.[4] The bureau had expanded its investigation in 1950 when Louis Budenz, an ex-communist, named

Pauling as a potential subversive in testimony that was later thoroughly discredited.[5] After years of surveillance, government agents could never prove that Pauling had even attended a Communist Party meeting.

Nevertheless, throughout the 1950s, agents of the U.S. government did their best to ruin Pauling's career. They prevented him from speaking and traveling, urged private donors to stop funding his lab, and persuaded his university to launch an internal investigation of his politics. When Pauling denied Party membership under oath, FBI chief J. Edgar Hoover responded by urging the Justice Department to prosecute him for perjury.[6]

It was Hoover's suspicions that lay behind the passport division's decision to prohibit Pauling from attending the scientific meeting held in his honor.[7] Some scholars have speculated that he suffered his greatest scientific disappointment as a result. Had he been allowed to attend the conference, he might have seen the X-ray images of DNA taken by British scientists, and he, rather than the Cambridge University team of James Watson and Francis Crick, might have solved the riddle of the double helix.[8] Despite his disappointment in DNA research, Pauling did win the Nobel Prize for chemistry in 1954. Some U.S. officials argued against allowing him to travel to Sweden to accept it.[9]

The story of the U.S. government's harassment of Linus Pauling is, at first glance, a perplexing mystery. Why, in the midst of the cold war, did government officials actively impede the work of one of its greatest scientists, a researcher who could help to advance the frontiers of American science and showcase the superiority of capitalism? The answer lies in the conspiracy theory of communist subversion. This theory prompted America's internal security agency to identify one of its most innovative minds as an enemy of the state.

There were real reasons for Americans to fear communist spies during the cold war. Communists had, after all, spied on the U.S. government, especially during the U.S.-Soviet alliance of World War II. But the combination of defections by some key spies, good counterintelligence work by the FBI, and a strict loyalty-security program effectively destroyed this conspiracy. By 1951, when Senator Joseph McCarthy made headlines by denouncing a conspiracy "so immense" at the highest levels of the U.S. government, there were no Soviet spies of any importance remaining within the government.

Just when the U.S. government was winning the war on Soviet espionage, many Americans became convinced that they were losing it, and losing badly. And they reacted with panic. The post–World War II Red Scare cost thousands of people their careers, cast suspicion on the highest officials of the government, and discredited progressive politics for a generation, all because some Americans feared a defunct conspiracy, a conspiracy that communist defectors and the FBI had already destroyed.

The public revelation of the real but obsolete conspiracy of communist espionage inspired one of the most consequential conspiracy theories in U.S. history. Conspiracy theorists exaggerated the story of the espionage plot until it became unrecognizable; in their telling, it became the explanation for America's supposed "impotency," as Joe McCarthy said, after World War II.

The public officials who promoted this conspiracy theory used all of the powers of the secret agencies of the government to smash the phantom conspirators. Ironically, when these public officials began to conspire against the supposed red plotters, they would lay the foundation for a new generation of conspiracy theories about the government.

FROM THE TIME they seized power in 1917, Lenin and the Bolsheviks worried about the "countless conspiracies and countless attempts against Soviet power by people who are infinitely stronger than us."[10] To combat these plots, the new Soviet state set up its own conspiratorial organizations, the most extensive and dreaded security agencies in the world at the time. Some of these Soviet agents began coming to the United States in the 1920s as part of a coordinated campaign to glean industrial secrets from U.S. businesses. The Soviets' industrial espionage program was extremely successful over the years, with one American chemist, Harry Gold of Philadelphia, earning the Order of the Red Star for his efforts in helping the Soviets to unravel the mysteries of synthetic rubber, nylon, and photo processing.[11]

In 1933, after the United States opened diplomatic relations with the Soviets, Soviet spies expanded their operations to include the U.S. government as well as American industry.[12] Because of their respect for U.S. power in the world, the Soviets were tantalized by the possibility of gaining an insider's view of the workings of U.S. foreign policy. "In world politics, the U.S. is the determining factor," Moscow officials wrote in one memo to their spies in America. "There are no problems, even those 'purely' European, in whose solution America does not take part because of its economic and financial strength."[13] To discover America's proposed solutions to these problems, Soviet agents posing as diplomats began to recruit American case officers, who were charged with finding and managing sources who worked in key U.S. government agencies.[14]

The most significant of these early case officers was a young New Yorker named Whittaker Chambers. A talented writer, Chambers took charge of a cell of secret communists in the Roosevelt administration in 1934 and encouraged them to steal information. Chambers's sources included some upwardly mobile young bureaucrats, including a lawyer in the Agriculture Department, Alger Hiss, who would later become a counsel to the Nye Committee and then a mid-ranking official at the State Department, and economist Harry Dexter White, who was later appointed assistant secretary of the treasury.[15]

But in the late 1930s, Stalin's fear of conspiracy helped to ruin many of the networks that his agents had built. Fearing enemies within, the Russians turned on some of their own best agents, snatching them off the street, charging them with treason against the Soviet state, and ordering them back to Moscow, where they were often tried and executed. The purges disillusioned and terrified many agents, including Chambers. In 1938, alienated from his former comrades and fearful that he might become a victim of the purges himself, Chambers left the Soviet underground and went into hiding. The next year, as the Soviets and the Nazis signed a nonaggression pact and World War II began in Europe, he told his story of secret communists within the government to an official in the Roosevelt administration.[16]

At first, the U.S. government failed to take Chambers seriously, as State Department officials and FBI agents found the tale told by the disheveled, mumbling defector less than credible. For his part, Chambers was ambivalent about informing on his old friends, and he was deliberately vague and somewhat hostile to his government interrogators. The FBI opened files on those he named but did not immediately pressure them to leave the government.[17] Chambers emerged from hiding and settled into a new career as a journalist at *Time*, where he told a few friends of his former life as a spy. Despite the dangers posed by this critical defection, Soviet espionage in the United States continued to thrive. New case officers went on to recruit dozens more American agents.

The war soon provided an unprecedented opportunity for Soviet spies in the United States. After the Nazis attacked the Soviet Union in June 1941, President Roosevelt opened the flow of Lend-Lease supplies and began shipping food, oil, Army boots, jeeps, machine guns, tanks, and fighter planes to the country that would ultimately lose more than twenty million lives fighting Hitler. Besides sharing supplies, the U.S. government also began to share some intelligence with the Soviets, even when Stalin refused to reciprocate. As the U.S. Joint Chiefs of Staff wrote in 1943, "Even if we get no information from the Russians it is still, on the narrowest view, to our advantage to put into the hands of the Russians the means of killing more Germans."[18]

But the U.S. government kept some secrets from Stalin, secrets that the Soviets tried to discover on their own. Wartime Soviet intelligence agents created a network of military, industrial, and government spies who funneled valuable information to the U.S.S.R. They put their greatest effort into infiltrating the atomic bomb project. Klaus Fuchs, a German refugee physicist hired by the British for the project, and Theodore Hall, a young American scientist, passed secret information on the bomb from their posts in Los Alamos.[19] Machinist David Greenglass provided some sketches that confirmed their data. Harry Gold, the Soviets' most significant industrial spy, worked as a courier for both Greenglass and Fuchs, slipping their documents under his coat after anxious meetings on busy bridges in Santa Fe or in cramped apartments in Albuquerque. Besides Fuchs and Hall, other nuclear scientists and engineers in Canada, Tennessee, Chicago, and Berkeley also helped the Soviets.[20] Thanks to the stolen data, the U.S.S.R. tested its own bomb in 1949, probably about one to two years earlier than it would have on its own.[21]

The FBI knew the general outlines of this atomic espionage conspiracy, though none of its details. Thanks to their surveillance of the Communist Party leader Steve Nelson, bureau agents had learned that a graduate student and a research fellow in the Berkeley radiation laboratory were passing information on the bomb project to Nelson and the Soviets. To try to catch these spies, the bureau stepped up its surveillance of Nelson and sent 125 additional agents to the San Francisco Bay Area.[22] It was foolhardy for the Soviets to use Nelson as a spy, because his role in espionage would later provide ammunition for those who argued that membership in the Communist Party was equivalent to treason.

The Soviets also received important military information from a ring of communist spies in New York headed by Julius Rosenberg. A thin, intense Stalinist, Rosenberg recruited a group of his fellow engineers, many of them friends from his college days in the Young Communist League. Rosenberg also recruited his brother-in-law, David Greenglass, after the young sergeant was stationed at Los Alamos, though Greenglass's knowledge was crude compared to the disquisitions on nuclear physics that the Russians received from Fuchs. Julius's wife, Ethel, helped him with his espionage, but was not a major spy in her own right.[23]

Besides the Rosenberg group and the atom spies, a third significant Soviet wartime spy ring provided key political and military information. Centered in Washington, D.C., this network was run by Elizabeth Bentley. The product of a long line of Republican Episcopalians in New Milford, Connecticut, Bentley later claimed that her idealism led her to the Communist Party. This was partly true, but she was also drawn to the excitement of belonging to an organization that horrified her family and hometown. The thirty-year-old Vassar graduate started her espionage in 1938 as an assistant to her lover, who was one of the top Soviet agents in the United States. When he died in 1943, she took over his job. She made twice-monthly trips from her home in Manhattan to Washington, where she met with sources, soothed their anxieties, and collected their documents. One of her agents received information directly from Chambers's old source, now a high-ranking Treasury Department official, Harry Dexter White, who continued to pass information to the Soviets despite the defection of his former case officer. She discreetly tucked rolls of microfilm into her knitting bag, which she shared with her Soviet controllers.[24]

Like most of the communist spies in this era, Bentley's sources received no money for their efforts. In fact, thanks to the hefty dues imposed by the Party, they paid for the privilege of working for what they saw as the utopian goal of worldwide communism. During the Depression, they had seen professionals selling apples to survive, children eating out of trashcans, and millions malnourished, while government officials destroyed food. "In that period of passionate conviction," explained one American communist, Hope Hale Davis, "I could not understand anyone's being merely a theoretical Marxist."[25]

Moreover, during the war, the Soviet Union was allied with the United States. Some Americans spied because they disagreed with their government's decision to withhold crucial information from their ally in the battle against fascism. In particular, the atomic spies disagreed with the U.S. government's refusal to share nuclear information with the Soviets, which, they believed, showed that Americans were conspiring to use the bomb to establish global hegemony. Alan Nunn May, a Canadian who spied on the atomic project for the Soviets, later insisted that he was trying to ensure the "safety of mankind" by preventing one power from monopolizing the bomb. In this view, sharing information brought safety, even survival; by contrast, secrecy bred fear, conspiracy, and domination.[26]

The official conspiracy theorists at the FBI chased after many of these spies, especially those in the atomic program. Though they had little success during the war, the hunt for red spies in the early 1940s would profoundly influence Hoover and the FBI and U.S.-Soviet relations for years to come.[27] Ever since the Bolshevik Revolution, Hoover had believed that communism was "the most evil, monstrous conspiracy against man since time began—a conspiracy to shape the future of the world."[28] As he received increasing numbers of reports of Soviet spying in the United States during the war, he found more evidence for his conviction that the communists were "masters of deceit," as he would title his 1958 book.

Then, just after the end of the war, Elizabeth Bentley knitted together all of the disparate strands of the conspiracy for Hoover. In 1945, teetering on the edge of panic and paranoia, Bentley grew convinced that the FBI was about to arrest her, which was not true, and that her thuggish Russian controllers were thinking of assassinating her, which was. In November 1945, she went to the FBI's New York field office to give a complete report to the bureau and to save herself from Stalin's assassins. The New York operatives sent an urgent telegram to Washington in the middle of the night alerting FBI headquarters to this stunning development: the voluntary defection of a woman who "furnished information relative to a Russian espionage ring with which she was affiliated and which is presently operating in this country."[29] At 2 a.m. panicked FBI clerks began rifling through files for evidence to corroborate her story.[30] Thus began the Great Spy Scare of the 1940s and 1950s.

As he read Bentley's statement, Hoover became more convinced that all American communists were engaged in a massive conspiracy to subvert and destroy the republic. She named dozens of Americans who had cooperated with Soviet intelligence during the war. Most of her sources were mid-ranking bureaucrats, but a few had held influential positions: Lauchlin Currie, one of a half-dozen special assistants to President Roosevelt, had passed along a few bits of information orally, she said, and Harry Dexter White had been a "valuable adjunct" who stole some documents and tried to influence policy. She had also heard that a man at the State Department named Hiss—she could not remember his first name; was it Eugene?— spied for Soviet military intelligence.[31] This confirmed the FBI's preexisting suspicion of Alger Hiss, whom Chambers had named years before.[32] In response to the new information from Bentley and from another defector in Canada, the FBI began to wiretap and spy on Hiss, and State Department officials successfully pressured him to leave the government.[33]

On November 30, 1945, the FBI presented Bentley with the results of her confession: a 107-page, typed statement packed with all of the names she had given them—those of her brutal controllers, her skittish government sources, and her former lovers and friends. At the last minute, she refused to sign. "She characterized the Americans' activities as being motivated by an ideology," an FBI memo explained, "and that they felt that the information they obtained was to help an ally." The agents persisted. They did not have to remind her that she had a selfish interest in helping the government. She had no immunity agreement, and wartime espionage, even for an ally, was a capital offense. Bentley finally signed the statement.[34]

But the FBI and the Justice Department prosecutors still had no case. It was Bentley's word against the people she accused, and she had not saved any documents to prove her accusations. To gather more evidence, the FBI decided to run her as a double agent: she pretended to continue working for the Soviets, while the bureau followed her and remained in the shadows, collecting evidence for future trials.

Unfortunately for the FBI's case, the Soviets learned immediately of Bentley's defection. The head of Soviet counterintelligence for the British secret service, Kim Philby, was one of a handful of American and British security officials to be briefed on Bentley. Philby also happened to be a Soviet mole himself. He informed Moscow of her defection while she was still giving her statement. Soviet officials immediately contacted all of her sources, and any agents who might have known her sources, and told them to stop spying. In response to this unprecedented security breach, they rolled up their spy networks in the United States.[35] A few years later, they reactivated some atomic and military spies who had not known Bentley, but the FBI soon either caught these agents or forced them to flee.

Philby's information gave the Soviets the chance to save their American spies. But though Soviet intelligence saved its agents from prison, it did so only by turning them into *ex*-agents. Any attempts to reestablish contact with their agents could "lead to fatal consequences," Moscow controllers wrote their new station chief in Washington. In the new era, the Soviets in America were reduced to clipping newspapers, complaining about anti-Soviet American movies, and reporting on internal embassy disputes.[36] The KGB later resumed spying in the United States, but only when it found some mercenary Americans willing to spy in return for huge payments. It would take many years for Soviet espionage in America to recover from the damage caused by this one defection.

ONCE BENTLEY EXPOSED the real conspiracy of Soviet espionage in the U.S. government, the government had to decide how to respond to what could be seen as a monumental security fiasco. The most important actors in this drama were the president and the FBI director, who had very different views on the magnitude and current significance of the communist conspiracy in the United States.

Although he would become a fervent cold warrior committed to stopping the expansion of Soviet communism throughout the world, in 1945 President Truman did not think that communists in the United States posed much of a threat. He distrusted the FBI, which he regarded privately as a "Gestapo," and disliked Hoover, who consistently exaggerated the Soviet espionage threat, in Truman's view.[37] The excitable Hoover deluged Truman with memos about every credible and not so credible rumor of communist sympathizers in the government. In one memo from 1946, for example, Hoover warned Truman about the alleged un-American tendencies of Undersecretary of State Dean Acheson, former vice president Henry Wallace, former undersecretary of war John McCloy, and many other eminent and patriotic Democrats.[38]

Bizarrely, while Truman received these unfiltered reports of unsubstantiated gossip, he never learned of the Army's successful code-breaking operation, known as Venona, in which military cryptographers deciphered Soviet wartime cables and found proof for some of Bentley's charges. The head of the Army Security Agency insisted that the president should never be told about Venona.[39] The president thus saw little proof of a *real* espionage conspiracy but heard many tales told by self-interested and alarmist conspiracists. Given this incomplete and biased data, Truman soon learned to be skeptical of everything Hoover told him.

Hoover reciprocated with unrestrained loathing for the president. According to one of his assistants, "Hoover's hatred of Truman knew no bounds."[40] The president infuriated Hoover by creating a new Central Intelligence Group (later the CIA) to handle foreign intelligence and limiting the bureau to domestic work. In Hoover's view, Truman did not understand the importance of the FBI to U.S. national security, in part because the president underestimated the danger of domestic communism.

Not surprisingly, given his disdain for the unfounded allegations that the FBI chief sent him almost daily, Truman paid little attention to Hoover's warnings about the treasonous activities of Harry Dexter White. Despite Bentley's and Chambers's charges, Truman nominated White to be the executive director of the International Monetary Fund in January 1946. To Truman, the stories about White were unbelievable. The famed economist was the architect of the premier capitalist postwar institutions, the IMF and the World Bank. Not only was he clearly devoted to global free trade and exchangeable, capitalist currencies, but he also worked with other American officials to ensure U.S. dominance of the postwar economic order.[41] Because he trusted White and doubted the FBI, Truman ignored Hoover's warnings about White's alleged Soviet sympathies until after he had sent his nomination to the Senate.[42] White would direct the IMF for less than a year before he resigned, in part because of pressure from the FBI.[43]

In Hoover's view, Truman's decision to promote White proved that his administration was infested with communist agents and their dupes. What else could explain the president's decision to name a suspected spy to such a high post? In response, Hoover started a covert war against his president, a sort of internal government conspiracy aimed at discrediting those who he thought refused to take the communist conspiracy seriously enough. He began leaking top-secret information to Republicans in Congress who suspected communist influence in the Truman White House, giving them files, suggesting witnesses for their investigations, and even sending them lists of questions to ask. As one FBI memo reported, the bureau wanted to use anticommunists in Congress "in order to properly and factually bring before the American public what Communist activity has been going on in the government for many years."[44] In this way, Hoover could expose the blunders of his enemies in the White House while controlling the release of the information so that the president and his aides, not the FBI, would take the blame for past mistakes.[45]

Increasingly paranoid about his enemies in the White House, Hoover even began to fear that Truman might be planning some sort of ploy to discredit Bentley's accusations, which, thanks to Philby, the FBI had not been able to prove and which were still secret as the presidential election of 1948 approached. He thought that Truman's attorney general might attempt to prosecute the Bentley case without corroborating evidence because he knew it would fail. As one FBI official explained, the president would "then be in a position in 1948 to say that such charges of Communist infiltration made by Republicans were investigated by the bureau and shown to be without foundation."[46] Hoover projected his own Machiavellian tendencies onto the president and resolved to fight him with all the weapons available to him.

By 1948, as the campaign began, Hoover took his crusade against the administration to its logical—and disloyal—conclusion: he began using his power to ensure that Truman was not reelected. He leaked his secret file on the president to Truman's Republican opponent, Thomas Dewey. Most of the file consisted of rumors of the president's corruption years earlier when he was a political boss in Missouri.[47]

Unlike earlier conspiracy theorists who suspected the government of various crimes, however, Hoover was not an antistatist. He believed that the state had an important role to play in protecting Americans from overt enemies abroad and concealed enemies at home. In fact, he thought the state—particularly his arm of the state—should have more secret power. He was, however, opposed to the administration temporarily in control of the state and determined to turn it out of office. As the election approached, he began giving congressmen one file that he thought they needed to protect the state's security and confront the current government. It was marked "Elizabeth Bentley, Internal Security, Espionage."[48] Hoover planned to make the Bentley case public, in the proper congressional venue and at the proper time. He could not, however, control his star witness.

BENTLEY HAD LED a rather glamorous life as a spy: good money, luxurious vacations, and frequent dinners in New York's best restaurants. But the FBI did not pay nearly as well as the KGB, and furthermore, it seemed to be making little progress on her case. After more than two years as a double agent, she began thinking about making her story public in hopes of landing a lucrative deal with a book publisher. When she mentioned her intentions to her FBI supervisors, however, they prohibited her from talking to reporters.[49] Hoover wanted to manage when and how the Bentley story reached the public. But in direct defiance of the FBI's orders, Bentley contacted an ex-communist reporter on New York's Scripps-Howard newspaper and began to tell her tale.[50]

The *New York World-Telegram* broke the story on July 20, 1948. Deciding that a good spy story would be even better with a suggestion of sex, the editors dubbed her the "blond spy queen." The story of the red queen, whose "gnawing pangs of conscience" had driven her to the FBI, created an instant sensation in Washington.[51] Within days, Bentley was on a train to Washington to testify before two congressional committees, including the House Un-American Activities Committee (HUAC).

Bentley's spy story served the interests of an increasingly powerful conservative lobby that was determined to discredit liberal officials and their policies by associating them with communists. Since its birth in 1938, HUAC had been crusading to destroy communist influence in the country, which meant, in the views of most HUAC members, the destruction of the New Deal itself. Its chairman, J. Parnell Thomas of New Jersey, claimed that New Dealers worked "hand in glove with the Communist Party," and a powerful Democratic member, John Rankin of Mississippi, dismissed civil rights for African Americans as "communistic bunk."[52] A new member of the committee, Richard Nixon of California, had recently defeated the popular incumbent congressman from his district by falsely implying that he was in league with subversives and communists.[53]

The committee received help from a loosely organized group of a few hundred journalists, priests, businessmen, and ex-communists that had been working diligently for years to expose what they saw as the hidden influence of communism in American life. The businessmen funded the anticommunist network, the journalists disseminated its message, and the ex-communists compiled lists of their former comrades to investigate.[54] Most important, Hoover and the FBI used the secret powers of the government to gather information on these alleged subversives and funnel it to the red hunters on HUAC. Like Hoover, most of the members of the network were sincere in their deep aversion to communism, but many of them also saw the political advantages of linking liberalism with Bolshevism.

Some of the leaders of the anticommunist network had already established careers as antigovernment conspiracists. John T. Flynn, a journalist and the Nye Committee consultant and early Pearl Harbor skeptic, continued his critique of statism with best-selling books. Flynn smoothly transferred his suspicion of Woodrow Wilson and Franklin Roosevelt to the newest Democrat in the White House. Soon he would begin constructing an ambitious theory linking the supposed Roosevelt treachery at Pearl Harbor to the triumph of communism in Asia.

In 1947, as the Republicans took control of Congress, Thomas took charge of HUAC, and he trolled for headlines by exposing communists in the movie industry. However, by 1948, Democrats sensed that the committee was losing public support. Truman felt confident enough to assail it as "more un-American than the activities it is investigating."[55] Then Bentley gave it new life.

Bentley's public charges before HUAC in August 1948 seemed straight out of pulp fiction. She told of surreptitious meetings on street corners, knitting bags bulging with microfilm, and secret formulas scrawled on scraps of paper. Most important, she alleged that more than twenty men and women in the U.S. government had betrayed their country and knowingly passed information to the Soviets, now the country's worst enemy. "We knew about D-Day long before D-Day happened," she said, drawing on her cigarette, "and we were right."[56] No one on the committee noted that top U.S. military officers had of course given a D-Day briefing to the Soviets before the invasion since they were American allies at the time.

Bentley's charges were sensational, but she had no proof for them. As a result, liberal commentators soon began painting her as a fantasist and a sociopath. They argued, in essence, that Bentley had middle-aged crushes on the men she accused and that she had responded to their rejections by inventing vicious lies.[57] But the Republicans on HUAC wanted to believe her, for she validated their dire warnings about the dangers of communists in America. If she was telling the truth, then there had indeed been communist traitors working in the New Deal administration. To many conservatives, her testimony seemed to give credence to the notion that the expansion of government power in the United States had actually been part of a communist plot. Desperate to find a corroborating witness, the committee staff decided to subpoena a man known in anticommunist circles for making similar charges. In Whittaker Chambers, the red hunters found their witness.

In a packed congressional hearing room, with the hum of movie cameras and the pop of flashbulbs in the background, the repentant ex-spy made his confession. Chambers supported Bentley's story, though he was as vulnerable as the spy queen to charges of delusional psychosis. Slouching and unkempt, he told the committee of his own long strange journey through the "insidious evil" of the communist underground. In the mid-1930s, he testified, he had supervised a group of American communists who had infiltrated the New Deal. According to Chambers, two of his agents had attained significant positions: Harry White, who had also been named by Bentley in her public testimony, and Alger Hiss, who had not. At this early stage, Chambers accused the men of being part of a "secret, sinister, and enormously powerful force" bent on enslaving Americans. He did not accuse them of spying.[58] However, he explained, every communist was a potential spy. "Disloyalty," he testified, "is a matter of principle with every member of the Communist Party."[59] White and Hiss angrily denied the charges and demanded the chance to respond.

Harry White gave the Democrats a great boost when he eloquently affirmed his innocence before HUAC. "The principles in which I believe, and by which I live," he testified, "make it impossible for me to ever do a disloyal act or anything against the interests of our country."[60] The brilliant economist's polished, confident demeanor contrasted favorably with Bentley's clearly mercenary performance and Chambers's gloomy mumblings. As White parried the committee's questions, the audience responded with enthusiastic applause. Three days later, he died of a massive heart attack. A few fringe anticommunists suggested that he had been "liquidated" by fellow communists or had faked his death and escaped to the Soviet Union.[61] But the liberal outrage following his death convinced most red hunters to drop the White case—for the moment.

As the most important accused spy still living, Alger Hiss took on tremendous symbolic power. A Harvard Law graduate who had impressed even his most distinguished professors, Hiss had always exuded the kind of self-confidence and quiet intelligence that prompted others to predict that he was bound for greatness.[62] In his testimony, Hiss denied even knowing Chambers, let alone sharing secrets with him in the 1930s. He relied on his résumé and his connections to support his contention that he was hardly "the concealed enemy," as Chambers called him, but a trusted friend of Supreme Court justices and Secretary of State Dean Acheson. He had advised Franklin Roosevelt at the wartime Yalta conference; he had served as temporary secretary general at the founding conference of the United Nations. He could not be a traitor.

Hiss's shrewdest antagonist on the committee was the freshman congressman from Orange County, Richard Nixon. Already a seasoned anticommunist, Nixon was as angered by Hiss's condescending attitude as he was by his alleged crimes. Nixon pressed the witness until Hiss finally admitted that he might have known Chambers under another name—but not, he insisted, as a fellow communist.

When Hiss dared his accuser to repeat his charges outside the privileged halls of Congress, Chambers obliged. "Alger Hiss," he told a panel of reporters on *Meet the Press*, "was a Communist and may be now."[63] In response, Hiss sued him for slander. He had no reason to believe that he would lose. After all, Chambers had never given any hint that he had been more resourceful than Bentley and saved documents to prove his claims.

The Hiss-Chambers case seemed destined to end in a standoff: both men insisted that they were telling the truth, but neither one was able to prove it. The Truman administration responded by vigorously counterattacking the spy hunters. The president assailed HUAC throughout his 1948 reelection campaign, agreeing with a reporter's characterization of its espionage inquiry as a "red herring."[64] After he won a surprising victory in November, Truman believed that he had the political muscle to smash the committee's conspiracy theories about the communization of America. He hoped to persuade the House to abolish HUAC in the next congressional session.[65]

But the mysterious Chambers had more surprises to reveal. As he met with his lawyers to plan his defense against Hiss's slander suit, he admitted that there was "something missing" in his earlier charges. Hiss was more than a communist: he had been a Soviet spy, Chambers said, and he had the papers to prove it. Chambers led HUAC investigators to the edge of his Maryland farm. He reached into a hollowed-out pumpkin and triumphantly extracted some microfilmed State Department documents dating from his spy days. He had hidden a stash of microfilm and papers—his life preserver, he called it—soon after his defection, and had just recently moved the microfilm to the pumpkin.[66] The documents included memos dating from the 1930s in Hiss's and White's handwriting.

THE "PUMPKIN PAPERS" became iconic to conservatives because they provided written proof of a real conspiracy by two New Dealers. These conservatives had argued for years that Roosevelt's liberalism was a form of treason; here, they believed, was the evidence they had long sought, in the form of yellowed notepaper and tiny strips of film.

Most historians now agree that the documents were real. There is convincing evidence that Hiss worked for the Soviets in the 1930s, and that he was still working for them as late as 1945.[67] He received a secret commendation from the Soviets soon after the Yalta conference.[68] Over the years, he gave the Soviets insight into the inner workings of the Roosevelt administration: which officials, for example, would be most likely to favor a Soviet request for a loan, and which ones were inveterate anticommunists.

However, as a midlevel functionary, Hiss did not have a lot of influence. Most historians have concluded that he played a small role at the Yalta conference. His one major suggestion there was, in fact, contrary to the interests of the Soviet Union: he recommended that the president deny Stalin's demand for three votes in the United Nations Assembly. Roosevelt ignored him.[69] In short, Hiss probably did steal documents and information for the communists, but his power to influence U.S. foreign policy was quite limited.

Like Hiss, White was indeed guilty of espionage. Newly released documents show that he met with Soviet agents and passed them some information.[70] Also like Hiss, he was not able to—or did not want to—change U.S. foreign policy to suit the Soviets.[71] Furthermore, in helping to create the International Monetary Fund, he ultimately strengthened capitalism throughout the world during the cold war. As his fellow communist economist (and spy) Harry Magdoff later said, "If Harry Dexter White was a Soviet spy ... he wasn't a very good one."[72]

President Truman and other liberal anticommunists tried desperately to calm public anxieties by insisting that the government had already caught and punished the conspirators. Most important, Truman expanded the loyalty program for government workers, which purged almost all of the potential ideologically motivated spies from the government (as well as thousands of innocents). A KGB officer complained to Moscow in 1950 that it was impossible to recruit new agents because of the "current fascist atmosphere in the U.S."[73] The Soviets were forced to abandon the Communist Party as a recruiting ground for spies and to begin the modern practice of paying Americans to spy for them.[74]

Yet in 1949 and 1950, a series of terrifying events gave credibility to the conspiracists' charges that enemies still lurked within the U.S. government. On September 23, 1949, President Truman announced that the Soviets had exploded their own atomic bomb. Some Republicans charged that Congress needed to discover and expel the traitors who had given the bomb to the communists and would continue to leak national secrets to America's enemies. "Plainly," said Representative Harold Velde, "Congress must act now unless we want to welcome a second Pearl Harbor with open arms."[75]

The next month, Mao and the Chinese communists forced their opponents to flee to Formosa. Anticommunist congressmen proclaimed that the communists had suddenly altered the global balance of power by adding a half-billion people to their side—and that treasonous Americans within the government had helped them do it. "Traitors in the high councils of our own Government make sure that the deck is stacked on the Soviet side of the diplomatic table," Congressman Nixon argued.[76]

Who had "lost" China, Nixon and others demanded to know? A New York jury seemed to provide part of the answer in January 1950, when it convicted Alger Hiss of perjury. To compound the public relations disaster for the Truman administration, Secretary of State Dean Acheson defended Hiss, saying that he would never turn his back on his friend. Republicans pounced on the statement as evidence of the incompetence and subversion within the White House. "This," said Congressman Nixon, "is only a small part of the whole shocking story of espionage in the United States."[77]

The next week, British officials announced that the Soviets had indeed stolen some of the information they needed to build a bomb. They arrested Klaus Fuchs for giving atomic secrets to the Soviets. Fuchs had been identified by U.S. Army code breakers who had been diligently trying to decipher Soviet telegrams dating from World War II. British agents confronted him and, after some resistance, he agreed to cooperate with the FBI. Fuchs's confession led investigators to his courier, Harry Gold, whose own voluble confession linked Fuchs, Greenglass, Julius Rosenberg, and some of Bentley's sources in a massive spying plot. The Soviets' inattention to one of the basic rules of spycraft—never let one courier handle the documents of different spy rings—led to the destruction of the remaining traces of the once-formidable Soviet espionage network in North America. "The circle was complete," wrote Robert Lamphere, the FBI agent in charge of the Fuchs-Gold case.[78] The battle was won.

Yet in destroying the espionage conspiracy, the FBI also exposed the plot's frightening dimensions. To some, this massive conspiracy seemed to explain not just the Soviets' luck in shaving a year or two off the time it took to make a bomb; not just their swift advances in synthesizing rubber, or processing film, or improving their airplanes. Instead, it explained nothing less than the course of recent world history.

By 1950 the United States seemed to be on the "losing side" of the cold war, in Whittaker Chambers's words. The communists successfully imposed their system on hundreds of millions of people and detonated the most powerful weapon in history. Many Americans wanted to know how the United States, the strongest and most virtuous country in the world, could suffer these reverses. There was only one possible explanation: concealed enemies, proven traitors like Hiss, White, and Fuchs, plus hundreds of their unknown comrades, must have weakened America from within. All of the elements of the conspiracy theory were in place. It remained for one man to put them all together and give them a malicious twist.

SENATOR JOSEPH McCARTHY actually brought two speeches with him to the Lincoln Day dinner in Wheeling, West Virginia, in February 1950. One speech was on federal housing policies; the other was on high treason committed by government officials. He decided to give the treason speech.[79] It was an issue that he had used, but not emphasized, in the past. McCarthy was facing an uphill battle for reelection in 1952. He needed some excitement to reignite his career, and, in the wake of Fuchs's confession and Hiss's conviction, he sensed that crying "Traitors!" could provide it.

The speech, delivered to a Republican women's group, presented the theme that McCarthy would exploit for the rest of his career. How, the senator wanted to know, had the United States come to its present condition of "impotency"? The only possible answer, he said, was that un-Americans were infesting the government, especially the Department of State. Alger Hiss was "representative of a group in the State Department," which still harbored 205 card-carrying communists. The rot started at the top, with Secretary of State Acheson, "a pompous diplomat in striped pants, with a phony British accent," defending the man who had allowed the sellout of the "Christian world to the atheistic world."[80]

McCarthy was not an original thinker. He had plagiarized much of his speech from several sources, including an address by Congressman Nixon and articles in right-wing newspapers.[81] Nor was he a true believer; unlike Hoover, he seemed to focus on communism not because he truly feared it but because he saw an opportunity for headlines and reelection. Though his charges were recycled, he attracted attention by making them current, rather than historical: there were 205 card-carrying communists in the State Department at that very minute, he claimed, and furthermore, he knew their names.

In fact, he did not. The figure of 205 was outdated and inflated, and McCarthy swiftly abandoned it, saying that he had been misquoted. He really meant, he said, that there were fifty-seven government employees who were "loyal to the Communist Party," as opposed to Party members. This number came from a 1948 congressional investigation that had compiled a list of alleged subversives. By 1950, this list included people who had left the government, had been cleared by FBI investigations, or had been charged with alcoholism or homosexuality, not communism.[82] The senator was accusing the Truman administration's loyalty program of unforgivable laxity, but his charges were simply not true.

As McCarthy flogged his story on a speaking tour, his alarming accusations appeared on the front pages of newspapers across the country. On February 20 he formally presented his charges to the Senate. For his text, he used the files from the previous investigation. But McCarthy substantially "improved" the evidence of conspiracy contained in the files. With a breathtaking disregard for the facts, he invented new accusations on the spot, dropped the modifiers "allegedly" and "reportedly," and changed words to convey a sense of certainty that the previous investigators had not shared ("may be" became "is"). At some points, as the historian Robert Griffith has said, "the enormity of his lie was staggering." McCarthy invented charges out of whole cloth, then insisted that he was just reading the information in executive branch documents provided to him by loyal Americans. "I am not evaluating the information myself," McCarthy said. "I am merely giving what is in the file."[83]

Republican leaders realized that McCarthy was misrepresenting old files as explosive new cases. Once, Senator Homer Ferguson, who had charged conspiracy and whitewash when he served on the Pearl Harbor investigation, interrupted McCarthy to ask him why he was taking the cases "out of order."[84] He knew that the senator was using an outdated list, but he encouraged him nevertheless. In the end, the Republican Party's strong support for McCarthy forced the Democratic majority in the Senate to authorize a formal investigation into his charges.

During the inquiry, headed by Senator Millard Tydings of Maryland, McCarthy continued his baseless attacks on Truman administration officials. Men and women who had sympathized with communism decades earlier, or simply associated with communists, were smeared as the latest Harry White or Alger Hiss. McCarthy leveled his most hyperbolic charges against an obscure State Department consultant named Owen Lattimore, who, the senator said, was the "top Russian espionage agent" in the United States and the "architect of our far eastern policy."[85]

The majority of senators on the Tydings Committee denounced McCarthy's charges as "perhaps the most nefarious campaign of half-truths and untruth in the history of this Republic." For the first time in U.S. history, the committee majority said, "we have seen the totalitarian technique of the 'big lie' employed on a sustained basis." The senator, the committee concluded, was perpetrating a "fraud and a hoax."[86]

Tydings had truth and justice on his side, but his timing was unfortunate. On the same day that he released his report charging McCarthy with lying about communist spies, the FBI announced that it had arrested Julius Rosenberg. He had committed, in J. Edgar Hoover's words, the "crime of the century." Rosenberg refused to cooperate, which prompted the FBI to arrest his wife the next month in hopes of pressuring him.

The summer of 1950 also marked the start of the Korean War. Americans were now fighting a shooting war with communists—and the communists had the bomb. What, McCarthy charged, were the real causes for the war? Plainly, he said, it was a case of treason by "Red counselors" in the State Department.

The Korean War and the arrest of the Rosenbergs gave credibility to McCarthy's charges. A wave of fear swept the country, with the Democratic Congress voting overwhelmingly to overturn Truman's veto of a bill that would put communists in concentration camps in a "national emergency." When Tydings lost his Senate seat in November, McCarthy seemed invincible. He built on his previous charges and dreamed up even more sensational ones.

McCarthy spun his most reckless conspiracy theories on the Senate floor in April 1951, when he named Secretary of Defense George Marshall and Secretary of State Dean Acheson as Soviet agents.[87] How else, he thundered, could anyone explain America's retreat from victory? "This must be the product of a great conspiracy, a conspiracy on a scale so immense as to dwarf any previous such venture in the history of man."[88]

Many Americans, Democrats and Republicans alike, were horrified by McCarthy's accusations against two cabinet officials who had honorably served their country for decades. No evidence has ever surfaced suggesting that Marshall, the revered commander of World War II, or Acheson, a veteran anticommunist diplomat, ever spied for the Soviet Union. Despite the absurdity of his charges, McCarthy maintained and even expanded his power. Fearful of losing votes, Republican presidential nominee Dwight Eisenhower declined to denounce McCarthy in the 1952 campaign, even though Marshall was his friend. When the Republicans won the White House and control of Congress that year, McCarthy received a committee chairmanship and a platform for his conspiracy mongering.

Other anticommunist conspiracists were exhilarated by McCarthy's fearless attack on the people they had long viewed as the enemies of the republic. "God bless Joe McCarthy," said John T. Flynn in one of his radio broadcasts.[89] Former senator Burton Wheeler, who lost his seat in 1946 in part because leftists accused him of participating in a pro-Nazi "plot against America," reveled in McCarthy's assaults on his tormenters. "When you are dealing with crooks and spies," Wheeler said, "you have to be tough and you have to stand up against the criticism of those who are being investigated."[90] In Wheeler's view, it was the investigators who were the victims, despite their control of congressional committees and the FBI, while the targets of the investigation allegedly held all the power.

The anticommunist conspiracists often drew on the same fears as the anti-interventionists. To old isolationists like Wheeler and Flynn, Hiss and White were dangerous precisely because they had devoted their public careers to working for internationalism. Once they were exposed as spies, many of the prewar anti-interventionists saw their role in the creation of international institutions like the United Nations and the International Monetary Fund as a cleverly disguised plot to advance the global interests of communism.[91] Extremists also pointed out that White was Jewish, and thus allegedly part of the international Jewish conspiracy to control the world's money supply.[92]

Some of the old anti-interventionists constructed a metaconspiracy theory linking Pearl Harbor to the origins of the cold war. They decided that White, not Franklin Roosevelt, had provoked the Japanese attack on Pearl Harbor (by allegedly writing the "ultimatum" given to the Japanese in November 1941). This was part of the Reds' long-term plan to manipulate the United States into fighting the world's most powerful anticommunist countries, Japan and Nazi Germany. In other words, Harry White tricked the country into joining World War II as part of a plot to help the communists take over the world.[93] It was quite a feat for an assistant secretary of the treasury, but his critics had no doubts about his ability to accomplish it.

Hiss also played a pivotal role in the plot, the conspiracists believed. The most important clue to Hiss's guilt, they believed, was his presence at FDR's side at Yalta, where the president effectively agreed to let the Soviets dominate Poland, which they had just liberated from the Germans, and allowed them to occupy parts of Asia. (Ironically, many of these anticommunist conspiracists had not worried about the fate of Eastern Europe or Asia when fascists or right-wing imperialists controlled these regions.)

Roosevelt gave Stalin nothing at Yalta that the Soviets "could not have taken in any event," as the historian John Gaddis has said.[94] But anticommunists saw a plot: according to them, Hiss was a "Svengali-like" manipulator who tricked the U.S. government into handing over Eastern Europe and much of Asia to communism. In their view, he wrote the Yalta agreement; he changed crucial language in the declaration on Poland; in fact, he stage-managed the entire conference. His crimes were "far worse than any theft of diplomatic documents," some authors maintained.[95] Alger Hiss was a chief conspirator in the plot to communize the world.

According to Flynn, the "most incredible conspiracy of our time" was not Pearl Harbor after all, but the secret efforts by traitors within the government to manipulate U.S. foreign policy for years to help Stalin. This conspiracy began at Pearl Harbor, continued at Yalta, and achieved its greatest victory in the communist takeover of China. "The sheer wickedness of this is so appalling," Flynn wrote, "that it is difficult to credit."[96]

In promoting their conspiracy theories, McCarthy and his supporters cleverly exploited old and new anxieties about America's internal enemies.

From the start, the Irish American McCarthy explicitly portrayed himself as an enemy of the self-satisfied, lazy, Anglophile American plutocracy. "McCarthyism," he said proudly, "is Americanism with its sleeves rolled."[97] Many of the "traitors" targeted by McCarthy were actually middle-class graduates of public schools in the Midwest.[98] But McCarthy and his supporters tried to conflate the hundreds of State Department employees with their dapper boss, Dean Acheson. According to McCarthy, Acheson was the "Red Dean of Fashion," who sported "a lace handkerchief, a silk glove, and ... a Harvard accent."[99] Conservative congressmen loved to portray Acheson as an arrogant dandy who was out of touch with the needs and values of "real" Americans.

McCarthy's genius was to combine old anxieties about rich men in fancy suits with new fears of the post–World War II age, such as homosexuality. By repeatedly implying that the accused spies were gay, the senator and his supporters reflected concerns about "unrestrained sexuality" in American life, as the historian K. A. Cuordileone has said.[100] Some writers even spoke of a "homosexual international" on the model of the Communist International, dedicated to subverting American values and spreading immorality across the globe.[101] On a more practical level, conservatives argued that homosexuals in the government were more inclined to become spies: they could be blackmailed, and since they lacked moral values to begin with, they could be easily subverted.[102]

But this theory was unfounded. A U.S. government study in 1991 found that only six of the 117 American spies uncovered since World War II had been homosexual, and sexual orientation did not play an important role in those cases.[103] Still, in the Truman years alone, more than four hundred suspected homosexuals lost their jobs in the State Department—more than twice as many gays and lesbians as suspected communists.[104] The historian David K. Johnson has estimated that the loyalty-security program cost as many as five thousand homosexual government workers their jobs by 1960.[105]

The draconian loyalty program was part of the Truman administration's attempt to respond to McCarthy's charges by appearing as tough and unyielding as possible. Truman set up his stringent security program, kicked "security risks" out of government by the hundreds, denounced communism in all its forms, and continued his firm anti-Soviet foreign policy. But he remained on the defensive while McCarthy mastered the art of the political attack. "I don't answer charges, I make them," McCarthy told a Senate subcommittee when it tried to raise the issue of his personal financial corruption.[106]

Many Republicans assumed that McCarthy would stop attacking the government once his party *was* the government. They had won the war against the party of "twenty years of treason"; now he could stop fighting his bloody battles. But McCarthy did not know how to function as a member of government. He excelled in the opposition, and he resolved to stay there. When he continued his investigations into the Eisenhower years, many members of his party began to abandon him. His crusade against Army officers for promoting a "Red dentist" in New Jersey backfired when the Army counterattacked in televised hearings and exposed him as a bully. The Senate censured him in 1954 for his "contempt and abuse" of the Senate, and he died in 1957.

McCarthy's extreme conspiracism had alienated many influential anticommunists, both liberal and conservative. "Those who are sympathetic to his cause," wrote the British author Evelyn Waugh to the conservative commentator William F. Buckley, "must deplore his championship of it."[107] Both *Time*, which loved to ridicule "chuckleheaded 'liberalism,'" and the *New York Times*, which *Time* regarded as a prime example of this sort of chuckleheadedness, labeled him a demagogue.[108] Television also helped to convince many moderate anticommunists that the senator had gone too far, as it showed his bullying tactics to a nationwide audience during the Army-McCarthy hearings and provided a platform for liberal journalists such as Edward R. Murrow of CBS News to criticize him.[109]

McCarthy's strongest supporters, though, viewed the mainstream media attacks on their hero as more evidence of the plotters' grip on the levers of power in the United States. Anticommunist conspiracists, despite their control of the FBI, several congressional committees, the Hearst, Patterson, and McCormick newspapers, and the Hollywood Blacklist, saw themselves as besieged victims of a powerful enemy. John T. Flynn, for example, wrote in 1949 that true patriots were "defenseless, voiceless, intimidated, and broke" because an insidious minority had "gotten into its hands a collection of weapons including the government treasury and payroll, the press, the radio, and all the great instruments of communication and opinion."[110] Flynn anticipated the New Right's attack on the "liberal media" by more than two decades.

Despite their fear of the supposedly leftist press, though, the anticommunist conspiracists did hope that the country could be saved if it awoke from its slumber and cast out the un-Americans. In this sense, their descriptions of the problem, and their solutions, were comfortingly simple: find and punish the conspirators. "History does not just happen," McCarthy once explained. "It is made by men—men with names and faces, and the only way the course of history can be changed is by getting rid of the specific individuals who we find are bad for America."[111]

To combat these individuals, men like Flynn, Gerald Nye, and Burton Wheeler—the most vociferous critics of excessive governmental power in the 1930s and early 1940s—came to embrace certain kinds of federal power by the mid-1950s. They saw the New Deal, with its promise of social security, labor union rights, and regulation of the excesses of capitalism, as a misguided, even feminized, form of government power. By contrast, the FBI and other internal security agencies were examples of necessary, muscular government powers. These former skeptics of the government became so worried about communists that they reversed their positions on government secrecy and on the FBI. Their jeremiads in the 1930s had been right: the internal security agency of the federal government was expanding its power. But now they were no longer the critics; they were the cheering section.

No one was happier about this turn of events than J. Edgar Hoover. Already authorized to spy on subversives by President Roosevelt, Hoover expanded his domestic spying programs dramatically in the 1950s and early 1960s. The threat was great, he said, and ordinary citizens could not and should not combat it directly. "To meet effectively the Communist subversive thrusts," Hoover wrote in 1962, "it is essential to employ highly professional counterintelligence measures....Modern-day counterintelligence ... is a task for experts."[112] Flynn, who called the state "the oldest villain in history," apparently saw no contradiction in supporting the expansion of state power in this area.[113]

Unhindered by any oversight, executive or congressional, Hoover's agents used intrusive surveillance methods on suspected subversives: wiretaps, bugs, burglaries, informants, and agents provocateurs. The FBI also began launching domestic covert actions known as "counterintelligence programs," COINTELPRO for short. Beginning in 1956, when the U.S. Supreme Court made it more difficult for the government to prosecute communists, Hoover started what a Senate committee later called a "sophisticated vigilante operation aimed squarely at preventing the exercise of First Amendment rights of speech and association."[114] Under COINTELPRO, the bureau recruited "informants"—a euphemism for "informer"—to infiltrate the dwindling ranks of the Communist Party, disrupt its plans, and discredit its members. Agents of COINTELPRO planted "snitch jackets," or false letters identifying a target as an informer, wrote anonymous poison pen letters, and spread rumors about political apostasies and marital infidelities. The bureau spared no expense in infiltrating the increasingly irrelevant communists. Hoover soon had fifteen hundred informants dedicated to spying on American communists—more than one agent for every five members.[115]

Hoover enlarged COINTELPRO to target hundreds of thousands of Americans he considered subversive. The agents moved far beyond suspicion of Communist Party membership to monitor law-abiding citizens who espoused—in the view of the FBI—vaguely defined communist sympathies. By 1960, the bureau maintained 432,000 files at its headquarters on dissident groups and individuals, and FBI field offices around the country collected an even larger number.[116] As before, the agents were not simply supposed to spy on the groups, but to promote paranoia and discord within them. To Hoover, these tactics were justified because he believed that the dissidents were part of a broad conspiracy to undermine law and order—and respect for institutions such as the FBI.

The countersubversive programs of the McCarthy era counted thousands of victims. The loyalty program, for example, cut short the careers of thousands of workers for the federal government and international organizations who had once been communists, defended communists, knew communists, or were allegedly vulnerable to communist blackmail because of their sexual orientation. Sylvia Meagher, an analyst with the World Health Organization, faced a hearing before a loyalty board simply because she questioned the legality of the loyalty program.[117] Harold Weisberg, a State Department analyst, lost his job in 1947 because of vague charges of "indirect association with representatives of foreign powers."[118] Both of these skeptics, and many others like them, would later help to organize the next generation of antigovernment conspiracy theorists.

One of the most prominent victims of this official repression was Linus Pauling. The years of FBI surveillance never produced any evidence of his disloyalty. "We have contacted every source we could find who might have useful information," one FBI official explained in 1958. "None has identified Pauling as [a] Communist Party member."[119] Still, the bureau monitored his mail and tracked his movements into the Nixon administration.[120] Even though his research suffered, Pauling refused to end his peace campaigns. In 1958 he published *No More War*, a call for the end of nuclear testing. He and thirteen other scientists sued the Defense Department to stop nuclear tests, and he spearheaded a drive by eleven thousand scientists to ask the United Nations to stop the tests in all member nations.[121]

A dangerous "subversive" in his own land, Pauling was hailed as a hero and a peacemaker abroad. In 1963, he won a second Nobel Prize for his role in ending aboveground nuclear tests. This time, the U.S. government, now headed by President John Kennedy, did not try to stop him from collecting his prize.

PAULING AND OTHER TARGETS of FBI surveillance during the Red Scare knew that the government was watching them. They also knew that many of the red hunters in the government relied on exaggerations and outright lies. To the victims of these lies and programs, the conservative anticommunist leaders seemed more than overzealous or misguided. They seemed to have a plan.

To some progressives, only one thing could explain the hysteria over domestic communism: a conspiracy by right-wingers to destroy the New Deal, discredit radical ideas, and smother the hope of progressive change in postwar America. According to Owen Lattimore, the man Joe McCarthy had called the "top Soviet spy in America," the real goal of the red hunters was to persuade Americans "that the man who thinks independently thinks dangerously and for an evil, disloyal purpose."[122] Some progressives, including former vice president Henry Wallace and former ambassador Joseph Davies, even came to believe in 1950 that anticommunist extremists were plotting an antigovernment coup.[123]

For his part, Pauling could not understand why the U.S. government had pursued the self-defeating policy of trying to destroy him. The answer, he decided, was that the anticommunist conspiracy theorists were themselves part of a great American conspiracy. Hoover, the FBI, and the "military-industrial complex" were conspiring to silence progressive American voices. The real un-Americans, Pauling believed, were the extreme anticommunists.[124] Hoover's official conspiracies and conspiracism had inspired an entirely different set of fears.

And so the right-wing antigovernment conspiracy theories of the 1950s helped to spawn left-wing antigovernment conspiracy theories of the 1960s. In a mirror image of Whittaker Chambers's "concealed enemies," left-wing conspiracists came to believe that concealed enemies on the right—the forces of reaction—had captured key parts of the government. If the real "masters of deceit" worked for powerful, secret agencies of the U.S. government, then there was no telling what they might do to achieve their reactionary goals. They might even try to kill the president.

4

The Dealey Plaza Irregulars:
The JFK Assassination and the Collapse
of Trust in the 1960s

IN FEBRUARY 1964, three months after the assassination that shattered her
world, Shirley Martin packed her four children and her dog into her car
and drove seven hours southwest to Dallas. With a recorder concealed in
her armpit and her kids in tow, she tracked down the people she was sure
could help her learn the truth. On this and several subsequent trips, she
interviewed more than fifty people who had information about the assassination of President John F. Kennedy, including the priest who gave him
the last rites, the woman who shared her house with the accused assassin, Lee Harvey Oswald, and his family, and the furniture salesman who
stood close to the limousine when the fatal shot hit. Mrs. Martin's husband used a stopwatch to check the FBI's time frame for Oswald's alleged
movements.[1] Before the assassination, Shirley Martin had been a housewife from Hominy, Oklahoma. But now she had a calling: she was going to
discover who had killed the president.

Martin was not alone. Maggie Field, a Beverly Hills housewife, filled
her spacious home with scrapbooks, file boxes, and seventy-five charts
detailing the names and locations of witnesses and other known facts of
the assassination.[2] A bookkeeper from Los Angeles, Lillian Castellano, sent
for a map of the Dallas sewer system to see if another assassin might have
hidden in a storm drain.[3] Sylvia Meagher, an analyst for the World Health

Organization in New York, spent six months making an annotated index to the official government report on the assassination, which she termed a "sleazy and insulting fantasy."[4]

These skeptics shared a common conviction: they were certain that their government was lying to them. At a time when 76 percent of the public trusted the government to "do what is right most of the time," these Americans believed that their government was working to cover up the truth—and that this cover-up could have tragic consequences.[5] "There are forces in this country who have gotten away with this thing, and will strike again," said Maggie Field. "And not any one of us is safe."[6]

These researchers of the Kennedy assassination not only believed that government officials had conspired, lied, and covered up aspects of the murder; they also believed that they could expose this conspiracy *on their own*. They could reenact key moments in the drama to check the official story; they could interview eyewitnesses and "earwitnesses" to determine the location of a second (or third, or fourth, or fifth) shooter. They developed a nationwide, grassroots network to pool their knowledge and prove that ordinary citizens could penetrate the national security state's culture of secrecy. "We are not alone," wrote Castellano to another researcher. "There are thousands of little people like you and I—all not satisfied—all wanting the truth."[7]

Unlike the anticommunist conspiracy theorists of the 1950s, the Kennedy researchers had no alliances with wealthy businessmen or government agencies. Indeed, they found themselves attacked by powerful interests. Yet without patrons or publishing contracts, they were determined to find the source of what one researcher called "this evil set loose on the world by the assassination of our president."[8] They formed local study groups, spent hours on the phone with each other, wrote letters of protest to the FBI, combed through the National Archives, and filled their garages with witness location charts and photography labs.

Over the years, they would convert millions to their cause. They had the virtues of dedication, diligence, and almost messianic belief in the righteousness of their cause. They also had the advantage of being partly right.

IT WAS NOT UNREASONABLE for ordinary Americans to believe conspiracy theories about the John Kennedy assassination, because, at the beginning, even the highest officials of the U.S. government considered them. Some of the most powerful men in the country feared the worst. "What raced through *my* mind," the new president, Lyndon Johnson, later said, "was that, if they had shot our president, driving down there, who would they shoot next? And what was going on in Washington? And when would the missiles be comin'? And *I* thought it was a *conspiracy*, and I raised that question. And nearly everybody that was *with* me raised it."[9] Richard Helms, chief of covert operations for the Central Intelligence Agency, also suspected a communist conspiracy. "It worried the hell out of everybody," Helms said later. "Was this a plot? Who was pulling the strings? And what was to come next?"[10] Attorney General Robert Kennedy, the president's brother, feared a different, home-grown conspiracy. He suspected that anti-Castro Cubans allied with the CIA might have taken revenge on Kennedy for failing to provide enough U.S. support at the Bay of Pigs. He confronted John McCone, the director of the CIA, and demanded to know if the agency had killed Kennedy.[11] McCone denied it.

These public officials suspected conspiracy because they had access to secret information: they knew that the Kennedy administration had conducted real conspiracies that might have provoked what happened in Dallas. In particular, they wondered about the role of the CIA's plots against Fidel Castro. The Eisenhower and Kennedy administrations had supervised at least eight attempts on Castro's life, using anti-Castro Cubans and mafia hit men as their tools. In fact, at the same moment that the Dealey Plaza assassin squinted through his rifle sight, a CIA officer was giving a poison-filled pen to a Cuban dissident in Paris, one of the agency's many plots to assassinate Castro.[12] The Castro plots raised the possibility that anti-Castro Cubans, mobsters, or Castro himself might have ordered the assassination.

One man, however, was absolutely certain that he knew what had happened, and it did not involve a conspiracy. J. Edgar Hoover made the first call to Robert Kennedy to tell him that his brother had been shot, with rather less excitement than "if he were reporting the fact that he found a Communist on the faculty of Howard University," Kennedy later said.[13] A few hours later, Hoover told the attorney general that he thought "we had the man" who had done the shooting.[14] As he explained to Robert Kennedy's assistant later that day, a communist sympathizer named Lee Oswald, a "nut" of the "extremist pro-Castro crowd," had been arrested by Dallas police after he had apparently killed a police officer.[15]

Hoover made up his mind within hours of the assassination that it would be best for the country—and, not incidentally, for himself and the FBI—to conclude that Oswald had acted alone. Besides his ideological preference for blaming an American communist for the assassination, Hoover also had professional reasons for declaring the case to be closed. After all, if Oswald was *not* a lone nut—if there had in fact been a plot to kill the president—then people might think that the FBI should have uncovered and stopped it. Ergo, Hoover quickly decided, there was no conspiracy. Ironically, the man who had done more than any American to spread the anticommunist conspiracy theory now became the nation's most fervent debunker of conspiracy theories.

Moreover, Hoover worried that a real investigation might prompt the excitable public to demand war with Russia—a war that could quickly go nuclear. Hoover pointed out to Walter Jenkins, a Johnson aide, that Oswald had recently visited the Cuban and Soviet embassies in Mexico City. He had even sent a letter to "the man in the Soviet Embassy who is in charge of assassinations and similar activities on the part of the Soviet government." Oswald had also defected to the Soviet Union and lived there for two years. Any discussion of conspiracy, Hoover concluded, might "complicate" the U.S. relationship with the Soviet Union.[16] Though he used euphemisms, Hoover's underlying point was clear: a thorough investigation could lead to conclusions that no one wanted to hear.

At first, it seemed that Hoover's lone gunman theory would be easy to prove. Investigators quickly found abundant evidence tying the suspect to the assassination. He had worked at the Texas School Book Depository on Dealey Plaza, where police found a sniper's nest, a Mannlicher-Carcano rifle, and three bullet casings on the sixth floor. A man fitting his description had shot and killed a Dallas police officer shortly after the assassination. Soon investigators would find proof that Oswald owned the Mannlicher-Carcano and that he had even posed for a picture while holding it. Moreover, the FBI had been watching Oswald for years, and agents knew that he was a violent, unstable sociopath prone to ideological extremism.

At various times in his short life, Oswald had been a U.S. Marine, an American communist, a Soviet communist, a professed anti-Soviet, a Castro supporter, and a member of an anti-Castro group—and sometimes he fit into two or more of these categories at the same time. Born in New Orleans in 1939, he had joined the Marines in the 1950s and served on an air base in Japan. While in the Marines, he subscribed to a Russian-language newspaper, earnestly plowed through *Das Kapital*, and talked of traveling to Cuba to join Castro's revolution.[17] In 1959 he defected to the country he viewed as paradise on earth, the Soviet Union. He worked in Minsk in a radio factory for two years, married a Russian woman, and started a family. But he grew increasingly disillusioned with life under communism, and in 1962 he returned with his wife, Marina, and their baby to the United States and moved to Texas.[18]

This erstwhile communist settled in an area known for its fanatical anticommunism. Dallas was the home of several right-wing leaders who believed that Kennedy was masterminding a conspiracy to turn the country over to the United Nations, which they believed was controlled by communists. The most prominent of these anticommunist conspiracists was Edwin A. Walker, a retired general who had been relieved of command in 1961 for indoctrinating his troops with extremist propaganda.[19] The general thought that the chief justice of the Supreme Court, Earl Warren, was plotting to destroy the United States by promoting civil rights and banning prayer in schools. "This is the conspiracy of the crucifixion by anti-Christ conspirators of the Supreme Court," Walker proclaimed in 1962, "in their denial of prayer and their betrayal of a nation."[20]

Oswald was a conspiracist of a different kind. Despite his alienation from Soviet communism, Oswald despised men like Walker, who was a "fascist," he told his wife. In April 1963, according to Marina, he became convinced that it was his destiny to kill Walker and save the world from the general's dangerous conspiracism. He ordered a rifle through the mail, stole up to Walker's home at night, and shot at him through a window. The general narrowly survived the assassination attempt. Later, Marina shut her husband in a bathroom to stop him from shooting Richard Nixon when the former vice president visited Dallas.[21]

By 1963 Lee Oswald had become convinced that the young revolutionary leader of Cuba represented the best hope for the future. After moving to New Orleans, Oswald formed a one-man chapter of a national pro-Castro organization, Fair Play for Cuba, and was arrested in the summer of 1963 for brawling with anti-Castro Cubans. He debated the leader of the local anti-Castro group on New Orleans radio. In September 1963, he took a bus to Mexico City, where he talked to officials at the Cuban and Soviet embassies. He wanted a visa to return to the Soviet Union, he said, and also permission to visit Cuba along the way. When both countries told him that it would take months to process the visas, he returned, full of fury, to Dallas, where Marina was living with friends.[22]

Despite his numerous pro-Castro statements, Oswald once joined an *anti*-Castro group, apparently in the hope of spying on its members. In Dallas he befriended a mysterious Russian baron who had fled the Bolsheviks. He expressed admiration for George Orwell's antitotalitarian novel, *Animal Farm*. Because of his unusual history, some scholars would later insist that Oswald was actually a fervent anticommunist.[23]

But those theories came later. At the time, it seemed clear that Oswald had seen himself as a warrior for communism. He had, after all, defected to Russia, passed out "Hands Off Cuba" flyers, and defended Fidel Castro to friends, acquaintances, and a radio audience in New Orleans. While in custody, he appeared to make a clenched-fist salute, recognized by militants as a symbol of revolution.[24]

In Washington after the assassination and Oswald's arrest, Hoover learned of the alleged assassin's past with a certain sense of vindication. In a way, Hoover had spent his entire life waiting for this moment. Early in his career, he had worked to deport the anarchist Emma Goldman, who, in his view, had inspired the crazed Marxist assassin of President William McKinley. More than forty years after Goldman's deportation he had caught the next presidential killer, another demented Marxist. As Hoover explained to a Justice Department official on the phone on the day of the assassination, "almost all" assassins had "some imaginary grievance," usually communist or anarchist. As an example, Hoover talked at length about McKinley's killer, Leon Czolgosz.[25]

Ironically, Hoover could not gloat in public. Because of their fear of nuclear confrontation with the Soviets, Hoover, Johnson, and other administration officials consciously underplayed Oswald's possible political motives. Indeed, when the White House heard that an assistant district attorney in Dallas was considering the idea of charging Oswald with perpetrating a "communist conspiracy," a Johnson aide immediately demanded that the district attorney's office delete any reference in the indictment to communism or conspiracies. The D.A. then called his assistant and yelled at him, "What the hell are you trying to do, start World War III?"[26] The federal authorities thus quashed any suggestion that Oswald was as ideologically motivated as Czolgosz. They wanted the

American public to see him as a generic psychopath, not an ideologically motivated one.

Though the Johnson administration wanted to prove the case in a quick and persuasive trial, it had not anticipated the incompetence of the Dallas police. Throughout Oswald's brief incarceration, the department was open and accessible to reporters and to the merely curious. Jack Ruby, a police informer and the owner of a local striptease club, wandered through the halls and even stood within three feet of Oswald at one point. In between interrogation sessions, the police moved the prisoner through the throngs of reporters, and he responded to their questions by claiming that he had not killed anyone. "I'm just a patsy!" he once shrieked.[27] As police moved Oswald to the county jail, Ruby pushed his way through the crowd and shot the accused murderer on live television.

The killing transformed the suspect from a figure of revulsion to one of mystery, especially when the nation learned that Ruby had friends in the mafia.[28] Was Oswald, after all, more than just "some silly little Communist," as Jacqueline Kennedy had called him privately?[29] Had he been silenced by the real conspirators? To many Americans, the murder required a government investigation of a possible conspiracy.

To Washington elites, though, the murder of Oswald required a different response: an official report naming him as the lone assassin. President Johnson agreed that it would be best for the country not to probe too deeply into the killing. To utter the word "conspiracy" in public, Johnson believed, might risk nuclear war. The new president believed that Castro might have ordered the killing—"I never believed that Oswald acted alone," he said later—but he did not really want to know for sure.[30] If he had proof that Castro was behind the murder, then he would be forced to invade Cuba, and the Soviets might respond by launching World War III. Moreover, rumors were flying that Johnson himself had ordered the killing so that he could assume the presidency. It was best for the survival of the world, not just for his own political future, if the conspiracy theories were quashed—immediately.

Just hours after Ruby killed Oswald, the deputy U.S. attorney general, Nicholas Katzenbach, who was effectively running the Justice Department for the grief-stricken Robert Kennedy, wrote a document outlining the government's goals. The Katzenbach memo would later be cited by many conspiracy theorists as evidence that the government never wanted a real investigation of the murder. In the memo, Katzenbach told President Johnson that the public must be satisfied "that Oswald was the assassin; that he did not have confederates who are still at large; and that the evidence was such that he would have been convicted at trial."[31] In other words, Johnson must convince the public of something he personally did not believe.

To accomplish this, Johnson decided to appoint a blue-ribbon commission to investigate the assassination. Just as President Roosevelt had appointed Supreme Court Justice Owen Roberts to head a probe of the intelligence failure at Pearl Harbor, Johnson created an independent board to reassure the public that the government was not hiding anything. Like Roosevelt, Johnson turned to the Supreme Court for the leader of this investigation. The Chief Justice, the liberal icon Earl Warren, did not want to take the job. But Johnson, known for his intense, high-pressure lobbying tactics, invoked the specter of nuclear holocaust to persuade him. "Now these wild people are chargin' Khrushchev killed Kennedy, and Castro killed Kennedy, and everybody else killed Kennedy," Johnson said. "Now we've had sixty FBI agents working for seven days, and they've got the story, and they've got the fingerprints, and they've got everything else. But the American people and the world have *got to know* who *killed* Kennedy and *why*, and somebody's got to evaluate that report. And if they don't, why, [if] Khrushchev moved on us, he could kill 39 million in an hour."[32] Faced with that harrowing prospect, Warren agreed to serve.

The FBI already knew who killed the president, Johnson said. *They've got the story*. The commission just needed to validate that story. After Warren reluctantly agreed to be the chairman, the president carefully chose the other members. The commission included two seasoned cold warriors, former CIA director Allen Dulles and John McCloy, the former high commissioner to Germany; two senators, Republican John Cooper of Kentucky and Democrat Richard Russell of Georgia; and two congressmen, Republican Gerald Ford of Michigan and Democrat Hale Boggs of Louisiana. As he selected his commissioners and cajoled them into serving, Johnson frequently used the argument about avoiding nuclear war.[33] Indeed, one scholar has argued that Johnson's determination to avoid an investigation into a possible communist conspiracy might have saved the world from a catastrophic nuclear exchange.[34]

The Warren Commission was not only created to discredit conspiracy theories about the communists. It was also designed to ensure that the assassination investigators did not discover the skeletons in the Kennedy administration's closet, especially Kennedy's plots against Castro. All seven commissioners were charter members of the Washington establishment who could be trusted to stick to the script given them by the president and the FBI. "All you're gonna do," Johnson told Richard Russell, "is evaluate a Hoover report that he's already *made*."[35] The president thought he could trust Russell and his fellow commissioners not to challenge that report, or to dig too deeply into the government's secrets.

And so the government began an investigation that was not really an investigation. Top officials realized that an aggressive inquiry would reveal explosive secrets—secrets about the competence of the FBI, the character of the slain president, and the morality of U.S. policy toward Cuba. Moreover, a real investigation of JFK's murder might lead to the ultimate horror: a nuclear exchange with Russia.

As a result, officials at the FBI, the CIA, and the White House decided to set limits on the investigation of the assassination. These leaders were not trying to protect the "real killers." Instead, they were statists trying to maintain Americans' trust in their system of governance. Ironically, their lies would shatter that trust.

BOTH THE CIA and the FBI had secrets that they hoped they could bury with Kennedy. The FBI's secret was mundane, but nevertheless vital to the men who ran the bureau. FBI officials hoped fervently that the Warren Commission would never discover the extent of the bureau's "gross incompetency," in Hoover's words.[36] The FBI had known before Kennedy visited Dallas that Oswald was violent, unstable, politically extreme, and employed at a warehouse on the president's motorcade route. Moreover, Oswald had threatened the U.S. government in person at the FBI field office in Dallas. The bureau had a system for monitoring people who might harm the government: it put their names on lists called the Security Index and the Reserve Index, which included tens of thousands of Americans. Linus Pauling was on one of them.[37] Oswald was not on either one.[38] Hoover's first priority was to cover up this embarrassing fact.

As a Soviet redefector, Oswald had fallen into the FBI's vast domestic surveillance net. Agents in Dallas and New Orleans had interviewed him three times in 1962 and 1963. Initially, the agents did not believe that Oswald merited more attention, and they closed his file. But when the

CIA notified the Dallas FBI office that Oswald had made mysterious visits to the Cuban and Soviet embassies in Mexico City, Special Agent James Hosty decided to reopen the case and interview the defector again. In early November 1963, Hosty made two attempts to talk to Oswald, but saw only Marina and a friend with whom she was staying.[39]

A few days after Hosty's visits to his wife, Oswald showed up at the Dallas FBI field office in a furious mood. When he learned that Hosty was out of the office, Oswald scrawled a two-paragraph note accusing Hosty of harassing his wife and threatening to take action against the FBI if he ever approached her again. When Hosty returned, he read the note and tossed it into a box on his desk. The FBI received these sorts of threats all the time. It was "no big deal," he decided.[40]

Hosty came to regret that decision. On the afternoon of the assassination, as he combed through his files at the field office, looking for clues to the killing, Hosty heard some horrifying news: Dallas police had just arrested one of his surveillance subjects, a violent, known political extremist whom he was supposed to monitor. He hurriedly briefed his supervisor, who ordered him to go to the police department and help with the questioning.[41]

When Hosty returned to the FBI field office he found Gordon Shanklin, the special agent in charge for Dallas, sitting at his desk, holding the Oswald note. "What the hell is this?" Hosty dismissed the note, saying it was "just your typical guff." This explanation infuriated his boss. "What the hell do you think Hoover's going to do if he finds out about this note!" he shouted. He ordered Hosty to type up a memo explaining his contacts with Oswald, then put the note and the memo in the "do not file" file—a Hoover-era designation for memos the FBI never wanted outsiders to see.[42]

On Sunday, November 24, after Ruby killed Oswald, Shanklin called Hosty to his office and handed him the note and his memo. "Here, take these," he said. "I don't ever want to see them again." Hosty started to tear up the documents. "No! Not here!" Shanklin protested. "I told you, I don't want to see them again. Now get them out of here." Hosty took the papers to the bathroom, tore them into tiny pieces, and flushed them down the toilet.[43] Later, the receptionist asked Hosty what had happened to the Oswald letter. "What letter?" he replied.[44]

When Hoover learned about the letter, he ordered an internal investigation of the bureau's failure in the Oswald case. He ultimately censured seventeen agents—men who offered "asinine" excuses, in his view—for their "gross incompetency." Some of the agents received letters of censure; others were transferred or suspended without pay. The agents all insisted that Oswald had not met the criteria for inclusion on the Security Index. Hoover scoffed at this defense. "They were worse than mistaken," he wrote. "Certainly no one in full possession of all his faculties could claim Oswald didn't fall within this criteria."[45] The punishments were kept secret, though. As the FBI assistant director explained, Americans might interpret the official rebukes as "a direct admission that we are responsible for negligence which might have resulted in the assassination of the President."[46]

But Hoover went beyond concealing the bureau's negligence. Opposed in principle to the whole idea of an investigation independent of the FBI, he did everything he could to thwart the work of the Warren Commission staff. As a later Senate inquiry concluded, the commission was "perceived as an adversary by both Hoover and senior FBI officials."[47]

FBI officials also failed to investigate new leads that might undermine the lone gunman theory. In particular, they showed a remarkable lack of interest in one bystander's wounds. On the day of the assassination, James Tague, who had been watching the motorcade, told a deputy sheriff that he believed he had been hit by fragments from a stray bullet. As the shots rang out, his face had been "stung" and wounded by small objects. Tague and the deputy found the place on the curb where a bullet, or a fragment of a bullet, had struck the curb and sent pieces of concrete into his face.

After noting his injury in a report, the FBI did not seem interested in Tague's story. Agents did not examine the curb until months after the assassination, when local officials, spurred on by news accounts, demanded that the FBI or the Warren Commission investigate the story. The commissioners had already finished their investigation when Tague's injury was brought to their attention, so staff members hastily added a paragraph suggesting that Tague might have been wounded by a fragment from the bullet that shattered the president's head, or by a fragment from a missed shot.[48] Many later critics found this explanation incredible and concluded that there must have been another shot and a second gunman.[49]

The fascination of the "Tague shot" for assassination researchers contrasts with the FBI's astonishing lack of curiosity about the path of the bullets. Within hours of Kennedy's death Hoover decided where the bullets came from. He did not care where they went.

According to one of his top deputies, "Hoover's main thought was always how to cover, how to protect himself."[50] In the Kennedy assassination, the way to protect himself was to ensure that the Warren Commission concluded that Oswald was a lone nut and there was no way the FBI could have stopped him. "The thing I am concerned about," Hoover said in a telephone call to presidential aide Walter Jenkins on the day Oswald was killed, "…is having something issued so we can convince the public that Oswald is the real assassin."[51] Oswald may have been the real assassin, but the FBI's refusal to consider alternatives ensured that conspiracy theories would flourish.

WHILE THE FBI was trying to cover up its incompetence, the CIA worked to protect far more significant secrets. In trying to hide its own attempts to murder foreign leaders, the CIA obscured the cold war context of the assassination and robbed it of its political meaning.

Many citizens had long believed that a powerful, centralized spy agency undermined American values of openness and limited government. In 1944, when the wartime spy chief William Donovan proposed a plan for the U.S. government's first centralized intelligence group, critics responded that a spy agency was an un-American idea. The *Chicago Tribune* lambasted Donovan's proposed intelligence agency as a "Gestapo" and quoted congressmen who foresaw the dawning of a totalitarian police state in Washington. "What is it they call that Russian spy system—the OGPU? It would certainly be nice to have one of those in our own country," one Republican senator commented dryly. Critics charged that the new agency would give too much power to the executive branch. The *Tribune* speculated that the new spy director could "determine American foreign policy by weeding out, withholding, or coloring information gathered at his direction."[52] These isolationist skeptics combined with military officers, who wanted to control intelligence themselves, and J. Edgar Hoover, who wanted to protect the FBI's bureaucratic turf, to kill the 1944 plan for a spy agency.[53]

But in 1947 President Truman decided to try again. He was convinced that the U.S. government needed a strong, central spy agency to compete against the Soviet Union in the cold war. To overcome Congress's fears that the new Central Intelligence Agency might be used against Americans, Truman promised that it would have no internal security or police functions and would not operate within the United States.[54] But although the law was clear that the CIA could not act at home, it was vague about its powers abroad. The CIA's charter contained an "elastic clause," which permitted it to perform "other functions and duties related to intelligence affecting the national security as the National Security Council may from time to time direct." By the early 1950s, these "other functions and duties" included the overthrow of democratically elected governments. By the early 1960s, they included assassination plots against foreign leaders.

Only a handful of government officials knew about the CIA's covert actions, but they had no doubt that they were justified. After all, the United States was facing "an implacable enemy whose avowed objective is world domination," as an influential, top-secret 1954 report on the CIA's expanded mission explained. There were "no rules in such a game." Perilous times required brutal methods. "If the United States is to survive," the report said, "long-standing American concepts of 'fair play' must be reconsidered. We must...learn to subvert, sabotage and destroy our enemies by more clever, more sophisticated and more effective methods than those used against us."[55]

The CIA was particularly eager to reconsider "American concepts of 'fair play'" in Cuba. Before Castro's revolution in 1959, the Caribbean nation had been a favorite spot for Americans seeking offshore opportunities for profit and sin. American mobsters controlled many of the casinos in Havana, as well as the thriving prostitution and abortion businesses. Throughout the 1950s, the Cuban dictator, Fulgencio Batista, had protected American businessmen of the legal and illegal variety.[56]

But after Castro toppled Batista's government, he closed the casinos and forced the mafia back to their homes in the United States. He soon began expropriating the Cuban holdings of American businesses, accepting aid from the Soviet Union, and ruthlessly purging his political opponents.

As Castro embraced the Soviets, American leaders reacted with increasing alarm. Besides their economic and ideological reasons for opposing Castro, U.S. officials also worried about the domestic political consequences of the Cuban Revolution. Ever since Joe McCarthy inveighed against the "conspiracy so immense," American politicians understood the dangers of appearing "soft" on communism. Because anticommunist extremists accused Truman of "losing" China, first Eisenhower and then Kennedy resolved not to lose Cuba. In this way, the anticommunist conspiracy theory of the 1950s prompted two successive presidents to adopt a Cuba policy that might have led to Kennedy's death.

Because American leaders feared provoking the Soviets with an all-out invasion of Cuba, the secret warriors at the CIA handled the attempts to overthrow Castro. In April 1961, the Kennedy administration tried to overthrow the revolutionary government with an army of Cuban exiles at the Bay of Pigs. The assault ended disastrously for the exile invaders and the United States, and Kennedy never tried to invade Cuba again. He did, however, continue Eisenhower's more secretive methods of getting rid of Castro. Kennedy intensified the CIA-sponsored sabotage operations in Cuba, dubbed "Operation Mongoose" (because it takes a mongoose to kill a snake). Agents tried to destabilize the Castro government with commando raids, espionage, and sabotage. At the same time, the CIA worked harder on its Eisenhower-era assassination plots, especially those using the mafia.[57]

CIA officials quickly realized that they shared certain interests with American mobsters in Cuba. The agency wanted to eliminate a threat to U.S. national security; the mafia, as one CIA report later said, wanted to regain its "gambling, prostitution, and dope monopolies."[58] It was logical, CIA covert operations chief Richard Bissell believed, that they should work together. In the last months of the Eisenhower administration, Bissell engaged Robert Maheu, a shady ex-FBI agent with contacts in the underworld, to arrange an assassination bankrolled by the U.S. government and carried out by the mafia. Maheu was a "cut-out," the man who would transact the details of the "dirty business" for the U.S. government so that government employees did not have to sully their hands.[59] Maheu in turn contacted Johnny Rosselli, a notorious Las Vegas mobster, and asked him to arrange a CIA-mafia deal.

In a suite at the opulent Fontainebleau Hotel in Miami Beach, a CIA officer met with two underworld bosses to discuss hiring them to murder a neighboring head of state. The CIA viewed Sam Giancana, the mob boss of Chicago, and Santo Trafficante, the mafia chieftain of Miami and formerly of Cuba, as "businessmen with interests in Cuba who saw the elimination of Castro as the first essential step to the recovery of their investments."[60] The attorney general saw them as two of the most dangerous men in the country and put them on his ten most-wanted list.[61] In one of many ironies, the FBI was hunting them down while the CIA was hiring them to commit crimes.

The U.S. government developed plans to drop poison pills in Castro's drinks and to plant an exploding seashell in his favorite scuba-diving bay. It customized a diving suit for Castro by dusting it with a skin-destroying fungus and contaminating its breathing tubes with the bacterium that causes tuberculosis. It also delivered guns and ammunition to teams of hit men. On November 22, 1963, as Kennedy was dying in Dallas, one of his CIA operatives was delivering a hypodermic needle concealed in a ball-point pen to a Cuban in Paris. The CIA planned for the Cuban to fill the pen with poison and stab Castro with it.[62]

After the Kennedy assassination, the agency abandoned this particular plan, but other plots continued. President Johnson later ended the program, claiming that he was horrified to learn that "we had been operating a damned Murder Inc. in the Caribbean."[63]

Although Johnson apparently did not approve of the Castro plots, President Kennedy and his brother Robert almost certainly did. CIA officials later testified that they had used "circumlocutious terms" in briefing top White House officials, but that everyone had known what they were talking about.[64] Indeed, CIA officials claimed that the attorney general had been the driving force behind the plots, furious at Castro for humiliating his brother at the Bay of Pigs. Richard Helms, the covert action chief at the time, said that Robert Kennedy had told him to "get rid" of Castro. "I heard him use those words," Helms said. "We had a whip on our backs. If I take off my shirt, I'll show you the scars."[65]

The Kennedys also had another source of information about the Castro plots: the all-knowing J. Edgar Hoover. Thanks to surveillance and detective work, Hoover's agents learned of the CIA's Castro plots, of Giancana's participation, and, most important for the president, of another link between Giancana and John Kennedy. As it happened, one of Giancana's mistresses, Judith Campbell, was also involved with President Kennedy. Hoover prepared a memo on the complicated relationships (titled "JUDITH E. CAMPBELL; ASSOCIATE OF HOODLUMS") and took it to a private meeting with the president in March 1962.[66] No record exists of the meeting, but one can assume that the FBI chief sketched the whole picture for the president: the mistress, the murder plots, and the mob connections. "J. Edgar Hoover has Jack Kennedy by the balls," Lyndon Johnson told some reporters privately.[67]

Although the American people did not know that their government was working with mobsters to kill Castro, the plots were common knowledge in Havana. Castro documented several U.S.-sponsored attempts on his life, and he later turned the evidence over to a U.S. senator. In September 1963 he issued an unmistakable threat against John Kennedy. "United States leaders," he said in an interview with the Associated Press, "should think that if they are aiding in terrorist plans to eliminate Cuban leaders, they themselves will not be safe."[68]

The Associated Press article on the Castro threat ran in several American newspapers, including the New Orleans *Times-Picayune*. Oswald, a dedicated newspaper reader, was in New Orleans at the time.[69] Did he read the story? Could he have decided to kill Kennedy because Kennedy was trying to kill Castro? Americans will never know. Because instead of investigating the potential link between the Castro plots and Kennedy's murder, the CIA immediately set out to cover it up.

Throughout the Warren Commission investigation, former CIA director Allen Dulles never told his fellow commissioners or their staff about the Castro plots. Years later commission staff members testified that knowledge of these plots would have profoundly influenced their investigation and conclusions. The CIA's secrets about the Castro plots, the former commission counsel Burt Griffin said, "lead not only to the issue of possible conspirators with Oswald, but also his motive."[70]

For his part, Lyndon Johnson was convinced that the Castro plots had led to Kennedy's assassination. Before his death in 1973, he told many people—his friends, his publisher, and at least four reporters—that he believed that Castro had organized a successful conspiracy to kill Kennedy. "Kennedy was trying to get to Castro, but Castro got to him first," he once said.[71] Robert Kennedy also seemed to connect the Castro plots to his brother's assassination, and to suffer from overwhelming guilt as a result.[72] To his closest friends he confessed doubts about the attempts to topple Castro. "I have myself wondered at times," he said, "if we did not pay a very great price for being more energetic than wise about a lot of things, especially Cuba."[73]

But Robert still refused to discuss publicly the possibility of a conspiracy. Finding the truth would not bring his brother back. The true story of their Cuba policy would also tarnish JFK's image, and that of the entire country, in the eyes of the world. There were some secrets, he believed, it was best never to reveal. When the Warren Commission asked Robert if he had any additional information that might shed light on the assassination, he replied that the commission had already received "all information relating in any way to the assassination of President John F. Kennedy *in the possession of the Department of Justice*."[74] It was an artfully worded letter. As Robert knew, the CIA was in possession of a great deal more information, but he, like Allen Dulles, declined to inform the commission of this.

ALL OF OFFICIAL WASHINGTON—the CIA, the FBI, the White House, and the Kennedy family—expected the Warren Commission to conclude that one sociopath had killed the president. The Warren Commission members and staff were generally willing to follow this scenario. But their determination to prove the lone gunman theory encountered two unanticipated problems.

Most later Kennedy assassination conspiracy theories would focus on two key pieces of physical evidence: the silent movie of the killing made by a bystander, local dressmaker Abraham Zapruder, and the president's body. In both cases, the U.S. government's examination of the evidence was rushed, incompetent, and unconvincing.

The Warren Commission started with the assumption that the assassin had fired three shots. This seemed relatively uncontroversial at first: the FBI had found three cartridge cases on the sixth floor of the book depository, and the majority of witnesses had heard three shots. In its initial report on the assassination, the FBI concluded that the three shots had all hit something: the first shot hit Kennedy in the neck, the second wounded Texas Governor John Connally, who was in the limousine with the president, and the third hit the president's head and killed him.

The Zapruder film captured the drama and all its grisly details on film. On the day of the assassination, Zapruder had clambered to the top of a concrete pillar midway up a grassy slope, hoping to use the added height to get a good picture of the presidential motorcade with his color movie camera. Unlike most of the other amateur photographers on the plaza that day, he kept filming even after he heard the gunshots. In its first frames, the two couples in the car, John and Jacqueline Kennedy and John and Nellie Connally, seem smiling and relaxed. Suddenly, Kennedy grabs his throat, then Connally slumps down. In its most disturbing sequence, the film shows Kennedy's head blown apart by a lethal shot.

Zapruder's twenty-six-second color movie helped to spawn generations of Kennedy assassination conspiracy theories. Even before it was released to the public in 1975, its still frames, reprinted in *Life* magazine the week after the assassination, raised troubling questions about the government's official narrative. At the same time, the film provided clues to an alternative narrative and seemed to give critics the power to solve the puzzle of the assassination themselves.[75]

The commission quickly discovered that the Zapruder film complicated its initial theory about the path of the bullets. In the movie, Connally reacts to his wounds less than two seconds after Kennedy. But an FBI marksman needed *more* than two seconds—at least 2.3—to fire two shots with Oswald's rifle. In other words, Oswald did not have enough time to take a separate shot at Connally. Either the same bullet hit both men, or different gunmen shot them. "To say that they were hit by separate bullets," a commission counsel said, "is synonymous with saying that there were two assassins."[76] Because the commission was committed to the one-assassin theory, the conclusion was obvious: one bullet must have hit both men.

But this conclusion forced the commission to posit an extraordinary path for this single bullet, the "magic bullet," as critics later called it. According to the commission's theory, this bullet struck Kennedy in the back, tore through his body, exited his throat, plowed into Connally's shoulder, came out his chest, wounded his wrist, and finally came to a stop in his thigh, where it rested until it fell out onto the governor's stretcher at Parkland Hospital, where it was later found by an orderly.[77]

The commission needed evidence to support its theory from the autopsy of the president: in other words, proof that the bullet in question had passed all the way through Kennedy's body. And here the investigators encountered problems that would later cast doubt on their work.

The autopsy was conducted at the Navy hospital in Bethesda, Maryland, which Jacqueline Kennedy chose because her husband had been in the Navy. At the hospital, in a tower suite high above the crowded, hectic morgue, Jacqueline and Robert Kennedy pressured the pathologists to finish their grim task as soon as possible. The attorney general and one of the late president's aides, Kenneth O'Donnell, repeatedly called the autopsy room and demanded to know when it would be over. James Humes, the head pathologist, later conceded that the family's interference served to "harass us and cause difficulty—of course it did, how could it not!"[78] Feeling pressed for time, the pathologists failed to take several routine steps, such as shaving the head, inspecting the clothing, and dissecting the wounds.[79]

Most important, the doctors did not trace the path of one of the bullets. The pathologists could not discover the path of the bullet that hit Kennedy in his back, nor could they find the bullet itself or its exit point. "It was bothering me very greatly, like nothing you can imagine," that they could not find the bullet or its exit wound, Humes later said.[80] However, they decided to put off that vexing question for another day.[81]

The Kennedy family's desire to keep the late president's secrets probably contributed to the doctors' rush to finish the autopsy prematurely. John Kennedy had suffered from Addison's disease, which was a treatable but serious disorder of the adrenal glands, and from repeated bouts of venereal disease. Selling himself as a youthful, energetic presidential candidate in 1960, he had consistently misled the public about his illnesses. His brother did not want the country to discover those lies.[82] The autopsy doctors, in other words, were handicapped by the Kennedys' desire to conceal certain facts about JFK's (live) body.

The next morning, Humes talked to one of the physicians who had treated the president in Dallas. He already knew that the emergency room doctors, in a desperate, doomed attempt to save the president's life, had performed a tracheotomy. But in talking to the Dallas doctor, Humes learned something astounding: the tracheotomy had obliterated an exit wound in Kennedy's neck. "The light came on," Humes explained, and he realized that the bullet must have entered the president's back and exited his neck.[83] He wrote this in his final report, which thus supported the single-bullet theory.

But the FBI agents at the autopsy were not privy to this enlightening conversation. According to their official report, the autopsy had proved that the problematic bullet had penetrated a short distance into Kennedy's body, and then apparently fallen out later at the hospital. It had not, in other words, barreled all the way through his body and gone on to hit Connally. The Warren Commission did not include the FBI report in its twenty-six volumes of hearings and exhibits, but in June 1966 a graduate student in physics at U.C. Berkeley requested it from the National Archives. Archivists mailed him a copy of the five-page report, and a controversy was born.[84]

In short, the forensic pathologists who conducted the autopsy and the FBI agents who observed it filed contradictory reports about the path of this bullet. For skeptics of the official story, the differing versions of the bullet's path would provide tantalizing hints of a conspiracy (though, one should note, a conspiracy burdened by a rather ineffective cover-up).

For his part, Connally, though an advocate of the lone gunman theory, was absolutely certain that he was hit by a second shot. "They talk about the 'one-bullet or two-bullet theory,' but as far as I'm concerned, there is no 'theory,'" he told *Life* magazine in 1966. "There is my absolute knowledge, and Nellie's too, that one bullet caused the President's first wound, and that an entirely separate shot struck me."[85] Indeed, many of the Warren Commission staff members did not believe the single-bullet theory at first, but ultimately embraced it as the only way to reconcile their interpretation of the Zapruder film with their conviction that Oswald had acted alone.

The commission's reconstruction of the assassination, in short, was shaped from the beginning by the members' determination to reach a prede-termined conclusion. It was unpersuasive even to the men who came up with it. This does not mean that their conclusion of a single bullet or a lone gun-man was wrong.[86] It does mean, however, that the commission was primar-ily a public relations exercise, as Robert Kennedy later told an aide, meant to placate the American public.[87] It was not meant to discover the truth.

The single-bullet theory was so unconvincing that even most of the commission members refused to believe it at first. Six of the seven mem-bers expressed doubts about it, with Allen Dulles the lone exception. Senator Richard Russell was so disgusted by the "magic bullet" theory that he initially rejected it in a separate dissent. As a senator, Russell was accustomed to the tradition of minority and majority reports. The Pearl Harbor Committee, for example, had issued two completely antithetical reports. Warren, however, wanted a unanimous report, and he was deter-mined to get it. He told Russell that his dissent would be noted in the report, and then simply ignored it.[88] The "unanimous" report said that there was no credible evidence of a conspiracy and that a single bullet hit Kennedy and Connally. Russell voiced his doubts to President Johnson in a candid phone conversation. "They said that they believe...that the Commission believe[s] that the same bullet that hit Kennedy hit Connally. *Well,*" Russell said, obviously irate that his views were misrepresented, "*I don't believe it.*" Johnson responded, "I don't either."[89]

THOUGH THE PRESIDENT and at least one of the commission members did not believe the Warren Report, they had utmost confidence in their ability to persuade the public to do so. At first, they seemed successful: the proportion of Americans who suspected a conspiracy dropped from 62 percent immediately after the assassination to 31 percent after the release of the report.[90] But from the start, there were some citizens who refused to accept the official version of the assassination, who thought that it "smelled awfully bad," in the words of one critic.[91] And they set out to prove that their government was covering up a conspiracy.

Around the country, from the day of the assassination, ordinary Americans began to clip and file stories about the investigation with the goal of finding the "real truth." Like Shirley Martin, the most ambitious traveled to Dallas to retrace Oswald's path or interview witnesses themselves.

The first skeptics labored in obscurity and isolation, but they soon began forming a grassroots network around the country. They identified each other through their impassioned letters to the editor charging conspiracy or through the angry articles they published in small, mostly left-wing publications. In October 1965, the first group of ten "Warrenologists" gathered in the Manhattan apartment of Sylvia Meagher, who knew more about the Kennedy assassination than anyone else in the world, according to her admiring fellow skeptics.[92] The East Coast critics corresponded with other researchers throughout the country in an increasingly specialized language: there was "LHO" (Oswald), the "TSBD" (Texas school book depository), and frequent references to "frame 313" and "CE 133-B," which identified frames of the Zapruder film and Warren Commission exhibits to insiders. Above all, they believed that the world had changed on "11/22/63."

The critics lived in different parts of the country, in small towns and large cities, in tiny apartments and rambling California ranch houses. They were businessmen, teachers, graduate students, and housewives. But despite their differences, the assassination researchers, as they called themselves, shared a common belief: they knew, beyond all possible doubt, that the U.S. government was lying to them.

The earliest Warren Report critics had been skeptical of the truthfulness of the federal government for years. A surprising number were direct victims of McCarthyism or had defended victims of McCarthyism. Meagher had successfully fought to keep her job in 1953 after investigators questioned her loyalty.[93] Harold Weisberg, who self-published an early critique of the Warren Report, *Whitewash,* and who went on to write *Whitewash II* and several other Kennedy assassination conspiracy books, had been fired by the State Department after a loyalty probe in 1947.[94] John Henry Faulk, who helped lead the Committee to Investigate Assassinations, lost his career in radio in the 1950s because of his alleged ties to communists. Two other directors of the committee, Fred Cook and Bud Fensterwald, actively opposed the Red Scare, Cook as a journalist and Fensterwald as a State Department analyst.[95] And chemist Linus Pauling, who had been spied on and harassed by the FBI, immediately suspected a government cover-up in the assassination.

Some of the skeptics even identified personally with the alleged assassin, who they suspected had been framed. The government's habit of demonizing leftists had cost some of them their friends, their jobs, and their privacy. They had been interrogated, humiliated, and spied on by federal agents, often for no reason other than their enthusiasm for labor rights or civil liberties. Could government agents have done even worse to Oswald?

Meagher was convinced that they had. From the moment she learned of the assassination, she believed that the government would find a convenient "communist" to blame.[96] Determined to find the truth, she devoted every spare minute to researching the murder. She molded the scattered, isolated assassination researchers into a unified movement.

When Meagher gathered the first group of researchers in her living room, the vast majority of Americans did not share their skepticism; they trusted their government to tell them the truth. They believed President Johnson and Defense Secretary Robert McNamara when they said that U.S. warships had been attacked without provocation in the Gulf of Tonkin in August 1964. They supported Congress's overwhelming vote to give the president a blank check to stop the advance of communism in Vietnam. Indeed, 1964—the year of the Warren Report, the Gulf of Tonkin Resolution, and Lyndon Johnson's landslide election victory—was the high point of Americans' trust in their government, with almost 80 percent saying they trusted officials to do the right thing most or all of the time.[97]

But as the Vietnam War turned into a quagmire and prominent senators began accusing the president of lying about the war, many Americans started listening to the critics' argument that the government was lying about the JFK assassination. The public's confidence in government began to fall by every measure beginning in 1965: growing numbers of Americans told pollsters that the government wasted "a lot of money," that it was run by "a few big interests," that it paid little attention to "what the people think," and, most important, that it could not be trusted to "do right most of the time."[98] In this atmosphere, more Americans became receptive to antigovernment conspiracy theories.

Several of the early critics had considered themselves politically liberal before the assassination, but now they saw liberals like Earl Warren as apologists for bureaucracy and for the failure of democracy in America. In the view of the skeptics, these complacent liberals, men who were now part of the establishment that liberalism was supposed to fight, used their control over information to construct a story of the JFK assassination that was a "demonstrable fraud."[99] The state had grown so big and powerful that it now had grabbed even the good liberals in its tentacles. Vincent Salandria, a lawyer and critic, told an interviewer in 1967 that he used to believe that liberals fought for equality and justice. "But as a consequence of this assassination," he explained, "I see the liberal as different. I see him as being more interested in protecting government, in even apologizing for government, surrendering the skepticism in favor of support for power."[100]

In the critics' view, their government lied about many things: about the dangers of nuclear fallout, the threat of communism, and, in time, the Vietnam War. It was not a great leap for them to believe that the government was lying about the murder of the president.

Why, though, did the government lie? Had Kennedy done something to threaten the interests of other government officials? The skeptics thought so. Kennedy had become a hero to Pauling when he signed the Nuclear Test Ban Treaty with the Soviet Union and Great Britain in 1963, thus ending the atmospheric nuclear tests that the scientist believed were leading to the premature deaths of millions of people. The treaty, Pauling had written to the president, "will go down in history as one of the greatest events in the history of the world."[101] Pauling also admired Kennedy's American University address in June 1963, in which he urged accommodation with the Soviet Union: "For, in the final analysis, our most basic common link is that we all inhabit this small planet. We all breathe the same air. We all cherish our children's future. And we are all mortal."[102]

The assassination researchers viewed the American University speech as Kennedy's "death warrant."[103] As Martin wrote to Meagher, "The Kennedys were moving (as fast as they dared) in the directions we wanted. As it was, the movement went too fast. He had to be killed."[104] Meagher agreed that after a "terrible beginning," Kennedy was "showing signs in the American University speech of growth and greatness."[105] Many critics came to believe that Kennedy was starting to confront what President Eisenhower had called the "military-industrial complex" in his farewell address in 1961.

Ironically, Kennedy had been the ultimate cold warrior, the candidate who mendaciously flogged the Republicans for allowing a "missile gap" to develop during Eisenhower's administration. His murderous anti-Castro policies might have provoked Oswald to act. But the researchers did not see Kennedy this way; to them, he was the one person challenging the military-industrial complex. And so, of course, "they" had to kill him.

Like earlier conspiracy theorists, the independent critics predicted dire consequences for the republic if the government's secrets and lies were not exposed. If Americans accepted the Warren Commission's conclusions, Salandria said, "it would mean that 1984 was with us and our experiment with democracy was ended....I couldn't live in a society that could pull a swindle of this kind."[106] A Los Angeles sign manufacturer, Raymond Marcus, agreed that the assassination should prompt Americans "to demand other answers. Maybe they'll ask about the Rosenbergs, Hiss, the whole Cold War. Maybe we can get clean and whole. But if this stays down, there's no hope."[107]

Besides their doubts about the government's actions during the cold war, the assassination critics shared the passionate conviction that they could discover the truth about Dallas on their own. They not only questioned the interventionist foreign policy of the liberal state, they also challenged the state's monopoly on expertise. Pauling, for example, pored over enlarged prints of Dealey Plaza, searching for shadowy assassins in the haze of photographic dots. Dismissing the Warren Commission's "scientific" studies and investigation, the researchers set out to prove that ordinary American citizens had as much authority to investigate the killing of the president as the government did—indeed, that their status as amateurs gave them *more* claim to authenticity and truth. "One of the things I have learned not to trust," said Meagher, referring to the Warren Report, "is the sentence you have to read several times to get its meaning." The smooth-talking government lawyers who composed awkward sentences about magic bullets and trajectories—all that "argle-bargle about the rifle," as Maggie Field said—failed to understand the basic absurdity of one "pristine" bullet causing seven wounds in two men.[108]

The skeptics saw this impenetrable prose as another example of a government trying to evade democratic controls and hiding important information from citizens. The officials seemed to be trying to cover up their mistakes—or their crimes—by producing a narrative that they hoped citizens would not question because they could not understand it.

In response, the critics conducted their own investigation, free from the "argle-bargle" of the state's experts. They took pictures of their sons posing with rifles in their backyards to prove their theory that the famous photo of Oswald with a Mannlicher-Carcano had been faked; they learned to use specialized tools to measure the angle from the sixth floor of the depository to the president's car; they studied the Zapruder film until they had memorized the four-hundred-odd frames and their corresponding numbers.

Their primary source material was, ironically, the very report that they condemned as a fraud and a lie. The Warren Report comprised, the *New Yorker* writer Calvin Trillin said, "the largest body of source material any armchair student of a crime has ever had."[109] It was not only a source: it was, Norman Mailer said, "a species of Talmudic text begging for commentary and further elucidation."[110] The critics mined the report for evidence to discredit it. The commission did not make this task easy, issuing only a name index for the twenty-six volumes of hearings and exhibits. The report was really a government archive of documents and testimony about the Kennedy assassination—but without an index, it was a closed archive. Meagher grew so frustrated with the lack of a subject index that she spent six months compiling one.[111] In the end, she produced an index with an attitude, with headings that pointed the intrigued reader to mistakes and contradictions as well as official stories. It soon became required reading for all assassination investigators.[112]

In the introductory note to her index, Meagher explained that she hoped her work would enable scholars "to test the assertions and conclusions in the Warren Report against their independent judgment."[113] They could use the report to attack the report. Her fellow researchers saw no contradiction in this. "There's enough evidence in the 26 volumes to hang the Commission three times over," said Maggie Field.[114] Their reliance on state-sanctioned information also showed the increasing difficulty of writing the history of political events without help, whether intentional or inadvertent, from the state.

The researchers worked anonymously for three years, but then two of the most articulate and well-connected critics succeeded in publishing, in the words of the comedian and filmmaker Woody Allen, the "nonfiction version of the Warren Report."[115] Mark Lane, a civil rights lawyer who had given hundreds of speeches since 1964 attacking the Warren Commission, wrote a manuscript that was rejected by fifteen publishers before it was finally published in 1966 as *Rush to Judgment*.[116] The book spent six months on the *New York Times* best-seller list. Edward Jay Epstein, a Cornell graduate student, published his master's thesis on the Warren Commission's failings, *Inquest*, that year.[117] Like Lane's book, Epstein's treatise was a phenomenal seller that helped to make criticism of the Warren Commission respectable. The critics' charges, Meagher said, were now making "the dramatic transition from taboo to dialogue."[118]

Though Lane and Epstein earned the headlines and royalties, they built on the research of a core of dedicated amateurs. David Lifton, a UCLA graduate student who later wrote his own best-selling book about the assassination, compared the critical community to a company with a public relations branch and a research-and-development branch. "The two puncture points at the top—what gets public attention—are Lane's book and Epstein's book," he explained. "The r.-and-d. program is being done by a bunch of amateurs."[119]

Many of these "amateurs" were women. In the past, when conspiracy theories flowed from the pens of prominent journalists or congressmen, most of the theorists tended to be men. But with the Kennedy assassination, the field was open to ordinary, untrained researchers—and to women. Meagher, for example, developed close friendships with other women who wanted to discover the truth about Kennedy's death. JFK's youth and good looks might have attracted more women to this particular conspiracy theory.

The Warren Commission's defenders quickly mobilized to attack these amateurs. With a few exceptions, most mainstream media outlets rushed to defend the Warren Report and to blast the critics as cranks and obsessives. "Who are the men [sic] who have created doubt about a document that in September, 1964, seemed to have reasonable answers?" asked the journalist Charles Roberts. "Are they bona fide scholars, as the review-ers took them to be, or are they, as Connally has suggested, 'journalistic scavengers?' "[120] The women came in for special criticism. The authors of one 1967 attack on the assassination researchers, for example, devoted a condescending chapter to the "housewives' underground," which implied that female researchers such as Meagher and Field were looking for mean-ing to fill their empty lives. Meagher was singled out as the "Housewives' Supersleuth," though she was a divorcée with a full-time salaried job.[121]

Top government officials also battled the critics. Because some of the most eminent men in the United States had served on the Warren Commission, the skeptics' attack on the report "cast doubt on the whole leadership of American society," an internal CIA memo concluded. The "whole reputation of the American government" was at stake. To coun-ter the critics, the memo urged CIA officials to seek out "friendly elite contacts" in the media and in Congress. The CIA should emphasize the selfish interests of the skeptics, whether financial or political, and suggest that "parts of the conspiracy talk appear to be deliberately generated by Communist propagandists."[122]

The CIA was partially correct: the Soviet Union did try to encour-age conspiracy theories about the Kennedy assassination by lauding the critics and planting some false stories in communist newspapers.[123] The agency was also correct that the leading Warren Report researchers were on the far left of American politics. But some government officials leaped to the conclusion that the critics were consciously serving Moscow, which was not true. One FBI report, for example, noted ominously that Harold Weisberg, the author of the *Whitewash* books, held "an annual celebra-tion of the Russian Revolution" at his Maryland chicken farm, evidently confusing a picnic celebrating the Jewish new year with a Bolshevik fete.[124] In a 1966 report to the president on seven critics of the Warren Report, Hoover stressed that they were all either suspected communists, associates of suspected communists, members of communist front groups, or, at the very least, former visitors to communist lands. Given their backgrounds, the FBI was not surprised that these authors had produced such "diaboli-cal" works as Weisberg's *Whitewash* series.[125]

By 1966, as public cynicism escalated, the critics found that their argu-ments resonated with millions of skeptical Americans. Journalists, intel-lectuals, and public officials called for a new investigation. As in 1950, the

American public was afraid that unknown conspirators had put the repub-lic in peril. And once again, as in 1950, a shrewd politician seized the oppor-tunity to shape—and to exploit—these fears.

LIKE JOE McCARTHY, Jim Garrison was a late convert to conspiracism. In the fall of 1966, when the New Orleans district attorney discovered Kennedy assassination conspiracy theories, the independent critics had spent more than two years combing through the Warren Commission hearings, examining the Zapruder frames, and interviewing eyewitnesses. The proportion of Americans who suspected a conspiracy climbed from 31 percent in late 1964 to 50 percent in December 1966.[126] Perhaps the best barometer of public opinion was *Life*, the glossy magazine of Middle America. *Life* had consistently supported the lone-gunman theory since it had published the still frames of the Zapruder film in November 1963. But three years later, in an article titled "A Matter of Reasonable Doubt," the magazine officially joined the ranks of the skeptics.[127] The *Saturday Evening Post*, an equally conservative publication, soon followed with its own story challenging the Warren Report.[128] The December 1966 issue of *Esquire* included a "primer" of thirty-five assassination theories, including the "evil forces theory," the "Dallas oligarchy theory," and the Manchurian candidate theory.[129] Garrison could sense that a movement was starting to form, and he wanted to lead it.

The flamboyant prosecutor had been controversial since his election in 1961. A six-foot, six-inch glad-handing politico known as the "Jolly Green Giant," Garrison was regarded locally as a fearless and somewhat erratic prosecutor. Though the military had discharged him for incapaci-tating neuroses, Garrison had still managed to earn a law degree and the votes of a majority of the New Orleans electorate.[130] He began his term by launching well-publicized raids of gay bars and houses of prostitution on Bourbon Street. The raids were not very effective, but they won him national publicity as an aggressive reformer. The *Saturday Evening Post* gushed that he "looked like Perry Mason and sounded like Eliot Ness" and portrayed him as a straight-talking, incorruptible populist hero. Despite the powerful enemies arrayed against him, he was determined to fight for the people, he told interviewers. "The only way anyone can stop me," he said, "is to kill me." Garrison framed his campaign against brothels in New Orleans as an assault on the local establishment and, in a somewhat bizarre logical twist, as a defense of individual rights. "People worry about the crime 'syndicate,' but the real danger is the political establishment, power massing against the individual," he said. "As an individual, I am not going to be pushed around by all the power in the state."[131] The big city prosecutor wielded some of the most arbitrary powers available to government officials, but like many conspiracists, he was blind to internal contradictions in his arguments.

Garrison first decided to investigate the Kennedy assassination during a plane ride in November 1966 with Senator Russell Long, the son of Huey Long, another self-proclaimed champion of the people and enemy of "the establishment." Senator Long told Garrison that the growing number of books and articles questioning the Warren Report had prompted him to have his own doubts. Garrison began to read the critics' books and devour the Warren Commission hearings. He had an excuse to reopen the case: Oswald had lived in New Orleans during the summer of 1963, but commission investigators had mostly ignored his activities there. As district attorney, Garrison could address that oversight and look for possible co-conspirators.[132]

The prosecutor began by interrogating several local residents who had contacted the FBI with leads shortly after the assassination. He was particularly interested in the tale of Dean Andrews, a New Orleans lawyer who had testified before the Warren Commission. Andrews claimed that Oswald had visited his law office a few times in the company of some "gay kids" from Mexico. On the day after Kennedy's death, Andrews said, a shadowy, bisexual figure named "Clay Bertrand" had asked him to defend Oswald.[133] The FBI had investigated Andrews's story and found it baseless; indeed, Andrews himself later admitted that he made up most of it.[134] But Garrison saw opportunity in Andrews's story, and he quickly identified "Bertrand" as a local businessman named Clay Shaw. Although Shaw did not look anything like Andrews's description of "Bertrand," his name was Clay and he was gay, which was close enough for Garrison.[135] In March 1967, Garrison made a splash on the front pages of newspapers across the country by arresting Shaw for conspiracy to murder President Kennedy.

At first, the Warren Report critics were thrilled that a public official with subpoena power was finally pursuing the case. Sylvia Meagher confessed that she had to repress her "almost irresistible" impulse to rush to New Orleans as soon as she heard Garrison intone "Let justice be done though the heavens fall."[136] Other assassination researchers did not repress these impulses. Many of them flew to New Orleans to serve as foot soldiers in Garrison's army of justice. Edward Epstein went through Shaw's papers for the prosecutor, Harold Weisberg searched for new witnesses, and Mark Lane held press conferences to herald Garrison's new leads.[137] They all wanted to help Garrison identify the real conspirators.

But just who were these conspirators? At first, Garrison was intrigued by the homosexuality of the supposed plotters. Seventeen years after McCarthy and other anticommunist conspiracists had vilified American diplomats as "pansies," Garrison resurrected the image of the homosexual enemy. He initially toyed with the idea that these men had committed a "homosexual thrill killing" and had targeted the president because they envied his virility.[138] Quickly, though, he discarded this theory in favor of one he found more compelling. Like McCarthy, Garrison came to believe that the real traitors to the republic were lodged in the heart of the federal government itself.

Garrison was the first prominent American to propose what would ultimately become the most widely believed JFK conspiracy theory: that elements within the U.S. government—most commonly, the CIA—had killed the president because he wanted to get out of Vietnam. In fact, Garrison's conspiracy theory was similar to one set forth by Soviet intelligence, and recent research has suggested this was no coincidence. Three days after Garrison arrested Shaw, European newspapers began running stories that identified Shaw as a CIA agent. Garrison read these stories and revised his conspiracy theory. He dropped the "homosexual thrill killing" angle and began to portray Shaw as a covert operative of a shadowy group within the federal government.[139]

As Max Holland has shown, the foreign newspaper stories that inspired Garrison were actually the products of a KGB disinformation campaign. Ironically, though President Johnson had tried assiduously to deflect suspicion from the Kremlin for Kennedy's assassination, Moscow's spies had been working just as hard to focus the blame on Johnson. For years, the KGB had been planting stories in the communist press alleging that the CIA and/or President Johnson had killed Kennedy.[140] When Garrison arrested Shaw, the KGB quickly adapted its story to fit the new circumstances and fingered the New Orleans businessman as part of the secret government plot.[141] Garrison picked up the European story, embroidered it with his own details, and announced that he was now on the trail of government-backed assassins.

In a different time—indeed, only a few months earlier—this conspiracy theory would have seemed incredible to most Americans. But Garrison, like McCarthy before him, chose the perfect moment to charge treason in high places. The month before Garrison arrested Shaw, the left-wing magazine *Ramparts* revealed that the CIA had been secretly funneling hundreds of thousands of dollars to a domestic organization, the National Student Association, a moderately liberal group of college student activists. Soon Americans learned that the CIA had also covertly funded numerous labor unions and cultural groups.[142] In other words, an agency prohibited by law from operating in the United States had been secretly trying to influence the country's cultural, economic, and political debates. As the editors of *Commonweal* wrote, "There is no point in complaining about a growing attachment of the New Left to 'conspiracy theories' when genuine conspiracies are popping up all around."[143] Right at this time of heightening skepticism of America's secret warriors, Garrison announced that Clay Shaw was part of a CIA conspiracy to kill the president.

Once Garrison decided that Shaw was a government operative, he began to spin grand theories about the killing. It was all connected to the cold war. Kennedy had been killed, Garrison said, "because he wanted peace." Oswald was actually a tool of the right; he had shrewdly been perfecting a communist cover since his high school days. His attempted assassination of Walker had been part of his act. "If you defect to Russia, pass out pro-Castro leaflets on street corners and take a pot shot at General Walker," Garrison reasoned, "who on earth would doubt you're a Communist?"[144]

In Garrison's view, the federal government had killed Kennedy because he opposed its plan to subvert American democracy and individualism. A "proto-fascist" state had taken over the country, with "an arrogant, swollen bureaucratic complex totally unfettered by the checks and balances of the Constitution" holding the real power. "In a very real and terrifying sense," he said, "our Government is the CIA and the Pentagon, with Congress reduced to a debating society."[145]

It was the invisible government of Charles Lindbergh again, but this time it was called the "military-industrial complex." Garrison drew on the traditional American fear of hidden plotters in the government and adapted it to the 1960s. His thesis was appealingly simple: Americans could no longer trust the federal government, which lied about everything. To combat the lies, real Americans must support truth-seekers like Jim Garrison. The conspirators in the government would be exposed, and the rightful rulers—those who were still alive, anyway—would be restored to power.

This was the mirror image of General Walker's conspiracy theory. Though Earl Warren was still the chief villain, this time the plotters were fanatical *anti*communists, and the victims were the ones who wanted peace with the communists. In Garrison's view, a cabal of CIA agents, military men, and defense contractors had united to kill the man who threatened their profits; they were, indeed, the modern merchants of death. This theory appealed to a number of Warren Report critics, who agreed with Garrison that the government's lies could have catastrophic consequences. "If I was basically in favor of our foreign policy," Raymond Marcus, an early skeptic, said in 1967, "I wouldn't be doing this work. But people have believed lies and those lies are going to kill us all."[146]

Those lies are going to kill us all. Ironically, President Johnson had tried to avoid a real investigation into Kennedy's murder because he was afraid that finding the truth might lead to Armageddon. The JFK conspiracy theorists saw the government "whitewash" as evidence of its willingness to *risk*—rather than avoid—a nuclear war. In another irony, they also saw the president who had escalated the secret war against Castro as a martyr for peace.

Ultimately, Garrison favored the emerging New Left theory that the chief conspirator was the man "who has profited most from the assassination—your friendly President! Lyndon Johnson."[147] Opponents of the Vietnam War hated Johnson as much as the isolationist right had hated Franklin Roosevelt; they believed that there was no limit to his evil.

As Garrison began his crusade, popular culture started to reflect this leftist hatred of President Johnson. In February 1967, an Off Broadway theater company produced a Macbeth parody, *MacBird!*, which featured a vice president with a Texas accent conspiring with his wife, Lady MacBird, to assassinate the president, John Ken O'Dunc. Written by a twenty-five-year activist, Barbara Garson, *MacBird!* had circulated in New Left circles as an underground script but could not find a publisher until Garson's husband set up his own company, Grassy Knoll Press, to bring it to the people. It sold 100,000 copies. Two ordinary citizens with contacts in the theater, a stage designer and a secretary, worked with Garson to produce the play in New York.[148]

Even after the play started rehearsals, the producers faced obstacles: a local TV news station spiked a report on *MacBird!*; New York fire marshals spent four hours poking around the theater, trying to find violations to justify shutting down the play; and a publisher refused to print the *MacBird!* brochure because of what he regarded as its sick and irresponsible conspiracy theory. "If those people think they can make a fortune out of a national tragedy," he said, "they're crazy."[149]

But they were not so crazy: the play was a hit, with "warm and responsive" sold-out audiences persuading legitimate publishers to bid for the right to produce slick editions of the play in English and French.[150] *MacBird!* was successful because Garson's counternarrative captured and intensified the "many dark fears and suspicions that are coming to light," explained Richard Christiansen of the *Chicago Daily News*. "As such," he continued, "it is only a sign of the general malaise eating away at the nation today, and there, at heart, is the real terror for us all."[151]

Garrison promoted himself as a hero to the fans of *MacBird!* and to the swelling ranks of disaffected leftists. These one-time liberals saw the current president as a right-wing warmonger who equated disagreement with sedition. "Flush out this filthy scum," Johnson/MacBird says in the play, "destroy dissent. It's treason to defy your president."[152] As the scholar John Kaplan noted in 1967, the leftist conspiracy theories blaming Johnson for Kennedy's murder helped to "ease the frustrations of Vietnam" and to punish Johnson for his perceived sins.[153]

But Garrison's cynical opportunism soon fractured the once-united assassination research community. Some of the early critics were shocked by his posturing, his wild swings from one conspiracy theory to another, and his unethical methods of investigation, including hypnosis and bribery. Meagher began to compare Garrison to the man most hated by assassination researchers: Earl Warren. "I do not see how we are to be saved," she wrote a friend, "merely by replacing one set of liars and charlatans with a new clique of liars, purveyors of fabricated evidence, and framers of innocent (though unpopular) people."[154]

The mainstream press also began to turn against Garrison. The *Saturday Evening Post*, an early fan of the crusading district attorney, published a troubling article that raised serious questions about Garrison's ethics and evidence.[155] In the *New Yorker*, Edward Epstein compared Garrison to Senator McCarthy. The unscrupulous prosecutor, he said, followed McCarthy's example of exploiting "inchoate fears" and "organizing a popular flight from reality."[156]

While Epstein, Meagher, and other researchers decried Garrison's hijacking of their movement, other critics maintained that he was still good for the cause. Garrison's supporters called themselves the Dealey Plaza Irregulars, after the crew of street urchins who assisted Sherlock Holmes, the "Baker Street Irregulars." They continued to support their Holmes, even when he claimed that sixteen gunmen had killed Kennedy from five different directions.[157] The Assassination Inquiry Committee, one of several new groups formed in the wake of Garrison's investigation, expressed irritation with the critics who attacked the prosecutor. "FOR GOD'S SAKE, SUPPORT JIM GARRISON!" the group's newsletter exclaimed. "It seems to us that Garrison is the only public official in the United States who is actively pursuing the truth of the assassination."[158] David Lifton, a critic who recoiled from Garrison's methods, said the Garrison supporters' motto seemed to be "Rally round the plot, boys. It's not much of a plot, but it's the only plot we've got."[159]

Garrison's greatest appeal was to the far left and, ironically, the far right. Although he publicly identified himself as a leftist, he enjoyed swapping theories with right-wing conspiracists. Their villains were different—Garrison blamed the "fascists," while the right-wing activists blamed the communists—but their description of the problem was similar. In the end, one of his aides later wrote, "all were prepared to agree that the spectral 'they' who controlled the nation were inimical to left and right alike."[160]

Liberal political leaders, with their faith in Earl Warren and in the liberal state, tended to be the most critical of Garrison's investigation. Until his own assassination in 1968, Robert Kennedy opposed Garrison's inquiry and all other public attempts to reopen the investigation of his brother's death. Although Robert Kennedy became a vocal opponent of the Vietnam War, he did not believe the conspiracy theory that the military-industrial complex had killed his brother for his peaceful views. Garrison responded by charging that Kennedy was more interested in his own political career than in finding the truth.[161] After Kennedy's murder by the Palestinian terrorist Sirhan Sirhan, though, Garrison "revealed" that the dead senator had actually been one of his secret supporters. Shortly before his assassination, unnamed "emissaries" from Robert Kennedy had secretly told Garrison that "there were many guns between him and the White House." As a result, the senator had to remain coy about the "real assassins" until he was in the position to punish them. Robert Kennedy knew, Garrison claimed, that there was a "force" in the United States dedicated to "disposing of any individual opposed to the Viet Nam war, our involvement in the Viet Nam war, or any sort of involvement in the cold war."[162]

By the summer of 1968, some assassination researchers were attempting to decipher the plots behind "K1" and "K2," the two Kennedy assassinations, which, they said, shared many similarities. Some conspiracists also connected the Kennedy assassinations with James Earl Ray's "alleged" murder of Martin Luther King Jr. in April 1968. Sirhan, Ray, and Oswald were all puppets of much larger forces dedicated to keeping the United States in Vietnam. The RFK and King assassinations never grabbed the public imagination the way Dallas did, partly because Sirhan and Ray survived their trials. But for hard-core JFK assassination researchers, the three murders formed a pattern that exposed the motive behind them all: the need to kill any leader who sought to thaw the cold war.

In 1969, after numerous delays, Garrison finally put Clay Shaw on trial for conspiracy to murder John Kennedy, the only person ever to stand trial for the crime. Shaw quickly became irrelevant to the case, however, and Garrison did not even bother to attend court on the days of his testimony.[163] Instead, the prosecutor subpoenaed the Zapruder film and showed it to the jury a total of fourteen times. However, he lacked any credible evidence to connect the defendant with the assassination. When the trial finally ended, the jury took less than an hour to acquit him. Garrison's critics were relieved that he had not succeeded in framing an innocent man. The prosecutor stood revealed, said the New Orleans *States-Item*, "for what he is: a man without principle who would pervert the legal process to his own ends."[164]

Garrison had a different explanation for his defeat. Until his death in 1992, he would accuse journalists, assassination researchers, government officials—indeed, everyone who challenged him—of working for the CIA. His opponents found themselves in the unenviable position of having to prove that they were not lying operatives of the secret state. Indeed, Garrison made these accusations in part because he knew they were hard to refute. According to one of his disaffected aides, Garrison had chosen to target CIA officials because "they can't afford to answer."[165]

As it turned out, the CIA did have some secrets about Clay Shaw. In 1979, when he was deposed in an unrelated lawsuit, former CIA chief Richard Helms revealed that Shaw had been an unpaid contact for the agency. Like thousands of businessmen in the early cold war, he had been debriefed by the agency's domestic contact division when he returned from foreign travels. Garrison seized on this testimony as proof for his charge that Shaw had been an "agent" of the CIA.[166]

Garrison's conspiracy theory achieved mythical status in 1991, when the filmmaker Oliver Stone made him the hero of his influential movie, *JFK*. The film confirmed most Americans' belief in a conspiracy: even before its release, only 11 percent believed that Oswald acted alone. (After the release, 10 percent believed in the lone gunman theory.)[167] Stone, like Garrison, contended that a cabal within the government had conspired to kill the president. So many Americans came to believe Garrison's theory, Max Holland has argued, that the Soviet disinformation campaign that inspired it might be "the single most effective active measure undertaken by the KGB against the United States."[168]

However, it was not just the KGB's and Garrison's lies that prepared Americans to believe in CIA conspiracy theories; it was also the lies of the U.S. government. Over the next several years, as congressional investigators dramatically revealed and documented those lies, even the most outrageous conspiracy theories about the government began to seem credible to many Americans.

EVER SINCE NOVEMBER 22, 1963, many Americans have ascribed transcendent importance to the assassination of John F. Kennedy. It was "the archetypal crime of parricide" that shook the nation to its core, according to a staff report of the National Commission on the Causes and Prevention of Violence.[169] The historian Christopher Lasch proclaimed it "a symbol of the country's thwarted promise, of former greatness overthrown, of the American dream in decline."[170] Many observers have concluded that it marked the beginning of the end of faith in the liberal state.

Besides their obvious distrust of government, the assassination conspiracy theories also reflect a loss of faith in all experts—in government *and* science—and in the whole idea of "expertise." When the amateur sleuths stuffed their tape recorders in their armpits and used their hardware store tools to measure bullet angles, they were demonstrating their distrust of authorities. After the initial attacks on the Warren Report, one assassination researcher explained, experts could "no longer claim undisputed privileged status among the myriad forms of human discourse. Indeed experts, by any measure, have become an endangered species."[171] The amateurs in the JFK investigation were rejecting the experts' view of a world-changing historical event. The struggle between the Warren Commission and its critics was a struggle over who could write the nation's history.[172]

Ironically, the government itself handed the critics the primary sources they needed to write this history. In July 1966, just as the first best-selling critiques of the Warren Report began appearing, President Johnson signed into law the Freedom of Information Act. "This legislation," he proclaimed, "springs from one of our most essential principles: a democracy works best when the people have all the information that the security of the Nation permits."[173] Warren Report critics would use the FOIA to pry information from what they saw as a sinister yet clumsy government that had neglected to destroy documentary evidence of its crimes.

As the amateur critics eagerly took on the challenge of writing about the Kennedy assassination, most academic historians steadfastly avoided the subject. As Max Holland has noted, historians have been quick to analyze and condemn Pearl Harbor conspiracy theories, but they have been reluctant to take on the hundreds of books on JFK conspiracy theories.[174]

This is unfortunate, because Kennedy's death cannot be understood without placing it in the historical context of the cold war. The cold war explains virtually everything about the assassination: it is, as Holland has written, the thread that connects all parts of the Kennedy drama. "Pull on that thread," Holland writes, "and primary mysteries unravel."[175] Conspiracists' favorite villains—anti-Castro Cubans, Castro, Soviet leaders, and mafia dons—were all cold war actors. Even the lone-gunman theorists must place the cold war at the heart of their explanation of the assassination, for Kennedy's Cuba policy, in the form of the Castro plots, provides the most likely explanation of Oswald's motive.

Some analysts have concluded that Kennedy thus caused his own death, that JFK was killed "by a political conspiracy his own actions may have helped set in motion," as Lasch argued.[176] The progressive journalist Alexander Cockburn predicted that Oswald might someday be recognized as a dedicated leftist who put a stop to murderous U.S. policies in the only way that he could.[177]

It is unfair, however, to blame Kennedy for his own murder. The Castro plots, which were set in motion by the Eisenhower administration, were the products of much bigger cold war forces than John Kennedy alone. Above all, they were the result of the anticommunist conspiracy theory that warped U.S. politics and policy. If Kennedy officials paid a high price for their covert foreign policies, as Robert Kennedy told close friends, they did so because the anticommunist extremists had made it politically impossible for them to accept the Cuban Revolution.[178] John Kennedy, who had begun his presidency with a ringing call to Americans to pay any price in the defense of liberty throughout the world, paid a much greater price than he ever could have imagined.

The American state also paid a very great price when its leaders decided to hide the political context of the assassination. High government officials—Lyndon Johnson, J. Edgar Hoover, and Earl Warren—did in fact carry out a conspiracy, though not the one so often attributed to them. It was a conspiracy to hide the truth about U.S. policy toward Cuba, and thus to obscure the historical context and the meaning of the assassination. Through their conspiracy, these dedicated statists undermined the credibility of the state.

Soon, a new set of statists would continue this trend. The assassination researchers believed that no president could ever be worse than Johnson. But the next president would make conspiracies and conspiracy theories central to the American system of governance.

5

White House of Horrors: Nixon, Watergate, and the Secret Government

THROUGHOUT HIS CAREER, Richard Nixon always worried that un-American forces were conspiring to subvert the republic. As the tapes of his Oval Office conversations reveal, he viewed himself as a soldier in the battle against "the liberal media," disloyal Democrats, the "intellectuals," and Jews. Then, in June 1971, all of these groups seemed to unite in one terrifying plot. "We're up against an enemy, a conspiracy," he told two of his top aides, Chief of Staff Bob Haldeman and National Security Adviser Henry Kissinger. "They're using any means. *We are going to use any means*. Is that clear?"[1]

The conspiracy in question was the leak of the Pentagon Papers, a top-secret study of the Vietnam War. The documents disclosed the U.S. government's lies about the war and its cynical disregard for American soldiers' lives. Daniel Ellsberg, a disillusioned former Pentagon and State Department analyst, secretly copied the papers and gave them to the *New York Times*, which began publishing them on June 13, 1971.

The Pentagon Papers case tapped a deep pool of resentment and hostility in the president. In private conversations with his aides, he repeatedly compared Ellsberg to Alger Hiss. In both cases, the men were part of a conspiracy of intellectuals, "left-wingers," and the "bastards" in the press determined to destroy the nation, the presidency, and Nixon personally.[2]

To combat this conspiracy, Nixon commanded his aides to begin a conspiracy of their own. They were to ruin Ellsberg in any way they could; his advisers suggested prosecution for espionage, but the president preferred to dig up some dirt on Ellsberg and then "convict the son of a bitch *in the press.*"[3] Responding to the president's repeated and emphatic orders, his aides set up a special unit within the White House to spy on and punish his enemies. They started with Ellsberg but soon moved on to other targets. Because they looked for leaks, they called themselves "the plumbers."

But these would be very bad plumbers, who planned to spring more leaks than they plugged. One of them, E. Howard Hunt, searched through classified historical documents to find—and then leak—embarrassing secrets from past Democratic presidential administrations. When he failed to find the evidence he sought, he fabricated it. As he worked to discredit Nixon's opponents from the past, he also helped to oversee a program of surveillance and harassment of the president's current enemies. The president's men did not want to indict Ellsberg alone; they wanted to convict all of the president's enemies, including every Democratic president since Franklin Roosevelt, in the court of public opinion.

In the Nixon administration, paranoia, conspiracy, and conspiracy theory became fundamental operating principles of the executive branch. Nixon's men believed in conspiracies, engaged in real conspiracies, and cynically promoted some conspiracy theories as a means to deflect attention from their crimes.

The disclosure of the "White House horrors," as Attorney General John Mitchell called the various abuses of the Nixon administration, prompted a wave of inquiries. Public officials, stunned by citizens' vocal distrust of government, scrambled to restore national morale by launching investigations of past administrations. The full extent of the government's paranoia about its citizens was revealed for all to see.

By the end of the 1970s, Americans knew more about their government's secrets and misdeeds than any people in history. And the more they learned, the more they suspected that the government was still hiding bigger, more explosive secrets.

NIXON HATED ALL of the members of what he regarded as the liberal establishment, but he particularly loathed Jews, Eastern elites, and reporters. The son of a grocer from Orange County, California, he had always been defensive about his degrees from Whittier College and Duke University Law School. As a young congressman and senator, Nixon had felt snubbed and patronized by Ivy League graduates, who despised him, or so he thought, because he did not have a degree from Harvard. He responded with contempt for the alleged phoniness and unscrupulousness of what he called "the intellectuals." The Hiss case confirmed his belief that "the intellectuals...basically, have no morals."[4] They hated him so much, he believed, that they would do anything to ruin him.[5]

He also despised the press. In 1952, when the *New York Post* revealed that a group of wealthy businessmen had given Senator Nixon a "secret fund" to help pay his personal expenses, Nixon nearly lost the Republican Party's vice presidential nomination. He recovered by going over the heads of journalists with his famous "Checkers" speech, in which he deftly transformed accusations of bribery into a vicious attempt to deprive his children of their cocker spaniel. The success of the speech enabled him to stay on the Republican ticket and claim the vice presidency in November, but the episode convinced him that "those sons of bitches are out to get me....They tried to get me, and they'll try to get anybody that had anything to do with the Hiss case."[6] In 1962, after he lost his race for the governorship of California, he erupted during his concession speech. "You won't have Nixon to kick around anymore, because, gentlemen, this is my last press conference," he snarled at the stunned journalists.[7] Once again, though, Nixon returned from the brink of political extinction. When he rebounded to win the presidency in 1968, he entered the Oval Office with a long list of enemies to attack and scores to settle.

The protests against the Vietnam War enraged President Nixon and strengthened his natural urge to hide behind a wall of secrecy. When he decided to expand the air war to neighboring Cambodia, for example, he kept the escalation secret—from Congress, the press, the public, and even most members of his administration. He knew that the bombing campaign would prompt antiwar protests, which he wanted to avoid. "My administration was only two months old," he wrote later, "and I wanted to provoke as little public outcry as possible at the outset."[8] He ordered the military to set up an elaborate system of false reports to mislead the public. When the *New York Times* ran a story disclosing the bombing, Nixon's Pentagon denied that it was taking place. The rest of the media, assuming that the administration would not lie outright, dropped the story.[9]

After the *Times* story on the secret bombing of Cambodia, the Nixon administration responded in ways that would ultimately cost the president his job. He ordered secret, illegal wiretaps on the phones of several journalists and administration staff members whom he suspected of leaking the Cambodia story. He had begun his descent into illegality by secretly expanding the war; then he ordered unconstitutional surveillance of the people who might have exposed his lies.[10]

Because Nixon believed that his predecessors had conspired against their enemies—indeed, that they had conspired against him personally—he thought that he was justified in ordering illegal activities. "On a thing like this," he once told an aide, "well, what the hell, you can break in, wiretap, what the hell."[11] He would later try to excuse his own crimes by arguing that presidents before him had engaged in conspiracies all the time.

Certainly, presidents before Nixon had approved domestic spying programs that most Americans later viewed as abuses of power. The FBI under Eisenhower, Kennedy, and Johnson had infiltrated liberal and radical groups, sabotaged their plans, and provoked them to violence in order to discredit them. Johnson initiated the CIA's Operation CHAOS, in which agents infiltrated antiwar groups, black power organizations, and even women's consciousness-raising collectives to determine if foreign communists were secretly directing them.[12]

But Nixon moved far beyond his predecessors and took the imperial presidency "toward its ultimate form," in the words of the historian Arthur M. Schlesinger, Jr.[13] Believing that the president was above the law, Nixon ordered the expansion of Operation CHAOS, even though the CIA repeatedly reported that it could find no evidence of foreign links to American dissenters.[14]

He also tried to set up a secret, interagency committee in the White House to centralize government surveillance, eavesdropping, and burglaries directed at U.S. citizens. It was called the "Huston Plan" after the twenty-eight-year-old ultraconservative Nixon aide, Tom Charles Huston, who conceived of it. But FBI chief J. Edgar Hoover, who was much too savvy to take illegal orders from an upstart committee of White House bureaucrats, refused to cooperate. When Hoover insisted that Nixon approve each illegal spying operation in writing, the president scuttled the plan.[15]

Nixon also used his executive powers to punish his personal enemies. His aides created an Enemies List, circulated it among various federal agencies, including the Justice Department and the Internal Revenue Service, and encouraged them to harass the people on the list. Those targeted included prominent officials, reporters, actors, football players, and singers who had incurred the wrath of the Nixon White House by publicly opposing the president.[16] Most important, Nixon set up the plumbers, a secret, ad hoc group within the White House, *outside* of the FBI and CIA and unknown to anyone beyond a select group of presidential aides, and then used this group to investigate and punish his enemies.

Nixon's mania for hiding his actions from his enemies infected everyone in his administration. Even the Joint Chiefs of Staff spied on the president because Nixon kept vital information from them. At the request of the joint chiefs, a Navy yeoman on the National Security Council staff stole documents from Kissinger's briefcase and secretly passed them along to the military leaders.[17] Adm. Elmo Zumwalt later explained the military spy ring against the president as the logical consequence of the atmosphere of fear in Nixon's White House. Zumwalt wondered how Nixon and his top aides could think that their obsession with secrecy "could have any other result than 'leaks' and 'spying' and all-around paranoia. Indeed," he continued, "they had created a system in which 'leaks' and 'spying' were everyday and essential elements."[18] The only way to fight this secrecy, the joint chiefs concluded, was to spy on the president and steal memos from his aides.

If the military chiefs—among the most powerful insiders in the country—felt forced to resort to subterfuge and theft of documents, it is not surprising that ordinary citizens came to the same conclusions. In 1971, angry opponents of the war grew convinced that they needed to steal and disclose secret government documents to expose government lies. In two separate, dramatic incidents, dissidents succeeded in obtaining and leaking documentary evidence of conspiracies by the government.

The first case took place on the night of March 8, 1971. As most Americans huddled around television sets to watch the fight between Joe Frazier and Muhammad Ali, a group of activists broke into the tiny FBI office in Media, Pennsylvania. The members of the Citizens Commission to Investigate the FBI searched quietly and rapidly through the file cabinets, looking for evidence that the government was spying on them. These activists, whose names remain unknown, spirited away about one thousand classified FBI files, including many with the mysterious notation

"COINTELPRO." About two weeks later, two prominent antiwar lawmakers and reporters at major newspapers received copies of the files in plain brown envelopes.[19] Most of the recipients accepted the FBI's judgment that the files were secret: the *New York Times* and the *Los Angeles Times* did not write about the documents, and the legislators returned their copies to the FBI. But *Washington Post* editors believed that the public had the right to know about the spying. The *Post* broke the first COINTELPRO story on March 24, 1971, revealing that the bureau had used mail carriers and a campus switchboard operator to eavesdrop on a radical professor at a Pennsylvania college.[20] Many subsequent stories over the next few years would reveal the massive efforts by the FBI to spy on and sabotage dozens of American groups and hundreds of thousands of individuals. J. Edgar Hoover's secrets were spilling out into the open.

Three months later, there was an even more significant breach of governmental secrecy: the *New York Times* began publishing the Pentagon Papers. Angered and disillusioned by the lies about the war, Daniel Ellsberg had decided to "expose and subvert the very process of presidential lying about war policy." In certain contexts, he had come to believe, "leaking could be a patriotic and constructive act." He copied the papers and, like the anti-FBI activists, tried to give them to antiwar senators to release. The senators, however, did not want to risk damaging their careers by exposing top-secret documents that did not even discuss current U.S. policy. Senator William Fulbright doubted whether the papers were really that significant. "Isn't it after all only history?" he asked Ellsberg.[21]

But Nixon understood that history could have explosive consequences for the present. Although the Pentagon Papers covered only the Kennedy and Johnson years, Nixon and his aides still thought that Ellsberg had undermined the president's war powers. One of Nixon's advisers, former congressman Donald Rumsfeld, believed that the Pentagon Papers represented a potentially catastrophic assault on the inherent authority of the presidency. "Rumsfeld was making this point this morning," Nixon's chief of staff, Bob Haldeman, told the president in an Oval Office conversation. He summarized Rumsfeld's argument: "To the ordinary guy, all this is a bunch of gobbledygook. But out of the gobbledygook, comes a very clear thing: you can't trust the government; you can't believe what they say; and you can't rely on their judgment; and the—the implicit infallibility of presidents, which has been an accepted thing in America, is badly hurt by this, because it shows that people do things the president wants to do even though it's wrong, and the president can be wrong."[22]

Nixon did not want the American people to think that the president could be wrong. Nor did he want current government employees to think that they could get away with another leak. The president had many of his own secrets to protect, such as the bombing of Cambodia. He was also certain that Ellsberg was part of a wider conspiracy to stop the war and destroy his presidency.

To ruin this conspiracy of leakers, Nixon planned to leak classified documents himself. *"That's the way it's done,"* he told his aides. In the Hiss case, he said in another conversation, "I had to leak stuff all over the place." This time, of course, he was in an even better position: as president, he could demand any secret document in the U.S. government. Nixon did not *know* of any particular conspiracy by his presidential predecessors, but he suspected that these conspiracies had happened and that the evidence for them was stashed in the government's vaults. "Let's have a little fun," he told Haldeman and Kissinger. He wanted to expose documents about Pearl Harbor ("I'm going to give that to the [Chicago] *Trib*....They hated Roosevelt"), the Cuban missile crisis, the supposed U.S. complicity in the assassination of South Vietnamese president Ngo Dinh Diem, and the disastrous CIA-sponsored invasion at the Bay of Pigs.[23]

To attract the most attention for these revelations, he wanted to find the right member of Congress—"We want somebody to be a McCarthy"—who was unprincipled enough to use the leaks to create a sensation. It would be best if one of the villains was Jewish, since he believed that Jews were "born spies," though his most frequently cited example of treachery, Alger Hiss, was not a Jew. "So that proves something," he told his aides. In a stunning example of Nixon's talent for projection, he added that a spy was despicable because he "puts himself above the law."[24] When he could not find a congressman tough enough to confront these conspirators, he decided to keep his countersubversive operations within the White House.

Nixon hoped that his overall strategy of revealing the dark secrets of the past would "take the eyes off Vietnam," he explained. "It gets them [the press] thinking about the past rather than our present problems. You get the point." In rewriting the past, he hoped to turn Americans against dead Democrats and, more generally, against the federal government as a whole. To divert attention from his own lies, Nixon planned to corrupt Americans' memory of previous presidents. He wanted one staff member to work full time combing through old government files to find evidence that his predecessors had routinely lied to the American people. He needed the right person for this job, someone who was "just as tough as I am for a change." In fact, he needed "an Ellsberg who's on our side; in other words, an intellectual who knows the history of the times, who knows what he's looking for," and who was smart enough to run the program from the White House "without being caught." His aides persuaded him that E. Howard Hunt was such a man. "Ideologically," counsel Charles Colson explained, "he is already convinced this is a big conspiracy."[25]

Hunt was a former CIA officer who had appeared, Zelig-like, at many major events in U.S. history, including the U.S. overthrow of the democratically elected government of Guatemala in 1954, the Bay of Pigs invasion, and, later, across the street from the Watergate building on the night of the famous break-in. Some conspiracy theorists would insist that they saw his face in a picture of three tramps near Dealey Plaza on November 22, 1963, though a congressional committee later determined that he was not there. A successful author of adventure yarns and spy novels, Hunt was smart, ruthless, intensely anticommunist, and passionately loyal to the president. These qualities recommended him to the Nixon aides looking for "an Ellsberg on our side."

Hunt embraced his new job as a presidentially authorized leaker. With scissors and paste, he faked cables that implicated Kennedy in Diem's murder and then leaked them to *Life* magazine (though he refused to let *Life* photograph the cables, and the suspicious editors decided not to publish the story).[26] Hunt also tried to tie the man who shot Alabama Governor George Wallace in May 1972 to the campaign of the likely Democratic presidential nominee, George McGovern. After the president himself told his aides to link the would-be assassin, Arthur Bremer, to prominent Democrats, Colson ordered Hunt to search Bremer's apartment and plant evidence. Later, Nixon asked Colson if Bremer was a left-winger or a right-winger. "Well, he's going to be a left-winger by the time we get through," Colson said.[27]

Hunt's other duties included an investigation of Senator Ted Kennedy, a Democratic presidential contender in 1972, in hopes of uncovering and leaking derogatory information. He also directed a burglary of the office of Ellsberg's psychoanalyst, hoping to find material that he could use to blackmail and discredit Ellsberg. Other plumbers searched for evidence of the lies, mistakes, and dirty deeds of Roosevelt, Truman, Kennedy, and Johnson.

The Nixon henchmen were strangely naïve in their faith that documentary evidence of past governing conspiracies lay hidden in government safes and that they could locate it quickly. The plumbers found themselves sifting through mountains of irrelevant papers—"It's like spooning out the ocean," Nixon aide John Ehrlichman explained to the president—and they never found the proof of conspiracies they sought.[28] They were determined to keep trying, though.

The Nixon administration, in short, tried to restore Americans' faith in the government and the "infallibility" of the presidency by proving the fallibility and dishonesty of previous presidents. The president's aides also tried to discredit and punish leakers with their own selective leaks. It was a strategy doomed to fail.

In the 1972 presidential campaign, one veteran plumber, an unstable former FBI agent named G. Gordon Liddy, moved from the White House to the Committee to Re-elect the President, where he helped oversee a vast, illegal program of espionage and sabotage against several Democratic candidates for president. Republican operatives burglarized the offices of Democratic candidates, eavesdropped on their conversations, stole their strategy documents, planted false rumors, and sabotaged their campaigns with everything from stink bombs to forged campaign letters. Senators Hubert Humphrey, Ed Muskie, and Ted Kennedy, as well as Governor Wallace, knew that some enemy was harassing them, but they assumed it was one of their rivals for the nomination. The Committee to Re-Elect the President paid for the crimes with an extensive, illegal fund-raising campaign involving bribery and extortion.

On June 17, 1972, a team of Liddy's men, all ex-CIA agents and veterans of the Bay of Pigs, broke into the offices of the Democratic National Committee in the Watergate office building to replace a malfunctioning bug they had installed two weeks earlier. This time, they got caught.

After the arrests at the Watergate, Nixon and his aides knew they had no choice but to launch a massive cover-up. A serious FBI investigation of the break-in could lead to exposure of other conspiracies directed from the White House, including the surveillance and sabotage of the Democratic candidates, the illegal fund-raising, the unconstitutional wiretaps, the Enemies List, and the secret bombing of Cambodia.

To cover up its crimes, the Nixon White House paid hush money to the burglars and lied repeatedly to the public. Nixon also ordered top CIA officials to try to convince the FBI to stop its investigation of the burglary; thus, he conspired to use federal agencies to obstruct justice. These orders, which were recorded on the voice-activated tape machines in the Oval Office, would become the most damning evidence of the president's participation in the cover-up conspiracy. But in addition to the "smoking gun" conversation about the cover-up, the Nixon tapes revealed an array of crackpot schemes by White House aides to deflect suspicion onto other groups. Colson, the president's counsel, proposed a particularly devious plan to spread a rumor that the CIA was responsible for the Watergate break-in. "I think that we could develop a theory as to the CIA if we wanted to," he told the president, because all of the burglars had once worked for the CIA, and several were Cuban. Nixon agreed that the burglars' ties to Cuba were a "plus" that made the CIA conspiracy theory seem credible.[29]

The cover-up was essential to Nixon's survival, but it also had some fatal flaws: there were too many men involved in it, and it turned out that some of them were more concerned about themselves than about a president who, at the end of the day, did not inspire much loyalty. Soon some of the conspirators turned against the president and testified before Congress and the special prosecutor. A federal grand jury named the president an "unindicted coconspirator" in the Watergate cover-up. In the end, the president's own voice, recorded on the tapes, sealed his fate. When the Supreme Court ruled that the president had to turn over the tapes of his conversations about Watergate to the special prosecutor, the president resigned on August 9, 1974. He would spend the rest of his life encouraging other conspiracists by insisting that government officials routinely lied and broke the law.

AT FIRST, NIXON'S resignation seemed to mark the end of an era. The new president, an unpretentious and self-effacing former congressman from Michigan, Gerald Ford, was anything but imperial. He commanded the White House band to replace "Hail to the Chief" with the "Michigan Fight Song." In the mornings, he padded down to the White House kitchen and toasted his own English muffins. Trying to distance himself from the disgraced man responsible for his own rise to power, Ford proclaimed, "Our long national nightmare is over." The nation welcomed the new president's populist style. "Everywhere," wrote *Time*'s Hugh Sidey, "there was a feeling that the American presidency was back in the possession of the people."[30]

But just a month into Ford's presidency, he ended this era of good feelings by issuing a "full, free, and absolute" pardon to his predecessor. Ford explained that he did not want to "prolong the bad dreams" of Watergate by reopening a "chapter that is closed."[31] In Ford's view, Watergate was only history, as Fulbright had said about the Pentagon Papers, and it was time to focus on the future.

Although Ford insisted that he had not made a deal with Nixon, many people believed that he had promised the pardon in return for the president's resignation. At the least, the pardon showed a remarkable lack of respect for the legal system that had put Ford in office. Sixty-two percent of the public opposed the pardon, and the president's approval rating dropped 21 points in a month, from 71 percent to 50 percent—the sharpest drop in the history of the Gallup poll to that point.[32] As the columnist Anthony Lewis concluded, the pardon produced the opposite of what Ford had hoped: "More rancor, more division, more cynicism about government and the law."[33]

The pardon persuaded many journalists and members of Congress that the nation's troubles did not end with Watergate. They worried that more secrets lurked below the surface of Washington politics, and that American democracy could not survive unless those secrets were exposed. CBS News reporter Daniel Schorr compared the mystery to an onion. "You peel off Watergate and you find the Plumbers and the Ellsberg break-in," he wrote. "Peel off the Plumbers and you find the 1970 Huston plan to use the CIA and FBI for domestic surveillance, wiretapping and break-ins. But what would you find if you peeled off another layer and had a close look at that secret world from which these things had been launched?"[34]

The first glimpse into this secret world came just a few months after Nixon's resignation, with a *New York Times* story on Operation CHAOS. At the CIA, some whistleblowers, appalled by the blatant illegality of the agency's domestic spying program, had leaked the outlines of the program to the reporter Seymour Hersh. On December 22, 1974, Hersh trumpeted his scoop on the front page of the *Times*. "HUGE C.I.A.

OPERATION REPORTED IN U.S. AGAINST ANTIWAR FORCES, OTHER DISSIDENTS IN NIXON YEARS," the four-column headline proclaimed. Hersh reported that the CIA had collected illegal files on at least ten thousand U.S. citizens. Members of Congress promised thorough investigations of what the *Times* later called "Son of Watergate."[35]

In the White House, the new president's aides were panicked by the prospect of more congressional investigations into executive branch abuses. Donald Rumsfeld, the new chief of staff, maintained the philosophy that he had explained to Bob Haldeman during the Pentagon Papers affair: it was best to quash any suggestion that the president could sometimes be wrong. Dick Cheney, Rumsfeld's deputy, was even more committed to the notion of restoring presidential power and secrecy. Three decades later, when he had become the villain of a new generation of conspiracy theories, Vice President Cheney would tell reporters that the Ford administration had witnessed "the nadir of the modern presidency in terms of authority and legitimacy."[36] Young Cheney was determined to reclaim this authority. He wrote numerous memos urging the president to stand firm against congressional attempts to "encroach" on executive power—and, more notably, to punish and intimidate journalists who probed too deeply into the nation's secrets.[37]

In a desperate attempt to avoid congressional inquiries, Ford set up a special commission headed by Vice President Nelson Rockefeller to investigate the charges in Hersh's story. But the public and Congress refused to be placated by a blue-ribbon panel. A plurality of Americans told pollsters that the Rockefeller Commission would just be "another cover-up."[38] Even after the commission issued a surprisingly tough report, both houses of Congress vowed to continue their own, independent investigations. These inquiries proved to be exactly what the Ford White House had feared: aggressive probes into decades of crimes by executive agencies. After discovering the lies of Watergate, these members of Congress resolved to find examples of other government conspiracies. Watergate had unlocked the door to the government's closet; the congressional investigators would put all of its skeletons on public view.

The Senate inquiry was headed by one of the most idealistic public officials in U.S. history. Frank Church of Idaho had an unshakable faith in the reality of national sin, the power of confession, and the possibility of redemption. Called "Senator Cathedral" and "Frank Sunday School" by his realpolitik critics, Church had spent his long and distinguished career battling for liberal causes. First elected to the Senate in 1956 at the age of thirty-two, he had fought for civil rights, civil liberties, and protections for organized labor. Like almost all senators of both parties in the 1950s, he had also supported an aggressive, anticommunist foreign policy.[39]

But Vietnam had prompted Church to question the underlying assumptions of the cold war. He turned against the war remarkably early, in 1964, and became a leader of the antiwar group in the Senate, challenging the policies of a president from his own party. Eventually he came to see the war as not merely a mistake but a "monstrous immorality," and his failure to stop it a sign that American democracy had failed.[40] The war persuaded him that the presidency had gained too much power at the expense of Congress. In the early 1970s, he began trying to reclaim the legislative branch's authority in foreign policy. He spearheaded congressional attempts to limit the scope of the war, to cut off its funding, and to expose multinational corporations' secret influence on U.S. foreign policy. In the mid-1970s climate of détente, with the Soviet Union no longer seeming as threatening as it had in the 1960s, many Americans supported Church's quest to challenge presidents and their interventionist foreign policies.

Church's outrage at presidential disregard for the Constitution was sparked anew by Hersh's exposé of Operation CHAOS. He set out to win the chairmanship of the committee investigating these charges. The winner of an American Legion speaking contest on the "American Way of Life" in high school, he strongly believed that citizens of a democracy usually make sound, moral decisions—but first their government has to give them accurate information and respect their right to dissent.[41] Without an open government, Church believed, corrupt officials could make selfish, immoral choices. "Secrecy corrupts," he explained, "and absolute secrecy corrupts absolutely."[42]

During fifteen months of investigation, the Church Committee uncovered secret government programs with comic book names and Orwellian intentions, including COINTELPRO, CHAOS, and Mongoose. The hearings produced sensational revelations and dramatic moments for the television cameras. For the COINTELPRO hearings, a Ku Klux Klan thug testified in a loose hood with large slits for his eyes. He explained that he had participated in assault and murder while working as an informant for the FBI, but the bureau had never used his information to prevent crimes.

Top CIA officials, many of them angry and defensive, testified about assassination plots and poison-dart guns, and mafia dons went behind closed doors to tell the committee their versions of the plots against Castro.

In an interim report with the imprimatur of the U.S. government, the Church Committee revealed to the nation the shocking details of more than a dozen CIA-sponsored murder attempts against Castro and other leaders.[43] Besides exposing the CIA's ties with the mob, the committee also revealed that President Kennedy had shared a "close friend" with mobster Sam Giancana at the same time that the agency was using Giancana to try to kill Castro.[44] The secrets that Robert Kennedy had tried so hard to hide were now splashed across the pages of the nation's newspapers.

The committee also disclosed the extent of the FBI's efforts to harass and discredit Martin Luther King Jr. Hoover had begun investigating King to discover if he was under communist influence, but the inquiry soon expanded far beyond the original purpose. At Hoover's direction, agents had wiretapped King's phones, bugged his hotel rooms, and did everything they could to take him "off his pedestal and to reduce him completely in influence," as one FBI memo put it.[45] The FBI peddled evidence of King's extramarital affairs to public officials and journalists. Just before King was to accept the Nobel Peace Prize in 1964, the assistant FBI director sent the new laureate his own copy of the evidence. King received a composite tape in the mail that included audio recordings of his alleged trysts. A letter sent with the tape concluded with this threat: "King, there is only one thing left for you to do. You know what it is.... You are done. There is but one way out for you."[46] The FBI, in other words, tried to persuade the internationally recognized leader of the American civil rights movement to kill himself.

Hoover was no longer around to explain his actions or shred the memos that documented them: he had died in his sleep in May 1972. Three years after his death, the news of his abuses shocked Americans who had known him through his heroic image in popular culture—an image that he had carefully cultivated for decades. The Hoover of countless radio shows, TV programs, movies, and comic books had been an incorruptible official who always put the nation's interest above his own. The truth about Hoover added to the public's sense that the government routinely deceived and manipulated its citizens. Members of Congress introduced bills to strip his name from the newly completed J. Edgar Hoover FBI building. "I see no reason," said Congressman Charles B. Rangel of New York, "why we should permanently enshrine a man who had little regard for one of the basic and fundamental principles upon which our Republic was founded."[47]

The Church Committee produced fourteen volumes of fearlessly worded and meticulously documented reports that would become essential sources for cold war historians and conspiracy theorists alike. The committee detailed the FBI's harassment of King and condemned COINTELPRO as "intolerable in a democratic society."[48] It was equally critical of the CIA's illegal programs, though the chairman, who had known and admired John Kennedy, refused to pin the blame for the Castro plots on him. Church insisted that JFK, at least, had not known about CIA abuses and called the agency a "rogue elephant on a rampage," though most of his committee and his staff quietly disagreed.[49]

The reports, however, merely documented past abuses; they did not prevent future abuse. Ultimately, Church failed in his quest to rein in the CIA. The next president, Jimmy Carter, tried to build on Church's legacy by asking Congress to spell out the limits of the CIA's powers with a new charter. Carter also appointed an iconoclastic CIA director, the tough-talking Adm. Stansfield Turner, who proclaimed that he would resign rather than carry out an illegal or unconstitutional order from the president.[50] But the reform era at the CIA did not last long. Congress never passed a new charter, or any substantive intelligence reforms, save the Foreign Intelligence Surveillance Act (FISA) of 1978, which set up a special court to approve electronic surveillance.[51] After the terror attacks of 2001, President George W. Bush nullified the only significant Church Committee reform when he secretly ordered government snoopers to bypass the FISA court.[52]

Church had inadvertently implemented one of Nixon's most Machiavellian directives: to document the illegal actions of agents of the U.S. government since World War II. And the senator had commanded more than a hundred staff members, not just Howard Hunt, to comb through old files for him. But whereas Nixon wanted to produce public cynicism, Church had hoped to educate and redeem American citizens by confessing—and then repudiating—the past sins committed in their name. "We must never become weary of being vigilant," the senator explained. "We dare not shrink from another *redemptive* investigation." To avoid an "Orwellian nightmare," the nation needed to confront the dark deeds of its past.[53]

Nixon, though, was a better student of the public mood than was the former choirboy from Idaho. After forcing the nation to confront its past, Church found that he had strengthened a trend he abhorred: the ultra-right, libertarian rejection of all governmental authority. The percentage of Americans who said they distrusted the government actually increased during and after Church's investigation.[54]

This distrust stemmed in part from the absence of justice following Church's revelations. There was confession, but no expiation. No one went to jail as a result of Church's disclosures. Nor was there much contrition—certainly not from former president Nixon, who would tell the interviewer David Frost in 1977, "Well, when the President does it, that means that it is not illegal."[55] The inherent difficulty of Church's project—discovery without justice, a (cold) war crimes trial with criminals but no convicts—convinced many Americans that public officials routinely committed crimes, covered them up, and escaped the consequences. Americans knew more about their government's secret activities, yet they also distrusted their government more than ever before. More information did not create more trust.

In the House of Representatives, another investigating committee came to quite different conclusions than Senator Church about the CIA, conclusions that were potentially even more disturbing. Though its investigation paralleled the simultaneous inquiry in the Senate, the House Intelligence Committee did not have the impact or authority of the Church Committee, partly because it was riven by partisan conflict and discredited by leaks. Yet the committee nevertheless conducted an extensive investigation and produced a hard-hitting report. Chaired by an irascible New York Democrat, Otis Pike, the House committee obtained secret cold war foreign policy documents that helped the members to assess responsibility for the CIA's assassination plots and coups against democratic foreign leaders. After examining these documents, the Pike Committee concluded in 1976 that the president had directed the CIA to undertake many of the actions that the nation now saw as morally reprehensible. "All evidence in hand," the committee's report said, "suggests that the CIA, far from being out of control, has been utterly responsive to the instructions of the President and the Assistant to the President for National Security Affairs."[56] Instead of a rogue elephant, the CIA was the president's lapdog.

By blaming the presidency rather than one particular president for recent scandals, the Pike Committee resurrected the ghost that Americans had tried to banish after Nixon's resignation. Pike concluded that many abuses were not merely the fault of Nixon or a few individuals at the CIA; instead, all presidents could abuse their power by using the secret tools at their disposal. In one interview, Pike maintained that this conclusion threatened some of Americans' most deeply held beliefs. In Watergate, he said, the American people were asked to believe that "their President had been a bad person. In this situation they are asked much more; they are asked to believe that their country has been evil. And nobody wants to believe that."[57]

PIKE'S EXPLANATION was rather simplistic. Many Americans concluded that some covert actions—the Castro plots, the bugging of King, or the overthrow of democratically elected governments—were morally wrong. But it was hardly fair to call the whole country evil. Clearly, these actions had been undertaken without public knowledge.

But if Pike's thesis was too easy, many Americans embraced an equally simple alternative. Why had their government done these shocking things? For many, the answer was obvious: the country itself was not evil, but it *was* ruled by an evil cabal.

After learning that Hoover's FBI had tried to persuade Martin Luther King to kill himself and that the CIA consorted with the mob to kill Castro, some Americans began to suspect government conspiracies behind every recent murder or scandal. As the journalist Rod MacLeish concluded, "American society has gone buggy on conspiracy theories of late because so many nasty demonstrations of the real thing have turned up."[58] Alger Hiss became a popular lecturer on college campuses as many Americans came to believe his conspiracy theory that the FBI had framed him.[59] Journalists considered possible CIA involvement in everything from the Watergate break-in to the slaying of Giancana as he scrambled eggs in his suburban Chicago kitchen before he was to testify to the Church Committee about the Castro plots.[60] "I suggest that two and two makes four," wrote the conservative columnist William Safire, "that Sam Giancana took seven .22-caliber slugs in his body...to keep him from telling all he knew."[61]

Some of Nixon's aides continued their campaign to spread conspiracy theories as a way to persuade the public that the former president was somehow a victim of Watergate. Charles Colson, who had first raised the possibility of pinning the Watergate break-in on the CIA in June 1972, seized the opportunity provided by the intelligence investigations to go on television to declare that the real villain behind the Watergate and Ellsberg burglaries was, in fact, the CIA.[62] Subsequent conspiracist books by journalists would suggest that the "real story" of the Watergate break-in involved professional spies and prostitution rings.[63]

Frank Church's mailbag overflowed with letters from concerned Americans who wanted him to look into CIA involvement in everything from the JFK assassination to New York City's financial problems. A Yale University professor urged the senator to investigate a power outage that abruptly silenced a televised speech by Democratic presidential nominee Jimmy Carter. In 1978, citizens asked Church to probe possible agency involvement in the mass murder-suicide of People's Temple members in Jonestown, Guyana.[64] Over at Langley, CIA officers responded to the new theories with glum resignation. "They're going to pin the crucifixion on us next," one said.[65]

Above all, the Church investigation breathed new life into conspiracy theories about the murders of John Kennedy and Martin Luther King Jr. Besides the Castro plots, congressional investigators revealed that the FBI had destroyed a threatening note from Oswald, the "Hosty note," days after the assassination, and that both the CIA and the FBI had withheld key evidence from the Warren Commission. By the end of 1976, the lone-gunman theory in the John Kennedy assassination was left "almost totally without adherents," according to Gallup pollsters. Moreover, 70 percent of Americans believed that King's convicted assassin, James Earl Ray, was part of a conspiracy. Only 5 percent of Americans accepted their government's version of both killings.[66]

Some public figures even suggested that the FBI itself might have plotted to kill King. After the Church Committee's disclosures, King's widow and some of his advisers called for reopening the investigation of his death.[67] The *Washington Post* agreed that the Church Committee's reports added "grotesque dimensions" to earlier doubts about Ray's guilt. "The very least one can wonder, considering the late FBI director J. Edgar Hoover's feelings about Dr. King," the *Post* wrote, "is whether he could have put his agency's whole heart into the investigation of the assassination."[68] Other Americans saw more sinister implications to the Church Committee revelations. The *Saginaw News* of Michigan admitted that it was "chilling" to wonder if the FBI had helped to plot King's murder. "Yet it is hardly more chilling," the editorialist concluded, "than testimony already a matter of record concerning alleged spy network involvement with organized crime in the field of international assassinations."[69]

Most prominent newspapers, newsmagazines, and network news shows still ridiculed the idea of a conspiracy in John Kennedy's assassination. As usual, the mainstream media, which believed official conspiracy theories without hesitation, regarded alternative, antigovernment theories as patently absurd. This condescending attitude persuaded many Americans that the media, like the government, could not be trusted. "To think that you still believe the Warren Report," wrote one reader to *Time* after the newsmagazine had published a story supporting the lone-gunman theory. "I do look forward to a future issue featuring the tooth-fairy story."[70]

In this atmosphere of cynicism, Jim Garrison, the disgraced, conspiracy-mongering former district attorney of New Orleans, found a new following. Everyone from cabdrivers to lawyers began stopping him on the street and saying, "You're right. You said it first."[71] A "new wave" of research into the JFK assassination began in 1975, building on the work of the early critics. In contrast to the earlier assassination researchers, many of whom had suffered during the McCarthy era, the new conspiracy theorists were young activists fresh from the antiwar movement. The first, graying generation of assassination skeptics began recruiting acolytes at the nation's universities. During a three-day conference at Boston University, for example, more than a thousand people packed into an auditorium in January 1975 to hear Mark Lane and other Warren Report critics. Over the next few months, Lane spoke at thirty-five colleges and helped to organize more than twenty assassination research groups at these schools.[72]

These researchers focused most of their attention on the John Kennedy assassination, but they also challenged the official stories about other recent political murders, including those of King and Robert Kennedy. Many of these new conspiracy theorists linked the three assassinations to the Vietnam War and Watergate. New Left leaders such as Carl Oglesby, former president of the Students for a Democratic Society, now looked back on Dealey Plaza as the place where American democracy had died. They focused on one enigmatic Watergate tape, the smoking gun tape of June 23, 1972. The release of this tape in 1974 had cost Nixon nearly all of his dwindling support in the Senate, for it proved conclusively that he had conspired to cover up the Watergate break-in. But beyond the evidence of cover-up, the tape was intriguing to many researchers because Nixon seemed to make mysterious references to other conspiracies. It was essential, Nixon told Haldeman on the tape, to stop the investigation of Watergate because more plots might be exposed. "Of course," Nixon growled, "this [E. Howard] Hunt, that will uncover a lot of things. You open that scab, there's a hell of a lot of things, and we just feel that it would be very detrimental to have this thing go any further." The president was probably referring to the Castro plots, but some skeptics believed that the "things" in question meant CIA complicity in Dallas.[73]

American movies helped to spread this "conspiracy fever," as *Commentary* put it, with a spate of films in the 1970s alleging that the U.S. government regularly conspired to commit murder and undermine democracy.[74] The producers of one of these movies, *Three Days of the Condor* (1975), explained that they wanted to "show how government institutions might be subverted from within to betray, not serve, the public trust."[75] According to their film, the CIA didn't fight evil, it embodied evil. Television shows and pulp novels also contributed to the "age of conspiracy" by featuring Nazi-loving CIA agents, mob-connected Justice Department officials, and tyrannical FBI directors who dreamed of suspending the Constitution.[76]

As popular culture began to prime Americans to look for conspiracies everywhere, the critics of the Warren Report finally got the chance to "see" the JFK assassination with their own eyes. Robert Groden, an optical technician who had worked at the photo lab that had processed the Zapruder film, showed a bootleg copy of the film on *Geraldo*, a nationally televised talk show, in March 1975.[77] Groden had spirited the film out of the photo lab and had been showing it at private screenings and assassination conferences for more than two years, but the *Geraldo* show marked the first time most Americans had seen it. Twelve years after the event, the public could see that Kennedy's head snapped back and to the left, in apparent defiance of the laws of physics if he had been shot from behind. They could also check the timing of the shots.

Members of Congress saw the film and began to voice their own doubts about the Warren Commission Report. Republican Senator Richard Schweiker, a member of the Church Committee, proclaimed that the Warren Report was "like a house of cards; it's going to collapse." He formed a subcommittee to examine the possibility that Kennedy had been killed by Castro, the Soviets, or anti-Castro Cubans. The senator favored no particular theory. "The only thing I'm certain about is that we don't know the truth about the Kennedy assassination," he said.[78]

A majority of the House of Representatives agreed with him. Convinced that the assassination deserved a full congressional investigation, the House voted in September 1976 to authorize a twelve-member select committee to delve into the John Kennedy and King assassinations. The Church Committee reports, with their revelations of the CIA's anti-Castro plots and the FBI's harassment of King, provided "substantial impetus" for the investigation, the new committee explained.[79] Thanks to Senator Church, the American people were finally going to learn what really happened on November 22, 1963.

AT LAST, THE CRITICS had won their fourteen-year battle: Congress had authorized a thorough investigation by the elected representatives of the people. Many of the Warren Report skeptics rushed to help the congressional investigators, much as they had poured their enthusiasm into Jim Garrison's probe years earlier. Eager to accept their help, the committee staff members organized a two-day conference with the leading critics.[80]

In an inquiry that lasted thirty months, cost $5.5 million, and employed 250 staff members, the House Select Committee on Assassinations used subpoena power to compel testimony from witnesses, mobsters, and even the "umbrella man," a person who, in the eyes of conspiracy theorists, seemed to signal someone by opening his umbrella as the motorcade went past.[81] In the end, the committee issued a massive report and twelve volumes of hearings and appendixes.[82]

Yet the committee failed to satisfy anyone—the critics, the few defenders of the Warren Report, or the public. On the one hand, the investigators concluded that no agency of the U.S. government had conspired to assassinate either Kennedy or King, and that the accused assassins, Oswald and Ray, were indeed guilty. Furthermore, they upheld the single-bullet theory in the JFK murder.

But the committee also contended that it had recently discovered new evidence of a fourth shot, and therefore of a second gunman in Dealey Plaza. The congressional investigators claimed that a motorcycle officer in the motorcade had inadvertently recorded the assassination when his radio transmitter got stuck in the "on" position. Acoustic experts said that they could hear a fourth shot on the "dictabelt" recording from his motorcycle. There was a conspiracy, the congressmen concluded, and it might have involved anti-Castro Cubans or American mobsters.[83]

Congress's extensive, footnoted, and authoritative conspiracy theory of the assassination was quickly demolished by a pornographic magazine and a drummer in a midwestern band. The Dealey Plaza Irregulars had always maintained that ordinary citizens could find the truth, and in this case, the girlie magazine *Gallery* provided the crucial clue. In 1979, *Gallery* included a plastic record of the dictabelt as an insert ("the historic recording of the JFK assassination 'gunshots' evidence that destroyed the lone assassin theory! A *Gallery* EXCLUSIVE"). Girlie magazines had historically provided a forum for Kennedy assassination theories, which were seen by most of the mainstream media as political pornography. A percussionist in an Ohio rock band, Steve Barber, bought the magazine with the insert and played the $33\frac{1}{3}$ RPM record repeatedly for four months until he heard something that the experts had missed: the faint echo of a voice picked up from another radio channel. "Hold everything secure until the homicide and other investigators can get there," Sheriff Bill Decker was saying. The tape, Barber concluded, had actually recorded sounds *after* the assassination; there was no audio record of the shots after all. A National Academy of Sciences investigation in 1982 upheld his analysis and discounted the acoustic evidence of conspiracy.[84] In this case, the experts agreed with the amateur.

Far from solving the mystery of the Kennedy assassination, the House committee's bungled investigation just raised more questions. "What the Committee gives us with one hand—a second gunman and a conspiracy—it tends to take away with the other," noted the *New York Times* columnist Tom Wicker.[85] The American people could read Wicker's scathing indictment of the committee in his foreword to the official paperback edition of the committee's final report. In other words, the mass-market version of the "definitive" investigation included an introduction denouncing that investigation. This did not bode well for public acceptance of the committee's work.

AFTER WATERGATE, public officials had tried desperately to restore Americans' faith in government. The House Assassinations Committee attempted to regain trust by finding evidence of conspiracy (but not by the government). Senator Church wanted to redeem the government by exposing (some) of its past sins and watching closely to make sure that it never sinned again. Congressman Pike expressed disgust at the bureaucrats in central intelligence who did the bidding of an evil president. President Ford and his aides wanted everyone to show respect and stop asking questions.

Yet the nightmare continued. By the 1980s, Americans no longer simply suspected that the government was undermining democracy. They were certain that it was guilty of much worse.

6

Trust No One: Conspiracies and Conspiracy Theories from the 1970s to the 1990s

WHEN BILL CLINTON won the presidency in 1992, he said he wanted to provide health care for all Americans, revive the economy, and build a "bridge to the twenty-first century." But the president also had other goals. Soon after his election, Clinton spoke with an old friend, Webster Hubbell, whom he planned to appoint to a high post in the Justice Department. As they talked privately, Clinton gave him some secret orders. "Webb," Clinton said to his golfing buddy, "if I put you over at Justice, I want you to find the answers to two questions for me. One, Who killed JFK? And two, Are there UFOs?" The president, Hubbell said, was "dead serious."[1]

By the 1990s, antigovernment conspiracy theories had become so mainstream that even the head of government took them seriously. Skepticism of the government pervaded American popular culture. *The X-Files*, which suggested a massive conspiracy between aliens and the government, was the cult television hit of the 1990s. Some Fox TV executives initially questioned whether viewers would believe in such extensive government conspiracies, but the network discovered in focus groups that most Americans never doubted the premise.[2] At the height of the show's popularity, Americans' distrust of the Warren Report hit its peak, with 90 percent of Americans doubting or rejecting outright the lone-gunman theory of the Kennedy assassination, and confidence in the executive branch dipped to its lowest point in history, with just 9 percent expressing a "great deal" of confidence in the presidency.[3] Two decades after Richard Nixon left office in disgrace, Americans' trust in their government continued to plummet.

Once again, Americans grew more suspicious of their government because they learned about secret government attempts to subvert American democracy. From the late 1970s to the 1990s, antigovernment conspiracy theories grew more credible and popular after the media and Congress discovered actual government conspiracies, from covert foreign policies to schemes involving drugs and secret medical tests. These plots were especially alarming to many because they targeted ordinary Americans rather than protest leaders.

The resulting skepticism transcended race and ideology. Suspicions about long-hidden government plots appealed to black separatists and white supremacists, to left-wing activists and right-wing militias, to anarchists and neofascists. Conspiracism bent the political spectrum and fused its extremes into an endless circle of paranoia. Soon after Clinton's directive to Hubbell, the Internet would spread conspiracy theories and allow theorists to link to one another's sites, thus proving that everything is connected and giving hope to those who believed, in the words of *The X-Files*, that "the truth is out there."

As the century neared its end, the antigovernment skeptics infused their theories with a millennial sense of urgency. "The wolf," said the popular conspiracy writer Milton William Cooper, "is at the door."[4] *The X-Files'* many devoted fans agreed with one character's assessment of the federal government in the show's fifth season: "No matter how paranoid you are," she explained, "you're not paranoid enough."[5]

PSYCHIATRISTS DEFINE PARANOIA in part as the "persecutory delusion" that one is being "conspired against, cheated, spied upon, followed, poisoned or drugged."[6] In the late 1970s, Americans discovered that this feeling of persecution was not always delusional. The revelation of CIA mind control experiments intensified antigovernment paranoia as the public learned of official plots to control the behavior of randomly chosen, ordinary Americans.

As with so many of the government's secret programs, agents began to experiment with mind control in response to feared communist conspiracies. Back in the 1930s, during the show trials of alleged counterrevolutionaries in Moscow, international observers grew alarmed when the defendants recited zombie-like "voluntary" public confessions of crimes they could not have committed. Over the next decade, communist leaders seemed to perfect their technique. In 1949, Cardinal Mindszenty, the anticommunist prelate of Hungary, made an eerie, robotic confession at his trial in Budapest. U.S. intelligence officers studied the cardinal's empty eyes and worried that the communists had developed the ultimate cold war weapon: a way to manipulate the human mind.[7]

How could the United States counter these diabolical techniques? In 1950, as President Truman deployed foot soldiers to the muddy fields of Korea, the CIA prepared to meet the enemy on the battlefield of the mind. In a program first codenamed Bluebird, then renamed MKULTRA, the agency set out to find a "chemical material" that could produce an "aberrant mental state" and "potentially aid in discrediting individuals, eliciting information, and implanting suggestions and other forms of mental control."[8] In other words, the CIA wanted to figure out how to make people do the government's bidding against their will. Over the next several years, the agency doled out $25 million to psychiatrists who used their unsuspecting patients as guinea pigs in a frightening cold war attempt to control human behavior.[9]

The public's first clue to the existence of MKULTRA surfaced in 1975. The Rockefeller Commission disclosed that the CIA had tested "potential behavior-influencing drugs" on an unknown number of "unsuspecting subjects in normal social situations" beginning in 1953. Ten years later, the CIA's inspector general had "questioned the propriety" of the program, which had devastating effects in some cases, and shut down the experiments with involuntary subjects. The agency stopped the tests with voluntary subjects four years later, in 1967.[10] By this time, the CIA had discovered that the human brain was remarkably resistant to external attempts to control it. Despite fears of a "Manchurian candidate," popularized by Richard Condon's 1959 novel and the 1962 movie, scientists had learned that it was impossible to "program" an unwilling subject.

Before it ended, though, MKULTRA prompted at least one victim to take his life. Frank Olson, a civilian biological warfare expert at Fort Detrick in Maryland, attended a three-day conference at a lodge in Maryland with CIA officers and other scientists in 1953. One of his colleagues dropped LSD into the after-dinner liqueur. The germ warfare specialist reacted severely to the drug and began to suffer from terrifying hallucinations. Over the next several days, he became increasingly agitated and unbalanced. When a CIA officer took him to New York to consult a psychiatrist there, Olson leaped to his death from the window of his tenth-floor hotel room.[11]

The Rockefeller Commission was troubled enough by the Olson case to feature it in its report. The commission did not name the man who had committed suicide, but it did give enough details for Olson's widow and three children to recognize him. The oldest son, Eric, voiced the family's outrage. "I'm very angry at the C.I.A., because they let us grow up thinking our father had 'inexplicably' committed suicide," he told the *New York Times*. CBS News, the *Washington Post*, and *People* magazine also did sympathetic stories about Olson and the "C.I.A. suicide that nearly smashed a family."[12]

The Church Committee investigated Olson's death and the drug-testing program, but it could find few relevant documents. CIA officials testified that they had shredded the records. But in July 1977, as they searched through old files in response to Freedom of Information Act requests, agency employees discovered five thousand MKULTRA documents. The CIA director, Adm. Stansfield Turner, immediately disclosed the documents to Congress as part of the Carter administration's policy of openness. Two Senate panels held hearings on those documents and the thousands more that workers soon discovered.[13]

The Senate hearings and a later investigation by the journalist John Marks provided more details of the mind control experiments. Forty-four universities and colleges participated in the drug-testing programs, along with research foundations and private companies, hospitals, and prisons.[14] In a bizarre twist, agents in the Bureau of Narcotics, the government's soldiers in the war on drugs, helped the CIA to set up a program to give drugs to unsuspecting U.S. citizens and then study their responses. In Greenwich Village and San Francisco, CIA officers hired prostitutes to lure their customers to CIA safe houses, where the hookers slipped LSD and other behavior-changing drugs into their drinks and agents observed their reactions. The agency called the program "Operation Midnight Climax." Besides LSD, the prostitutes also dropped laxatives in the drinks of their unsuspecting customers, dusted them with itching powders, and surprised them with stink bombs. The CIA never followed up to see if the involuntary subjects suffered from the drugs; indeed, the agency never even knew their names.[15] As the 1977 hearings showed, top U.S. "security" officials used "safe" houses to test dangerous drugs on random and unknowing citizens. "If you happened to be at the wrong bar at the wrong place and time, you got it," Senator Richard Schweiker observed.[16]

The hearings also disclosed the most notorious example of mind control experiments run amok. In the 1950s and 1960s, the CIA paid an internationally prominent psychiatrist to erase the memories of his patients before attempting to reconstruct their shattered psyches. Dr. Ewen Cameron, a New York doctor who commuted to work in Montreal, prescribed cocktails of LSD, PCB, amphetamines, and barbiturates for the Canadians in his care; put them into a drugged sleep for weeks at a time; deprived them of all sensory stimulation in black chambers; convulsed them with electroshocks ramped up many times their usual power; and bombarded them with "psychic driving" messages on endless audio loops. Many of his patients came to Cameron with mild anxiety or depression disorders but became hysterical after weeks of his "depatterning" experiments. Cameron justified these experiments as a way to destroy "deviant" personalities and reprogram them for the public good.[17]

The revelations of the mind control experiments helped to create a new genre of conspiracy theories. By the early 1980s, suspicious citizens reinterpreted every recent puzzling event as the product of a CIA brainwashing or drug-testing experiment. As skeptics studied recent assassinations, they concluded that many of the killers seemed oddly robotic. Was Sirhan Sirhan, Robert Kennedy's assassin, a tool of these mad CIA scientists? What about the lovesick sociopath who shot Reagan, or the two lonely women who tried to kill Gerald Ford, or the seemingly demented J. D. Salinger fan who killed John Lennon?[18] Critics even suggested that the suicide-murder of more than nine hundred People's Temple members in Jonestown, Guyana, in 1978 might have been a CIA "brainwashing laboratory whose specimens spilled into public view."[19] It might also have been "cover" for a CIA plot to kill Congressman Leo Ryan, a vocal CIA critic who was assassinated by People's Temple fanatics as he tried to flee Guyana and expose the cult. "I believe that it is possible," said one of Ryan's aides, Joseph Holsinger, "that Jonestown may have been a mind-control experiment, that Leo Ryan's congressional visit pierced that veil and would have resulted in its exposure, and that our government, or its agent the CIA, deemed it necessary to wipe out over nine hundred American citizens to protect the secrecy of the operation."[20]

Although it sparked a brushfire of antigovernment conspiracy theories, the revelation of the CIA's mind control program was mainly of historical interest. The operation was, after all, defunct. Moreover, elected officials had never approved nor played a role in the program. But in the 1980s, Americans learned of current, continuing government conspiracies that, like Watergate, were centered in the White House itself and raised new questions about the subversion of American democracy.

THE GOVERNMENT CONSPIRACY known as Iran-contra began with an official conspiracy theory, and once again, as with so many official conspiracy theories of the twentieth century, this one involved communism. In President Ronald Reagan's view, the United States was confronting a terrifying global conspiracy run from the heart of an "evil empire." He portrayed the cold war in Manichaean terms, calling it a battle between "right and wrong and good and evil."[21]

In Reagan's view, these evil conspirators grew increasingly bold in the 1980s. The communists were flooding Central America "in a sea of red, eventually lapping at our own borders."[22] Reagan saw the new communist government of Nicaragua, which had been reluctantly tolerated by the Carter administration, as "a cruel clique of deeply committed Communists at war with God and man from their very first days."[23] If the Nicaraguan government remained in power, Reagan memorably warned, it would provide "a privileged sanctuary for terrorists and subversives just two days' driving time from Harlingen, Texas."[24]

Congress initially agreed with Reagan's official conspiracy theory and voted to support a group of anticommunist counterrevolutionaries in Nicaragua known as the contras. Created from the remnants of the national guard of Nicaragua's previous dictator, Anastasio Somoza, the contras attempted to subvert the communist government by assassinating public officials and destroying Nicaragua's infrastructure. But the contras' terrorist tactics made them increasingly unpopular in the United States, and in 1982 Congress began limiting their funds. In 1984 Congress completely stopped the flow of U.S. aid to the contras.[25]

Reagan, however, was determined to continue supporting the contras, whom he called the "moral equal of our Founding Fathers."[26] But because the contra war was unpopular with the public, he decided to subvert the law covertly, rather than making it a prominent issue in his reelection campaign in 1984. He directed his national security adviser, Robert McFarlane, to find ways to keep the contras together "body and soul": in other words, to find a way around the law.[27] McFarlane delegated this task to the Central American action officer on his staff, Marine Lt. Col. Oliver North.

North was an ambitious, charismatic young operative with a moist-eyed love of his country and an unshakable certainty that he knew what was best for it. He had "the sunny, undimmed confidence of a man who lacks insight into his own weaknesses," the White House speechwriter Peggy Noonan later said.[28] Contemptuous of the Democratic Congress, which he blamed for losing the Vietnam War, North eagerly sought ways to subvert the will of Congress and to continue funding the contras.

At first, North tried to privatize and outsource the contra war by soliciting contributions from wealthy individuals and foreign countries. Once he had his slush fund, he set up a conglomerate to buy guns and fly them down to Central America. He called this company "the Enterprise." Some of the contras apparently took advantage of the secrecy of the project and used Enterprise planes to import drugs to the United States.[29] As Senator Daniel Inouye later remarked, the Enterprise was "a shadowy government with its own air force, its own navy, its own fund-raising mechanism, and the ability to pursue its own ideas of the national interest, free from all checks and balances and free from the law itself."[30]

Hidden from Congress's view, the Enterprise grew in the darkest recesses of the national security state. Congress required the CIA to report its covert actions to legislative overseers in a timely fashion, but the National Security Council staff had no overseers except the president. The CIA tried to avoid direct involvement with the Enterprise for the good reason that it did not want to report to Congress that it was breaking a law passed by Congress. But CIA Director William Casey clearly directed North from the wings.

The Reagan administration's secret funding of the contras was illegal and unconstitutional, but at least it was consistent with Reagan's publicly stated policies. This was not the case with the other half of the Iran-contra scandal. At the same time as he managed the covert war in Nicaragua, North also sold arms to a government regarded by most Americans as the moral equivalent of the Evil Empire.

The spiritual leader of Iran, Ayatollah Ruhollah Khomeini, was a uniquely feared and hated figure in the United States, named by *Time* magazine as "man of the year" for 1979 because he "towered malignly over the globe." The ayatollah "gave the 20th century world a frightening lesson in the shattering power of irrationality, of the ease with which terrorism can be adopted as government policy."[31] As Khomeini's menacing eyes glared from magazine covers in the early 1980s, he became the face of evil to many Americans stunned by the surge of anti-American demonstrations around the world.

As *Time* and the Reagan administration charged, Khomeini was indeed guilty of promoting terrorism. In 1984 and 1985, the Iranian ally Hezbollah began to seize individual U.S. citizens in Lebanon and hold them hostage, demanding, in return, the release of Islamic prisoners jailed in Israel. In 1985, as the militants held seven Americans hostage in Beirut, an Iranian businessman approached U.S. officials and suggested that he could arrange for the release of the hostages. In return, the Iranian government wanted the U.S. government to sell it arms.

National Security Adviser McFarlane could have responded to the businessman's proposition in a number of different ways. He could have pointed out that the U.S. government banned arms sales to Iran, for the good reason that it supported terrorists such as the kidnappers in Lebanon. He might have noted that the United States was leading a propaganda campaign, "Operation Staunch," to persuade other countries to stop selling arms to Iran. He could have told the businessman that the United States never negotiated with terrorists, and that the president had explicitly called Iran part of a "confederation of terrorist states...a new, international version of Murder, Incorporated."[32]

But McFarlane did not say any of those things. Instead, he arranged, with Reagan's written approval, secret arms-for-hostages trades with Iranian government officials, who then pressured the kidnappers to release some hostages (though the terrorists promptly captured some more).[33] Despite the Reagan administration's public insistence that it would never negotiate with terrorists, it essentially arranged to pay a kind of ransom to the kidnappers. McFarlane put North in charge of the arms-for-hostages trades, which continued after Adm. John Poindexter replaced McFarlane as national security adviser.

After months of coordinating the Iran and the contra operations, North got the "neat idea" to merge them.[34] The contras needed money; the Iranian arms deals brought profits. So he decided to divert the profits from the arms-for-hostages deals and give them to the contras. Investigators later spent months trying to determine if Reagan had approved this diversion of funds. Although North said that the president had given his approval, Reagan denied it, and investigators never found any documentary proof.

In 1986 both of North's secret operations leaked to the media, creating a crisis for the administration. A joint congressional investigation and an independent counsel soon revealed the frightening and bewildering contours of the scandal: Swiss bank accounts and suitcases full of chemically treated cash; private businessmen, mercenaries, arms dealers, and drug runners on the payroll of the U.S. government; public officials flying on a secret mission into Tehran and begging for help from the nation that called the United States the Great Satan.

North also claimed that CIA Director Casey had even more grandiose plans for the future. In highly publicized testimony before Congress, North swore that Casey had discussed the idea of using illegal weapons sales to fund a permanent, secret foreign policy group unknown to Congress. In North's words, Casey wanted an "off-the-shelf, self-sustaining, stand-alone entity"—a covert agency outside of the CIA—that could carry out the CIA director's wishes without the knowledge of democratic overseers.[35] Casey died before he could respond to North's charges.[36]

The Iran-contra scandal exposed a government that had been run, as the congressional committee's majority report said, by a "cabal of zealots."[37] The Reagan administration, said Democratic Representative Louis Stokes, included "government officials who plotted and conspired...who lied, misrepresented and deceived. Officials who planned to superimpose upon our government a layer outside of our government, shrouded in secrecy and only accountable to the conspirators."[38]

Moreover, Iran-contra represented what conspiracy theorists since the First World War had feared the most: the ultimate executive usurpation of power. The Iran-contra conspirators had not subverted the government; they *were* the government. "We usually think of a junta as planning to overthrow a president," explained the political scientist Theodore Draper. "This junta came into being to overthrow an established constitutional rule of law, with the help of a president."[39] Reagan had clearly understood the implications of his actions. At one secret meeting, he seemed to accept the argument that evading Congress by soliciting foreign money for the contras might be an impeachable offense. "If such a story gets out, we'll all be hanging by our thumbs in front of the White House," he said.[40]

Unlike the Watergate conspirators, who had recorded their crimes on audiotape, the Iran-contra plotters left a contradictory and fragmentary documentary record. They took to heart the lesson that hard-line defenders of executive secrecy learned from Watergate: just burn the tapes. North spent weeks shredding documents before Reagan's attorney general seized his office and protected the files. The colonel proudly admitted that he had held a "shredding party" and destroyed the evidence. "I think I shredded most of that," he said, with a smirk, to congressional investigators. "Did I get 'em all?"[41]

As the details of the scandal came to light, Reagan's approval rating went into free fall and Americans' faith in their government dipped to Watergate-era levels.[42] Senator Daniel Patrick Moynihan claimed that in the history of the republic there had never been "so massive a hemorrhaging of trust and integrity."[43]

Some of the president's supporters, however, insisted that his political opponents had exaggerated the significance of Iran-contra. In the congressional investigation's minority report, a group of Republican representatives and senators conceded that the president made mistakes, including his decision to secretly subvert the contra aid law. In general, though, the Republican representatives found the president too *weak* in defending his foreign policy powers, such as when he "acceded too readily and too completely to waive executive privilege for our Committees' investigation." The main problem in Iran-contra, the minority seemed to say, was the Congress's failure to accept the president's role as the nation's "foreign policy leader."[44] Eight Republicans, including Wyoming's congressman, Dick Cheney, signed the minority report. During the Iran-contra hearings, Cheney went even further, explaining that he sympathized with Reagan's decision to ignore Congress and even his own State Department. Sooner or later, he said, most presidents decide that the "only way to get anything done, to cut through the red tape, to be able to move aggressively, is to have it done, in effect, inside the boundary of the White House."[45]

Though most Americans disagreed with Cheney's analysis, the president's approval ratings did eventually recover from the scandal, largely because of Reagan's sudden and unexpected willingness to help thaw the cold war at the end of his second term. But Americans' trust in the government rebounded only slightly in 1989, and then fell to even lower levels in the years to come.[46] Although several leading Iran-contra figures were convicted of felonies, they never served time in jail, thanks to court reversals on technicalities and last-minute pardons by Reagan's successor, President George H. W. Bush. Once again, the revelations of government crimes had brought partial confessions but no penance or redemption.

Skeptics found it difficult to decide which part of Iran-contra scared them the most: the government-within-a-government, the contempt for democracy, or the bald-faced hypocrisy of a tough-talking administration willing to sell arms to the ayatollah. For many Americans, though, the scandal had one clear message: government officials routinely lied and broke the law.

If they inveighed against terrorism while selling arms to terrorists, if they fought a "war on drugs" while easing the path for drug runners, what else might Reagan's secret warriors be hiding? "We're told by our leadership to be resolute against terrorism, yet they make deals," one science fiction writer told the *New York Times*. "People have lost trust in reality and they're looking for something else."[47] In the wake of the scandal, old antigovernment conspiracy theories took on contemporary twists.

ON THE SURFACE, the soldiers of Oliver North's Enterprise might not seem to have an obvious connection to little green men from outer space. But inventive skeptics soon suggested otherwise. In the 1980s, conspiracists dusted off a decades-old mystery in the New Mexico desert, imbued it with cosmic significance, and "proved" its likelihood by linking it to real Reagan administration conspiracies. In Roswell, antigovernment conspiracy theorists found the ultimate explanation for government deception and cover-ups.

The Roswell "incident" occurred at the dawn of the nuclear age and the cold war, just months after President Harry Truman had officially announced his administration's intention to fight communism all over the globe. At the beginning of the summer of 1947, the first summer of the cold war, hundreds of Americans began calling newspapers, radio stations, and government agencies to report mysterious, unidentified objects hovering in the night sky. By early July, a wave of "flying disk" sightings had rippled across the American West. Many of these early witnesses assumed that they were seeing secret U.S. or Soviet military vehicles, not ghostly ships from another planet.[48]

As newspapers breathlessly reported each new saucer sighting, a rancher in southeastern New Mexico stumbled upon a puzzling find. On the remote stretches of his property, he discovered a pile of sticks, tinfoil, thick paper, and smoky-gray rubber, all stuck together with scotch tape. After he called the nearby Army Air Force base at Roswell, the public relations officer for the base announced that the Army had obtained the remains of a mysterious "flying disc." But the next day, the commanding general for the region denied the saucer story. The strange debris had a mundane origin: it was just the remains of an ordinary weather balloon.[49]

In subsequent decades, conspiracy theorists would report this story in quotation marks—as in, the "weather balloon" story—and indeed, it was not the truth. The "weather balloon" had been part of a top-secret U.S. military project to detect possible Soviet nuclear tests. In 1946 and 1947, the Army Air Force had launched thousands of these high-flying balloons, puffed full with helium to pull their loads of instruments into the stratosphere. The devices strained to hear the high-altitude sound waves of Soviet atomic detonations.[50] When one of these balloons smashed into the sands of the New Mexico ranch, the military decided to hide the project's real purpose. The "weather balloon" story was born. And the public accepted the story for three decades.

But after Vietnam, Watergate, and the Church Committee revelations, writers uncovered the long-buried story of the crash in the desert and found it teeming with conspiratorial possibilities. The first Roswell conspiracy book appeared in 1980, thirty-three years after the original event. In *The Roswell Incident*, William L. Moore and Charles Berlitz, who had previously written books on the alleged teleportation of a World War II ship and on the Bermuda Triangle, managed to link nuclear fears and suspicion of the government with a quasi-religious hunger for supernatural communion. According to *The Roswell Incident*, which the anthropologist Charles Ziegler calls "Version 1" of the Roswell myth, the "weather balloon" was actually an alien spaceship that had been flying over New Mexico to monitor the U.S. military's atomic research.[51] A lightning strike downed the craft and the crash killed the aliens on board. The government swiftly covered up the accident because it wanted to prevent a mass panic and, more important, because it wanted to conceal the alien technology found at the crash site. After studying the debris, military officers believed that they had found the "ultimate secret weapon."[52]

The first version of the Roswell theory was standard conspiracist fare: it featured evil generals, killer technology, and lying politicians, but no evidence for its assertions. Then, seven years later, in the midst of the worst government scandal since Watergate, Roswell researchers suddenly produced the evidence to support their thesis.

In May 1987, as dramatic testimony before the Iran-contra investigating committee dominated the headlines, three authors announced that an informant had provided them with proof of the Roswell conspiracy. According to their account, an anonymous whistleblower had sent them several top-secret documents, including a copy of a 1952 memo to President-elect Dwight Eisenhower. Stamped "TOP SECRET: MAJIC EYES ONLY," the memo allegedly briefed the president on a complex plot involving a flying saucer crash at Roswell, the military's recovery of four decomposed alien bodies, the weather balloon cover story, and a massive governmental cover-up, codenamed Operation Majestic-12, or MJ-12.[53] Some conspiracists saw the hand of MJ-12, or perhaps of their alien controllers, in the Kennedy assassination.

Later, other researchers denounced the MJ-12 documents as fakes. In one case, the forgers, showing an impressive command of earlier conspiracy theories, had cribbed much of Gen. George Marshall's 1944 letter to Thomas Dewey disclosing the Pearl Harbor "Magic" intercepts, with names and dates changed and "magic" becoming "majic."[54]

But though they lacked creativity, the MJ-12 forgers clearly understood the contemporary political context. In all significant respects, MJ-12 was the Enterprise of the early cold war. According to the documents, a small group of men at the top of the U.S. government, many of them uniformed military officers, had formed a secret government—a government within the government—as part of a massive conspiracy to deceive the public. As in Iran-contra, a few documents had survived to testify to the truth, but most had been shredded.

The Roswell authors' charge that government officials had stolen alien technology raised another, more important question: *What were they doing with that technology?* Throughout the 1980s, as automatic teller machines and checkout scanners spread throughout the United States, some activists worried that the military could use computer microchips to track and control citizens. Meanwhile, in the skies over vast stretches of the American West, the U.S. military tested the Stealth Bomber, a plane so cleverly designed that it was invisible to enemy radar. Perhaps government agents had found these technologies in the debris of alien crafts and were using them to discover new ways to control the people. Perhaps, some skeptics speculated, the aliens were tutoring the CIA on new mind control techniques.

The implications of these new antigovernment theories could be unbearable to contemplate. After all, with earlier conspiracy theories, if the CIA killed the president, then the truth-seekers could expose the malefactors and toss them out of office. But if *aliens* killed the president, or if the CIA controlled Americans' minds, then it was much more difficult to plan an effective response. Some bold conspiracists connected the alien and brainwashing theories and suggested that mind control was "the ultimate abduction."[55]

Although many of the theories were preposterous, they did spring from actual congressional investigations of real government conspiracies. Theorists did not imagine that the CIA had dropped drugs into the drinks of random Americans, or that executive branch officials sold arms to terrorists, opened the nation's gates to drug runners, and conspired to create a secret government-within-a-government; these things had really happened.

Soon, though, some Americans began to examine these real conspiracies and to hypothesize about even more ambitious plots yet to be unveiled. When the Iran-contra hearings revealed CIA ties to drug dealers, some theorists leaped to an even more terrifying conclusion: that the U.S. government deliberately allowed drug trafficking as a means to control African Americans.

LIKE THE OTHER antigovernment conspiracy theories of the 1980s, rumors of government-sanctioned drug dealing had rumbled through American communities for decades. During the Vietnam War, some African Americans argued that the government imported drugs to pacify militant blacks. In the 1970s, this rumor became painfully credible to many African Americans as they read frightening headlines about official plots against the powerless.

In 1972, the Associated Press publicized the Tuskegee syphilis experiment, in which the U.S. Public Health Service denied potentially life-saving treatment to four hundred syphilitic black men from 1932 to 1972 so that doctors could learn more about the disease.[56] For many African Americans,

Tuskegee became a metaphor for the government's callous disregard for their lives. "A lot of people don't even know exactly what Tuskegee was," one community organizer told the *Los Angeles Times* in 1997, "but it has become mythological. They know it was against black people, and it was bad."[57]

After the Tuskegee revelations, journalists uncovered more examples of unethical government medical experiments. To study the effects of radiation on the human body, government workers persuaded boys in reformatories to eat oatmeal laced with radioactive calcium. In Nashville, government doctors urged pregnant women to drink cocktails that fizzed with radioactive iron. In prisons in the West, government scientists bombarded prisoners' groins with radiation and then studied their peeling, shrunken scrotums. Government doctors even injected plutonium directly into the veins of eighteen Americans who they thought were going to die soon anyway. The subjects of these government experiments were poor and powerless, and many, including all of the Tuskegee victims, were black.[58]

Some African Americans saw these programs as the newest episodes in a shameful history of white American assaults on black bodies, from slavery to lynching to Tuskegee.[59] They knew that other government conspiracies, like the FBI's counterintelligence programs, also targeted African Americans. In fact, the more African Americans knew about history, the more likely they were to believe in contemporary conspiracies against them.[60]

To some, the spread of crack throughout urban America in the 1980s seemed to be another such conspiracy. Smokable cocaine, or crack, was much cheaper than the powdered form of the drug and thus opened up marketing opportunities for dealers.[61] Crack ravaged inner-city America and prompted the National Urban League in 1989 to declare substance abuse to be "the single major leading social, economic, and health problem confronting the African-American community."[62]

The federal government responded to the surge in crack use by passing draconian drug laws designed to lock up the dealers, who were overwhelmingly black. Under mandatory minimum sentencing laws passed in the 1980s, the predominantly white sellers of powder cocaine received much less time in prison than crack dealers who had sold similar amounts of drugs.[63]

Crack devastated African American communities, and the government's response to the "plague" forced millions of black men into prison. How could this happen? For many African Americans, the answer seemed obvious: the government worked with smugglers in Central America to bring crack into black communities to control them.

Once again, the Iran-contra scandal made the most outrageous anti-government conspiracy theories seem believable. In 1987 and 1988, as Iran-contra unfolded, Senator John Kerry of Massachusetts chaired a major investigation into the links between drug dealers and the Nicaraguan contras. In December 1988 the Kerry Committee issued an eleven-hundred-page report documenting the contras' efforts to sell drugs to pay for their war and U.S. officials' knowledge of these crimes. "It is clear," the report said, "that individuals who provided support for the Contras were involved in drug trafficking, the supply network of the Contras was used by drug trafficking organizations, and elements of the Contras themselves knowingly received financial and material assistance from drug traffickers." The committee also concluded that several U.S. agencies, including the CIA, knew about the trafficking but chose to look the other way.[64]

Most public officials and journalists ignored or scoffed at the Kerry Committee report because it relied on the testimony of drug dealers. As the committee's chief investigator explained, it could hardly do anything else. "Bring me a Lutheran pastor who was there when the drugs were unloaded in Miami," said Jack Blum, "and I'll call him as a witness."[65]

Although the mainstream media dropped the CIA-crack story after the release of the Kerry Report, many African Americans saw it as proof that the U.S. government intentionally imported drugs to destroy black America. In 1990, 60 percent of African Americans told pollsters that it was likely or possible that "the government deliberately makes sure that drugs are easily available in poor Black neighborhoods to harm Black people." By contrast, only 16 percent of whites believed this suggestion of government-sponsored misery.[66]

The mainstream media seemed uninterested in pursuing the CIA-drug links until August 1996, when a regional newspaper suddenly revived the story. The *San Jose Mercury News*, a Knight-Ridder newspaper known for its aggressive investigations, published a story by the reporter Gary Webb that linked the contras and the CIA with drug dealers in a "Dark Alliance" against poor Californians. Webb reported that CIA agents deliberately ignored and then covered up evidence that contras were selling crack cocaine in Los Angeles ghettoes. The cocaine that flowed into California "helped spark a crack explosion in urban America," Webb explained.[67]

Webb never claimed that the CIA was engaged in a conspiracy to spread drugs in African American neighborhoods. The agency was far too incompetent, he believed, to carry out such a complicated plot. But he did believe that individual agents' conscious decisions to allow the contras to sell drugs "boomeranged back to the streets of America, in the long run doing far more damage to us than to our supposed 'enemies' in Central America," as he explained in a memo to his editors.[68]

Webb was a well-known investigative journalist who had won several awards, including the Pulitzer Prize, for his hard-hitting articles on mobsters, corrupt politicians, incompetent bureaucrats, and dishonest businessmen. He had come of age in the 1970s, when young journalists ached to become the next Bob Woodward or Carl Bernstein by exposing government conspiracies. Some of his colleagues idolized him for his sensational stories and his legendary refusal to compromise his principles; others found him self-important and inclined to push his stories beyond where the facts would take them. In this case, Webb's key assertions were true: some CIA agents *did* turn a blind eye to drug trafficking by their anticommunist allies. But Webb's interpretation of those facts—that one contra-led drug ring helped start the crack epidemic—was less defensible. The *Mercury* packaged the story in a salacious manner, with a graphic that superimposed a man smoking a crack pipe on the CIA logo.

Although the nation's most prestigious papers, including the *New York Times*, the *Washington Post*, and the *Los Angeles Times*, initially ignored the stories, talk radio helped Webb and the fans of the series bypass the elite newspapers and television networks. Hosts of these shows deluged Webb with requests for interviews. He obliged by giving more than one hundred radio interviews over the next two months.

The Internet was even more important than talk radio for Webb's story. "Dark Alliance" was the first online, interactive exposé. Located in the heart of the Silicon Valley, the *Mercury* wanted to stretch the boundaries of traditional newspaper publishing. The format was revolutionary for the time: readers could not only read Webb's piece but click on links to see the documents he had unearthed.

With the *Mercury*'s pioneering use of the Web as an interactive publishing tool, the trend toward citizen involvement in investigating government conspiracies, first evident in the Kennedy assassination, now reached its zenith. Those interested in a possible CIA-crack conspiracy did not have to mail each other smudged clippings; anyone in the world with Internet access could log on to the *Mercury* Web site, read Webb's story, and judge its accuracy by clicking on the links to the official documents. Even those Americans who were not yet connected to the Web had easier access to the stories in the new digital era. For example, at one hair salon in New York that catered to African Americans, clients could pick up printouts of Webb's stories on the reading rack, right next to *Ebony* and *Essence*.[69] Hosts of African American talk radio shows read excerpts from the series on the air and urged their listeners to log on to the *Mercury* Web site to learn more. Thanks to the series, the "Black Telegraph," said the *Time* columnist Jack E. White, referring to the term for the informal communication network among African Americans, "moved into cyberspace."[70]

To many African Americans, "Dark Alliance" provided evidence of yet another government conspiracy against them. "We've always speculated about this," said one Washington, D.C., talk radio host. "Now we have proof."[71] The Rev. Jesse Jackson, the NAACP, the Congressional Black Caucus, and Maxine Waters, an African American congresswoman from Los Angeles, called for official investigations. Residents of South Central Los Angeles, a predominantly African American neighborhood, held marches and candlelight vigils to demand a government inquiry into Webb's story. African American activists sealed off the entrance to CIA headquarters in Langley with yellow crime scene tape.[72]

In response, CIA Director John Deutch took the unprecedented step of confronting the angry skeptics in person. Appearing at a town hall meeting in South Central Los Angeles, packed with hundreds of hostile, suspicious inner-city residents, Deutch insisted that the CIA as an institution never consciously ignored evidence of drug trafficking by its agents. He was drowned out by boos and catcalls. "Why should we believe you today," asked one middle-class black man, "when you say certainly this could never happen in Los Angeles, when the CIA's done this stuff all over the world?"[73] Deutch's promise of an internal investigation did not satisfy the crowd. "You think you can come down here and tell us that you're going to investigate yourselves, and expect us to believe something is actually gonna happen?" one woman yelled at him. "How stupid do you think we are?"[74]

The growing popularity of the *Mercury* series finally prompted the top-tier newspapers to address it—and to dismiss it as misleading and inaccurate. The *Los Angeles Times*, the *Washington Post*, and the *New York Times* published front-page stories attacking both the series and African Americans' embrace of it, which the newspapers perceived as evidence of African American paranoia.[75] The assaults on his story disgusted Webb. "This is like reading *Pravda*," he said on Los Angeles radio.[76] Many African Americans could not understand why the mainstream media found the story incredible. As one Washington resident said, the "white press is pointing fingers at the black community, saying we're paranoid and quick to see conspiracy at every turn of the corner. Where have they been for the last 30 years? Can I just mention the Tuskegee syphilis study, COINTELPRO, Watergate, Iran-contra. Hello, America?"[77]

By focusing on the stories' weakest element—the charge that a contra drug ring helped to cause a nationwide crack epidemic—the large papers missed the most disturbing aspects of the revelations. Even if the CIA did not cause the drug explosion in the United States, neither did it deserve a medal for valorous service in the government's supposed "war on drugs." The historian Peter Kornbluh called the attack on Webb's stories "one of the most wasteful expenditures of journalistic resources" in recent journalism history. "If that much energy … had been expended on the true scandal of contras and drugs," Kornbluh continued, "Gary's reporting would have been significantly expanded."[78]

For some readers, the big papers' attacks on Webb confirmed their longtime suspicion of the media. For others, including Webb himself, the attacks were unexpected and disillusioning. The *Mercury* editors were terrified by the big newspapers' collective decision to push them to the margins of respectable journalism. Stung by the critiques, the *Mercury* backed away from the series and apologized for its alleged flaws. Webb's bosses reassigned him to an obscure bureau. He quit the paper and never found another job in mainstream journalism.

An internal CIA investigation later confirmed Webb's most important point: that some agency officials deliberately ignored evidence that its contra allies were trafficking in drugs.[79] "Dark Alliance" forced the CIA to admit publicly that some of its agents worked with anticommunist drug smugglers at the height of the war on drugs. The *Los Angeles Times* did not run a story on the report.

Partly because the major newspapers treated Webb with contempt, he quickly became a hero to conspiracists throughout the nation. His censure by the journalism establishment proved what they had suspected for years: the fourth estate was in league with the government to hide disturbing facts from the public. Earnest tipsters located the underemployed Pulitzer Prize winner in Sacramento and tried to convince him to expose everything from the identity of the anthrax serial killer to the CIA's attempts to control their brain waves. Webb was irritated by the attention and adulation from the conspiracists. He did not want to be associated with crazy extremists, or to have his own reporting dismissed by historians as "conspiracy mongering."[80] When another reporter mentioned conspiracy theories in a conversation with Webb in 1998, he erupted. "I don't believe in fucking conspiracy theories," he responded. "I'm talking about a fucking conspiracy."[81]

Unable to find a job on a major daily, Webb sank into depression, divorced his wife, and pushed away many of his old friends. On December 10, 2004, he watched his favorite movie, *The Good, the Bad, and the Ugly*, played his favorite album, *Ian Hunter Live*, and tossed a poster with a quotation hailing the integrity and independence of journalists ("There should be no fetters on reporters, nor must they tamper with the truth, but give light so the people will find their own way") into the trash. Then he shot himself in the head.[82] Admiring conspiracists from all over North America came to his funeral to pay him homage. A few of them called the Sacramento coroner to ask if someone might have faked the suicide to cover up his murder.[83]

Many of Webb's fans came from the left. Embittered survivors of the protest movements of the 1960s, they took refuge in conspiracy theories that helped to explain why their dreams had died. In particular, his stories resonated with some African Americans, who interpreted his reporting as evidence for earlier theories about government-sponsored drug rings.

Yet the impact of Webb's stories and his death stretched beyond the political left. His suicide saddened Pacifica radio listeners and militia sympathizers alike, who saw him as a rare journalist willing to speak truth to power. Admiration for Webb connected Americans who, by any rational political calculus, should despise one another. John Birch Society supporters joined with graying hippies to celebrate his determination to expose the lies of what activists of the right and the left called the "secret government."

The story of how a radical journalist became the hero of racist militia members helps to explain the strange fusion of the political extremes after

Iran-contra. As the journalist Michael Kelly explained in a 1995 article, there were surprising similarities between the radical left and the paranoid right in post–cold war America. Extremists of all stripes feared one thing above all: "the boundless, cabalistic evil of the government and its allies."[84] What Kelly termed "fusion paranoia" would become the preeminent trend of conspiracism at the end of the millennium as both left and right found a common enemy to fight in their defense of the republic: their own government.

WEBB'S ADMIRERS on the right drew on the ideas and strategies of earlier white supremacist movements. Calling themselves the Patriot movement, these activists of the 1990s had roots that stretched back to the neofascist organizations of the 1970s and 1980s. Groups like the Order, the Aryan Nations, and the Posse Comitatus spread the "Christian identity" belief that people of color were subhuman "mud people" and that Jews were the spawn of Satan.[85] Right-wing extremists firebombed synagogues, robbed banks, terrorized government officials, and assassinated liberal spokesmen throughout the 1970s and 1980s. In many ways, these far-right groups were mirror images of the leftist revolutionary groups of the same era. They organized in secretive cells, mixed ammonium nitrate bombs in their cellars, and hoped to provoke government oppression, which, they reasoned, would radicalize the masses and generate sympathy for the terrorists.[86] But these groups were on the fringes of American life. The FBI estimated that the Posse Comitatus had between twelve thousand and fifty thousand members, while the Order was far smaller.[87]

After the end of the cold war, these fringe groups helped to lay the foundation for a much larger movement. Building on the doctrines of the neofascists, the Patriot movement leaders emphasized a secular, libertarian form of government bashing. White supremacy took a backseat to a more marketable grievance: the threat posed to American citizens by their government.

The Patriot movement comprised an eclectic assortment of antiabortion activists, antienvironmentalists, nationalists, unapologetic racists, survivalists, and gun rights advocates. Some members of this loosely organized movement were registered Republicans who worried about what they saw as assaults on gun rights but believed it was possible to reform the system from within; others were hard-core conspiracists who believed that the republic was already lost because "insiders" had taken over the government and were undermining the Constitution.[88] Unlike the more mainstream leaders of the Christian right, the Patriot leaders rejected alliances with corporate elites and with most conservative political leaders, whom they viewed as part of the plot.

The Patriots appealed to millions of Americans who agreed with their basic premise that the government was taking away their God-given and constitutional rights. Scholars estimate that as many as five million Americans joined Patriot organizations or supported Patriot candidates for office. A much smaller subset of this group, about twenty thousand to sixty thousand Americans, joined the armed militias of the movement, which prepared for war against the government.[89]

In the view of Patriot leaders, the end of the cold war in 1989 and the impending end of the millennium in 2000 were bookends for the most dangerous period in U.S. history. They worried that government security agents, rendered redundant by the fall of the Soviet Union, would spy on and oppress Americans. Indeed, some conspiracists believed that this had already happened. The conspiracist guru and militia activist Milton William Cooper explained that a bomb shelter in Virginia initially built to house public officials in the event of nuclear war hid a shadow government that exercised the real power in the country. The program to protect Americans, he warned, "has actually been turned against us."[90]

The end of the cold war also opened up a new—and, to some, a frightening—economic universe. As the barriers to global free trade collapsed throughout the 1990s, some nationalists worried that the United States might lose its distinctive identity. When President George H. W. Bush spoke glowingly of a "new world order" in 1991, conspiracists seized on the "secretly coded" speech as evidence of the internationalists' plan to destroy the republic. Bush's repetition of the code phrase "must...be considered in light of the fact that he is a Skull & Bones alumni [sic] and a dedicated and loyal servant of the Secret Brotherhood," wrote the conspiracist Texe Marrs. This Brotherhood was a "small clique, or committee, of plotters" who "possess more power and authority than any other group in all of human history," but who apparently needed to communicate by placing code words in public speeches.[91]

Marrs and other conspiracists thought they knew the precise date of this impending catastrophe: the start of the new millennium, they believed, would bring the ultimate battle between good and evil.[92] During the cold war, many had assumed that the communists would be the villains in this apocalyptic drama. After the fall of communism, they were forced to recast the play, with the U.S. government itself now starring as the Antichrist. As in the McCarthy era, the Enemy was indeed within. But this time, these enemies controlled more than a few midlevel bureaucrats in the State Department; they controlled the FBI, the military, and the Federal Emergency Management Administration.

But it was the Bureau of Alcohol, Tobacco, and Firearms (ATF) that served as the insiders' most important tool, the right-wing conspiracists believed. To subdue the American people, the government first needed to take their guns. In their view, ATF agents were the shock troops of totalitarian revolution. By the early 1990s the conspiracists saw signs that this revolution had begun.

The event that inspired the birth of the American militia movement took place on a remote mountaintop in northern Idaho in 1991. Randy Weaver was a survivalist, a fundamentalist Christian, and a Second Amendment enthusiast who had tried to separate from American society and government by moving his family to the Idaho wilderness. Weaver could not escape the reach of federal weapons laws, though; he was arrested after he sold a sawed-off shotgun to an ATF agent at a white supremacist gathering. Believing that the agent had entrapped him and seeing all gun laws as unconstitutional, Weaver refused to appear for his federal trial on illegal weapons charges. Instead, he holed up with his family and a friend in his tiny cabin in Ruby Ridge. When federal marshals approached the cabin, both sides began shooting. Weaver's fourteen-year-old son, Samuel, and a marshal were killed. The government responded with a massive show of force, with hundreds of federal agents barricading the rural outpost. Weaver surrendered after an eleven-day siege, but not before an FBI sniper had killed his wife, Vicki, as she held their infant daughter in her arms.

For many Americans on the right, Ruby Ridge symbolized the "tyranny of government," as John Trochmann, a right-wing activist and conspiracist, explained. Weaver's supporters helped to organize the American militia movement at a meeting in Estes Park, Colorado, two months after the siege ended.[93] To the hundreds of Americans at that meeting, the government had tricked Weaver into breaking an unjust law, then assaulted his family in their home. The only way to respond to such police-state tactics, they believed, was to organize eighteenth-century-style militias to restore the republic.

The siege at Ruby Ridge angered the militia activists, but the events at Waco the next year truly enraged them. Outside of that Texas city, on a stretch of prairie called Mount Carmel, an apocalyptic Adventist sect known as the Branch Davidians prepared for the "end times" by stockpiling illegal weapons in their wooden fortress. The cult's polygamous leader, David Koresh, combined Christian fundamentalism with secular survivalism. In February 1993, when the ATF tried to search the compound for banned weapons, the Davidians resisted with deadly force. Four ATF agents and an unknown number of Davidians died in the shootout. The FBI responded to the murder of their fellow federal officers with hundreds of agents, tanks, helicopters, searchlights, and stereo speakers intended to blast the Davidians out of the compound with unbearably loud music.

After fifty-one days of tense negotiations, Attorney General Janet Reno, convinced that the Davidians were abusing the children in the fort, decided to force them out. As an armored vehicle poked a hole in the compound walls and began pumping in tear gas, a fireball exploded. At least eighty adults and children died in the ensuing inferno, which was broadcast live on television.[94] A special investigation by former senator John C. Danforth criticized the FBI for trying to hide evidence that the tear gas was flammable, but concluded that the Davidians had started the fire themselves.[95]

Right-wing conspiracists, however, alleged that the FBI set the fire and then shot the victims as they tried to run from the flames. The "tyrannical regime" of the Clinton administration had targeted the Davidians because of their unorthodox religious views and their refusal to submit to arbitrary gun laws. In the conspiracists' view, their government was willing to do anything to control Christians and their guns—even burn them alive. With the "Waco Holocaust," explained one Waco conspiracy Web site, the U.S. government "proclaimed itself to be the enemy of the people."[96]

The militias saw the 1993 passage of the Brady Law as the next stage in the government's plot to confiscate citizens' weapons of resistance. The law mandated a waiting period before consumers could buy handguns. Once Americans, thus disarmed, could no longer resist, the conspiracists concluded, government agents would summon the forces of the United Nations and the New World Order. "Fear the Government That Fears Your

Guns" was the motto on a popular bumper sticker sold by the American Justice Federation, a right-wing conspiracist group specializing in theories about what really happened at Waco.[97]

Some conspiracists did more than fear the government; they wanted to destroy it, along with the people who worked for it. The ultimate fantasy of antigovernment terrorism was expressed in *The Turner Diaries*, a neo-Nazi, futuristic novel written in 1979 by William Pierce under the pseudonym Andrew Macdonald. Early in the novel, the protagonists blow up FBI headquarters with a homemade fertilizer bomb concealed in a truck. Later, the hero destroys the Pentagon, the government's "nerve center," by smashing into it with a plane loaded with a nuclear bomb.[98]

One of the most devoted fans of *The Turner Diaries* was a young Gulf War veteran named Timothy McVeigh. A militia sympathizer, McVeigh was a walking compendium of antigovernment conspiracy theories. In the pre-Internet days of the early 1990s, he networked with other right-wing activists by attending gun shows around the country, where he collected assault rifles along with conspiracist books and theories about government cabals. Setting up his own table at the shows, he sold ATF baseball caps that had been suggestively pierced with bullet holes. He also hawked discounted copies of *The Turner Diaries*.[99] McVeigh had distrusted the federal government before Waco, but the siege of the Branch Davidians pushed him to the outer fringes of conspiracist paranoia. Convinced that federal agents had gassed, incinerated, and shot the Davidians because of their defense of their Second Amendment rights, he vowed to seek revenge. "ATF, all you tyrannical mother fuckers will swing in the wind one day, for your treasonous actions against the Constitution of the United States," he wrote in a letter he hoped federal agents would find. During the siege, he made a pilgrimage to Waco, where a student journalist photographed him sitting on a car and selling antigovernment bumper stickers ("WHEN GUNS ARE OUTLAWED, I WILL BECOME AN OUTLAW"). Shortly afterward, McVeigh visited Area 51 in Nevada, where right-wing extremists believed the government had stashed alien bodies and technology.[100]

On April 19, 1995, the second anniversary of the tragedy at Waco and the 220th anniversary of the battle of American colonists against British imperial forces at Lexington and Concord, McVeigh carried out an attack against the government he saw as tyrannical. Wearing a T-shirt that celebrated the assassination of the president who symbolized the creation of a national government, Abraham Lincoln, and that quoted Thomas Jefferson's advice that "the tree of liberty must be refreshed from time to time with the blood of patriots and tyrants," he drove a rented Ryder truck to Oklahoma City and parked it in front of the Alfred P. Murrah Federal Building. At 9:02 he leaped from the cab of the truck, ran to a nearby car, and sped away. One minute later, the truck exploded with a force that ripped apart the nine-story building, tore a massive crater in the ground, and murdered the federal workers, their children in the day care center, and the visitors inside ("collateral damage," McVeigh called the children and visitors, using a Pentagon phrase from the Gulf War for civilian casualties of bombings). He killed 168 people in the worst terrorist attack in the country's history up to that point. McVeigh later explained that he had cast himself as Jedi Knight Luke Skywalker in *Star Wars*, with the federal government as the Evil Empire and the Murrah Building as the Death Star.[101] In his world, an obscure office building in Oklahoma was the site of imperial power and repression.

Despite McVeigh's confession, right-wing conspiracists speculated that government agents had planned a "Reichstag fire" and planted the bomb themselves, or used mind control techniques on McVeigh. ATF agents in Oklahoma City, they insisted, had been told to stay away from work that day.[102] In any event, they claimed, the dead workers "were the real terrorists," as William Pierce, author of *The Turner Diaries*, explained. "When a government engages in terrorism against its own citizens, it should not be surprised when some of those citizens strike back and engage in terrorism against the government."[103] President Clinton offered a different perspective. "The bombing in Oklahoma City," he said to the nation on television that afternoon, "was an attack on innocent children and defenseless citizens. It was an act of cowardice, and it was evil. The United States will not tolerate it. And I will not allow the people of this country to be intimidated by evil cowards."[104]

As his secret request to Webb Hubbell had shown, the president sometimes questioned the truthfulness of the U.S. government. But he believed that there was a great difference between questioning some official narratives—Who really killed JFK?—to believing that the government was actively plotting against its citizens. "If you say that government is in a conspiracy to take your freedom away," he explained, "you are just plain wrong."[105]

SOME AMERICANS DISAGREED with the president. They did not see McVeigh as "evil"; instead, they found him to be worthy of their sympathy, or even admiration. And it was not just white supremacists with cellars full of assault rifles who respected McVeigh. He had many defenders on the left. Like Gary Webb, McVeigh helped to fuse the fears of the political extremes.

At first glance, the extreme left and the far right of the 1980s and 1990s shared little common ground. The activists on the far right despised socialism while often preaching white supremacy, anti-Semitism, misogyny, fundamentalist Christianity, and homophobia. They opposed the use of state power for any purpose except protecting the social and economic order.[106] By contrast, activists of the far left were often hostile to organized religion and passionate about using government to protect the rights of people of color, gays, and women. They were also eager to expand government power in certain areas, such as health care. Moreover, though both groups sometimes shared a common rhetoric, the same words could mean very different things. For the left, "government terrorism" meant American bombs falling on foreign civilians; for the right it meant gun control laws, the income tax, and the Bureau of Land Management.

And yet, despite these obvious differences, as the end of the millennium approached activists of the right and the left shared a common terror that the republic was in peril. Iran-contra had caused liberals and even a few right-wing activists to fear "the secret government," which was the title of both a compelling 1987 Bill Moyers documentary on PBS and an alarming 1989 book by the militia leader Milton William Cooper. Although many self-described conservatives applauded Oliver North, Cooper wrote for a constituency that saw the scandal as a sign that the "insiders" had already taken over the government. Perhaps, Cooper suggested, Congress's failure to punish the president proved that the New World Order was coming sooner than anyone thought. In Iran-contra, Cooper noted, "the Congress even seemed to go out of its way to duck the issues that were just under the surface. Could it be that Congress knows the whole thing and won't touch it?" The "whole thing" involved the control of the government by aliens, who were hiding their weapons under the testing sites at Area 51 in Nevada. "It is the only scenario," he wrote, "that answers all the questions and places the various fundamental mysteries in an arena that makes sense."[107] He used the Iran-contra hearings and Church Committee reports to "prove" his theory.

Cooper's alarm over Iran-contra was not unique among right-wing activists. According to the conspiracy theory analyst Chip Berlet, the mainstream press received help in uncovering the details of Iran-contra from many unlikely right-wing sources, including career military men, who resented the influence of the CIA; anti-Semitic intelligence analysts, who decried the influence of Israel in Reagan's White House; and fringe conspiracists such as perennial presidential candidate Lyndon LaRouche. Berlet worried about the consequences of this left-right alliance against the CIA. In 1992 he warned that "some of the classic scapegoating conspiracy theories of the far right" were influencing allegedly leftist analyses of U.S. foreign policy and domestic surveillance.[108]

As one example, Berlet cited the mélange of left and right in Oliver Stone's film *JFK*. Because it alleged that Kennedy was killed because he wanted to withdraw from Vietnam, most reviewers saw it as a leftist film. But many progressive commentators noted the film's "right-wing paranoid theories," which were blended with the leftist conspiracy theories.[109] Stone proposed a massive plot involving generals, industrialists, anti-Castro Cubans, and homosexuals, indiscriminately mixing left-wing theories about a military-industrial complex conspiracy with the right-wing arguments spouted by an ally of Holocaust deniers, Fletcher Prouty (called "Mr. X" in the film).[110] Alexander Cockburn, a columnist for the *Los Angeles Times* and the *Nation*, contended that the film illustrated the "crippling nuttiness of what passes in many radical circles for mature analysis and propaganda." In Stone's version of history, Cockburn argued, "left ultimately joins hands with right."[111]

This fusion conspiracism was also evident in the popular responses to Ruby Ridge and Waco. Both sieges had consequences far beyond the militia movement: they convinced millions of Americans that government agents routinely conspired against nonconformists. A CBS made-for-television movie, for example, portrayed the Weavers as creepy but harmless eccentrics who did nothing to deserve the government assault on their family.[112] Similarly, support for the Davidians also crossed ideological lines, with one feminist pacifist calling theirs a "loving, committed, interracial community and family, something all too rare in our isolated, alienated, bigoted world."[113] A poll showed that 61 percent of Americans believed that federal officials, not the Davidians, started the fire at Waco.[114] To Americans in and beyond the militias, Waco and Ruby Ridge symbolized government assaults on American families in their homes.[115] The FBI's excesses in these two cases managed to transform rather unsympathetic characters—a polygamist and a white supremacist—into misunderstood victims of governmental tyranny.

Gore Vidal, who for decades had been defending the American republic against the "American Global Empire, our old republic's enemy," was another leftist intellectual who empathized with the Weavers, the Davidians, and McVeigh.[116] In a November 1998 article on the "shredding" of the Bill of Rights, Vidal described Vicki and Sam Weaver as victims of "cold-blooded federal murder" and the Waco fire as the "FBI slaughter of the innocents." He challenged the government's definition of "terrorist," adding that "most of today's actual terrorists can be found within our own governments, federal, state, municipal."[117]

In prison before his execution, McVeigh read Vidal's article with interest. He began corresponding with the author and ordered a volume of his collected essays, *United States*. In these essays, Vidal ruminated, among other things, on various Kennedy assassination conspiracy theories, declared that President Wilson had "arranged a war which neither Congress nor nation wanted," and speculated that Howard Hunt might have forged the diary of the man who shot George Wallace.[118] McVeigh was impressed by these meditations on the subversion of the republic by corporate elites and imperial executives. "I think you'd be surprised," he wrote Vidal in 1999, "at how much of that material I agree with."[119]

After the execution, Vidal tried to justify McVeigh's terrorism in a long, respectful article in *Vanity Fair* magazine. McVeigh, he said, seemed "to have stumbled into the wrong American era." He would have made a fearsome abolitionist or Union soldier, fighting the good fight against slaveholders and rebels. "But he was stuck where he was and so he declared war on a government that he felt had declared war on its own people." Like McVeigh's favorite author, *The Turner Diaries'* William Pierce, Vidal argued that McVeigh had been driven to extremes by the repressiveness of the state.[120]

The anarchist terrorist known as "the Unabomber" also admired McVeigh. Theodore Kaczynski killed three people and wounded twenty-three more in an eighteen-year bombing campaign. The Unabomber's ideology was difficult to classify: his "manifesto," which railed against industrialization, technology, and the loss of individual freedom, contained elements of right-wing reaction, yet he also inspired admirers on the extreme left with his anarchist views and his dedication to propaganda of the deed.[121]

Kaczynski met McVeigh in the exercise yard of the supermax federal prison in Colorado, where they sat in separate wire-mesh pens. At first, Kaczynski was reluctant to engage McVeigh in conversation because he feared that a friendship with a neofascist mass murderer might project the wrong image. But when they began talking, he discovered that McVeigh "sounded like a liberal." Like Vidal, Kaczynski came to believe that McVeigh had missed his historical era, because "America since the closing of the frontier has had little room for adventurers." Also like Vidal (and like William Pierce), Kaczynski tried to excuse McVeigh's crime by insisting that "our politicians and our military kill people in far larger numbers than was done at Oklahoma City."[122]

As they sat in the cages in the yard of the country's most secure prison, the two antigovernment terrorists discussed their common political ground and agreed that "certain rebellious elements on the American right and left respectively had more in common with one another than is commonly realized." It was impossible, the neo-Nazi told the anarchist, to tell left from right any more.[123]

As the new millennium approached, scholars noted that conspiracy had become "the default assumption in an age which has learned to distrust everything and everyone," in the words of the cultural theorist Peter Knight.[124] In 1995, a jury acquitted O. J. Simpson of the murder of his wife and her friend because its members believed his lawyers' theory that a conspiracy of racist cops had framed him. Hillary Clinton invoked a "vast right-wing" conspiracy to explain the looming impeachment of her husband in 1998. Popular movies featured presidents who staged fake wars on soundstages to avoid domestic problems and CIA drug-testing victims under assault from black helicopters.[125]

The X-Files was the ultimate expression of 1990s fusion paranoia. The television series creator, Chris Carter, explained that Watergate was "the big bang of my moral universe," but his plots, featuring global conspiracies and a government-within-a-government, owed more to Iran-contra.[126] The show, which aired from 1993 to 2002, followed FBI agents Fox Mulder and Dana Scully as they sought to discover the truth about government cover-ups of alien visitation and horrific medical experiments.[127] Like the popular conspiracist writer Milton William Cooper, *The X-Files* sometimes suggested that aliens controlled the government, and sometimes suggested that human plotters in the government were trying to *get Americans to think* that aliens controlled the government. "For years," Agent Scully suggested, "we've been nothing more than pawns in a game;…it was a lie from the beginning."[128] The show's message resonated with many viewers. Polls showed that 71 percent of Americans agreed that the government knew more about UFOs than it acknowledged.[129]

Mulder and Scully were 1990s versions of the amateur sleuths of the Kennedy assassination, pounding the pavement in Dallas with recorders hidden in their armpits. True, they had official roles as FBI agents, but they fought the FBI hierarchy, which was part of the conspiracy. This conspiracy grew more complicated and nefarious as the series progressed, as the apparent leaders of the plot turned out to be mere pawns themselves.

Like the Kennedy assassination researchers, Mulder and Scully could never quite solve the central mystery of the conspiracy. Although one of the slogans of the show contended "The truth is out there," the writers played with the notion of "truth." Mulder seemed to think that he could explain everything if only he could open the right door or find the right file—that he could avenge his father and his sister, who had apparently been victimized by the conspiracy, and restore some imaginary idyll. But the show repeatedly foiled Mulder, insisting that each new truth he discovered was at best only partial and in fact probably another layer of ruse. The show seemed to contend that all reality was a vast and incomprehensible conspiracy that resisted logic (and Mulder). Nobody controls the game, and the truth is in fact *not* out there. The show rotated the "truth" slogan with a few others, including "Trust no one" and "Everything dies"—including, apparently, logic.

The endless twists and turns of the *X-Files* conspiracy embraced the demands of series television, because, of course, if Mulder ever found the truth, the series would be over. But the show also reflected the anxieties of the 1990s: the government is a conspiracy; Americans *think* they can uncover this conspiracy; the plotters always foil them. Self-consciously post-Dallas, post-Watergate, post–Iran-contra, and post–cold war, *The X-Files* combined the Kennedy assassination, Nixon's White House horrors, Tuskegee, Ruby Ridge, Waco, and Roswell into one gigantic government plot against the people.

The Soviets were gone, but the national security state that grew up to fight them survived. "Because there's not nuclear missiles pointed at our heads, you can't consolidate your fears there anymore," explained Glen Morgan, a co-executive producer of the show during its first two seasons.[130] Public trust in the government dropped to even lower levels in the 1990s than in the 1980s, with just 21 percent of Americans, a historic low, expressing a great deal of faith in their government in 1994.[131] Lacking borders, these fears flooded the cultural landscape.

As *The X-Files* entered its eighth season in the twenty-first century, it seemed that conspiracism about the U.S. government had reached its height. Until, that is, Dick Cheney, unapologetic defender of secret government conspiracies and executive power, came back to the White House.

7

Cabal of Soccer Moms:
9/11 and the Culture of Deceit

THE FOUR WIDOWS from New Jersey were nervous as they sat down to meet with the man they privately called "everyone's favorite war criminal."[1] It was late 2002, and the women and other 9/11 family members had just won their long battle to force President George W. Bush to appoint a blue-ribbon commission to investigate the unanswered questions of the terrorist attacks of September 11, 2001. Their husbands died in those attacks, and these widows, known collectively as the "Jersey Girls," wanted desperately to discover if the 9/11 conspiracy involved more people than the hijackers from Osama bin Laden's al Qaeda terrorist group.

But when the president appointed former secretary of state Henry Kissinger, one of the strongest advocates of official secrecy in U.S. government history, as chair of the inquiry, the women wondered whether the commission would wage an aggressive fight for truth. They worried that Kissinger might try to turn the investigation into a whitewash that exonerated his friends in the Bush administration and the Saudi clients of his international consulting business.

Kristen Breitweiser, a petite, thirty-two-year-old blonde with a scrubbed face and carelessly tied ponytail, took the lead. She and the other three Jersey Girls came from upscale, Republican suburbs across the state line from New York, and two of them had voted for Bush in 2000. But the administration's opposition to an exhaustive investigation of 9/11 had convinced them that Bush did not want to discover the whole truth about the events of that day. They looked like amiable soccer moms, but, as the president's supporters would soon learn, they should never be underestimated.

After introductions and small talk, Breitweiser, an attorney who had practiced for just three days before quitting, and other family members asked Kissinger to disclose his client list. Visibly irritated, Kissinger mumbled about confidentiality. He grudgingly conceded that perhaps "a lawyer" could look at the list. "Kristen's a lawyer," one of the other widows piped up. Kissinger stiffened in irritation. Then another Jersey Girl, Lorie Van Auken, asked him if he represented clients who might present a conflict of interest—such as, for example, the bin Laden family. Kissinger knocked over his coffee cup and "nearly fell off the couch," Breitweiser remembered.[2] He soon resigned from the commission.

The president's supporters were outraged that the widows had effectively vetoed his choice to lead the investigation, and they quickly mobilized to assail the Jersey Girls as manipulative narcissists who reveled in the attention brought by their victimization. The tone of these and subsequent attacks was always the same: How did these women dare to dictate the terms of an investigation to the president of the United States?[3] When the widows met with the *New York Post* to complain about a particularly vicious editorial against them, the *Post's* editor, Bob McManus, expressed amazement that they had gotten an appointment. "I don't even know who you people are, who you may *think* you are," he said, "and frankly, I don't know how you *even got in the building*."[4]

The Bush supporters were angry because the Jersey Girls had done far more than get in the building: they had successfully disputed the power of the mainstream media and political elites to define the meaning of 9/11. In time, they would reject the findings of the official commission that they had demanded and begin considering and popularizing "revisionist" theories about 9/11 that diverged from the official conspiracy theory sanctioned by the White House. They worried that a small group of executive branch officials—a cabal of neoconservatives—was trying to cover up damning, perhaps even horrifying, secrets about 9/11. "We felt that the country was at risk from terrorists and from incompetence," Van Auken explained in a 9/11 documentary. "And maybe worse."[5]

Real government conspiracies and cover-ups made these revisionist theories more believable. The popularity of alternative 9/11 conspiracy theories rose as Americans' trust in their president fell. By 2006, this distrust had become so widespread that more than one-third of Americans believed that their own government either planned and executed or consciously took no action to stop the worst mass murder in U.S. history.[6]

INITIALLY, TO MOST AMERICANS, the conspiracy behind the 9/11 attacks seemed nefarious but relatively small, consisting of nineteen hijackers and the al Qaeda leader bin Laden, who had been protected by the weak Taliban regime in Afghanistan. This conspiracy theory supported a vigorous but (relatively) limited response from the U.S. government: invading Afghanistan, capturing the plotters, and deposing the Taliban.

Then, about three months later, some administration officials began suggesting a different, more far-reaching plot behind September 11, a plot that required a more extensive response from the U.S. government. On December 9, 2001, Vice President Dick Cheney said on NBC's *Meet the Press* that it had been "pretty well confirmed" that Mohammed Atta, one of the hijackers, had met with a "senior official of the Iraqi intelligence service" in Prague several months before the attacks. Ominously, Cheney implied that there might be continuing links between al Qaeda and Iraq's Saddam Hussein, who, the vice president stated categorically, had been "aggressively" adding to his existing stocks of weapons of mass destruction. Clearly, "given the vulnerability of the United States that's now been demonstrated, given the increasing linkage, if you will, between terrorist[s] and weapons of mass destruction," Cheney explained, U.S. officials had to consider "how we proceed to make certain that the United States is not vulnerable to that kind of an attack."[7]

The danger to the United States posed by Iraq's regime had been a standard argument for neoconservatives for years before 9/11. In 1997, many future Bush administration leaders, including Cheney, Defense Secretary Donald Rumsfeld, Deputy Defense Secretary Paul Wolfowitz, and Cheney's chief of staff, I. Lewis Libby, had called for the United States to expand its military and to impose "an international order friendly to our security, our prosperity, and our principles."[8] These men and others had united to form a think tank, called the Project for a New American Century (PNAC), to lobby for this aggressive post–cold war foreign policy. But to expand its power in the Middle East, the U.S. government first needed to oust Saddam Hussein. In 1998, several PNAC leaders, including Rumsfeld and Wolfowitz, publicly called on President Bill Clinton to remove Hussein from power. Iraq was "almost certain" to acquire weapons of mass destruction, they said, and to use these weapons to threaten U.S. security.[9]

In 2000, the PNAC laid out in extensive detail its ambitions for "rebuilding America's defenses." In a seventy-six-page report, the authors argued for a more interventionist foreign policy that would strengthen U.S. power around the world and intimidate those rogue regimes like Iraq that refused to accept American dominance. They acknowledged, and lamented, the difficulties of persuading the public to bear the burdens of the New American Century. Unless, that is, "some catastrophic and catalyzing event, like a new Pearl Harbor," awakened the American people to the need for military expansion.[10] Advocates of Iraqi "liberation" were almost wistful about the prospect of a crisis that would prompt U.S. intervention in Iraq. "Ideally, the first crisis would be something with Iraq," Kenneth Adelman, a Bush-Cheney adviser, told the journalist Nicholas Lemann after Bush's election. "It would be a way to make the point that it's a new world."[11]

Some neoconservatives had warned for years that Hussein might use terrorist proxies to carry out a new Pearl Harbor. For example, the political scientist Laurie Mylroie, a fellow at the American Enterprise Institute and former assistant professor at Harvard, saw Saddam's hand behind many terrorist attacks of the 1990s. Mylroie blamed Saddam for the 1993 World Trade Center bombing and, despite Timothy McVeigh's confession, for the Oklahoma City bombing in 1995. She had offered her assistance to McVeigh's lawyers, who regarded her as a "fanatic." Stephen Jones, McVeigh's lead attorney, compared Mylroie to *The Da Vinci Code* people." "She had this one grand theory," he said. "I didn't see it."[12] Like many neoconservatives, including her friend Wolfowitz, Mylroie concluded that Hussein was the chief conspirator behind the 9/11 attacks. "No reasonable person" could believe otherwise, she said on CNN.[13]

But reasonable people did think otherwise. Most U.S. intelligence professionals were astounded that anyone would link the secular, modernizing, though brutal, dictator of Iraq with the religious zealots in al Qaeda. Just hours after the attacks, Richard Clarke, the U.S. counterterrorism chief, was "incredulous" when the president directed him to investigate Saddam's possible links to the terrorists. "But, Mr. President, al Qaeda did this," Clarke protested. The president responded "testily" that Clarke should investigate the possible Saddam link anyway.[14]

Like Clarke, many U.S. counterterrorism officials were stunned by the Bush administration's persistent suggestions that Iraq might have directed the 9/11 attacks. CIA analysts doubted the claim about the alleged Iraqi–al Qaeda meeting in Prague from the beginning. The only supposed evidence for the meeting was a surveillance photo outside the Iraqi embassy in Prague showing an Iraqi agent with an unidentified husky man in a leather jacket. "We knew right away that's not Atta," said one U.S. counterterrorism official. The man in the picture "looked sort of like an Albanian thug. Atta was a little scrawny guy." Moreover, FBI agents found evidence from Atta's bank and cell phone records that he was in the United States in the days surrounding the alleged meeting.[15] In short, according to the agency's top Middle East specialist, Paul Pillar, U.S. intelligence "never offered any analysis that supported the notion of an alliance between Saddam and al Qaeda."[16]

Yet administration officials persisted in manufacturing the link.[17] Over the next year, Cheney used increasingly definitive language to tie Iraq to al Qaeda. In March 2002 he stated that Mohammed Atta had "in fact" met with Iraqi intelligence in Prague.[18] By September, this Prague meeting had become one of many; there were, Cheney said, "a number of contacts" between Saddam and al Qaeda before the attacks.[19]

These official pronouncements about "contacts" and "facts" helped to transform many Americans' understanding of 9/11. Right after September 11, only 3 percent of Americans blamed Iraq for the attacks.[20] But they trusted the president and vice president to tell them the truth about terrorist threats. The surge of patriotism after the attacks helped to reverse, at least temporarily, the long-term slide in Americans' trust in their government. In the last national poll on government trust before the attacks, taken in March 2001, only 29 percent of Americans said they trusted the government to do the right thing most of the time. After September 11, those numbers more than doubled, to 64 percent.[21] Citizens of democracies typically "rally round the flag" and support their government in times of crisis.[22] In this context, Bush administration officials had a great deal of power to persuade Americans to believe their theory.

By August 2002, after months of administration arguments, the proportion of Americans who blamed Saddam for 9/11 leaped from 3 percent to 53 percent.[23] In September 2003, nearly 70 percent of Americans believed the administration's conspiracy theory.[24]

In proposing the Saddam–al Qaeda conspiracy, the administration was making an argument about history. September 11 was, after all, in the past. But this historical interpretation also pointed the way to future policies. The administration was suggesting that the next Iraq–al Qaeda conspiracy would bring the unthinkable.

In the administration's view, Iraq gave al Qaeda the one thing it needed most: a state sponsor capable of building the factories required to enrich vast quantities of uranium. Although Hussein might hesitate to launch nuclear missiles from Iraq, he could still slip bombs to terrorists and kill tens of thousands of Americans "without leaving any fingerprints," President Bush said.[25]

According to Cheney, Saddam was not only supporting terrorists but was also "actively pursuing nuclear weapons at this time," despite the rigorous inspections after the Gulf War in 1991.[26] Indeed, Cheney reported that the United States had "irrefutable evidence" that Saddam had reconstituted and accelerated his nuclear weapons programs.[27] National Security Adviser Condoleezza Rice vividly spelled out the implications: "We don't want the smoking gun to be a mushroom cloud."[28] President Bush also used the smoking gun–mushroom cloud image, first suggested by a creative White House speechwriter.[29]

In his State of the Union address for 2003, the president presented a terrifying scenario. Bush said that Saddam had tried to buy aluminum tubes to enrich uranium, and, even more ominously, he had also "recently" sought to buy "significant quantities" of uranium from Africa. Iraq could conceivably develop a nuclear bomb and give it to al Qaeda. "It would take one vial, one canister, one crate slipped into this country," the president said, "to bring a day of horror like none we have ever known."[30]

The next month, in a riveting speech to the United Nations, Secretary of State Colin Powell presented evidence that Saddam was stockpiling biological and chemical weapons, trying to build nuclear bombs, and improving his "sinister" links to al Qaeda. "Our concern," Powell said, "is not just about these illicit weapons. It's the way that these illicit weapons can be connected to terrorists and terrorist organizations that have no compunction about using such devices against innocent people around the world."[31]

United Nations weapons inspectors reported that they could find no "evidence or plausible indication of the revival of a nuclear weapons program in Iraq."[32] The chief inspector, Hans Blix, asked for more time to complete the inspections, which would "not take years, nor weeks, but months."[33] But administration officials dismissed these pleas, claiming that the international inspectors had, as Cheney said, "consistently underestimated or missed what Saddam Hussein was doing."[34]

Having conjured the dragon, the administration set out to slay it. On March 19, 2003, U.S. and British troops, along with a coalition of other nations, began the war against Iraq. The initial phase of the war went well for coalition forces, which advanced to a swift and decisive victory. Hussein went into hiding outside Tikrit in a dirt hole six feet underground, from which U.S. soldiers would drag him, enraged and bedraggled, in December. The Iraqis used only conventional weapons against the invasion forces; U.S. soldiers did not need the suits and masks they carried in case of chemical or biological attacks.

In the early weeks, the American public supported the invasion overwhelmingly.[35] At the height of the war's popularity, on May 1, 2003, the president flew in a fighter jet to a cinematic landing on the deck of the U.S.S. Abraham Lincoln off the coast of California. Under a banner proclaiming "Mission Accomplished," Bush once again linked Iraq with September 11. "With those attacks," he said, "the terrorists and their supporters declared war on the United States, and war is what they got."[36] The U.S. government had ostensibly identified, captured, and punished the 9/11 conspirators. Or some of them, anyway: bin Laden was still at large.

The Bush administration remained confident that it could mold and control public perceptions of 9/11 and the war. One administration official later explained this worldview to the reporter Ron Suskind. "We're an empire now, and when we act, we create our own reality," the unnamed official explained. "And while you're studying that reality—judiciously, as you will—we'll act again, creating other new realities, which you can study too, and that's how things will sort out. We're history's actors . . . and you, all of you, will be left to just study what we do."[37]

BUT THE BUSH ADMINISTRATION began to lose some control over the 9/11 narrative just eight months after the attacks. In May 2002 reporters revealed that FBI agents in Phoenix and Minneapolis had separately warned Washington in the months before the attacks that terrorists might be training in U.S. flight schools.[38] A Phoenix agent even recommended that the FBI check the visas of foreigners attending the schools—a recommendation that, if it had been implemented immediately, might have detected at least one and perhaps three of the 9/11 hijackers.[39] Top FBI officials had shown little interest in the reports and had turned down the Minnesota agents' request for a search warrant to examine the computer of a would-be pilot they had detained, Zacarias Moussaoui. The U.S. government later charged Moussaoui with being the intended "twentieth hijacker."[40] The implications of the stories were alarming: if FBI officials had been more alert, they might have thwarted the plot.

Although the president had not read the Phoenix and Minneapolis memos, he did know more about the terror attacks than he admitted at the time. In an explosive report, also in May 2002, CBS News revealed that the CIA had warned President Bush a month before the attacks that bin Laden was poised to strike in the United States, perhaps by directing his followers to hijack airplanes.[41] Administration officials insisted, though, that the intelligence community's warnings did not specify that the terrorists would use the planes as weapons. "I don't think anybody could have predicted that these people would take an airplane and slam it into the World Trade Center, take another one and slam it into the Pentagon; that they would try to use an airplane as a missile, a hijacked airplane as a missile," explained National Security Adviser Condoleezza Rice.[42] She later admitted that "somebody did imagine it"; in fact, U.S. intelligence agents had warned of terrorist plots to use hijacked planes as missiles at least a dozen times in recent years.[43] "How is it possible," Kristen Breitweiser later asked, that "we have a national security advisor coming out and saying we had no idea they could use planes as weapons when we had FBI records from 1991 stating that this is a possibility?"[44]

In the summer of 2002, investigators for a joint congressional committee on 9/11 uncovered more errors and apparent contradictions in the Bush administration's story. The committee, chaired by Democratic Senator Bob Graham, found evidence in San Diego that an FBI informant had been friendly with two of the hijackers. Indeed, the informant had even rented a room to them. But the FBI insisted that the informant had known nothing about his friends' deadly plans and refused to let the committee talk to him. When Senator Graham handed an FBI agent a subpoena to give to the informant, the agent "leaned back from the subpoena as if it were radioactive." One agent told Graham that White House officials had ordered the FBI to snub the committee.[45]

Graham and his staff were even more alarmed by another discovery: that a Saudi government spy had funneled more than $40,000 to the two San Diego hijackers. In Graham's opinion, the hijackers had indeed benefited from a state sponsor, but not the one touted by the Bush administration. Instead, it was "our supposed friend and ally Saudi Arabia."[46] Graham's committee wrote twenty-eight pages on the possible links between the hijackers and some Saudi intelligence agents, but these pages were blacked out on the president's orders.[47]

Besides its reluctance to follow the leads to Saudi Arabia, the Bush administration refused to give the committee documents and generally "slow-walked and stonewalled" the investigation, in Senator John McCain's words.[48] Vice President Cheney encouraged the president to deny information to the committee, just as he had advised President Ford thirty years earlier during the Church Committee investigation.[49] Angered by the executive branch attempts to derail and discredit his committee, Senator Graham even suspected that the White House might have deliberately leaked secret information on National Security Agency intercepts to the press and then, in a diabolically clever move, blamed the leak on the committee. "I am not by nature a conspiracy theorist, but the fact that we were hit with this disclosure at the moment we began to make things uncomfortable for the Bush administration has stuck with me," Graham wrote later.[50]

As Graham's opponents dismissed the inquiry as a leak-prone, partisan witch hunt, the media "pounded" the committee with unfavorable coverage.[51] The 9/11 skeptics clearly needed someone more sympathetic than a Democratic senator with presidential ambitions to demand answers, someone who could dramatize the personal costs of the government's failure on 9/11 to protect its citizens.

As the committee's public hearings began in September 2002, the cameras focused on the first witness, a small woman with a frightened expression and a nervous twitch in her chin. Kristen Breitweiser looked like a suburban mother who had wandered inadvertently into a congressional hearing room, yet her role as the opening speaker was no accident. She had spent months filling two-inch binders with her research on 9/11's mysteries. And she was determined to get answers to her questions.

Breitweiser began by asking the committee members to "find in my voice the voices of all of the family members of the 3,000 victims of

September 11th." She would never know the precise details of how her husband, Ron, had died, but she knew his death had not been easy. Rescue workers had found part of his left arm at ground zero, with his wedding ring still on his finger, charred but intact. "I wear it on my right hand," Breitweiser said, fighting to hold back tears, "and it will remain there until the day I die."[52]

As audience members wept openly in sympathy, Breitweiser proceeded quickly to a list of questions she wanted the committee to answer: Why did FBI headquarters ignore the Phoenix memo? Why weren't FBI officials more interested in Moussaoui? Why didn't military jets shoot down the hijacked airplanes? Why wasn't the second tower evacuated after the first was hit? Most important, were the hijackers under surveillance before the attacks? In essence, she demanded to know what U.S. agents and elected officials knew, and when they knew it.[53]

The widows wanted to force the government to respond to those questions. In part, they wanted to find some meaning in their husbands' deaths and to believe that their loved ones had not died in vain. They also wanted to punish the U.S. government officials whose mistakes had contributed to the catastrophe. "We need people to be held accountable for their failures," Breitweiser explained to the investigating committee.[54]

Despite the media's interest in the widows and their questions, it soon became clear that the congressional investigators would not be able to answer them. As Republicans grew confident of victory in the 2002 elections, they knew that the inquiry would end soon. A Republican majority in Congress would shut down any real investigation of a Republican White House. Some Republicans on the investigating committee began to try to "run out the clock," in Graham's view, changing procedures and questioning staff reports, until a new chairman could take over.[55] The White House also obstructed the committee's work by refusing to declassify documents. Given these limits, the widows and other 9/11 family members became convinced that there was only one way to get answers to their questions: continue to pressure Congress and the president to appoint an independent 9/11 commission.

The four mothers from New Jersey began a feverish lobbying campaign on Capitol Hill. As single mothers of young children, their new public roles were not always easy. In between cheering at soccer games and helping with homework, they lobbied, testified, and dashed between New Jersey and Washington.

Although they were new to the game, the widows quickly grasped how to use their personal stories to force legislators and reporters to reopen the wound of 9/11 with another investigation. At a typical meeting with lawmakers, one Jersey Girl, Patty Casazza, would pass around pictures of company parties for Cantor Fitzgerald, the investment firm that employed her husband and more than six hundred other victims of September 11. "All of these men playing volleyball in the pool are dead," Casazza would say. "See these guys on the tennis court? They are all dead. And those dads playing basketball with their sons? Dead." After a long pause, Casazza would yield the floor to Breitweiser, who would follow up with a "laundry list" of demands from the victims' families.[56]

Moreover, the Jersey Girls were careful to present themselves as *female* victims, robbed of their husbands and providers and forced into single parenthood because of their government's failure to protect them. Breitweiser and her friends resisted any attempt to define them as anything but grieving widows and struggling single mothers. At one congressional hearing, Breitweiser bristled when she saw her nameplate identifying her as "Ms. Breitweiser." One of the other widows took out a marker and quickly added an "r" between the "M" and "s."[57]

Breitweiser and her friends consciously adopted the persona of the Jersey Girl, with all of its connotations of resourcefulness and independence. Tom Waits wrote the original "Jersey Girl," which became a hit for Bruce Springsteen in the 1980s, but the term long predated the song. It suggested a certain New Jersey working-class scrappiness and an affinity for straight talk, in contrast to snobbish Manhattanites. As a writer for *Newsweek* said in one of the first references to the women by their nickname in the national press, the Jersey Girls were "feisty young widows" who had become "increasingly radicalized" by the Bush administration's failure to answer their questions.[58] The widows embraced the term because it conveyed the image they wanted: that of ordinary American women— "just four moms from New Jersey," they called themselves at first—who were speaking truth to power.[59] It was, of course, a carefully constructed and somewhat disingenuous image they chose to project; they were affluent, stay-at-home mothers before the attacks, not struggling working girls. But this image helped the women to attract more attention from the mainstream media, which in turn supported their campaign to pry loose more information from the government.

At first, to many lawmakers, these bereaved widows in their somber suits and pearls seemed far from threatening. But if a lawmaker refused to do the right thing—which, in the widows' view, meant voting for a 9/11 commission—these Jersey Girls would set their jaws and morph into hardened politicos. Breitweiser would inform the recalcitrant lawmaker that she had set up several media interviews to discuss his stand on the commission. "We'd be more than happy to share the fact that you are supporting us on this position," she would say. "If not, we'll make it abundantly clear to your constituents that national security is not a top priority for you."[60]

After Breitweiser's testimony before the investigating committee, the White House made a "complete 180-degree turnaround in a week's time," she remembered triumphantly, and the president agreed to an independent commission.[61] Conservative columnists, infuriated by the widows' refusal to follow the president's script, began a series of increasingly vitriolic attacks on the women, culminating with the judgment from the conservative pundit Ann Coulter that the Jersey Girls were "witches" and "harpies" who were enjoying their husbands' deaths.[62] Some suggested that the women were Democratic Party operatives—in effect, the agents of a partisan conspiracy against the president.[63] They were a cabal of soccer moms, in league with Democratic presidential candidate John Kerry and his minions.

By demanding answers to their questions, the Jersey Girls were challenging the official story of 9/11. Breitweiser realized that this was the White House's primary objection to an independent investigation. "What the White House wanted was control," she wrote, "control over a more sweeping and damning account of 9/11; they wanted to turn that factual account into a shortened, distilled, and less damning fairy tale."[64]

The feminist author Susan Faludi argues that the president's supporters were also outraged that the widows refused to play their assigned roles in what she calls a "compensatory gender narrative." They were supposed to be the "perfect virgins of grief," expressing gratitude to the federal government for keeping them safe. Instead, they accused government officials of failing to protect their husbands on 9/11 and their children in the future.[65]

Feminists certainly respected the widows' success at challenging Washington's male power brokers. The "girls" who objected to the term "Ms." became *Ms.* magazine's women of the year.[66]

WHEN THE JERSEY GIRLS began their fight for an investigation, they sometimes found it hard to persuade their fellow citizens that their president might intentionally lie or cover up the truth. But as Americans learned more about how their country came to be at war in Iraq, growing numbers began to find the notion of a Bush-Cheney conspiracy all too likely.

In the spring and summer of 2003, U.S. search teams hunted throughout Iraq for the all-important weapons of mass destruction. They found none. Once, the U.S. military heralded the discovery of two "mobile biological weapons labs"—"We found the weapons of mass destruction," the president said—but these turned out to be trailers packed with machinery to make hydrogen for weather balloons.[67]

The specialized search teams sent to find the weapons, led by David Kay and then by his successor, Charles Duelfer, concluded definitively that, contrary to administration claims, Iraq had *not* reconstituted its nuclear program and did not have any caches of chemical or biological weapons. "We were almost all wrong," Kay told Congress in January 2004.[68] (By "we," Kay meant U.S. government officials; it turned out that the UN inspectors, much derided by Cheney, had been almost all right.) The post–Gulf War sanctions and inspections had worked.

If there were no weapons of mass destruction, why had the Bush administration insisted that there were? Administration officials blamed the CIA for providing bad intelligence. But soon a series of insiders came forward with different stories, charging that the White House and the Pentagon had deliberately misused intelligence and misled the American people. The male experts joined the female amateurs in challenging the Bush administration's official narrative.

The first prominent insider to accuse the administration of lying would soon realize the consequences of challenging the Bush White House. In 2002 the CIA sent Joseph Wilson, a former ambassador who had served his country in hotspots around the world, to Niger to investigate charges that Iraq had tried to buy uranium there. Wilson was a logical choice: he had served in Niger before and had studied its uranium trade. His wife, Valerie Plame Wilson, worked as a covert operative for the CIA on weapons of mass destruction. After his week in Niger, Wilson told the CIA that the charges were baseless.

But as he listened to the president's State of the Union address in January 2003, Wilson was puzzled by the president's reference to Iraq's supposed quest for uranium in Africa. It must be a different African country, he decided; the president could not still be recycling the discredited Niger accusations. But when the war began, Wilson became convinced that the Bush administration was intentionally using false charges and faked documents to bolster its case for war.[69]

On July 6 Wilson fired the opening salvo in the former insiders' war on the administration. In an op-ed piece in the *New York Times* headlined "What I Didn't Find in Africa," Wilson described his trip to Niger and his findings. He charged that administration officials had "twisted" the intelligence on Iraq's nuclear weapons program "to exaggerate the Iraqi threat."[70]

Wilson's claims were potentially explosive: they could cause the American public to distrust the president and undercut support for the war. He was suggesting, in essence, a Bush administration conspiracy to "lie the country into war," as Franklin Roosevelt's critics had said about their president and Pearl Harbor. "It really comes down to the administration misrepresenting the facts on an issue that was a fundamental justification for going to war," Wilson told the *Washington Post*. "It begs the question, what else are they lying about?"[71] More than thirty years earlier, Donald Rumsfeld and Bob Haldeman had warned President Nixon about men like Wilson who challenged presidential authority. The words Haldeman had used to describe Daniel Ellsberg could also apply to Wilson. Just like Ellsberg, Wilson was showing the public that "you can't trust the government; you can't believe what they say ... and the president can be wrong."[72] That was not the message presidents wanted the public to hear.

Just as the Nixon administration had gone after Ellsberg, the Bush administration moved to attack Wilson. The president's top political adviser, Karl Rove, and the vice president's chief of staff, I. Lewis Libby, began calling reporters and denouncing Wilson as an attention seeker, a liar, and a beneficiary of nepotism. A week later, the *Chicago Sun-Times* columnist Robert Novak disclosed that Valerie Plame Wilson worked as a CIA officer and implied that she had arranged a junket to the poverty-stricken African nation for her husband. By publishing her name, Novak ruined Plame's career as a covert operative—and quite possibly endangered her life. In 2006 a federal jury convicted Libby of lying to investigators about the operation to discredit Wilson, but the president commuted his sentence. The whole saga—the leak, the lies, and Libby's escape from punishment—convinced more Americans that the administration held itself above the law.

In January 2004 another former insider joined Wilson and charged that the administration's deceptive claims were part of a pattern. Former treasury secretary Paul O'Neill revealed in *The Price of Loyalty* that Bush had been planning to attack Iraq from the first days of his administration, months before 9/11. "It was all about finding *a way to do it*," O'Neill said. "That was the tone of it. The President saying, 'Fine. Go find me a way to do this.'"[73]

Then the 9/11 Commission gave a public platform to the man who would become the most important critic of the Bush administration's version of 9/11—and of its justification for war. In March 2004 the former counterterrorism czar Richard Clarke gave blistering public testimony to the commission about the administration's failure to anticipate the attacks. Clarke's book, *Against All Enemies*, which came out one week before his testimony, painted a picture of an administration obsessed with Iraq and shockingly unconcerned with bin Laden, whom Paul Wolfowitz had dismissed as "this little terrorist in Afghanistan."[74]

Clarke aggressively promoted his version of 9/11 on the television news shows. In his book, sworn testimony, and media appearances, he portrayed an administration that willfully ignored its own intelligence experts. "On the issues that they cared about," he wrote, "they already knew the answers, it was received wisdom."[75] Like many conspiracy theorists, they refused to consider facts that did not support their preconceived ideas.

The 9/11 widows and other victims' families embraced Clarke as a rare truth-teller from a White House generally uninterested in discovering the truth. His public apology to the families—"Your government failed you ... and I failed you"—acknowledged, for the first time, that the government needed to apologize.[76]

In the two years following Clarke's testimony, other insiders came forward to charge that Bush administration officials, and especially the vice president, had "cherry-picked" intelligence to support their predetermined course for war. Paul Pillar, the CIA's top officer for the Middle East from 2000 to 2005, went public with his argument that the administration had "misused" intelligence "to justify a decision already made."[77] According to Pillar, White House officials had rejected any intelligence that failed to fit the case for war and exaggerated the significance of the questionable intelligence that supported it.

More forcefully, Lawrence Wilkerson, who had been Colin Powell's chief of staff, described his former boss's speech before the United Nations as "a hoax on the American people, the international community and the United Nations Security Council."[78] A Vietnam War veteran and former director of the Marine Corps War College, Wilkerson charged that Powell had been used by a "cabal" led by Cheney and Rumsfeld.[79]

Top-secret British documents supported Pillar's and Wilkerson's charges that Bush administration officials had conspired to deceive the American people about the case for war. Several memos from Prime Minister Tony Blair's government, known collectively as the Downing Street memos, were leaked to the London press in May 2005. In the most significant memo, the head of the British secret service told Blair in July 2002 that Bush was set on war and *"the intelligence and facts were being fixed around the policy."*[80]

In other words, the intelligence community did not mislead the White House, as Bush administration officials insisted; instead, administration officials intimidated and manipulated the intelligence community into supporting its deceptive case for war. This was a real conspiracy: a conspiracy to perpetrate a fraud on the American public by lying about the intelligence for war.[81]

As the public learned that government officials had lied about Saddam's weapons of mass destruction, the 9/11 Commission demolished the other pillar of Bush's justification for war: the alleged Saddam–bin Laden link. In June 2004 the commission stated definitively in a report that there was no "collaborative relationship" between Iraq and al Qaeda.[82] The president's own commission had disproved his conspiracy theory.

The percentage of Americans who believed that Saddam was involved in 9/11 began to fall, dropping from 69 percent before the release of the 9/11 Commission report to 22 percent afterward.[83] Even more striking, the numbers of Americans who believed that Bush deliberately lied about the case for war climbed sharply, from 31 percent in June 2003 to 53 percent in October 2005. Subsequent polls showed that a majority of Americans continued to believe for years that their president lied them into war.[84] And if he lied about WMDs and the Saddam–al Qaeda conspiracy on 9/11, what else did he lie about?

As it turned out, the White House did not have unlimited power to construct reality and to write contemporary history. With the official story of the attacks and the subsequent war under assault, the 9/11 skeptics began to respond with their own, revisionist histories of that traumatic day.

SOME FRINGE CONSPIRACISTS had begun telling alternative stories about 9/11 from the moment they tore themselves away from the televised images of carnage and switched on their computers to discuss the attacks with their virtual friends. Veteran conspiracy theorists of the far right had seen the fingerprints of the usual suspects on the attacks from the very beginning. The Ku Klux Klan leader David Duke argued that agents of Israel had either carried out the attacks or "at the very least they had prior knowledge"; the John Birch Society blamed communists, the "global power elite," and the forces of the New World Order.[85]

Over time, though, it was the left rather than the radical right that proved most influential in spreading alternative 9/11 conspiracy theories in the United States. The president's opponents on the left believed that Bush owed his presidency to the subversion of democracy in the 2000 election. Because five Supreme Court justices had "selected, not elected" him to his office when they decided to halt the recount of the ballots in Florida, he seemed illegitimate to his opponents from the beginning. Later, in the 2004 election, charges of fraud in Ohio convinced some Democrats that the Republicans would stop at nothing to keep power.[86] Like FDR's enemies after Pearl Harbor, some of Bush's critics were convinced that he was capable of anything, even the mass murder of his fellow citizens.

The antigovernment 9/11 conspiracy theorists fell into two major categories: those who believed that the Bush administration knew in advance about the attacks but decided not to stop them, and those who believed that the U.S. government actually carried out the attacks. These rival theories were known as LIHOP and MIHOP, for "let it happen on purpose" and "made it happen on purpose."

The LIHOP theories were more popular in the movement's early days, when the critics were isolated and unsure of themselves. In the LIHOP story of 9/11, bin Laden planned the attacks and the al Qaeda hijackers carried them out, but they could not have succeeded without protection from U.S. government officials, who ordered U.S. air defenses to "stand down" before and during the attacks. Congresswoman Cynthia McKinney, a Georgia Democrat, helped to publicize the LIHOP doubts in a widely reported interview on Pacifica Radio's *Democracy Now* in March 2002.

"What did this Administration know, and when did it know it about the events of September 11?" she asked, adapting Senator Howard Baker's famous question from Watergate to recent events. "Who else knew and why did they not warn the innocent people of New York who were needlessly murdered?"[87]

For most skeptics, though, LIHOP was unsatisfying. The supposed masterminds of LIHOP had successfully sabotaged the air defenses of what the theorists believed was an otherwise invincible military superpower. If the plotters were that good, would they leave anything to chance? Would they sit back and allow "Arabs in caves" to plan and execute the plot?[88]

The MIHOP theorists did not think so. They regarded the LIHOP believers as weak liberals, unable to accept the radical consequences of their inquiries. In the MIHOPpers' view, there was only one significant question, as the longtime Kennedy conspiracist Jim Marrs pointed out: "Whose conspiracy was it?"[89] There were many possible answers, including a Mossad MIHOP, an Illuminati MIHOP, a Peak Oil MIHOP, a New World Order MIHOP, and even an MJ-12 and the Aliens MIHOP.[90] There was an all-encompassing MIHOP perpetrated by a "rogue network of moles, patsies, and a commando cell in the privatized intelligence services, backed by corrupt political and corporate media elites."[91] The most popular version, though, was the Bush-Cheney MIHOP.

The alternative theorists rejected the label "conspiracy theorist." As one 9/11 Web site explained, activists believed that the term was "an attempt to discredit all those who seek the truth on the events of 9/11 and to intimidate everyone who questions the official account."[92] They preferred "conspiracy factualist" or "9/11 truth activist" or the more concise "truther," and they considered themselves part of the "9/11 Truth Movement."

The first major 9/11 Truth book appeared in France just six months after the attack. *L'Effroyable Imposture,* by the French philosopher Thierry Meyssan, argued for a Bush-Cheney MIHOP, charging that the Bush administration used bin Laden as its agent in the attacks to justify repression at home, expansion overseas, and an oil pipeline in Afghanistan. In his instant best-seller, Meyssan claimed that secret agents on the ground used remote control to pilot the planes that hit the World Trade Center, and that a missile, not a plane, hit the Pentagon.[93]

As other authors joined Meyssan in charging conspiracy, some skeptics began forming grassroots groups to challenge the official narrative.

In September 2002 a group of researchers from around the country met in New York City to form the 9/11 Truth Alliance. These researchers created an email discussion list, a newsletter, and an organizing committee. They traded theories in conference calls.[94] Over the next few years, local groups of 9/11 researchers sprouted in large cities and small communities around the nation. Activists in Davis, California, for example, could attend monthly meetings, view screenings of 9/11 films, participate in Truth Action demonstrations by holding signs at major traffic intersections, and pick up literature and DVDs at a table at the local farmers' market.[95]

Although the grassroots groups inspired some activists, the real medium for the truth movement's message was the Internet. As 9/11 activists began to spin their theories, the Internet was moving into its second phase, sometimes called Web 2.0. New software tools made it easier for people to create their own content: to write blogs, make movies, and "create citizen media."[96] This user-generated content leveled the playing field for alternative conspiracy theorists. In the age of digital democracy, anyone with access to the Web could post theories or treatises.

The most important of the 9/11 Web sites first appeared in May 2002, as the mainstream media began revealing inconsistencies in the official story of 9/11. "Paul Thompson," a pseudonymous recent Stanford graduate in San Francisco, created the Complete 9/11 Timeline (complete911timeline .org). A hyperlinked, annotated list of thousands of 9/11 actors and events, the site allowed researchers to search and access news stories from all over the world about the attacks. It soon became an essential tool for 9/11 researchers.

The History Commons, a group dedicated to allowing "people at the grassroots level to assume a dominant role in public and private sector oversight," sponsored Thompson's Web site. The group, and some visitors to the Web site, believed that the "corporate media" had abandoned their role as government watchdogs, so it was incumbent upon citizens to take on this duty themselves.[97] By reading the entries in the time line and clicking on the links, researchers could construct a narrative different from the one produced by the government. Like the Bush administration, they were also free to cherry-pick their evidence to support a predetermined theory.

Now people all over the world could take disparate parts of the 9/11 story and make their own sense of them. They could even challenge government officials in public forums and then post visual records of these confrontations on the Internet.[98] Skeptics did not need a Harry Elmer Barnes, or a *Chicago Tribune*, or a Frank Church, or even an Oliver Stone to write a counternarrative for them: the Internet, for better and for worse, had democratized government information. By linking to one another's sites, they could help each other find the truth.

They could also help each other "see" the truth. In a revolutionary contribution to the art of spreading alternative conspiracy theories, the 9/11 researchers crafted visual arguments with a twenty-first-century tool: the YouTube documentary. Produced on cheap laptops and stuffed full of still images and film scrounged from the Internet, these digital movies could help transform unknown theorists into the Jim Garrison or John T. Flynn of their day. The most influential piece of propaganda for 9/11 conspiracists was not a book or a Web site but a documentary produced by a twenty-two-year-old film school reject on his Compaq Presario. Dylan Avery of Oneonta, New York, made *Loose Change* with two of his friends for $2,000 and uploaded it onto the Internet. Within eighteen months of its debut in April 2005, more than ten million people worldwide had watched its compelling visuals and shocking story line.[99]

Like many 9/11 documentaries, *Loose Change* drew much of its power from the horrifying images of the attacks: the terrified faces of the rescue workers running from the crumbling skyscrapers, the United Airlines jet slicing into the South Tower, and the flames licking the Pentagon's smoldering rubble. Just as watching the Zapruder film seemed to thrill many JFK "assassinologists," 9/11 conspiracy documentaries gave viewers the opportunity to dwell on images of death and destruction without guilt.

Avery's voiceover knitted together the most outrageous 9/11 theories to suggest a monstrous conspiracy. After all, enough "loose change" can add up to real money. This conspiracy might have included explosives experts, who rigged the towers for demolition; U.S. military officers, who launched a missile at the Pentagon; and shadowy agents at the Cleveland airport, who ushered the as yet unharmed passengers of United 93 (which did not crash in Pennsylvania) into a NASA research center. To spread the word, Avery encouraged his fans to burn DVDs of his film and distribute them for free.[100]

Loose Change started a brushfire of enthusiasm for alternative 9/11 theories, especially among young adults who loved its hip soundtrack and its implicit message of rebelling against authority. But many 9/11 activists despised its indiscriminate embrace of every conceivable 9/11 plot. Some alternative theorists created Web pages debunking both the "official story" and *Loose Change* at the same time.[101] These theorists hated the media's tendency to lump all the skeptics together as an undifferentiated army that included "no-planers" along with the more "mainstream" researchers.[102]

The 9/11 truth movement was indeed diverse. A visitor to Thompson's time line Web site could click on thousands of links to construct dozens of potential stories of 9/11. The loose change of 9/11 questions could add up to a massive plot, or to nothing at all. In this postmodern moment for conspiracy theories, individuals could pick and choose the facts to construct a 9/11 story to support their own beliefs. Contrary to the Bush administration official in the Suskind article, *Loose Change* demonstrated that you did not need to be an empire to create your own reality.

Some researchers, such as Senator Graham, pointed to tantalizing hints of Saudi involvement. Others highlighted a story from India claiming that an agent of the Pakistani intelligence service wired money to one of the hijackers just days before the attack.[103] These stories suggested additional conspirators in the hijacking plot but did not necessarily question the visual or physical evidence of the attacks.

Other truthers were very suspicious of the buildings' collapse. Like the Kennedy assassination conspiracy theorists, some 9/11 skeptics immersed themselves in the physical evidence of the alleged conspiracy. As they watched the towers crumble into dust on their computer screens, they were struck by several apparent "oddities": Why did the towers fall so fast and so symmetrically, into their own "footprints"? If jet fuel burns at 1,500 degrees Fahrenheit and steel melts at 2,800 degrees, why did they fall at all? Many in the truth movement focused on the mysterious collapse of a third building, World Trade Center 7, which abutted the twin towers and contained the offices of several government agencies, including the CIA. The falling debris from the twin towers damaged WTC 7 severely and ignited raging fires that the New York Fire Department chose not to fight. But the skeptics found this the most significant mystery of all: How could a forty-seven-story building collapse simply because of fire? Did "they" blow it up to conceal the financial evidence of their crimes, or perhaps the control panels for the explosions in the twin towers?

The government engaged a "Who's Who of experts" to try to answer the question of why the towers fell.[104] Two government agencies, the Federal

Emergency Management Administration and the National Institute of Standards and Technology, issued reports on the twin towers' collapse; the NIST study alone filled more than ten thousand pages.[105] The airplane crashes, combined with the fires, weakened the steel columns until they buckled, the government studies concluded. But the skeptics dismissed those studies as deliberately misleading. They found the government's long delay in issuing a definitive report on WTC 7 as another sign of conspiracy. The skeptics also rejected an extensive study by writers for the magazine *Popular Mechanics* that supported the government's account.[106]

While they regarded the government's experts with disdain, the 9/11 theorists relied on the handful of their own experts who supported their cause. "I have scientists on my side," boasted Avery of *Loose Change*.[107] On the question of the towers' alleged demolition, for example, the alternative theorists cited studies by the movement's favorite physicist, Steven E. Jones, who suggested that World Trade Center 7 and the towers were brought down by explosives, not by damage from crashes and fires.[108] In 2007, when the meltdown of a section of a California highway following a fiery truck crash seemed to undermine Jones's theories, some 9/11 skeptics dismissed the crash as a government plot designed to discredit the movement.[109]

The controlled-demolition theory envisioned a huge cast of characters, including the president and vice president, the CIA, the FBI, the Federal Aviation Administration, the Air Force, Arab "patsies," and dozens of workers crawling through the Trade Center towers to place explosives. It was much more extensive than, say, shooting a president in a motorcade or concealing intelligence about an impending Japanese attack on the Pacific Fleet.

But the controlled-demolition theorists did not try to divine the details of the plot. For the most part, they contented themselves with pointing out the weaknesses of the official story rather than attempting to construct a detailed narrative of an alternative plot. "One must not be distracted by the *how* of an event but instead should focus on the *who* and the *why*," said Jim Marrs.[110] To answer these questions, they turned to the history of "state-sponsored false flag terrorism." And here they found an astounding gift in the U.S. National Archives, courtesy of the John F. Kennedy Assassination Review Board and, indirectly, the director Oliver Stone. It was the perfect historical precedent for their theories.

Back in the early 1990s, after the success of Stone's *JFK*, Congress created the Assassination Review Board, which was charged with reviewing and declassifying the official record of the Kennedy assassination. The board broadly defined this record to include any documents that could "enhance the historical understanding" of the assassination, even if they did not discuss the event itself.[111] The board released thirty-three thousand relevant documents, including one memo from the Joint Chiefs of Staff to Defense Secretary Robert McNamara in 1962, in which the chiefs proposed "Operation Northwoods."

Northwoods was an alarming example of government madness from the height of the cold war. In March 1962, as American leaders worried about the potential dangers presented by Fidel Castro, the U.S. Joint Chiefs proposed launching terrorist attacks against their own people and blaming them on Castro. The pseudo-Cuban terrorists would shoot down an airliner, set off bombs in major U.S. cities, sink an American ship, and start "riots" outside the Guantánamo naval base. Kennedy vetoed the proposal.[112]

In the Northwoods plan, Kennedy's joint chiefs saw themselves as history's actors. Like the unnamed Bush administration official in Suskind's famous article, they planned to create their own reality. In the 1962 case, this meant a "communist" attack on a plane filled with "passengers."[113]

The plan stayed buried until 1997, when the review board quietly declassified it. In 1998, the National Security Archive, a private research institution, put the Northwoods memos on the Internet. Three years later, and just months before the September 11 attacks, the best-selling author James Bamford helped to publicize Northwoods by featuring it in his book on the National Security Agency, *Body of Secrets*.[114]

Many 9/11 conspiracists embraced the Northwoods memos as unassailable historical proof that their theories of U.S. government-sponsored terrorism were horrifyingly plausible. Above all, the Northwoods documents convinced conspiracists that the Truth Was Out There: like Agent Mulder of *The X-Files*, they could discover memos explicitly describing evil government plots in, of all places, the National Archives.[115] Evidence for official conspiracies lay hidden within the most secret files of the government. It was up to the Mulders and Scullys of America, or, in this case, the Jim Marrses and the Paul Thompsons, to find it.

Once the skeptics proved to their satisfaction that there were historical precedents for a 9/11-style conspiracy, they moved to their next question:

Who benefited from 9/11? And, here, of course, the answer was obvious: the Bush-Cheney White House.

Bush administration officials seemed to get everything they wanted after 9/11: a concentration of power in the executive, a war to topple Saddam, and the opportunity to monitor and intimidate their critics. This seemed to be especially true for Cheney, who was the "maestro" of the plot, in the view of some conspiracists.[116] Since his days in the Ford administration, Cheney had worked to expand presidential power and restore the imperial presidency. Beginning with his struggle against the Church Committee, he lobbied for more government secrecy and surveillance of dissenters. During the Iran-contra scandal, he signaled his disdain for checks on presidential power. Most notably, his fellow neoconservatives at the Project for a New American Century called for Saddam's ouster and for a newly aggressive U.S. foreign policy, though they worried that the American people might not support these goals unless there was a "new Pearl Harbor."

As if on cue, the new Pearl Harbor occurred on 9/11 and gave Cheney the opportunity to accomplish all of these goals.[117] After the attacks, the Bush administration reclassified documents, refused to release new government documents as required by the Freedom of Information Act, expanded governmental surveillance powers with the USA Patriot Act, and brushed aside the only meaningful reform to come out of the Church Committee, the Foreign Intelligence Surveillance Act's requirement for warrants for national security wiretaps on American citizens. The Bush White House took the opportunity to rehabilitate Iran-contra figures, even appointing John Poindexter, a convicted felon, head of the Defense Department's Total Information Awareness Office. The terrorist attacks legitimized a president whom many saw as illegitimate; they led to a war that achieved the neoconservatives' foreign policy goals; and they ensured Bush's reelection.

Some leftist intellectuals looked at this pattern and declared that Cheney and Bush had "hijacked catastrophe" to achieve their goals.[118] In a sense, they got lucky. But the 9/11 alternative conspiracy theorists accused them of much more. To many skeptics, these facts led to an obvious conclusion: the country was lied into war by a cabal of neocons. They did not just get lucky on 9/11: they made their own luck. The "cabal of zealots" denounced by the majority in the Iran-contra report were back in power, and this time they had conspired to murder their own people.

By 2006, alternative 9/11 theories had entered the American mainstream. Celebrities such as the actor Charlie Sheen and the talk show host Rosie O'Donnell helped to spread the alternative theories and persuade many Americans to consider them. On the daytime television talk show *The View*, hosted by women and aimed at a largely female audience, O'Donnell got into a highly publicized fight with the show's resident conservative, Elisabeth Hasselbeck, about 9/11's unanswered questions. In an unusually political discussion for a television talk show, O'Donnell said that it was "beyond ignorant" for someone to claim that WTC 7 collapsed because of fire. Hasselbeck rejected O'Donnell's theory as "the unthinkable."[119]

But millions of Americans were thinking about it. The first national poll on alternative 9/11 conspiracies, conducted by Scripps Howard News Service in the summer of 2006, found that 36 percent of Americans believed that Bush administration officials either helped the terrorists or consciously took no action to stop them. Sixteen percent embraced the most extreme theory: that explosives, not airliners, brought down the towers. Moreover, a *majority* of Americans ages eighteen to twenty-nine had joined the LIHOP or MIHOP camps.[120] For these young Americans, 9/11 was their Dallas: it fascinated them, it mystified them, and it explained everything. "This is our Kennedy assassination," said Korey Rowe, the twenty-three-year-old producer of *Loose Change*.[121]

THE JERSEY GIRLS were among those who had begun to wonder about the extent of their government's prior knowledge of the 9/11 plot. Ironically, the investigation for which they had fought so hard, conducted by the 9/11 Commission, only intensified their doubts. The commission failed to answer many of the families' questions, especially about the two hijackers who lived in San Diego with the FBI informant. Was the government trying to cover up links between the hijackers and Saudi or Pakistani intelligence? The families were also furious that the commission stopped short of blaming any U.S. government official for the tragedy. Despite the scale of the catastrophe, CIA Director George Tenet, FBI Director Robert Mueller, and National Security Adviser Condoleezza Rice all kept their jobs. Tenet, who presided over the worst intelligence disaster in U.S. history, even received the Presidential Medal of Freedom, the nation's highest award for civilians.

The Jersey Girls did not advocate a single alternative conspiracy theory. Breitweiser focused on the mysteries surrounding a Pentagon operation called "Able Danger," which allegedly identified four of the hijackers years before the attacks but was shut down by the Bush administration.[122] The other three Jersey Girls appeared in a 9/11 documentary suggesting the U.S. military deliberately allowed al Qaeda leaders to escape to Pakistan during the battle of Tora Bora in late 2001.[123] Mostly, though, the widows were furious that their government did not seem to want to learn the truth about 9/11—because the truth would not serve its interests.

Early on, the Jersey Girls and other skeptics had seen worrisome signs that President Bush seemed determined to control the course of the 9/11 Commission. The White House frequently refused to let the commission see critical documents, or allowed only selected commissioners to review them. Former Democratic senator Max Cleland, the most aggressive questioner on the panel, resigned from the commission, later explaining that he knew it "was ultimately going to be a sham."[124] Throughout the inquiry, the commission chair and vice chair, former New Jersey governor Tom Kean and former Indiana congressman Lee Hamilton, made it clear that they did not want the final report to "point fingers."[125] But, as one 9/11 family member said, the families thought that the government "should point fingers" and fire those responsible for the disaster.[126]

The 9/11 commissioners' choice for staff director seemed to confirm their lack of interest in an aggressive inquiry. As the lead investigator, the historian and political scientist Philip Zelikow helped determine the questions that the commissioners tried to answer—and those they should avoid. Yet Zelikow was not a disinterested party: he had served on President Bush's transition team and his foreign intelligence advisory board. A personal friend of Rice, he had written a book with her.[127] He had also written a national security strategy paper on preemptive war that the administration used to justify its invasion of Iraq.[128]

Throughout the investigation, some commissioners and staff members viewed Zelikow as a Bush administration "plant" or "mole" who was secretly channeling information to White House officials. Some staff members even believed that Zelikow was trying to rewrite commission reports to imply a link between Iraq and al Qaeda. When he began receiving phone calls from Karl Rove, speculation about his White House contacts started to "spread wildly through the commission," according to the reporter Philip Shenon.[129] This speculation eventually reached the Jersey Girls.

Because Zelikow had authority over the commission's eighty staff members, the story "told by the 9/11 commission became the story that Zelikow wanted to tell," Breitweiser complained. It was also the story that the Bush administration wanted to tell. For his part, Zelikow resented the 9/11 widows' suggestions that he could not direct an unbiased investigation because of his previous links to the Bush administration. "That's right, Kristen," he exploded once at Breitweiser. "Everything is connected. The hip bone is connected to the thigh bone is connected to the knee bone is connected to the ankle bone. It is all connected!"[130]

Zelikow angrily insisted that his connections to Bush did not suggest that he was part of a conspiracy to limit the investigation. Yet the president and his aides had repeatedly implied that Saddam Hussein's "contacts" and "connections" with al Qaeda meant that Iraq was somehow responsible for 9/11.[131] When independent investigators proved that those connections did not exist, the widows considered other plots. As before in U.S. history, official conspiracism helped to breed alternative conspiracy theories. Perhaps, as Breitweiser suggested, the list of 9/11 conspirators was "a bit more lengthy and all-inclusive than anyone might have imagined."[132] Perhaps it even included the official conspiracy theorists themselves.

Conclusion

IN JUNE 2006, about five hundred members of the 9/11 Truth movement gathered in Chicago to listen to lectures and panel discussions on the unanswered questions of the September 11 attacks. The *New York Times* described the group as a collection of "professors, chain-saw operators, mothers, engineers, activists, used-book sellers, pizza deliverymen, college students, a former fringe candidate for United States Senate, and a long-haired fellow named hummux (pronounced who-mook) who, on and off, lived in a cave for 15 years." The *Times* explained that friends and family members of the "truthers" thought that they might be "completely nuts." It was clear that the reporter shared this view.[1]

American scholars, public officials, and journalists frequently use the metaphor of illness when they discuss alternative conspiracy theorists. The experts see the conspiracist worldview as a pathology, a form of disease afflicting the body politic. In their view, the conspiracists suffer from paranoia, as Richard Hofstadter said, or from a kind of social leprosy, in the view of the *Times*. Their illness, for most observers, casts them to the margins of our culture.

But by stopping at diagnosis and finger-pointing, these analysts of conspiracy theories miss an opportunity to understand the sources of the illness. Most important, their attempts to contain the disease tend to exacerbate rather than alleviate it. To find a cure, we need to understand why conspiracy theories are endemic to American democracy, how they become epidemic, and which environments allow them to thrive. And here we must turn from psychology to political history.

From World War I to the present, U.S. government actions have helped to create these conspiracy theories in three ways. First, officials often promoted conspiracy theories of their own. From Woodrow Wilson to George W. Bush, they argued that sinister powers were pouring the "poison of disloyalty" into our national arteries, or that enemies were plotting to bring "a day of horror like none we have ever known." To combat this evil, the official conspiracy theorists argued, citizens must give more power to their government. Often, though, Americans responded by rejecting these officials' self-interested arguments while embracing their conspiracist view of history. The citizens agreed that there was a plot, but they identified different villains.

Second, government officials provided fodder for conspiracism by using their powers to plot—and to conceal—real conspiracies. Operation Northwoods, MKULTRA, and the arms-for-hostages trades were real conspiracies against democracy and individual rights. When U.S. government agents dropped LSD into the drinks of ordinary citizens or offered a suitcase full of cash to mafia gunmen to turn their sights on Fidel Castro, they made the most outrageous conspiracy theories seem plausible.

Third, public officials have fed citizens' antigovernment paranoia by actively suppressing alternative views. The government agents who smashed the printing plates of Charles Lindbergh's books or put the tape recorder under Martin Luther King Jr.'s bed were trying to control dissidents and maintain trust in the U.S. government. But exposure of their actions only intensified the public's fears. The story of the dynamic relationship between these conspiracy theorists, the official and the alternative, is a tragedy of American democracy.

In the case of 9/11, the Bush administration officials' response to the terror attacks followed the model established in World War I and perpetuated and refined through the cold war. They promoted conspiracy theories (there were "a number of contacts"). They plotted conspiracies (the "intelligence and facts were being fixed around the policy"). They expanded executive power, repressed dissent, and lied and covered up the truth of what they had done. All of these actions worsened rather than allayed the American public's distrust of its government.

The response of U.S. citizens to the Bush administration's handling of the 9/11 attacks was also predictable: Americans demanded the right to investigate and write an alternative history. "To me," said Father Frank Morales, a leader of New York 9/11 Truth, "this is about history. History and truth, the nature of truth in a not particularly truthful age." Jersey Girl Lorie Van Auken agreed that the "conspiracy people," whom she initially tried to avoid, were on a distinctly American quest: "If you ask me, they're just Americans, looking for the truth, which is supposed to be our right."[2] But is Van Auken correct? Do Americans have a "right" to the truth from their government?

Americans have always believed that each citizen has as much right to discover and assert the truth as do government authorities. For many citizens, living throughout this nation's history, this search has become the noblest cause of their lives—nothing less than a quest to expose the worst crimes in American history and, in the process, save the country. Without their efforts, they thought, the republic would perish. As Jim Garrison explained, "There is no way to survive if we do not bring out the truth."[3] Moreover, conspiracy theorists believed that the stakes got higher with each supposed government atrocity. One conspiracist Web site describes the alleged deceptions at Pearl Harbor as the "mother of all conspiracies (at least until 9/11)."[4]

In some ways, these citizen researchers do help to keep American democracy healthy and inform the public debate. In Sylvia Meagher's living room, in Gary Webb's tiny newspaper bureau, in congressional hearing rooms from the 1930s to the present, and even on Hollywood soundstages, skeptics demanded more information from their government. As a result, they helped to uncover the nation's history. Oliver Stone's *JFK* proposed some absurd theories, but it prompted Congress to demand the release of thousands of documents related to the Kennedy assassination. Without Stone, there would be no Operation Northwoods documents on the Internet. Maybe, as Webb Hubbell discovered, we cannot know with complete certainty who killed JFK, but thanks to the Dealey Plaza Irregulars, we can find out who tried to kill Castro, and how.

In this sense, conspiracy theories can constrain increasingly centralized executive power. The framers of the U.S. Constitution were afraid to give too much authority to the presidency; that's why they created checks and balances within the system. But these countervailing powers have been weakened over time. In the early twenty-first century, Americans discovered that the mainstream media were often reluctant to challenge executive secrecy and question presidential narratives. Employed by a shrinking number of media outlets, afraid of being labeled "conspiracy theorists" and thus cut off by their official sources, reporters often serve as stenographers to power. By calling attention to these failings, alternative conspiracy theorists can play a useful role by demanding more transparency in the U.S. government. Conspiracists, at their best, have inserted themselves into the system of checks and balances.

Yet the costs of conspiracy theories far outweigh their benefits. Too often, conspiracists press their analysis beyond the realms of facts and logic and in doing so inject toxins into the public discourse. In the 9/11 case, both types of conspiracists, the official and the alternative, constructed narratives about an event, and then constructed ever more elaborate justifications for believing in those stories. This was not so much a leap from the undeniable to the unbelievable, as Richard Hofstadter said, as a slow march toward self-delusion (and the deliberate deluding of others). Conspiracists can sometimes be like children who tell lies and must make up greater and more detailed lies when they fear discovery. Dick Cheney spoke of a "contact" that was "pretty well confirmed," which then became a "fact," which ultimately became a "number" of contacts. The invasion of Iraq flowed from this kind of tortured reasoning. Other theorists often followed a similar trail of logic. They started from the undeniable fact that Franklin Roosevelt or Lyndon Johnson or George W. Bush did not want a real investigation into a national tragedy. Then they moved, step by step, down the path of supposition until they were convinced that the president did not want to investigate a murder because he was, in fact, the murderer.

Alternative conspiracy theorists can sometimes hinder the process of historical discovery by refusing to change their position when the facts they discover undercut their favorite theories. As a result of the Kennedy researchers' efforts, for example, historians have learned of conspiracies and cover-ups in the Kennedy and Johnson administrations, but not the ones the critics usually emphasize. The conspiracists never propose the possibility, more likely on the basis of the evidence, that it was Kennedy's staunch *anti*communism that got him killed. Instead, in their view, he was the one person standing up to the evil plots of the military-industrial complex. Nor do they ever suggest that it was Johnson's more appealing qualities, such as his concern about nuclear war, that prompted him to shut down a real investigation of the assassination.

Despite their rhetoric about finding the "truth," the alternative theorists often tend to be ideologues who force every piece of evidence to fit their preconceived theses. When professional historians or pundits point out the errors in their logic, the conspiracists dismiss their critics as "gatekeepers" with a vested interest in restricting the flow of information.[5] Some of these anticonspiracists have discovered that the alternative theorists could be just as zealous as the "cabal" they were trying to expose.[6]

Antigovernment conspiracists also sometimes concentrate on obscure physical details of the alleged conspiracy and miss more significant issues. The 9/11 "truthers," for example, have spent a lot of energy trying to unravel a supposed controlled-demolition plot that, in the end, seems absurdly convoluted. Some analysts have noted that the 9/11 researchers could perhaps do more to help the republic by focusing on current events. "The main question I have about the Sept. 11 conspiracy is—why bother?" wrote the columnist Jon Carroll. "We have a conspiracy to undermine the Constitution of the United States. It's in the papers; it requires no knowledge of engineering."[7] In other words, the Bush administration was not even trying to conceal its effort to amass unprecedented authority in the executive branch. Yet the conspiracy theorists were more interested in making accusations and identifying the government as irredeemably evil than enacting reforms, which fundamentally undercuts the salutary effects of their questioning and research.

Finally, conspiracy theorists often fail to distinguish between those who are hiding the truth and those who are trying to uncover it. Again and again, they decide that the public officials or researchers who are questioning the government are actually in league with the conspirators, plotting to distract and mislead the truth seekers. In February 2008, the *Dallas Morning News* asked for the public's participation in interpreting a cache of Kennedy assassination documents recently discovered in a safe at the Dallas district attorney's office. The newspaper's editors scanned all the documents, put them on the Internet, and asked readers to tell them what they meant: "Take a look, and let us know if you see something interesting."[8] But some conspiracy theorists found this experiment in participatory journalism to be more evidence of a plot. "What is going on with this sudden public involvement?" one reader asked. "Secret documents are found and now the public is allowed to riffle through them all we want. What are we being distracted from now?"[9]

Despite these complications, there are possible treatments. If official conspiracies are the cause of the disease of conspiracism, then transparency surely is the cure. There's an old saying that the cure for the ills of democracy is more democracy. As the philosopher John Dewey explained, this phrase signals the necessity of returning to the idea of democracy, "of clarifying and deepening our apprehension of it, and of employing our sense of its meaning to criticize and remake its political manifestations."[10]

Of course, the U.S. government can never be completely open, for a modern state needs to keep some secrets to survive. Franklin Roosevelt, for example, could not have allowed a real investigation of Pearl Harbor without revealing to the Japanese that the Americans had broken some of their codes. Moreover, as the *Dallas Morning News* case shows, total transparency will not calm all fears, as some skeptics will never believe that government officials or the media are disclosing everything they know.

But excessive secrecy breeds distrust, which can make it impossible for democracy to flourish. By contrast, transparency causes government officials to hesitate before they engage in real conspiracies—and, at the same time, restores Americans' trust in their government. Opening the government to public scrutiny would have helped to avoid many of the most corrosive conspiracy theories of the twentieth century. If Woodrow Wilson and Franklin Roosevelt had informed the public about their growing conviction that the United States would soon join the world wars, they would have deprived their critics of one of the best arguments against them: that they "lied" the country into war. Similarly, if George W. Bush and his advisers had not manipulated and misled the American public before the invasion of Iraq, they would have avoided many of the worst conspiracy theories about 9/11. Thanks to the American tradition of openness, official conspiracies nearly always come to light, and when they do they undermine the careers and the power of the conspirators. As Richard Nixon, one of the preeminent conspiracy theorists of the twentieth century, said in his farewell address, "Always remember others may hate you, but those who hate you don't win unless you hate them, and then you destroy yourself."[11]

Nixon did not understand the irony of his words, and the extent to which his own hatred and fear had led to his downfall. His failure to grasp the consequences of his secret actions was not unusual. Government officials know that secrecy is power, and most want to maintain that power, no matter how thoroughly those secrets contribute to social and institutional pathologies by degrading democracy, promoting public cynicism, and ultimately harming their own reputations. When a reporter asked Earl Warren if his commission would release the testimony from its investigation of John F. Kennedy's death, he responded in a way that assassination researchers found chilling. "Yes, there will come a time," he said. "But it might not be in your lifetime."[12] A generation of conspiracy theories spread from this one germ, from this assumption that the American people could not be trusted with the truth.

When citizens such as Lori Van Auken cannot trust their government to tell the truth, when they are convinced that public officials routinely conspire, lie, and conceal their crimes, they become more susceptible to that dread disease, conspiracism. They become less likely to trust the government to do anything: to conduct fair elections, say, or spend their tax money, or protect their children or their planet. The result is a profoundly weakened polity, with fewer citizens voting and more problems left unaddressed for a future generation that is even more cynical about the possibility of reforms.[13]

If Americans want to prevent conspiracy theories from spreading, they need public officials and journalists who challenge and demand proof of the executive branch's version of history. They need strong oversight laws such as the Foreign Intelligence Surveillance Act, which was passed in the wake of the Church Committee hearings but gutted by the Bush administration. They require watchdogs who can question the false narratives without replacing them with baseless rumors of their own. Above all, Americans must hold their government accountable. In some cases, conspiracy theories are a way of accomplishing this. In other cases, though, they become another barrier separating the people from the truth, obscuring more than they reveal.

Citizens of a democracy must be wary of official and alternative conspiracists alike, demanding proof for the theories. Yet Americans should be most skeptical of official theorists, because the most dangerous conspiracies and conspiracy theories flow from the center of American government, not from the margins of society.

Since the First World War, officials of the U.S. government have encouraged conspiracy theories, sometimes inadvertently, sometimes intentionally.

They have engaged in conspiracies and used the cloak of national security to hide their actions from the American people. With cool calculation, they have promoted official conspiracy theories, sometimes demonstrably false ones, for their own purposes. They have assaulted civil liberties by spying on their domestic enemies. If antigovernment conspiracy theorists get the details wrong—and they often do—they get the basic issue right: it is the secret actions of the government that are the real enemies of democracy.

Notes

INTRODUCTION

1. Thomas Hargrove and Guido H. Stempel III, "Anti-Government Anger Spurs 9/11 Conspiracy Belief," Scripps Howard News Service, August 2, 2006, available at http://newspolls.org/story.php?story_id=55, viewed February 2, 2008.

2. Chairman, Joint Chiefs of Staff, "Justification for US Military Intervention in Cuba," March 13, 1962, cover memo and appendixes, available at http://www.gwu.edu/~nsarchiv/news/20010430/. For analysis of Northwoods, see Bamford, *Body of Secrets*, 82–91.

3. Joint Chiefs of Staff, "Justification for US Military Intervention in Cuba."

4. Memo by General Lansdale, "Meeting with the President, 16 March 1962," available at http://www.gwu.edu/~nsarchiv/bayofpigs/press3.html, viewed March 20, 2008.

5. See *Loose Change*, directed by Dylan Avery, at http://video.google.com/videoplay?docid=7866929448192753501, viewed March 20, 2008.

6. Tarpley, *9/11 Synthetic Terror*, 99.

7. Daniele Ganser, "The 'Strategy of Tension' in the Cold War Period," in Griffin and Scott, *9/11 and American Empire*, 99.

8. For the best surveys of conspiracy theory in U.S. history, see Hofstadter, *Paranoid Style*; Davis, *Slave Power Conspiracy* and *Fear of Conspiracy*; D. H. Bennett, *Party of Fear*; Goldberg, *Enemies Within*; Rogin, *Ronald Reagan, the Movie*.

9. Hofstadter, *Paranoid Style*.

10. Davis, *Fear of Conspiracy*, xiii.

11. For an interesting discussion of how Hoover effectively became the nation's internal security minister, see Frank Donner, "Hoover's Legacy," *Nation*, June 1, 1974.

12. On conspiracy theories as narratives, see Fenster, *Conspiracy Theories*. See also Jameson, "Cognitive Mapping"; Knight, *Conspiracy Culture*. On narrative, see H. White, *Content of the Form*.

13. Didion, *White Album*, 11.

14. Hagedorn, *Savage Peace*, 65–66.

15. For discussions of the "merchants of death" theories about World War I, see M. W. Coulter, *Senate Munitions Inquiry*; Wiltz, *In Search of Peace*. Some important refutations of Pearl Harbor conspiracy theories include Alvin D. Coox, "Repulsing the Pearl Harbor Revisionists: The State of Present Literature on the Debacle," *Military Affairs* 50, no. 1 (January 1985): 29–31; John Zimmerman, "Pearl Harbor Revisionism: Robert Stinnett's *Day of Deceit*," *Intelligence and National Security* 17, no. 2 (Summer 2002): 127–46; Stephen Budiansky, "Closing the Book on Pearl Harbor," *Cryptologia* 24, no. 2 (April 2000): 119–30; Philip H. Jacobsen, "A Cryptologic Veteran's Analysis of 'Day of Deceit,'" *Cryptologia* 24, no. 2 (April 2000): 110–18. On communist spies and McCarthyism, see Sibley, *Red Spies in America*; Schrecker, *Many Are the Crimes*; Haynes and Klehr, *Venona*. The most complete refutation of JFK conspiracy theories is Bugliosi, *Reclaiming History*. On Nixon's crimes, see Kutler, *Abuse of Power* and *The Wars of Watergate*. On conspiracy theories after Iran-contra, see Barkun, *Culture of Conspiracy*. Finally, there are many Web sites and books debunking 9/11 conspiracy theories, including Dunbar and Reagan, *Debunking 9/11 Myths*.

16. Kutler, *Abuse of Power*, 8.

17. President George W. Bush, Address to the United Nations General Assembly, November 10, 2001, available at the American Presidency Project, http://www.presidency .ucsb.edu.

18. U.S. Senate, Select Committee to Study Governmental Operations with Respect to Intelligence Activities (hereafter Church Committee), *Final Report*, book 2, 23n.

19. Sibley, *Red Spies in America*, 2–3; Whitehead, *FBI Story*, 90.

20. Church Committee, *Final Report*, book 2, 20.

21. Ibid., book 3, 34.

22. Ibid., book 2, 47.

23. "Stolen Documents Describe FBI Surveillance Activities," *Washington Post*, March 24, 1971.

24. Robert Phillips, foreword to Schwartz, *Ego*, x.

25. Hofstadter, *Paranoid Style*, 38.

26. Ronald Inglehart, "Extremist Political Positions and Perceptions of Conspiracy: Even Paranoids Have Real Enemies," in Graumann and Moscovici, *Changing Conceptions*, 231–44. For more on who believes conspiracy theories, see Robins and Post, *Political Paranoia*; Pipes, *Conspiracy*; Showalter, *Hystories*.

27. M. Moore, *Dude*, 2.

28. Quoted in Michael Powell, "The Disbelievers," *Washington Post*, September 8, 2006.

CHAPTER 1

1. Lindbergh, *Why Your Country Is at War*, 6. For the story of the smashing of the plates, see Walter Eli Quigley, "Like Father, Like Son," *Saturday Evening Post*, June 21, 1941; Larson, *Lindbergh of Minnesota*, 233–34. See also Quigley's introduction to the 1934 edition of Lindbergh's antiwar book, *Your Country at War* (Philadelphia: Dorrance). For general discussions of the suppression of dissent in World War I, see Murphy, *World War I*; Preston, *Aliens and Dissenters*.

2. Lindbergh, *Banking*.

3. The budget and employment data come from *Statistical History of the United States: From Colonial Times to the Present* (New York: Basic, 1976), 1114, 1102. The main U.S. agencies charged with suppressing dissent were the Bureau of Investigation, the Military Intelligence Division of the War Department, and the Secret Service.

4. J. M. Cooper, *Warrior and the Priest*, 277.

5. "President's Annual Address to Congress," *New York Times*, December 9, 1914.

6. "President Wilson's Speech," *New York Times*, January 9, 1915.

7. "Text of President's Speech," *New York Times*, May 11, 1915.

8. O'Rourke and Williamson, *Globalization and History*, 2.

9. Leuchtenberg, *Perils of Prosperity*, 15; Lafeber, *American Age*, 273.

10. For examples of the Wilson administration's secret sympathy for the British, see House to Wilson, May 25, 1915, "House Material—Diary, Letters," Records of the Special Committee Investigating the Munitions Industry (hereafter Nye Committee files), box 333; House to Wilson, January 13, 1916, "House Material—Diary, Letters," Nye Committee files, box 333, National Archives, Washington, D.C.

11. Devlin, *Too Proud to Fight*, 140.

12. Quoted in Barnes, *In Quest*, 99.

13. "Text of the President's Statement to the Public," *New York Times*, March 5, 1917. See also Ryley, *Little Group*.

14. *Congressional Record*, 64th Cong., 2d sess., 5007. For more on Norris's opposition to the war, see Lowitt, *George W. Norris*, chapters 3 and 4.

15. See Link, *Wilson: Campaigns*, 340–77.

16. *Congressional Record*, 65th Cong., 1st sess., 214.

17. Quoted in Hofstadter, *Paranoid Style*, 8.

18. See W. I. Cohen, *American Revisionists*, 12–13. See also "Pacifism in the Middle West," *Nation*, May 17, 1917, 595–97.

19. Wilson's Fourteen Points address to Congress, January 8, 1918, available at the American Presidency Project, http://www.presidency.ucsb.edu.

20. Quoted in Todd, *Wartime Relations*, 17.

21. Wilson, speech in Washington Monument Grounds, June 14, 1917, available at the American Presidency Project, http://www.presidency.ucsb.edu.

22. Wilson message to Congress, April 2, 1917, available at the American Presidency Project, http://www.presidency.ucsb.edu.

23. Wilson, third annual message, December 7, 1915, available at the American Presidency Project, http://www.presidency.ucsb.edu.

24. Wilson message to Congress, April 2, 1917, available at the American Presidency Project, http://www.presidency.ucsb.edu.

25. Quoted in Peterson and Fite, *Opponents of War*, 228.

26. Chafee, *Free Speech*, 74–75.

27. Gentry, J. *Edgar Hoover*, 79.

28. "All Disloyal Men Warned by Gregory," *New York Times*, November 21, 1917.

29. Quigley, "Like Father, Like Son," 27. See also Lynn Haines, "Sire of the Eagle," *Nation*, December 28, 1931, 730–32; Haines and Haines, *Lindberghs*, 279–94; Margaret S. Ernst, "Lindbergh's 'Bolshevik' Father," *Nation*, June 15, 1927, 666; Larson, *Lindbergh of Minnesota*, 236–43; "Honorable Lindbergh, M.C.," *American Monthly* 20, no. 7 (October 1927): 3–6; Salisbury, *Journey*, 16.

30. Wheeler with Healy, *Yankee*, 135–39; Work, *Darkest before Dawn*.

31. Wheeler with Healy, *Yankee*, 140.

32. Ibid., 139–41, quotes on 141, 140.

33. Beard and Beard, *Rise of American Civilization*, 640.

34. For discussions of historians' contributions to wartime propaganda, see C. Hartley Grattan, "The Historians Cut Loose," *American Mercury* 11 (1927): 414–30; Selig Adler, "The War-Guilt Question and American Disillusionment, 1918–1928," *Journal of Modern History* 23 (March 1951): 1–2; Blakey, *Historians*; Todd, *Wartime Relations*, 13–70; and Gruber, *Mars and Minerva*, chapter 4.

35. Paxson, Corwin, and Harding, *War Cyclopedia*.

36. Novick, *That Noble Dream*, 208.

37. Sidney Fay, "New Light on the Origins of the World War, I. Berlin and Vienna, to July 29," *American Historical Review* 25, no. 4 (July 1920): 628. On Barnes, see Justus D. Doenecke, "Harry Elmer Barnes: Prophet of a 'Usable' Past," *History Teacher* 8, no. 2 (February 1975); W. I. Cohen, *American Revisionists*; Goddard, *Harry Elmer Barnes*; Roy Turnbaugh, "The FBI and Harry Elmer Barnes: 1936–1944," *Historian* 42, no. 3 (May 1980): 385–98; and Richard T. Ruetten, "Harry Elmer Barnes and the 'Historical Blackout,'" *Historian* 33, no. 2 (February 1971): 202–14.

38. Harry Elmer Barnes, "Woodrow Wilson," *American Mercury* 1 (April 1924): 484. Wilson's psychobiographer agrees with Barnes on this point. See E. Weinstein, *Woodrow Wilson*, 317.

39. Barnes, *In Quest*, 94.

40. Selig Adler reviews this literature in "The War-Guilt Question."

41. Barnes, *In Quest*, 105.

42. Barnes, "Woodrow Wilson," 484.

43. J. K. Turner, *Shall It Be Again?* 418.

44. Sir Gilbert Parker, "The United States and the War," *Harper's* 136 (March 1918): 521–31.

45. The literature on House is vast. I have found the most helpful analyses to be David Esposito, "Imagined Power: The Secret Life of Colonel House," *Historian* 60, no. 4

(Summer 1998): 741–56; Charles E. Neu, "Woodrow Wilson and Colonel House: The Early Years, 1911–1915," in J. M. Cooper and Neu, *Wilson Era*, 248–78; Lasch, *New Radicalism*, 228–50; E. Weinstein, *Woodrow Wilson*, 265–78; J. M. Cooper, *Warrior and the Priest*, 242–45, 291–96; Hodgson, *Woodrow Wilson's Right Hand*.

46. Seymour, *Intimate Papers*, 45.

47. Ibid., 128.

48. J. M. Cooper, *Warrior and the Priest*, 293–94.

49. See Esposito, "Imagined Power."

50. Quoted in E. Weinstein, *Woodrow Wilson*, 275.

51. Irwin Hoover, "The Case of Colonel House," *Saturday Evening Post* 207 (July 14, 1934), 16.

52. Oswald Garrison Villard, "More Revelations of Colonel House," *Nation*, December 5, 1928, 595.

53. Oswald Garrison Villard, "Issues and Men," *Nation*, April 9, 1938, 414.

54. C. Hartley Grattan, "The Walter Hines Page Legend," *American Mercury*, September 1925, 46.

55. *New York Times*, August 9, 1925.

56. C. Hartley Grattan, "Walter Hines Page—Patriot or Traitor?" *Nation*, November 25, 1925, 512.

57. Harry Elmer Barnes, "Why America Entered the War," *Christian Century* 42 (November 19, 1925): 1441.

58. A Google search with the words "Colonel House" and "Illuminati" turns up sixteen hundred hits, including grandconspiracy.com, conspiracyarchives.com, and truthseeker .com.

59. Quoted in R. Cohen, *When the Old Left Was Young*, 83.

60. On Detzer, see Rosemary Rainbolt, "Women and War in the United States: The Case of Dorothy Detzer, National Secretary WILPF," *Peace and Change* 4 (Fall 1977): 18–27; Rhodri Jeffreys-Jones, "Dorothy Detzer and the Merchants of Death," in *Changing Differences*, 65–83.

61. Detzer, *Appointment*, 3.

62. Ibid., 153–63.

63. Harry Elmer Barnes, introduction to Engelbrecht and Hanighen, *Merchants of Death*, viii.

64. M. W. Coulter, *Senate Munitions Inquiry*, 15.

65. "Munitions Makers Assailed by Ford," *New York Times*, March 8, 1934.

66. M. W. Coulter, *Senate Munitions Inquiry*, 22–25.

67. "Mr. Nye's Termites," *Chicago Tribune*, January 21, 1936.

68. Whittaker Chambers claimed that Soviet intelligence first activated Hiss as a spy when he got his job on the Nye Committee and directed him to use his post to obtain secret State Department documents. See Chambers, *Witness*, 336, 375. Nye was under the impression that Hiss was writing a book about the committee. Hiss might possibly have used this excuse to explain why he took notes and removed documents from the committee

offices. See letter, Nye to James Monahan, July 10, 1935, folder "Women's International League," box 27, Nye Committee files.

69. U.S. Senate, Special Committee Investigating the Munitions Industry, *Hearings* (hereafter Nye Committee hearings), part 1, 375; part 5, 1134–35.

70. R. Cohen, *When the Old Left Was Young*, 95.

71. Twenty-six percent said that the United States had a "just cause," and 18 percent said it entered "for its safety." The rest gave "other reasons" or did not know. Gallup, *Gallup Poll*, 189, 192–93.

72. See the numerous reports and depositions in an untitled folder in box 158 of the Nye Committee files.

73. Nye Committee hearings, Part 26, 7786, 7941–84. See also Chernow, *House of Morgan*, chapter 10.

74. "New History and Old," *Time*, January 20, 1936.

75. On Jack Morgan, see Chernow, *House of Morgan*, 165–475; Forbes, *J. P. Morgan*.

76. Letter, Bryan to Wilson, August 10, 1914, unnamed folder, box 151, Nye Committee files; letter reprinted in *New York Times*, January 8, 1936.

77. "Morgan Testifies as Nye Bares Data on War Loan Curbs," *New York Times*, January 8, 1936.

78. McAdoo to Wilson, August 21, 1915, "Wilson Papers—Originals," box 333, Nye Committee files.

79. Lansing to Wilson, September 6, 1915, "Confidential," box 150, Nye Committee files.

80. Lawrence Brown to Raushenbush, July 11, 1935, in folder 120, box 154, Nye Committee files. Emphasis added.

81. Warburg letter quoted in Stephen Raushenbush, "Confidential Memorandum," June 27, 1935, Box 150, Nye Committee files.

82. McAdoo to Wilson, August 21, 1915, "Wilson Papers—Originals," box 333, Nye Committee files. On Warburg, see Chernow, *Warburgs*, 158–62; P. Roberts, "Conflict of Loyalties." On Wilson administration disgust with Warburg and Miller, see folder "House Papers," box 333, "Report on Inspection of House-Wilson Correspondence and House Diary," April 24–27, 1935, Nye Committee files.

83. Sir Cecil Spring-Rice, British ambassador, told Sir Edward Grey that a Jewish cabal had taken over U.S. financial policy. "Since Morgan's death, the Jewish banks are supreme and they have captured the Treasury Department by the small expedient of financing the bills of the Secretary of the Treasury...and forcing upon him the appointment of the German, Warburg, and the Federal Reserve Board which he dominates." Quoted in Chernow, *Warburgs*, 161.

84. Some Americans were angry at the Nye Committee's failure to conflate "bankers" with "Jews." For an example of an anti-Semite angry at the Nye Committee's refusal to blame the Jews, see the letter from "an American Patriot," September 13, 1934, "Anonymous Correspondence," box 1, Nye Committee files.

85. For scholarly discussions of the Morgan role in Allied financing, see Burk, *Britain, America*; Chernow, *House of Morgan*, chapter 10; Lamont, *Ambassador from Wall Street*,

67–85; Priscilla Roberts, "'Quis Custodiet Ipsos Custodes?' The Federal Reserve System's Founding Fathers and Allied Finances in the First World War," *Business History Review* 72, no. 4 (Winter 1998): 585–620; John Milton Cooper, "The Command of Gold Reversed: American Loans to Britain, 1915–1917," *Pacific Historical Review* 45 (May 1976): 209–30.

86. Nye Committee hearings, part 26, 7866. See also part 28, 8579.

87. Ibid., part 26, 7866.

88. Ibid., 7873; "J. P. Morgan Denies Letting Pound Slip to Force 1915 Loan," *New York Times*, January 11, 1936.

89. Nye Committee hearings, part 26, 7886.

90. Ibid., 7911.

91. Raushenbush to Homer Bone, November 11, 1935, "Bone, Senator," box 161, Nye Committee files.

92. Beard, *Devil Theory*, 12–13.

93. Wilson's Fourteen Points address to Congress, January 8, 1918, available at the American Presidency Project, http://www.presidency.ucsb.edu.

94. U.S. Senate, Foreign Relations Committee, Hearings, *Treaty of Peace with Germany*, August 19, 1919, published in *New York Times*, August 20, 1919.

95. The transcript of the hearings indicates that Nye said that Wilson had "falsified," but a newspaper reported that Nye said Wilson had lied. For the quote in the hearings, see Nye Committee hearings, part 28, 8512. See also part 21, 6003–05; W. S. Cole, *Senator Gerald P. Nye*, 89.

96. Nye Committee hearings, part 28, 8517.

97. *Congressional Record*, 74th Cong., 2d sess., 503–10.

98. Connally, *My Name Is Tom Connally*, 214; "Glass Assails Nye on Wilson Charge," *New York Times*, January 18, 1936.

99. *Congressional Record*, 74th Cong., 2d sess., 504.

100. Arthur Krock, "Ghosts of War Figures Stalk at Nye Hearing," *New York Times*, January 16, 1936.

101. "Wilson's Honesty Defended by Hull," *New York Times*, January 18, 1936.

102. Nye Committee hearings, part 28, 8634.

103. William Stone to Raushenbush, July 11, 1935, folder "120," box 154, Nye Committee files. See also Raushenbush to Stone, July 11, 1935, in the same folder.

104. Nye Committee hearings, part 26, 7893.

105. Beard, *Devil Theory*, 120–22.

106. *Congressional Record*, 74th Cong., 1st sess., 13784.

107. Raushenbush to William Stone, September 18, 1935, folder "120," box 154, p. 10, Nye Committee files.

108. See, for example, Wiltz, *In Search of Peace*.

109. Elliott Roosevelt, *Roosevelt Letters* 156.

110. See Koistinen, *Military-Industrial Complex*, chapter 2.

111. Raushenbush to Stone, September 18, 1935, 10.

112. Ibid., 7.

CHAPTER 2

1. Roosevelt's address to Congress, December 8, 1941, available at the American Presidency Project, http://www.presidency.ucsb.edu.

2. Berg, *Lindbergh*, 431.

3. "Through the Mill," *Time* 44, November 20, 1944, 23. Congresswoman Luce was a "consistent internationalist," as her husband's magazine reported, but very anti-Roosevelt and anti–New Deal.

4. Higgs, *Crisis and Leviathan*, 21; *The Statistical History of the United States*, 1102, 1114, 1127, 1110.

5. Kennedy, *Freedom from Fear*, 379.

6. Gallup, *Gallup Poll*, 1: 51, 83, 154.

7. Flynn quoted in Moser, *Right Turn*, 93. Wheeler's comments are in Wheeler, *Yankee*, 319, 331. For a general discussion of why some old progressives turned against Franklin Roosevelt, see O. Graham, *An Encore*, especially 32–34.

8. *Congressional Record*, 75th Cong., 1st sess., 7695, 7692.

9. On the Reorganization Act, see Polenberg, *Reorganizing Roosevelt's Government*; Hart, *Presidential Branch*, 26–37.

10. Eleanor Roosevelt, *This I Remember*, 2.

11. Quoted in W. F. Kimball, *Juggler*, 7.

12. Flynn to Robert E. Wood, November 11, 1941, "America First Committee—Robert E. Wood," box 21, John T. Flynn Papers, University of Oregon, Eugene (hereafter Flynn Papers).

13. Lindbergh to Robert Theobald, September 29, 1957, "Lindbergh, Charles," box 5, Robert Theobald Papers, Hoover Institution, Stanford, California.

14. Gallup, *Gallup Poll*, 1: 276.

15. Leigh, *Mobilizing Consent*, 75.

16. W. S. Cole, *Roosevelt and the Isolationists*, 454.

17. Herzstein, *Roosevelt and Hitler*, 78.

18. W. S. Cole, *Roosevelt and the Isolationists*, 277.

19. Press conference no. 575, September 1, 1939, in *Complete Presidential Press Conferences of Franklin D. Roosevelt* (New York: Da Capo Press, 1972), 14: 132.

20. Campaign address at Boston, October 30, 1940, available at the American Presidency Project, http://www.presidency.ucsb.edu.

21. The quote is from Alterman, *When Presidents Lie*, 16. See also Heinrichs, *Threshold of War*, 11.

22. Flynn to Wood, November 11, 1941.

23. See Flynn's book, *As We Go Marching*. See also Barnes to Flynn, September 16, 1943, "B," Box 17, Flynn Papers.

24. Quoted in Dallek, *Franklin D. Roosevelt*, 187. See also Greenbaum, *Men against Myths*, chapter 4.

25. W. S. Cole, *Roosevelt and the Isolationists*, 217. For a discussion of Roosevelt's image as a dictator, see Alpers, *Dictators*, 26–28, 29–34, 205–8. See also Patterson, *Congressional Conservatism*, 13.

26. H. Donovan, *Roosevelt to Reagan*, 20.

27. Alpers, *Dictators*, 4.

28. "Congress Ranks Split on Accord," *New York Times*, September 4, 1940.

29. See, for example, Schlesinger, *Imperial Presidency*, 108–9; Heinrichs, *Threshold of War*, 11.

30. Quoted in W. S. Cole, *Roosevelt and the Isolationists*, 375.

31. Doenecke, *Storm on the Horizon*, 1–8. See also Stenehjem, *An American First*.

32. "President's Call for Full Response on Defense," *New York Times*, December 30, 1940.

33. A rare exception among midwestern Republican progressives, Norris himself was an interventionist by this time.

34. Anderson, "Senator Burton K. Wheeler," 250, 207.

35. Wheeler speech, January 12, 1941, "Lend Lease" folder, box 30, America First Committee Files, Hoover Institution, Stanford, California (hereafter America First Committee Files).

36. "Lindbergh's Statement before the Foreign Relations Committee," *New York Times*, February 7, 1941.

37. *Congressional Record*, 77th Cong., 1st sess., 1111.

38. Mass mailing by Wheeler to America First Committee members, undated, "Lend Lease" folder, box 30, America First Committee Files.

39. Jonas, *Isolationism*, 231.

40. Hugh S. Johnson, "Is Britain Fighting Our War?" in Schoonmaker and Reid, *We Testify*, 100.

41. See R. Douglas Stuart to John T. Flynn, December 11, 1940, "America First Committee," Box 21, Flynn Papers.

42. Quoted in Dinnerstein, *Antisemitism in America*, 129.

43. W. S. Cole, *America First*, 175, 180; Moser, *Right Turn*, 138–39.

44. Amos Pinchot to Stanwood Menken, October 4, 1941, folder "Colonel Lindbergh's Des Moines speech," box 282, America First Committee Files.

45. On American anti-Semitism, see Quinley and Glock, *Anti-Semitism in America*; Gerber, *Anti-Semitism in American History*; Dinnerstein, *Antisemitism in the United States* and *Antisemitism in America*; Baldwin, *Henry Ford*.

46. Jonas, *Isolationism in America*, 234.

47. Quoted in ibid., 234.

48. Burton K. Wheeler, "Marching Down the Road to War," in *Vital Speeches of the Day* 6, no. 22 (September 1, 1940): 692.

49. Annual message, January 6, 1941, available at the American Presidency Project, http://www.presidency.ucsb.edu.

50. Fireside chat, December 29, 1940, available at the American Presidency Project, http://www.presidency.ucsb.edu.

51. Annual message, January 6, 1941, available at the American Presidency Project, http://www.presidency.ucsb.edu.

52. Roosevelt campaign address in Brooklyn, November 1, 1940, available at the American Presidency Project, http://www.presidency.ucsb.edu.

53. Brinkley, *Voices of Protest*, 109.

54. Anderson, "Senator Burton K. Wheeler," 185.

55. See, for example, "Man & Wife of the Year," *Time*, January 3, 1938.

56. "Chinese Coverage," *Time*, December 27, 1937.

57. Heinrichs, *Threshold of War*, 6–10. Roosevelt never made an official decision to embargo oil, but U.S. bureaucrats refused to give export licenses to Japan after the president froze Japanese assets in the United States. See Heinrichs, *Threshold of War*, 133–41.

58. Kennedy, *Freedom from Fear*, 512.

59. For a discussion of the effects of the European war on Roosevelt's Asian policy, see ibid., 509–15.

60. Beard, *President Roosevelt*, 517.

61. Philip H. Jacobsen, "Radio Silence and Radio Deception: Secrecy Insurance for the Pearl Harbor Strike Force," *Intelligence and National Security* 19, no. 4 (Winter 2004): 695–718.

62. Prange, *At Dawn We Slept*, 86.

63. U.S. Congress, Joint Committee on the Investigation of the Pearl Harbor Attack, *Hearings*, part 14, 1328, 1406.

64. Prange, *At Dawn We Slept*, 402–3, 406.

65. Congress, *Pearl Harbor Attack*, part 10, 4662. See also Costello, *Days of Infamy*, 202.

66. Budiansky, *Battle of Wits*, 6–9, David Kahn, "United States Views of Germany and Japan in 1941," in E. R. May, *Knowing One's Enemies*, 476–501; David Kahn, "The Intelligence Failure of Pearl Harbor," *Foreign Affairs* 70, no. 5 (Winter 1991): 138–53. Robert Stinnett has argued that the United States did break the naval codes, but many scholars have persuasively rebutted his charges. See note 178 below. John Costello argues that military leaders' decision to focus on the diplomatic rather than the naval code "cost the U.S. Navy the best chance it ever had of alerting Pearl Harbor." See Costello, *Days of Infamy*, 336.

67. Congress, *Pearl Harbor Attack Report*, 223.

68. D. Kahn, *Codebreakers*, 60–61.

69. Prange, *At Dawn We Slept*, 559.

70. *Congressional Record*, 77th Cong., 1st sess., 9522.

71. Dower, *War without Mercy*, 36, 105.

72. Letter from R. O. Archer to Alben Barkley, October 5, 1945, "On the Pearl Harbor Investigation—A," box 324, RG 128, Records of the Joint Committee on the Pearl Harbor Attack, National Archives, Washington, D.C.

73. Rosenberg, *Date*, 11–14.

74. *Congressional Record*, 77th Cong., 1st sess., 9660.

75. Melosi, *Shadow*, 26–27.

76. For an analysis of the Roberts Commission and four other national security commissions, see Kitts, *Presidential Commissions*.

77. For the report, see Congress, *Pearl Harbor Attack*, part 41, 1–21.

78. Barnes to Callander, November 11, 1958, "November 1–November 29, 1958," box 50, Harry Elmer Barnes Papers, University of Wyoming, Laramie (hereafter Barnes Papers).

79. Barnes to Thackrey, May 26, 1940, folder "May 1, 1940–May 31, 1940," box 25, Barnes Papers.

80. See Earl Welch to Barnes, January 6, 1942, "January 1, 1942–March 31, 1942," box 28, Barnes Papers, and Barnes's reply of January 12 in the same file.

81. William L. Neumann to Harry Elmer Barnes, June 8, 1943, file "June 1, 1943–July 28 1943," box 29, and Tansill to Barnes, April 20, 1943, file "April 1, 1943 to May 28, 1943," box 29, Barnes Papers.

82. Wood to Barnes, September 17, 1943, "August 2, 1943 to September 30, 1943," box 29, Barnes Papers. Wood at first promised to fund the revisionists' project, then backed out.

83. Barnes corresponded with and encouraged Morgenstern, *Pearl Harbor*; Tansill, *Back Door to War*; Beard, *President Roosevelt*; and Theobald, *Final Secret*. He also edited the collection of revisionist essays in *Perpetual War for Perpetual Peace*.

84. On Flynn, see Moser, *Right Turn*; Stenehjem, *An American First*; Radosh, *Prophets on the Right*, 197–273; Kazin, *Populist Persuasion*, 172–74.

85. "Mr. Flynn Speaks for Himself," *New Republic*, February 3, 1941. See also Bruce Bliven to Flynn, November 4, 1940, "New Republic," box 19, Flynn Papers.

86. Barnes to Flynn, September 16, 1943, box 17, file "B," Flynn Papers.

87. Kimmel, *Admiral Kimmel's Story*, 5–6; "Admiral Husband E. Kimmel Dies," *New York Times*, May 15, 1968.

88. Melosi, *Shadow*, 54–55.

89. Kimmel to Stark, February 22, 1942, "Facts and Correspondence about Admiral Kimmel's Retirement," box 30, Husband E. Kimmel Papers, University of Wyoming, Laramie (hereafter Kimmel Papers).

90. For an astute account of the congressional battles over the extensions for the statutes of limitation, see Melosi, *Shadow*, chapter 5.

91. "Memorandum of Interview with Admiral King in Washington," December 7, 1944, "Memoranda, 1944," box 35, Kimmel Papers.

92. Smith to Rugg, June 23, 1944, "Pearl Harbor, 1944–1945," box 745, Robert A. Taft Papers, Library of Congress, Washington, D.C. (hereafter Taft Papers). Martin Melosi discusses Smith's advice in *Shadow*, 73–74, 77.

93. "Memorandum on the Issue of Foreign Policy in the Campaign," undated, "Pearl Harbor, 1944–45," box 745, p. 4, Taft Papers.

94. Moser, *Right Turn*, 164.

95. Barnes to Barton, August 23, 1944, "July 5–September 30, 1944," box 30, and Barnes to Barton, July 28, 1944, in the same file and box, Barnes Papers.

96. Barton to Barnes, August 8, 1944, "July 5–September 30, 1944," box 30, Barnes Papers.

97. "Senators Dispute on Foreign Policy," June 20, 1944, *New York Times*; "Why Is Kent Case Reopened Now?" *Christian Century* 61 (September 13, 1944), 1045. See also "The Case of Tyler Kent," *Newsweek*, September 18, 1944, 47–48.

98. In 1972, the British government released documents showing Kent's claims to be false.

99. *Congressional Record*, September 6, 1944, 7668–70.

100. Flynn, *Truth*, 23.

101. "J'Accuse 1944," *Chicago Tribune*, October 23, 1944.

102. Flynn to Mr. Weir, November 6, 1944, "Pearl Harbor pamphlets," box 9, Flynn Papers.

103. The Navy had already begun its own internal investigation of Pearl Harbor before Congress ordered it to start one. Adm. Thomas Hart and his assistants had been interviewing key naval personnel since February 1944. The Navy had begun the Hart inquiry in part because of Kimmel's crusade to clear his name and in part because top brass feared that many of the principals might be killed in battle before they could answer questions. When Congress insisted on a new Navy investigation, Hart combined his efforts with the congressionally mandated Navy Court of Inquiry.

104. Dewey to William Mitchell, November 1, 1945, "Gov. Dewey Correspondence File," box 326, RG 128, Records of the Joint Committee on the Pearl Harbor Attack.

105. For Dewey's speech, see "Roosevelt Record 'Desperately Bad,' Dewey Declares," *New York Times*, September 26, 1944.

106. Dewey to Mitchell, November 1, 1945.

107. Ibid. For the complete text of Marshall's letter to Dewey, see D. Kahn, *Codebreakers*, 605–7.

108. Wohlstetter, *Pearl Harbor*, 177; D. Kahn, *Codebreakers*, 604–8.

109. D. Kahn, *Codebreakers*, 604–8, 562–73.

110. R. N. Smith, *Thomas E. Dewey*, 427, 429–30.

111. Barnes to Wood, September 22, 1943, "August 2 1943 to September 30 1943," box 29, Barnes Papers.

112. Church Committee, *Final Report*, book 2, 23–24.

113. Ibid., 24. See also book 3, 393–97. For a detailed analysis of Roosevelt's expansion of the FBI, see Kenneth O'Reilly, "A New Deal for the FBI: The Roosevelt Administration, Crime Control, and National Security," *Journal of American History* 69, no. 3 (December 1982): 638–58.

114. Quoted in MacDonnell, *Insidious Foes*, 164.

115. Quoted in Donner, "Hoover's Legacy," 679.

116. Ibid., 678.

117. Church Committee, *Final Report*, book 2, 33.

118. Quoted in Gentry, *J. Edgar Hoover*, 226.

119. See Richard W. Steele, "Franklin D. Roosevelt and His Foreign Policy Critics," *Political Science Quarterly* 94, no. 1 (Spring 1979): 15–32. For other discussions of the Roosevelt administration's attempts to monitor and discredit its enemies, see Ribuffo, *Old Christian Right*, chapter 5; G. S. Smith, *To Save a Nation*, epilogue; Douglas M. Charles, "Informing FDR: FBI Political Surveillance and the Isolationist-Interventionist Foreign Policy Debate," *Diplomatic History* 24, no. 2 (Spring 2000): 211–32.

120. Church Committee, *Final Report*, book 2, 36.

121. O'Reilly, "New Deal for the FBI," 648.

122. W. S. Cole, *Roosevelt and the Isolationists*, 532.

123. O'Reilly, "New Deal for the FBI," 651, 653; Steele, "Franklin D. Roosevelt," 22.

124. Flynn to Senator Bennett Clark, February 15, 1940, "U.S. Congress, Senate, A-K," Box 20, Flynn Papers.

125. Ribuffo, *Old Christian Right*, 198–215.

126. Barnes to "Roger," April 8, 1944, "April 3–June 29, 1944," box 30, Barnes Papers.

127. See John Moser, "'Gigantic Engines of Propaganda': The 1941 Senate Investigation of Hollywood," *Historian* 63, no. 4 (Summer 2001): 731–51.

128. Flynn to Nye, August 29, 1941, "America First—Motion Picture Investigation," box 21, Flynn Papers.

129. See, for example, Flynn, *Smear Terror*, 30. Albert Fried notes that this type of accusation is "standard anti-Semitic fare." Fried, *FDR and His Enemies*, 204.

130. Flynn, "Confidential Memorandum for members of the Executive Committee," September 16, 1941, folder "America First Committee—Motion Picture Investigation," box 21, Flynn Papers.

131. L. M. Birkhead to George H. Whipple, March 11, 1941, "Friends of Democracy," box 28, America First Committee Files.

132. See also David George Kin (pseudonym for David Plotkin), *Plot against America*. For scholarly analyses of the antifascist movement, see MacDonnell, *Insidious Foes*; John Earl Haynes, *Red Scare*, chapter 2; and Ribuffo, *Old Christian Right*, chapter 5.

133. *Congressional Record*, 78th Cong., 1st sess., 486, 475.

134. See "Diary—Under Cover," December 30, 1943, "Carlson," box 24, and Robert E. Wood to Flynn, January 6, 1944, in same file and box, Flynn Papers.

135. Report, no date, "Carlson," box 24, Flynn Papers.

136. Notes, "Plans Thus Far," no date, "Carlson," box 24, Flynn Papers.

137. Ibid.

138. Flynn to Wallace, October 14, 1944, "Lend-Lease," box 28, Flynn Papers.

139. Congress, *Pearl Harbor Attack*, part 39, 321, 175–76.

140. See Melosi, *Shadow*, 112–21.

141. Goodwin, *No Ordinary Time*, 602, 612.

142. "Ted" (Thackrey) to Barnes, April 17, 1945, "April 7 to June 27, 1945," box 31, Barnes Papers.

143. Melosi, *Shadow*, 124.

144. Congress, *Pearl Harbor Attack*, part 39, 139. Emphasis added.

145. See the *Tribune* for September 2, 1945. The *Tribune*'s White House correspondent, Walter Trohan, later claimed that he had told Flynn about Magic. Trohan said he had been certain that the United States had broken the Japanese code in 1941 but had been unable to publish his scoop because of wartime censorship. Trohan claimed that he "turned the full story" over to Flynn and put him in touch with his military sources after Flynn had sniffed out "a corner of the story." Trohan, *Political Animals*, 167. There is no other evidence for Trohan's version of events, though.

146. *New Republic*, September 24, 1945, 373, quoted in Doenecke, *Not to the Swift*, 94.

147. McCormick to Flynn, September 14, 1945, and Flynn to McCormick, September 17, 1945, in "McCormick," box 18, Flynn Papers.

148. For a discussion of the debate on creating the congressional committee, see Melosi, *Shadow*, 132–39.

149. Harry Elmer Barnes uses this term to describe Percy Greaves in Barnes, *Perpetual War*, 408.

150. "Pearl Harbor's 'Missing Papers,'" *U.S. News*, November 16, 1945, 99.

151. "Secrets in FDR's Papers," *U.S. News*, November 16, 1945, 15.

152. John Chamberlain, "Pearl Harbor," *Life*, September 24, 1945, 111.

153. "Pearl Harbor Secrets," *Newsweek*, November 26, 1945, 38.

154. Ibid., 37.

155. For Marshall's testimony, see Congress, *Pearl Harbor Attack*, part 3, 1049–1439 and 1499–1541, part 11, 5175–5200.

156. Ibid., part 7, January 22, 1946, 2922. For Short's complete testimony, see part 7, 2921–3231. For Kimmel's testimony, see part 6, 2497–2663, 2701–2915.

157. The winds code is discussed at length in the congressional hearings. See ibid., part 8, 3555–3813, 3842–3927, part 9, 3930–4599, and part 10, 4628–4828. Roberta Wohlstetter gives one of the best scholarly analyses of it in *Pearl Harbor*, 214–18.

158. See Flynn's "'Winds' Code Key to New Deal Guilt," *New York Journal-American*, December 13, 1945, and his untitled manuscript, February 3, 1947, in "Truth Sources— Flynn Articles," box 8, Flynn Papers.

159. See "'Winds' Code Story Hit by New Witness," *New York Times*, February 7, 1946.

160. "Counsel and His Staff Quit the Pearl Harbor Inquiry," *New York Times*, December 15, 1945. See also Mitchell's "Memo for Congressman Murphy," November 9, 1945, "Navy Administrative File," box 330, RG 128, Records of the Joint Committee on the Pearl Harbor Attack.

161. "The Pearl Harbor Trial," *New Republic* 113 (November 26, 1945), 710.

162. "Isolationists Use Pearl Harbor to Attack F.D.R. Policies," *Foreign Policy Bulletin* 25 (November 30, 1945): 4.

163. *Congressional Record*, 79th Cong., 1st sess., 10446.

164. Rosenberg, *Date*, 40.

165. "Truman Says Public Must Share Blame for Pearl Harbor," *New York Times*, August 31, 1945.

166. "The Pearl Harbor Trial," *New Republic* 113 (November 26, 1945), 710.

167. George H. E. Smith to Homer Ferguson, August 31, 1945, "Pearl Harbor, 1944–45," box 745, Taft Papers.

168. Ibid.

169. Chamberlain, "Pearl Harbor," 110.

170. Congress, *Pearl Harbor Attack*, Report, July 20, 1946, 251.

171. Ibid., 570.

172. Ibid., 499.

173. Morgenstern, *Pearl Harbor*; Beard, *President Roosevelt*; Tansill, *Back Door to War*. For reviews of the Pearl Harbor conspiracy literature, see Mintz, *Revisionism*; Rosenberg, *Date*, 40–46; Doenecke, *Not to the Swift*, 91–112; Zimmerman, "Pearl Harbor Revisionism," 127–46.

174. Flynn to Barnes, April 29, 1957, "B," box 17, Flynn Papers.

175. Barnes to Callander, November 11, 1958.

176. Barnes, "The Public Stake in Revisionism," *Journal for Historical Review* 1, no. 3 (Fall 1980): 205, available at www.ihr.org. For a discussion of Barnes's role in promoting Holocaust denial, see Lipstadt, *Denying the Holocaust*, 67–83.

177. Theobald, *Final Secret*.

178. The major conspiracy books since the 1970s include Stinnett, *Day of Deceit*; Bartlett, *Cover-Up*; Toland, *Infamy*; Wilford, *Pearl Harbor Redefined*. See also Timothy Wilford, "Watching the North Pacific," *Intelligence and National Security* 17, no. 4 (Winter 2002): 131–64. Some important refutations of these conspiracy theories include Coox, "Repulsing the Pearl Harbor Revisionists," 29–31; Zimmerman, "Pearl Harbor Revisionism"; Budiansky, "Closing the Book on Pearl Harbor," 119–30; Jacobsen, "Cryptologic Veteran's Analysis of 'Day of Deceit,'" 110–18; and Jacobsen, "Radio Silence and Radio Deception."

179. Flynn to William Borah, January 7, 1938, "U.S. Congress, Senate, A-K," box 20, Flynn Papers.

180. Smith to Ferguson, August 31, 1945.

181. *Congressional Record*, 78th Cong., 1st sess., 478.

182. "The Indictment," *Chicago Tribune*, September 3, 1945.

183. Flynn to Clark, February 15, 1940.

184. Memo, February 19, 1944, "Carlson," box 24, Flynn Papers.

185. Wheeler to Flynn, December 31, 1943, "Wheeler," box 24, Flynn Papers.

CHAPTER 3

1. Hager, *Force of Nature*, 391, 400.

2. "Statement by Linus Pauling," April 22, 1952, in folder "Linus Pauling—anti-communist hysteria," in the safe at the Linus Pauling Papers, Oregon State University, Corvallis (hereafter Pauling Papers). See also Kathryn Olmsted, "Linus Pauling: A Case

Study in Counterintelligence Run Amok," in L. Johnson, *Handbook on Intelligence Studies*, 269–78.

3. See Tolson to director, November 26, 1947, FBI file 100–353404–2, in box 2.025, folder 25.1, Pauling Papers.

4. Quoted in report, "Linus Carl Pauling," October 21, 1952, FBI file 100–353404–27, box 2.025, folder 25.1, Pauling Papers.

5. Memo, Special Agent in Charge (SAC), New York to director, August 8, 1950, FBI file 100–353404–7, box 2.025, folder 25.1, Pauling Papers. On Budenz's credibility, see Robert M. Lichtman, "Louis Budenz, the FBI, and the 'List of 400 Concealed Communists': An Extended Tale of McCarthy-Era Informing," in *American Communist History* 3, no. 1 (June 2004): 25–54.

6. Memo, FBI director to attorney general, December 9, 1953, FBI file 100–353404–37, box 2.025, folder 25.1, Pauling Papers.

7. Report, "Linus Carl Pauling," October 21, 1952, FBI file 100–353404–27, box 2.025, folder 25.1, Pauling Papers.

8. Kutler, *American Inquisition*, 90–91; Judson, *Eighth Day*, 132. Hager, *Force of Nature*, 414, disagrees with this analysis.

9. Hager, *Force of Nature*, 454.

10. Andrew and Mitrokhin, *Sword and the Shield*, 29.

11. On Gold's industrial espionage, see Sibley, *Red Spies*, 109–13.

12. A. Weinstein and Vassiliev, *Haunted Wood*, 23.

13. Ibid., 33–34.

14. For the best overviews of Soviet spying in America, see Sibley, *Red Spies*; A. Weinstein and Vassiliev, *Haunted Wood*; Haynes and Klehr, *Venona*; Andrew and Gordievsky, *KGB*; Andrew and Mitrokhin, *Sword and the Shield*.

15. For more on Chambers, see Tanenhaus, *Whittaker Chambers*.

16. See Berle, *Navigating the Rapids*, 249–50, 598; Chambers, *Witness*, 463; Levine, *Eyewitness*, 192–95.

17. Ladd to Hoover, December 29, 1948, vol. 13, no. 659, p. 2, Hiss-Chambers File, FBI; Tanenhaus, *Whittaker Chambers*, 170.

18. Quoted in Sibley, *Red Spies*, 93.

19. On Hall, see Albright and Kunstel, *Bombshell*.

20. See Sibley, *Red Spies*, chapter 4; William J. Broad, "A Spy's Path: Iowa to A-Bomb to Kremlin Honor," *New York Times*, November 12, 2007. In addition, the Soviets may have had another significant source at Los Alamos who has not yet been identified. There has been some debate among scholars about whether J. Robert Oppenheimer was among the Los Alamos scientists who passed information to the Soviets. Jerrold Schecter and Leona Schecter assert that he was; Gregg Herken and Katherine Sibley think that it was unlikely. See Schecter and Schecter, *Sacred Secrets*, 47–51; Sibley, *Red Spies*, 137; Herken, *Brotherhood*, 93. See also A. Weinstein and Vassiliev, *Haunted Wood*, 216.

21. Holloway, *Stalin and the Bomb*, 108, 137–38, 222–23.

22. Sibley, *Red Spies*, 148.

23. For discussions of Rosenberg's spy ring, see ibid., 98–105; S. Roberts, *Brother*; Feklisov, *Man behind the Rosenbergs*; Haynes and Klehr, *Venona*, 295–303; Walter Schneir and Miriam Schneir, "Cryptic Answers," *Nation*, August 14–21, 1995, 152–53. The limited references to Ethel Rosenberg in the Soviet archives are reprinted in A. Weinstein and Vassiliev, *Haunted Wood*, 217, 331. Julius Rosenberg's KGB case officer, Alexander Feklisov, said that Julius worked for him, but that Ethel was not an active spy.

24. See my biography of Bentley, *Red Spy Queen*.

25. Hope Hale Davis, "Looking Back at My Years in the Party," *New Leader*, February 11, 1980, 13.

26. Quoted in Romerstein and Breindel, *Venona Secrets*, 199. For more on the motivations of communist spies, see Craig, *Treasonable Doubt*, 271; Albright and Kunstel, *Bombshell*, 288–89; Olmsted, *Red Spy Queen*, 55–56.

27. Sibley, *Red Spies*, 5.

28. Whitehead, *FBI Story*, 43.

29. Teletype, New York to director and SAC, 65–56402–1, Nathan Gregory Silvermaster File, FBI (hereafter Silvermaster File).

30. Memo, Simon to Ladd, November 8, 1945, 65–56402–8, Silvermaster File.

31. November 30, 1945, 65–56402–220, 25, 105, Silvermaster File.

32. Ladd to Hoover, December 29, 1948, vol. 13, no. 659, p. 2, Hiss-Chambers File, FBI; Tanenhaus, *Whittaker Chambers*, 170. Igor Gouzenko, a clerk in the Soviet embassy in Canada who defected in September 1945, also told his debriefers that an unnamed aide to Secretary of State Edward Stettinius was a Soviet agent.

33. G. E. White, *Alger Hiss's Looking-Glass Wars*, 50.

34. November 30, 1945, 65–56402–43, Silvermaster File.

35. A. Weinstein and Vassiliev, *Haunted Wood*, 104–7.

36. Ibid., 287.

37. Gentry, *J. Edgar Hoover*, 319, 356; Harvey Klehr and John Earl Haynes, response to Robert D. Novak's "Did Truman Know about Venona?" http://hnn.us/articles/1706.html#klehr, accessed March 20, 2008.

38. Memo reprinted in Moynihan, *Secrecy*, 63–68.

39. Moynihan, *Secrecy*, 70–71. See also the Novak article and the response by Haynes and Klehr cited in note 37.

40. Sullivan with Brown, *Bureau*, 38.

41. Skidelsky, *John Maynard Keynes*, 467.

42. R. J. Donovan, *Conflict and Crisis*, 174. In the Eisenhower administration, Attorney General Herbert Brownell resurrected the scandal and blasted Truman for promoting a spy.

43. Craig, *Treasonable Doubt*, 201.

44. Memo, Jones to Ladd, January 16, 1947, 65–56402–2296, 4, Silvermaster File.

45. See my discussion of this conflict in *Red Spy Queen*, 116–17.

46. Memo, Jones to Ladd, January 16, 1947, 65–56402–2296, 6, Silvermaster File.

47. Gentry, *J. Edgar Hoover*, 357.

48. O'Reilly, *Hoover*, 105; Gentry, *J. Edgar Hoover*, 357; Pearson, *Diaries*, 58–59.

49. Memo, SAC New York to director, December 22, 1947, 65–56402–3019, Silvermaster File.

50. Memo, Fletcher to Ladd, April 3, 1948, 65–56402–3185, Silvermaster File.

51. Nelson Frank and Norton Mockridge, "Red Ring Bared by Blond Queen," *New York World-Telegram*, July 21, 1948, 1.

52. Goodman, *Committee*, 65; U.S. House, Committee on Un-American Activities, *Hearings Regarding Communist Espionage in the United States* (hereafter HUAC hearings), 548.

53. Paul Bullock, "'Rabbits and Radicals': Richard Nixon's 1946 Campaign against Jerry Voorhis," *Southern California Quarterly* 55, no. 3 (1973): 319–59.

54. See Schrecker, *Many Are the Crimes*, chapter 2.

55. Goodman, *Committee*, 240.

56. HUAC hearings, 525; "The Network," *Time*, August 9, 1948, 16.

57. See, for example, A. J. Liebling, "The Wayward Press," *New Yorker*, August 28, 1948; Joseph Alsop, "Miss Bentley's Bondage," *Commonweal*, November 9, 1951; Kempton, *Part of Our Time*, 219–20.

58. See Tanenhaus, *Whittaker Chambers*, 220–21; "Red 'Underground' in Federal Posts Alleged by Editor," *New York Times*, August 4, 1948.

59. "Red 'Underground.'"

60. HUAC hearings, 879.

61. Craig, *Treasonable Doubt*, 215; Burnham, *Web of Subversion*, 158.

62. Kempton, *Part of Our Time*, 20.

63. Quoted in Tanenhaus, *Whittaker Chambers*, 277.

64. R. J. Donovan, *Conflict and Crisis*, 414.

65. O'Reilly, *Hoover*, 125.

66. Tanenhaus, *Whittaker Chambers*, 289–304; Chambers, *Witness*, 754.

67. On Hiss's guilt, see A. Weinstein, *Perjury*; A. Weinstein and Vassiliev, *Haunted Wood*, 5–8; White, *Alger Hiss's Looking-Glass Wars*; Eduard Mark, "Who Was 'Venona's' 'Ales'? Cryptanalysis and the Hiss Case," *Intelligence and National Security* 18, no. 3 (Autumn 2003): 45–72; John Ehrman, "Once Again, the Alger Hiss Case," *Studies in Intelligence* 51, no. 4 (December 2007), available at https://www.cia.gov/library/center-for-the-study-of-intelligence. A few scholars say his guilt has not been proved. See the article by the late John Lowenthal, "Venona and Alger Hiss," *Intelligence and National Security* 15, no. 3 (Autumn 2000): 98–130; David Lowenthal and Roger Sandilands, "Eduard Mark on Venona's 'Ales': A Note," *Intelligence and National Security* 20, no. 3 (September 2005): 509–12. See also the Alger Hiss Web site, algerhiss.com. On the use of the communist espionage cases by post–cold war conservatives, see Maurice Isserman and Ellen Schrecker, "'Papers of a Dangerous Tendency': From Major Andre's Boot to the VENONA files," in Schrecker, *Cold War Triumphalism*, 149–73.

68. Haynes and Klehr, *Venona*, 171–72.

69. Alterman, *When Presidents Lie*, 71. Allen Weinstein argues that Hiss played an important role at Yalta and was privy to many secret documents. However, he does not argue that Hiss influenced U.S. policy in a meaningful way. Weinstein, *Perjury*, 313–14.

70. The definitive discussion of White is Craig, *Treasonable Doubt*. For a different view, see James Boughton and Roger J. Sandilands, "Politics and the Attack on FDR's Economists: From the Grand Alliance to the Cold War," *Intelligence and National Security* 18, no. 3 (Autumn 2003): 73–99. Besides stealing government memos, White also may have enabled the Soviets to steal American money—or, as he probably viewed it, to obtain a just settlement from the U.S. government for the twenty million people the Soviets had lost in fighting their common enemy. Although most of the relevant documents are still unavailable, some writers contend that he may have masterminded a complex scheme that enabled Soviet soldiers in occupied Germany to redeem occupation currency for $250 million in hard American cash. For differing views on the occupation currency scandal, see Schecter and Schecter, *Sacred Secrets*, 119–23; Craig, *Treasonable Doubt*, 113–34.

71. Craig, *Treasonable Doubt*, 263.

72. Quoted in ibid., 147.

73. A. Weinstein and Vassiliev, *Haunted Wood*, 293–300, quote on 299.

74. John Earl Haynes and Harvey Klehr argue that some historians have exaggerated the decline of Soviet espionage in the United States after 1945. They argue, "We still only know bits and pieces about what happened to Soviet espionage in the postwar world," and cite Judith Coplon, the Rudolf Abel network, and the Jack Soble network as evidence that significant spying continued into the cold war period. However, they do agree that there was at least some decline in ideologically motivated spying. Haynes and Klehr, *In Denial*, 220–25, quote on 221.

75. Quoted in Oshinsky, *Conspiracy*, 102.

76. *Congressional Record*, 81st Cong., 2d sess., 1007. For a discussion of the partisan uses of the Yalta conference, see Theoharis, *Yalta Myths*.

77. Quoted in Griffith, *Politics of Fear*, 48.

78. Lamphere with Shachtman, *FBI-KGB War*, 177.

79. R. M. Fried, *Nightmare in Red*, 121; Steve Neal, "Speech That Painted the Nation Red," *Chicago Sun-Times*, February 8, 2000.

80. Senate, *Congressional Record*, 81st Cong., 2d sess., 1957. McCarthy later claimed that he had been misquoted, but reporters at the speech said he had used the figure 205. Griffith, *Politics of Fear*, 49–51.

81. Griffith, *Politics of Fear*, 48–49.

82. Oshinsky, *Conspiracy*, 109–11; Griffith, *Politics of Fear*, 51.

83. Griffith, *Politics of Fear*, 56–57.

84. Senate, *Congressional Record*, 81st Cong., 2d sess., 1980.

85. See "Lattimore Named as 'Top Soviet Spy' Cited by M'Carthy," *New York Times*, March 27, 1950.

86. "Excerpts of Text of Majority Report on Charges by Senator McCarthy," *New York Times*, July 18, 1950.

87. McCarthy's admirers insist that he never called Marshall and Acheson traitors. But the speech, though contradictory at times, quite clearly depicts the men as consciously working for a foreign power. "If Marshall were merely stupid," McCarthy said, "the laws

of probability would dictate that part of his decisions would serve America's interests." At another point he said, "We have our Acheson. Or perhaps I should say their Acheson." McCarthy, *America's Retreat*, 138, 134.

88. Ibid., 135–36.

89. Quoted in Moser, *Right Turn*, 180.

90. Quoted in Anderson, "Senator Burton K. Wheeler," 333.

91. See Kubek, *Communism at Pearl Harbor*, 15–22; Burnham, *Web of Subversion*, 132, 150–58. See also Schecter and Schecter, *Sacred Secrets*, 118–24.

92. Mullins, *Federal Reserve Conspiracy*, 141–42.

93. Kubek, *How the Far East Was Lost*, 17–21; Kubek, *Communism at Pearl Harbor*, 20; Fish, *Memoir*, 99; Schecter and Schecter, *Sacred Secrets*, 22–45.

94. Gaddis, *We Now Know*, 56. See also LaFeber, *American Age*, 421; Clemens, *Yalta*, 290.

95. DeToledano, *Seeds of Treason*, xiv, xiii. Richard Nixon and Joseph McCarthy used similar language.

96. Flynn, *Lattimore Story*, 33.

97. Rovere, *Senator Joe McCarthy*, 8.

98. Of the eighteen "China hands" in the State Department in 1944, only one, says the historian Gary May, fit "the pattern of eastern-based wealth and education." May, *China Scapegoat*, 109.

99. Quoted in Cuordileone, *Manhood*, 46.

100. Ibid., xi.

101. D. K. Johnson, *Lavender Scare*, 34.

102. Cuordileone, *Manhood*, 53.

103. D. K. Johnson, *Lavender Scare*, 115. One British official who spied for the Soviets, Guy Burgess, was both a communist and a homosexual; his case received a lot of publicity in 1951, when he and a fellow spy, Donald Maclean, fled their posts at the British embassy in Washington and defected to the Soviet Union. But Burgess was not blackmailed into espionage, and the British did not experience a comparable red scare or lavender scare. On Burgess's homosexuality and its relation to his espionage, see Fred Sommer, "Anthony Blunt and Guy Burgess: Gay Spies," in Hekma, Oosterhuis, and Steakley, *Gay Men*, 273–93.

104. Cuordileone, *Manhood*, 64; D. K. Johnson, *Lavender Scare*, 76.

105. D. K. Johnson, *Lavender Scare*, 166.

106. Rovere, *Senator Joe McCarthy*, 39.

107. Quoted in introduction to Buckley and Bozell, *McCarthy*, xi.

108. "Demagogue McCarthy," *Time*, October 22, 1951, cover; "The M'Carthy Speech," *New York Times*, October 28, 1952. For an astute discussion of the press coverage of McCarthy, see Strout, *Covering McCarthyism*.

109. For a nuanced analysis of McCarthyism and television, see Doherty, *Cold War, Cool Medium*.

110. Flynn to Styles Bridges, March 1, 1949, folder "U.S. Congress, Senate, A-K," box 20, Flynn Papers.

111. Quoted in Herman, *Joseph McCarthy*, 192.

112. Hoover, *Study of Communism*, 185.

113. Flynn, *Lattimore Story*, 112.

114. Church Committee, *Final Report*, book 3, 3.

115. Gentry, *J. Edgar Hoover*, 442.

116. Church Committee, *Final Report*, book 2, 46–47.

117. See the documents in "Loyalty Case (1953–54)," box 10, Sylvia Meagher Papers, Weisberg Archive of the Beneficial-Hodson Library at Hood College, Frederick, Maryland (hereafter Meagher Papers).

118. Quoted in "One Man vs. One Government," *Frederick News-Post*, December 25, 2005.

119. Memo, A. H. Belmont to L. V. Boardman, April 10, 1958, FBI file 100–353404–148, box 2.206, folder 26.1, Pauling Papers.

120. See summary, April 25, 1973, FBI file 100–353404–424, box 2.029, folder 29.2, Pauling Papers.

121. Hager, *Force of Nature*, 532.

122. Lattimore, *Ordeal by Slander*, 224.

123. Richard M. Fried, "The Idea of 'Conspiracy' in McCarthy-Era Politics," *Prologue* 34, no. 1 (2002): 43–44.

124. Hager, *Force of Nature*, 524.

CHAPTER 4

1. The unprocessed Sylvia Meagher papers at Hood College in Frederick, Maryland, contain letters between Meagher and other Warren Report critics. This summary of Martin's activities is compiled from the folders labeled "Martin, Shirley (1966)" and "Martin, Shirley (1966–68)," in box 10, Meagher Papers, and from Lewis and Schiller, *Scavengers*, 60, 57.

2. Various letters in folder "Field, Maggie, 1965" and "Field, Maggie, 1966–67," box 9, Meagher Papers; Lewis and Schiller, *Scavengers*, 65.

3. For Castellano's investigations, see "Castellano, Lillian," box 8, Meagher Papers; Lewis and Schiller, *Scavengers*, 77.

4. Meagher to Castellano, October 6, 1965, "Castellano," box 8, Meagher Papers.

5. Virginia A. Chanley, "Trust in Government in the Aftermath of 9/11: Determinants and Consequences," *Political Psychology* 23, no. 3 (2002): 472.

6. Quoted in Kelin, *Praise*, 464.

7. Castellano to Mr. Corson, December 29, 1964, folder "Castellano, Lillian," box 8, Meagher Papers.

8. Ibid.

9. Transcript of Johnson phone conversation with Bill Moyers, December 26, 1966, in Holland, *Kennedy Assassination Tapes*, 363.

10. Quoted in Evan Thomas, "The Real Cover-Up," *Newsweek*, November 22, 1993, 66.

11. Thomas, *Robert Kennedy*, 277.

12. According to the CIA's inspector general, "It is very likely that at the very moment President Kennedy was shot, a CIA officer was meeting with a Cuban agent…and giving him an assassination device for use against Castro." Church Committee, *Alleged Assassination Plots Involving Foreign Leaders*, 89.

13. Manchester, *Death of a President*, 257.

14. Hoover to Tolson et al., November 22, 1963, FBI file 62–109060–59, JFK Collection, National Archives, College Park, Maryland (hereafter JFK Collection).

15. Hoover recounts his conversation in a memo to Tolson et al., November 22, 1963, FBI file 62–109060–57, JFK Collection.

16. Oswald had actually sent a letter to a functionary in the embassy in hopes of getting a visa. He had, however, also talked to a KGB agent in Mexico City who might have been responsible for some assassinations, in the FBI's view. Hoover apparently confused the two men. Jenkins to Johnson, "Mr. J. Edgar Hoover said as follows," November 24, 1963, record 179–30003–10201, JFK Collection.

17. Testimony of Nelson Delgado, Hearings before the President's Commission on the Assassination of President Kennedy (hereafter Warren Commission Hearings), 8: 228–65.

18. On Oswald, see McMillan, *Marina and Lee*; Davison, *Oswald's Game*; Bugliosi, *Reclaiming History*, 513–788.

19. "I Must Be Free…," *Time*, November 10, 1961.

20. "Walker Demands a 'Vocal Protest,'" *New York Times*, September 30, 1962.

21. Nixon was not actually in Dallas on the day in April 1963 that Lee took his gun and told his wife he was going to "have a look" at him, though the newspapers were reporting an impending visit from Lyndon Johnson. Possibly Marina or Lee confused the current vice president with his predecessor, but Marina was certain that her husband had been contemplating killing a public official that day. For Marina's testimony on the Nixon incident, see Warren Commission Hearings, 5: 387–95; for her testimony on the Walker shooting, see 1: 16–18.

22. Oswald's activities in Mexico City are the subject of intense debate, largely because the CIA has been reluctant to release files relating to Oswald. For the House Select Committee on Assassinations' investigation of the Mexico City trip, see the report by staff members Dan Hardway and Edwin Lopez, "Oswald, the CIA, and Mexico City," undated, released 1996, available at http://www.aarclibrary.org/publib/jfk/hsca/lopezrpt/contents .htm, viewed March 20, 2008. For interpretations of the evidence, see Posner, *Case Closed*, chapter 9; Russo, *Live by the Sword*, chapter 10. For the recent efforts of a journalist to uncover the CIA's links to Oswald, see Jefferson Morley, "What Jane Roman Said," available at http://mcadams.posc.mu.edu/morley1.htm, viewed March 20, 2008. Morley is currently suing the CIA to release records he believes might relate to the assassination. See letter by Anthony Summers et al., *New York Review of Books*, August 11, 2005.

23. For example, see Wrone, *Zapruder Film*, 107, 146–47.

24. Alexander Cockburn says that Berkeley radicals recognized, with outrage, the meaning of Oswald's salute when they saw it on television on November 23. Cockburn, "Propaganda of the Deed," *New Statesman and Society* 6, no. 279 (November 19, 1993)

30–31. The police detective who tried to get a statement from Oswald as he died later said that Oswald had made a second clenched-fist salute. It was, the detective said, the accused assassin's last gesture. Summers, *Not in Your Lifetime*, 407 n37; Davison, *Oswald's Game*, 254.

25. Hoover recounts his conversation in a memo to Tolson et al., November 22, 1963, FBI file 62–10960–57, JFK Collection.

26. Russo, *Live by the Sword*, 333; Posner, *Case Closed*, 348n.

27. See Seth Kantor's handwritten notes, which are reproduced in Warren Commission Hearings, 20: 366.

28. Gerald Posner concludes that Ruby's ties to organized crime were tenuous and unimportant. Posner, *Case Closed*, 361–65. Anthony Summers presents the case for a mob conspiracy in *Not in Your Lifetime*, 330–61.

29. Manchester, *Death of a President*, 407.

30. Leo Janos, "The Last Days of the President," *Atlantic Monthly*, July 1973, 39.

31. "Memorandum for Mr. Moyers," November 25, 1963, FBI 62–109060–1399, JFK Collection.

32. Transcript of Johnson conversation with Thomas Kuchel, November 29, 1963, in Holland, *Kennedy Assassination Tapes*, 194. Johnson described his unrecorded conversation with Warren to Kuchel.

33. In addition to the conversation with Warren cited above, see the following transcripts in Holland, *Assassination Tapes*: Johnson's conversation with Speaker of the House John McCormack, November 29 (164); House Minority Leader Charles Halleck (178); House Majority Leader Carl Albert (181); Richard Russell (197, 201, 205–6).

34. Russo, *Live by the Sword*, 348.

35. Holland, *Kennedy Assassination Tapes*, 200. Russell was a little surprised by Johnson's bluntness. "Well, I don't think we oughta move that fast on it," he responded.

36. Handwritten note on memo from Gale to Tolson, December 10, 1963, FBI 67–798–3050, JFK Collection.

37. See Sullivan to Bland, March 12, 1962, FBI file 100–353404–289, folder 27.2, box 2.207, Pauling Papers.

38. See Gale to Tolson, December 10, 1963.

39. Hosty with Hosty, *Assignment Oswald*, 49–51.

40. Ibid., 29.

41. Hosty testimony, Warren Commission Hearings, 4: 461–62.

42. Hosty, *Assignment Oswald*, 29–30.

43. Ibid., 59–60; U.S. House, Subcommittee on Civil and Constitutional Rights of the Committee on the Judiciary, *Destruction of the Lee Harvey Oswald Note*, 36–175.

44. Testimony of Nanny Lee Fenner, receptionist, Dallas field office, in ibid., 43.

45. Gale to Tolson, December 10, 1963.

46. Addendum by Cartha Deloach in ibid.

47. Church Committee, *Final Reports*, book 5, 47.

48. President's Commission on the Assassination of President Kennedy, *Report* (hereafter *Warren Report*), 116.

49. Warren Commission members John S. Cooper and Richard Russell also doubted the commission staff's reconstruction of the "shot that missed." See McKnight, *Breach of Trust*, 292–93.

50. Sullivan with Brown, *Bureau*, 52.

51. Jenkins to Johnson, November 24, 1963.

52. Walter Trohan, "New Deal Plans Super Spy System," *Chicago Tribune*, February 9, 1945; Walter Trohan, "Super-Spy Idea Denounced as New Deal OGPU," *Chicago Tribune*, February 10, 1945.

53. Troy, *Donovan*, 222–28; Rudgers, *Creating the Secret State*, 21–25; Riebling, *Wedge*, 58–60; Ranelagh, *Agency*, 44, 55–56; Gentry, *J. Edgar Hoover*, 266.

54. Riebling, *Wedge*, 61–62, 76–77; Ranelagh, *Agency*, 104–5.

55. Doolittle Committee report quoted in Church Committee, *Final Report*, book 4, 52–53nn.

56. On Cuba's ties with the United States, see Paterson, *Contesting Castro*, especially 15–65; Hinckle and Turner, *Deadly Secrets*.

57. On Operation Mongoose, see Church Committee, *Alleged Assassination Plots Involving Foreign Leaders*, 71–180.

58. CIA inspector general report quoted in ibid., 81.

59. Church Committee, *Alleged Assassination Plots*, 127, 126.

60. CIA inspector general report quoted in ibid., 75.

61. Church Committee, *Alleged Assassination Plots*, 77.

62. The Castro plots are described in ibid., 71–90.

63. Janos, "Last Days of the President," 39.

64. Church Committee, *Alleged Assassination Plots*, 94. The Church Committee's complete analysis of the extent of Kennedy's knowledge of the plots is on 116–80.

65. Quoted in Thomas, "Real Cover-Up," 74.

66. "Judith E. Campbell," Evans to Belmont, March 20, 1962, FBI file 62–116606, folder 96, JFK Collection.

67. Quoted in Reeves, *President Kennedy*, 288.

68. "Castro Warns U.S. on Meddling with Cuba," *Los Angeles Times*, September 9, 1963.

69. Posner, *Case Closed*, 168, 168n.

70. Church Committee, *Final Report*, book 5, 73.

71. "Johnson Is Quoted on Kennedy Death," *New York Times*, June 25, 1976. For a discussion of Johnson's conspiracy theories, see Russo, *Live by the Sword*, 376–78.

72. See Russo, *Live by the Sword*, 381–86; Thomas, *Robert Kennedy*, 154, 283–87.

73. Wofford, *Of Kennedys and Kings*, 426.

74. Belin, *Final Disclosure*, 217–18. Emphasis added.

75. For analysis of the Zapruder film and its cultural meaning, see Wrone, *Zapruder Film*; Lubin, *Shooting Kennedy*.

76. Epstein, *Inquest*, 43.

77. *Warren Report*, 87–109.

78. U.S. House, Select Committee on Assassinations (HSCA), *Hearings*, 7: 15.

79. Ibid., 7: 17; Posner, *Case Closed*, 304.

80. Dennis L. Breo, "JFK's Death—The Plain Truth from the MDs Who Did the Autopsy," *Journal of the American Medical Association* 267, no. 20 (May 27, 1992): 2799.

81. This was not unprecedented in the history of presidential assassinations: the doctors who operated on the dying William McKinley also never found one of the bullets. See Rauchway, *Murdering McKinley*, 11. However, the sciences of surgery and pathology had improved greatly between 1901 and 1963. Oswald, for example, received a thorough and meticulously documented autopsy.

82. On JFK's poor health, see Hersh, *Dark Side of Camelot*, 5, 231–33. On the cover up of his illnesses at the autopsy, see Russo, *Live by the Sword*, 326–27.

83. Breo, "JFK's Death," 2799.

84. Lifton, *Best Evidence*, 101–2. For the complete FBI report, see J. Thompson, *Six Seconds*, appendix G, 296–98.

85. "A Matter of Reasonable Doubt," *Life*, November 25, 1966, 48.

86. In 1979, a House investigation found evidence of a conspiracy but still validated the single-bullet theory. Its evidence for conspiracy was later discredited. See chapter 5.

87. Thomas, *Robert Kennedy*, 284.

88. Russo, *Live by the Sword*, 372–73.

89. Holland, *Kennedy Assassination Tapes*, 250.

90. Sheldon Appleton, "Trends: Assassinations," *Public Opinion Quarterly* 64, no. 4 (Winter 2000): 514.

91. Lewis and Schiller, *Scavengers*, 72.

92. Notes on meeting of Warrenologists, October 3, 1965, "Sunday meeting 10/3/65," box 27, and letter, Raymond Marcus to Kenneth Auchincloss, August 20, 1966, "Marcus, Raymond," box 10, both in Meagher Papers.

93. See folder labeled "Loyalty Case," box 10, Meagher Papers.

94. FBI report on Harold Weisberg, November 8, 1966, FBI file 62–109060–4250, JFK Collection.

95. Fred J. Cook, "The Irregulars Take the Field," *Nation*, July 19, 1971, 40.

96. Meagher, *Accessories*, xxi.

97. Teixeira and Rogers, *America's Forgotten Majority*, 46; Lipset and Schneider, *Confidence Gap*, 17.

98. Lipset and Schneider, *Confidence Gap*, 17, 25.

99. Calvin Trillin, "The Buffs," *New Yorker*, June 10, 1967, 66.

100. Ibid., 46, 48.

101. Pauling to Kennedy, August 1, 1963, box 198, folder 198.3, Pauling Papers.

102. Pauling clipped and filed the text of the speech. See box 198, folder 198.3, Pauling Papers.

103. Meagher to Shirley Martin, December 30, 1965, "Martin, Shirley," box 10, Meagher Papers. Maggie Field called the speech Kennedy's "death knell." Note, undated, from Mrs. Joseph A. Field, "Field, Maggie, 1965," box 9, Meagher Papers.

104. Martin to Meagher, December 28, 1965, "Martin, Shirley," box 10, Meagher Papers.

105. Meagher to Martin, September 20, 1966, "Martin, Shirley," box 10, Meagher Papers.

106. Trillin, "Buffs," 66.

107. Ibid., 68.

108. Lewis and Schiller, *Scavengers*, 65.

109. Trillin, "Buffs," 44.

110. Mailer, *Oswald's Tale*, 351.

111. Lewis and Schiller, *Scavengers*, 73.

112. Even the FBI wanted a copy. See Jones to Wick, October 25, 1966, FBI file 100–442665, and Director to SAC, NY, October 24, 1966, 62–109090–494, JFK Collection.

113. Meagher, *Subject Index*, iv.

114. Lewis and Schiller, *Scavengers*, 65.

115. Jolie Solomon, "True Disbelievers," *Newsweek*, November 22, 1993, cited in Goldberg, *Enemies Within*, 120.

116. For Lane's search for a publisher, see Lewis and Schiller, *Scavengers*, 47.

117. Epstein, *Inquest*.

118. Trillin, "Buffs," 43.

119. Ibid., 45.

120. C. Roberts, *Truth*, 119.

121. Lewis and Schiller, *Scavengers*, 70–71.

122. CIA memo, "Countering Criticism of the Warren Report," 201–289248, April 1, 1967, JFK Collection.

123. Andrew and Mitrokhin, *Sword and the Shield*, 225–30.

124. FBI report on Harold Weisberg, November 8, 1966, in Hoover to Marvin Watson with attachments, November 8, 1966, FBI file 62–109060–4250, JFK Collection, National Archives, Maryland; Liam Farrell, "One Man vs. One Government," *Frederick News-Post*, December 26, 2005.

125. Hoover to Marvin Watson.

126. Appleton, "Trends: Assassinations," 514.

127. "A Matter of Reasonable Doubt," *Life*, November 25, 1966, 38–48B.

128. Richard Whalen, "The Kennedy Assassination," *Saturday Evening Post*, January 14, 1967, 19–25, 74.

129. "A Primer of Assassination Theories," *Esquire*, December 1966, 205–10, 334–35.

130. Posner, *Case Closed*, 423; Lambert, *False Witness*, 225–26, 238–40.

131. James Phelan, "The Vice Man Cometh," *Saturday Evening Post*, June 8, 1963, 67, 70–71.

132. Lambert, *False Witness*, 40–42.

133. Dean Andrews testimony, Warren Commission hearings, volume 11: 326, 331, 335.

134. Phelan, *Scandals*, 161. See Andrews's full testimony in the Warren Commission Hearings, 11: 326–39, to appreciate his instability and frequent contradictions.

135. Lambert, *False Witness*, 47.

136. Meagher to Garrison, April 22, 1967, "Garrison, New Orleans, 1967," box 15, Meagher Papers.

137. David Lifton, "Is Jim Garrison Out of His Mind?" *Open City* (Los Angeles underground newspaper), May 31 and June 6, 1968, available at http://mcadams.posc.mu.edu/lifton1.htm; Edward Epstein, "Reporter at Large," *New Yorker,* July 13, 1968, 52.

138. Phelan, *Scandals,* 150; James Phelan, "A Plot to Kill Kennedy? Rush to Judgment in New Orleans," *Saturday Evening Post,* May 6, 1967, 21–25. Interestingly, one of Garrison's recent biographers has found evidence to confirm contemporaneous rumors that the prosecutor himself was bisexual—and a child molester. Lambert, *False Witness,* 232–38.

139. Max Holland, "The Demon in Jim Garrison," *Wilson Quarterly* 25, no. 2 (Spring 2001), 10–17.

140. The consequences, of course, were not comparable. Johnson feared that nuclear war would result if the Soviets were blamed for the assassination. The Soviets, by contrast, knew that blaming Johnson and the CIA for the murder were relatively risk-free propositions for them.

141. See Max Holland's articles: "The Lie That Linked CIA to the Kennedy Assassination," *Studies in Intelligence,* Fall/Winter 2001, available at https://www.cia.gov/library/center-for-the-study-of-intelligence; "The Demon in Jim Garrison"; "The JFK Lawyers' Conspiracy," *Nation,* February 20, 2006, 20–22.

142. Tom Braden, "I'm Glad the CIA Is 'Immoral,'" *Saturday Evening Post,* May 20, 1967, 10, 12.

143. "The CIA Nightmare," *Commonweal,* March 3, 1967, 612.

144. "Jim Garrison's Playboy Interview," originally published in *Playboy,* October 1967, available at http://www.jfklancer.com/Garrison2.html, viewed March 20, 2008.

145. Ibid.

146. Quoted in Trillin, "Buffs," 68. Marcus was echoing John Connally's cry, "They are going to kill us all," on November 22.

147. Brener, *Garrison Case,* 221.

148. Garson, *MacBird!,* ix–x.

149. "Program Printer Rejects 'M'Bird!,'" *New York Times,* January 11, 1967. See also "WCBS-TV Withholds 'MacBird!' Segment," *New York Times,* January 30, 1967; "Ready, MacBird!," *New York Times,* February 19, 1967.

150. "'M'Bird!' Gets Off to Flying Start," *New York Times,* February 22, 1967; "Major Publisher in Paris Bids for 'MacBird!' Rights," *New York Times,* January 18, 1967.

151. Quoted in Garson, *MacBird!,* unpaginated front matter.

152. Garson, *MacBird!,* 74.

153. John Kaplan, "The Assassins," *Stanford Law Review* 19, no. 5 (May 1967): 1146.

154. Meagher to Penn Jones, July 29, 1967, "Jones, Penn, 1966–67," box 10, Meagher Papers.

155. Phelan, "Plot to Kill Kennedy?"

156. Epstein, "Reporter at Large," 60.

157. Epstein, *Assassination Chronicles,* 215–16.

158. *Assassination Inquiry Committee Newsletter* 1, no. 4 (August 17, 1968), box 198, folder 198.4, Pauling Papers.

159. Lifton, "Is Jim Garrison Out of His Mind?"

160. Tom Bethell, "Was Sirhan Sirhan on the Grassy Knoll?" *Washington Monthly*, March 1975, 38.

161. Lambert, *False Witness*, 124.

162. "Garrison Interview," *Assassination Inquiry Committee Newsletter* 1, no. 1 (June 24, 1968), box 198, folder 198.4, Pauling Papers.

163. Lambert, *False Witness*, 140; Kirkwood, *American Grotesque*, 403–11.

164. Quoted in Kirkwood, *American Grotesque*, 472.

165. William Gurvich quoted in CBS News transcript published in S. White, *Should We Now Believe*, 276.

166. Holland, "Lie That Linked CIA to the Kennedy Assassination."

167. Appleton, "Assassinations," 513, 515.

168. Holland, "Demon in Jim Garrison."

169. Kirkham, Levy, and Crotty, *Assassination and Political Violence*, 73.

170. Christopher Lasch, "The Life of Kennedy's Death," *Harper's*, October 1983, 32.

171. Ronald F. White, "Apologists and Critics of the Lone Gunman Theory: Assassination Science and Experts in Post-Modern America," in Fetzer, *Assassination Science*, 407. See also Lasch, "Life of Kennedy's Death," 39.

172. For more on this point, see Zelizer, *Covering the Body*, 101–20; Simon, *Dangerous Knowledge*, 8–27.

173. Quoted in Wrone, *Freedom of Information Act*, 52.

174. Max Holland, "After Thirty Years: Making Sense of the Assassination," *Reviews in American History* 22, no. 2 (June 1994): 191. See also Allen R. Vogt, "The Kennedy Assassination and the History Teacher," *History Teacher* 20, no. 1 (November 1986): 7–8.

175. Max Holland, "Cuba, Kennedy, and the Cold War," *Nation*, November 29, 1993, 655.

176. Lasch, "Life of Kennedy's Death," 40.

177. Cockburn, "Propaganda of the Deed," 30.

178. Wofford, *Of Kennedys and Kings*, 426.

CHAPTER 5

1. Kutler, *Abuse of Power*, 8. Emphasis in original.

2. See transcript of conversation between Nixon and Haldeman on June 14, 1971, available at National Security Archive, http://www.gwu.edu/~nsarchiv/NSAEBB/NSAEBB48/nixon.html, viewed March 20, 2008. See also Kutler, *Abuse of Power*, 1–42.

3. Kutler, *Abuse of Power*, 10. Emphasis in original.

4. Nixon conversation with Bob Haldeman, June 14, 1971, National Security Archive.

5. For some telling examples of Nixon's hatred of Eastern elites, see Summers with Swan, *Arrogance of Power*, 17–18.

6. Ibid., 79.

7. Quoted in Ambrose, *Nixon*, 671.

8. Nixon, *RN*, 382.

9. See Schell, *Time of Illusion*, 32; Ellsberg, *Secrets*, 428.

10. For a discussion of the effect of the secret bombing of Cambodia on Nixon's view of the war, see Schell, *Time of Illusion*, 34.

11. Kutler, *Abuse of Power*, 62.

12. Church Committee, *Final Report*, book 3, 681–732.

13. Schlesinger, *Imperial Presidency*, 422.

14. Church Committee, *Final Report*, book 3, 699.

15. See Church hearings, vol. 2, *Huston Plan*; Theoharis, *Boss*, 419–23.

16. On the Enemies List, see Schell, *Time of Illusion*, 188–89; Lukas, *Nightmare*, 12–13, 18.

17. On the military spy ring, see Colodny and Gettlin, *Silent Coup*, 5–31; James Rosen, "Nixon and the Chiefs," *Atlantic Monthly*, April 2002, 53–59.

18. Zumwalt, *On Watch*, 375.

19. Allan M. Jalon, "A Break-In to End All Break-Ins," *Los Angeles Times*, March 8, 2006.

20. "Stolen Documents Describe FBI Surveillance Activities," *Washington Post*, March 24, 1971.

21. Ellsberg, *Secrets*, 206, 357.

22. Conversation between Nixon and Haldeman on June 14, 1971.

23. Kutler, *Abuse of Power*, 10 (emphasis in original), 7, 8, 13, 23.

24. Ibid., 11; Conversation among Richard Nixon, Ron Ziegler, and Bob Haldeman, July 5, 1971, available at http://tapes.millercenter.virginia.edu/transcripts/index.php/Nixon/537–004, viewed March 20, 2008, quoted in Kenneth J. Hughes Jr., "How Paranoid Was Nixon?" August 13, 2007, available at http://hnn.us/articles/41698.html. See also Kenneth J. Hughes Jr., "Nixon vs. the Imaginary 'Jewish Cabal,'" September 24, 2007, available at http://hnn.us/articles/42970.html, both viewed March 20, 2008. Ellsberg's grandparents were all Jewish, but he was raised as a Christian. Ellsberg, *Secrets*, 22.

25. Kutler, *Abuse of Power*, 8, 5, 14.

26. Emery, *Watergate*, 71–73. John Dean was astounded to find a faked cable in Hunt's safe after Hunt's Watergate arrest. See Dean, *Blind Ambition*, 115.

27. Kutler, *Abuse of Power*, 38. See also George Lardner Jr., "Behind the Statesman, A Reel Nixon Endures," *Washington Post*, June 17, 1997.

28. Kutler, *Abuse of Power*, 36.

29. Ibid., 61.

30. Hugh Sidey, "Notes from an Open White House," *Time*, August 26, 1974, quoted in Rozell, *Press*, 47.

31. President Ford's address to the nation, September 8, 1974, available at the American Presidency Project, http://www.presidency.ucsb.edu.

32. "Ford's Gallup Rating Off 21 Points after Pardon," *New York Times*, October 13, 1974.

33. Anthony Lewis, "The System Scorned," *New York Times*, September 9, 1974, quoted in Rozell, *Press*, 56.

34. Daniel Schorr, "My 17 Months on the CIA Watch," *Rolling Stone*, April 8, 1976, 32.

35. "Son of Watergate," *New York Times*, September 18, 1975.

36. Cheney quoted in Scott Shane, "Recent Flexing of Presidential Powers Had Personal Roots in Ford White House," *New York Times*, December 30, 2006.

37. Draft memo, "CIA—the Colby Report," Cheney to Ford, December 27, 1974, folder "Intelligence—the Colby Report," box 5, and meeting notes for May 28 and 29, 1975, folder "Intelligence—*New York Times* articles by Seymour Hersh, 5/75–6/75 (1)," box 6, both in Richard Cheney Files, Gerald R. Ford Library, Ann Arbor, Michigan.

38. Louis Harris, "35% Support Ford-Named CIA panel," *Washington Post*, February 17, 1975.

39. On Church, see LeRoy Ashby and Rod Gramer's excellent biography, *Fighting the Odds*.

40. Quoted in ibid., 394.

41. "The American Legion National High School Oratorical Contest," series 8.1, box 1, folder 5, Frank Church Papers, Boise State University, Boise, Idaho (hereafter Church Papers).

42. Press conference, July 8, 1975, series 7.9, box 4, folder 1, Church Papers.

43. See chapter 4 for a discussion of these plots.

44. Church Committee, *Alleged Assassination Plots*, 129.

45. Church Committee hearings, 6: 31.

46. Church Committee, *Final Report*, book 2, 221. For the most complete examination of the FBI's harassment of King, see Garrow, *FBI*.

47. U.S. Congress, House, *Congressional Record*, 94th Cong., 2d sess., 1435. See also Senate Bill 1489 introduced that year.

48. Church Committee, *Final Report*, book 3, 3.

49. John Crewdson, "Church Doubts Plot Links to Presidents," *New York Times*, July 19, 1975. For one committee member's dissent on the rogue elephant theory, see Walter Mondale's comments in volume 2 of the Church Committee hearings, September 25, 1975, 108.

50. S. Turner, *Secrecy and Democracy*, 28.

51. For a fuller explanation of my argument that the investigations did not produce real reforms, see my *Challenging the Secret Government*, 176–81. For other perspectives, see L. Johnson, *Season of Inquiry*; Smist, *Congress Oversees*, 275.

52. James Risen and Eric Lichtblau, "Bush Lets U.S. Spy on Callers Without Courts," *New York Times*, December 16, 2005.

53. Frank Church, address at Idaho State University, Pocatello, February 18, 1977, series 7.9, box 4, folder 3, Church Papers.

54. Sixty-two percent agreed that "you cannot trust the government to do right most of the time" in 1974. This increased to 63 percent in 1976, 68 percent in 1978, and 73 percent in 1980. Lipset and Schneider, *Confidence Gap*, 17.

55. Frost, "*I Gave Them a Sword*," 183.

56. U.S. House, Select Committee on Intelligence, *CIA: The Pike Report*, 189.

57. Oriana Fallaci, "Otis Pike and the CIA," *New Republic*, April 3, 1976, 10.

58. Rod MacLeish, "Conspiracy Theories," *Washington Post*, August 5, 1975.

59. See G. E. White, *Alger Hiss's Looking-Glass Wars*, chapter 5.

60. For examples of these charges, see Charles Colson on the *CBS Evening News*, February 5, 1975; the story on Giancana's death leading the *CBS Evening News* on June 20, 1975; and William Safire, "Murder Most Foul," *New York Times*, December 22, 1975.

61. Safire, "Murder Most Foul."

62. *CBS Evening News*, February 5, 1975.

63. See Colodny and Gettlin, *Silent Coup*; Hougan, *Secret Agenda*. See also David Greenberg's discussion of the revisionist works in *Nixon's Shadow*, chapter 5.

64. See letters to Church in series 3.2.2, box 4, and series 2.6, box 1, Church Papers. See also my discussion of this phenomenon in Olmsted, *Challenging the Secret Government*, 99–102.

65. "Week in Review," *New York Times*, June 22, 1975.

66. Gallup, *Gallup Poll*, 930, 927–31.

67. Andrew Torchia, "Conspiracy Killed King, Widow Says," *Washington Post*, November 28, 1975; Leon Dash, "Rights Leaders Ask Probe of Dr. King Assassination," *Washington Post*, November 28, 1975.

68. "The King Review," *Washington Post*, November 27, 1975.

69. *Saginaw News*, November 20, 1975, in *Editorials on File 1975* (New York: Facts on File, 1975), 1427.

70. Laura Kittrell of Dallas, letter to the editor, *Time*, December 15, 1975.

71. "Jim Garrison and His War with the CIA," *Washington Star News*, April 18, 1975, in "New Wave (1975) press clips," box 22, Meagher Papers.

72. George O'Toole, "New Demands for Better Answers," *Saturday Evening Post*, September 1975, 46; Mark Lane, "The New Explosion of Controversial Research," *Saturday Evening Post*, September 1975, 50.

73. Oglesby, *Yankee and Cowboy War*, 47–80, quote from tape on 47. For later examples of connections among "the whole Bay of Pigs thing," Dallas, and Watergate, see Vankin, *Conspiracies*, 155.

74. Jacob Cohen, "Conspiracy Fever," *Commentary*, October 1975.

75. Dino de Laurentiis Corporation, "Dino de Laurentiis Presents Three Days of the Condor" (Beverly Hills: Dino de Laurentiis, 1975).

76. Jenkins, *Decade of Nightmares*, 55. For another insightful discussion of 1970s popular culture, see Ryan and Kellner, *Camera Politica*. See also Russell Baker's discussion in his column titled "Black Hat for Uncle Sam," *New York Times*, December 13, 1975.

77. Wrone, *Zapruder Film*, 67–69.

78. "Schweiker Predicts Collapse of Warren Report on Kennedy," *New York Times*, October 16, 1975.

79. HSCA, *Final Report*, 9.

80. Letter, G. Robert Blakey to Sylvia Meagher, September 8, 1977, "HSCA Correspondence," box 15, Meagher Papers.

81. HSCA, *Hearings*, 4: 429–53.

82. The report and hearings are online at http://www.aarclibrary.org/publib/jfk/hsca/contents.htm, viewed March 20, 2008.

83. HSCA, *Final Report*, 3–4.

84. Summers, *Not in Your Lifetime*, 17; Steve Barber, "The Acoustic Evidence: A Personal Memoir," available at http://mcadams.posc.mu.edu/barber.htm, viewed March 20, 2008; "New Study on Slaying of Kennedy Doubts 2d Gunman Was Involved," *New York Times*, May 15, 1982. D. B. Thomas published an article in 2001 claiming that the acoustic evidence did indeed suggest a second gunman, but his findings remain controversial. See Thomas, "Echo Correlation Analysis and the Acoustic Evidence in the Kennedy Assassination," *Science and Justice* 41 (2001): 21–32; Michael O'Dell, "The Acoustic Evidence in the Kennedy Assassination," available at http://mcadams.posc.mu.edu/odell, viewed March 20, 2008.

85. U.S. House, *Final Assassinations Report*. The foreword is not paginated.

CHAPTER 6

1. Hubbell, *Friends*, 282.

2. Delasara, *PopLit*, 16.

3. The Harris Poll, 1995, available at http://www.harrisinteractive.com/harris_poll/index.asp?PID=646, viewed May 23, 2008. On JFK polls, see Sheldon Appleton, "The Polls—Trends: Assassinations," *Public Opinion Quarterly* 64, no. 4 (Winter 2000): 515.

4. M. W. Cooper, *Behold a Pale Horse*, 3.

5. "Unusual Suspects," *The X-Files*, season five, 1997.

6. American Psychiatric Association, *Diagnostic and Statistical Manual*, 200.

7. "Mind-Control Studies Had Origins in Trial of Mindszenty," *New York Times*, August 2, 1977.

8. Richard Helms memo from April 3, 1953, quoted in U.S. Senate, Select Committee on Intelligence and Subcommittee on Health and Scientific Research of the Committee on Human Resources, *Joint Hearings on Project MKULTRA*, 79.

9. On MKULTRA and its predecessors, see Marks, *Search for the "Manchurian Candidate."*

10. Commission on CIA Activities within the United States, *Report*, 227–28.

11. See Marks, *Search for the "Manchurian Candidate,"* chapter 5; Ted Gup, "The Coldest Warrior," *Washington Post Magazine*, December 16, 2001; Eric Olson's Web page, www.frankolsonproject.org, viewed March 20, 2008.

12. Seymour Hersh, "Family Plan to Sue C.I.A. Over Suicide in Drug Test," *New York Times*, July 10, 1975; *People*, July 28, 1975.

13. Testimony of Stansfield Turner before Senate, *Joint Hearings on Project MKULTRA*, August 3, 1977; "C.I.A. Says It Found More Secret Papers on Behavior Control," *New York Times*, September 3, 1977.

14. Senate, *Joint Hearings on Project MKULTRA*, 12.

15. Marks, *Search for the "Manchurian Candidate,"* chapter 6.

16. Senate, *Joint Hearings on Project MKULTRA*, 22.

17. H. M. Weinstein, *Psychiatry and the CIA*; Marks, *Search for the "Manchurian Candidate,"* chapter 8.

18. See, for example, Vankin, *Conspiracies*, 171.

19. Ibid., 178.

20. Quoted in Jonathan Vankin and John Whalen, "The Jonestown Massacre: CIA Mind Control Run Amok?" available at http://www.hiddenmysteries.org/mind/research/re020600a.html, viewed March 20, 2008.

21. President Ronald Reagan, remarks at the annual convention of the National Association of Evangelicals, March 8, 1983, available at the American Presidency Project, http://www.presidency.ucsb.edu.

22. Reagan, remarks to Jewish leaders, March 5, 1986, available at the American Presidency Project, http://www.presidency.ucsb.edu.

23. Reagan, radio address to the nation, March 8, 1986, available at the American Presidency Project, http://www.presidency.ucsb.edu.

24. Reagan, remarks at a White House meeting for supporters of United States assistance for the Nicaraguan Democratic Resistance, March 3, 1986, available at the American Presidency Project, http://www.presidency.ucsb.edu.

25. The best summaries of Iran-contra include Draper, *Very Thin Line*; Walsh, *Iran-Contra* and *Firewall*; Inouye and Hamilton, *Report of the Congressional Committees Investigating the Iran-Contra Affair*. Schaller, *Reckoning with Reagan*, has an excellent short summary of the scandal in chapter 6.

26. Reagan speech, "Remarks at the Annual Dinner of the Conservative Political Action Conference," March 1, 1985, available at the American Presidency Project, http://www.presidency.ucsb.edu.

27. Testimony of Robert McFarlane to the U.S. House, Select Committee to Investigate Covert Arms Transactions with Iran and U.S. Senate Select Committee on Secret Military Assistance to Iran and the Nicaraguan Opposition (hereafter Iran-contra hearings), part II, July 14, 1987, 225; Oliver North testimony reproduced in U.S. House, Select Committee to Investigate Covert Arms Transactions with Iran and U.S. Senate Select Committee on Secret Military Assistance to Iran and the Nicaraguan Opposition, *Taking the Stand*, 373.

28. Noonan, *What I Saw*, 236.

29. For example, in his diary entry for August 9, 1985, Oliver North wrote, "Honduran DC-6 which is being used for runs out of New Orleans is probably being used for drug runs into U.S." For this document and a trove of others on U.S. officials' knowledge of narco-trafficking by the contras, see the Oliver North file online at the national security archive, http://www.gwu.edu/~nsarchiv/NSAEBB/NSAEBB113/index.htm#doc1, viewed March 20, 2008.

30. Moyers, *Secret Government*, 24.

31. "The Mystic Who Lit the Fires of Hatred," *Time*, January 7, 1980.

32. Ronald Reagan, remarks at the annual convention of the American Bar Association, July 8, 1985, available at the American Presidency Project, http://www.presidency.ucsb.edu.

33. For Reagan's approval of the Iran initiative, see John Poindexter, memorandum for the president, "Covert Action Finding Regarding Iran," with signed finding attached, January 17, 1986, in Kornbluh and Byrne, *Iran-Contra Scandal*, 232–35. For a narrative of the arms-for-hostages trades, see Inouye and Hamilton, *Report*, part 3.

34. U.S. House, Select Committee to Investigate Covert Arms Transactions with Iran and U.S. Senate Select Committee on Secret Military Assistance to Iran and the Nicaraguan Opposition, *Taking the Stand*, 346.

35. Ibid., 443.

36. The independent counsel noted that North was not a very credible witness on this point. Walsh, *Final Report*, 212.

37. Inouye and Hamilton, *Report of the Congressional Committees Investigating the Iran-Contra Affair*, 34.

38. Iran-contra hearings, part II, July 14, 1987, 161.

39. Theodore Draper, foreword to Kornbluh and Byrne, *Iran-Contra Scandal*, xiii.

40. Minutes, National Security Planning Group Meeting on Central America, June 25, 1984, reproduced in ibid., 82.

41. U.S. House, Select Committee to Investigate Covert Arms Transactions with Iran and U.S. Senate Select Committee on Secret Military Assistance to Iran and the Nicaraguan Opposition, *Taking the Stand*, 19.

42. Reagan's approval rating fell from 70 percent in mid-1986 to 44 percent at the height of Iran-contra in February 1987. ABC News poll, http://abcnews.go.com/sections/politics/DailyNews/poll_reagan010806.html, viewed March 20, 2008. The standard poll used to measure public confidence in the government is the American National Election Studies series, which has asked the same question of Americans at two-year intervals since 1964. The question is: How much of the time do you think you can trust the government in Washington to do what is right—just about always, most of the time, or only some of the time? In 1964, 76 percent of Americans answered "just about always" or "most of the time." In 1974, that percentage had fallen to 36. It had risen to 44 percent in 1984, but dropped to 38 percent in 1986. Virginia A. Chanley, "Trust in Government in the Aftermath of 9/11: Determinants and Consequences," *Political Psychology* 23, no. 3 (2002): 472.

43. Quoted in Draper, *Very Thin Line*, 22.

44. Inouye and Hamilton, *Report of the Congressional Committees Investigating the Iran-Contra Affair*, 389, 376.

45. Iran-contra hearings, part II, July 10, 1987, 26.

46. Chanley, "Trust in Government in the Aftermath of 9/11," 472.

47. William J. Broad, "'Urge to Investigate and Believe' Sparks New Interest in U.F.O.'s," *New York Times*, June 16, 1987.

48. Charles A. Ziegler, "Mythogenesis," in Ziegler, Saler, and Moore, *UFO Crash at Roswell*, 6–7, 13. See also Peebles, *Watch the Skies*.

49. Ziegler, "Mythogenesis," 9. See also chapter 4, "The Roswell Incident," in Goldberg, *Enemies Within*; McAndrew, *Roswell Report*.

50. For a complete analysis of the top-secret atomic program, see Charles B. Moore, "The Early New York University Balloon Flights," in Ziegler et al., *UFO Crash at Roswell*, 74–114. See also McAndrew, *Roswell Report*.

51. Ziegler, "Mythogenesis," 17. The *National Enquirer* did an article on Roswell in 1978, but Moore and Berlitz wrote the first book-length examination of the incident.

52. Berlitz and Moore, *Roswell Incident*, 126.

53. On MJ-12, see Friedman, *Top Secret/Majic*.

54. Gerald K. Haines, "CIA's Role in the Study of UFOs, 1947–90," *Studies in Intelligence* 1, no. 1 (1997), n. 93. For a transcript of Marshall's letter to Dewey and the similar MJ-12 document, see http://www.cufon.org/cufon/marshall.htm#notes, viewed March 20, 2008. For further discussion of the MJ-12 documents, see Peebles, *Watch the Skies*, 264–68.

55. "Mind Control: The Ultimate Abduction," headline on the cover of *UFO: The Science and Phenomena Magazine* 18, no. 1 (February/March 2003).

56. See Jones, *Bad Blood*.

57. Jonathan Peterson, "U.S. to Admit Its Tuskegee Study Betrayal," *Los Angeles Times*, May 15, 1997.

58. Welsome, *Plutonium Files*.

59. See P. A. Turner, *I Heard It*.

60. Anita M. Waters, "Conspiracy Theories as Ethnosociologies: Explanation and Intention in African American Political Culture," *Journal of Black Studies* 28, no. 1 (September 1997): 118. See also R. C. Smith and Seltzer, *Contemporary Controversies*, chapter 5.

61. Craig Reinarman and Harry G. Levine, "Crack in Context," in Reinarman and Levine, *Crack in America*, 2.

62. Randolph N. Stone, "The War on Drugs: The Wrong Enemy and the Wrong Battlefield," *National Bar Association Magazine*, December 1989, 18, quoted in Lusane, *Pipe Dream Blues*, 4.

63. See D. Cole, *No Equal Justice*, 142. See also Troy Duster, "Pattern, Purpose, and Race in the Drug War," in Reinarman and Levine, *Crack in America*, 266.

64. U.S. Senate, Committee on Foreign Relations, Subcommittee on Terrorism, Narcotics, and International Operations, *Drugs, Law Enforcement, and Foreign Policy*.

65. Quoted in Schou, *Kill the Messenger*, 73.

66. Jason DeParle, "Many Blacks See Ills as Part of Conspiracy," *New York Times*, October 29, 1990; Waters, "Conspiracy Theories as Ethnosociologies," 117.

67. Gary Webb, "America's 'Crack' Plague Has Roots in Nicaragua War," *San Jose Mercury News*, August 18, 1996. The entire "Dark Alliance" series is on-line at several sites, including http://www.narconews.com/darkalliance/drugs/start.htm, viewed March 20, 2008. See also Webb, *Dark Alliance*.

68. Gary Webb, "The Mighty Wurlitzer Plays On," in Borjesson, *Into the Buzzsaw*, 300.

69. Tim Golden, "Though Evidence Is Thin, Tale of C.I.A. and Drugs Has a Life of Its Own," *New York Times*, October 21, 1996.

70. Jack E. White, "Crack, Contras and Cyberspace," *Time*, September 30, 1996.

71. Quoted in ibid.

72. Webb, "Mighty Wurlitzer," 302–3.

73. Quoted in Cockburn and St. Clair, *Whiteout*, 88.

74. B. Drummond Ayres, "CIA Chief Denies Crack Conspiracy," *New York Times*, November 16, 1996; Webb, "Mighty Wurlitzer," 304.

75. See Roberto Suro and Walter Pincus, "The CIA and Crack: Evidence Is Lacking of Alleged Plot," *Washington Post*, October 4, 1996; "Tale of CIA and Drugs Has Life of Its Own," *New York Times*, October 21, 1996; Jesse Katz, "Tracking the Genesis of the Crack Trade," *Los Angeles Times*, October 20, 1996. For analysis of the media coverage, see Jack E. White, "Caught in the Middle," *Time*, May 26, 1997; Knight, *Conspiracy Culture*, 148–52; Peter Kornbluh, "The Storm over 'Dark Alliance,'" *Columbia Journalism Review*, January/February 1997.

76. Webb, *Dark Alliance*, 453.

77. Golden, "Though Evidence Is Thin."

78. Quoted in Schou, *Kill the Messenger*, 146.

79. Andrew Marshall, "CIA Turned a Deliberate Blind Eye to Contras' Drug Smuggling," *Independent*, November 7, 1998; Schou, *Kill the Messenger*, 183–84; Webb, "Mighty Wurlitzer," 307–8; CIA Inspector General, *Allegations of Connections between CIA and the Contras in Cocaine Trafficking to the United States: Report of Investigation— Volume II: The Contra Story*, October 8, 1998, available at https://www.cia.gov/library/ reports/general-reports-1/cocaine/contra-story/report-of-investigation-volume-ii-the-contra-story-2.html, viewed March 20, 2008.

80. Conversation with the author, May 27, 2003.

81. Quoted in Charles Bowden, "Introduction," in Schou, *Kill the Messenger*, vii.

82. Schou, *Kill the Messenger*, 4.

83. "Reporter's Suicide Confirmed by Coroner," *Sacramento Bee*, December 15, 2004.

84. Michael Kelly, "The Road to Paranoia," *New Yorker*, June 19, 1995, 64.

85. Berlet and Lyons, *Right-Wing Populism*, 270–73; Gibson, *Warrior Dreams*, 218–30.

86. See, for example, Macdonald, *Turner Diaries*, 42.

87. Berlet and Lyons, *Right-Wing Populism*, 271.

88. On the militias and the larger Patriot movement, see Berlet and Lyons, *Right-Wing Populism*; Barkun, *Culture of Conspiracy*; Lamy, *Millennium Rage*; Stern, *Force upon the Plain*; Mulloy, *American Extremism*; Bennett, *Party of Fear*, chapter 16.

89. Berlet and Lyons, *Right-Wing Populism*, 288, 289.

90. M. W. Cooper, *Behold a Pale Horse*, 115–19.

91. T. Marrs, *Dark Majesty*, 32, 18; George H. W. Bush, speech to Congress, January 16, 1991, available at the American Presidency Project, http://www.presidency.ucsb.edu. For a discussion of New World Order conspiracy theories, see Barkun, *Culture of Conspiracy*, chapter 3.

92. T. Marrs, *Dark Majesty*, 32. On the American right and the millennial myth, see Lamy, *Millennium Rage*; Boyer, *When Time Shall Be No More*.

93. Stern, *Force upon the Plain*, 35–37, quote on 37.

94. The precise number of the dead is unknown because of the devastation caused by the fire.

95. Danforth, *Interim Report to the Deputy Attorney General Concerning the 1993 Confrontation at the Mt. Carmel Complex, Waco, Texas*.

96. Waco Holocaust Electronic Museum, http://www.web-ak.com/waco/cover/c_pag202.html, viewed March 20, 2008.

97. Stern, *Force upon the Plain*, 61.

98. Macdonald, *Turner Diaries*, 38–40, 201–4. For a discussion of the climactic scene, see Gibson, *Warrior Dreams*, 223.

99. Michel and Herbeck, *American Terrorist*, 121; Stern, *Force upon the Plain*, 192.

100. Michel and Herbeck, *American Terrorist*, 179–80, 120, 155–56; Barkun, *Culture of Conspiracy*, ix.

101. Michel and Herbeck, *American Terrorist*, 3, 234, 224–25.

102. Stern, *Force upon the Plain*, 205–7.

103. Quoted in ibid., 206.

104. President Bill Clinton, Remarks on the Oklahoma City Bombing, April 19, 1995, available at the American Presidency Project, http://www.presidency.ucsb.edu.

105. President Bill Clinton, remarks at the Michigan State University Commencement Ceremony, May 5, 1995, available at the American Presidency Project, http://www.presidency.ucsb.edu. For a discussion of Clinton's response, see Hamm, *Apocalypse in Oklahoma*, 58, 222.

106. See Sara Diamond's definition of right-wing movements in *Roads to Dominion*, 8.

107. M. W. Cooper, "The Secret Government," reprinted as chapter 12 in *Behold a Pale Horse*, 223, 196.

108. Berlet, *Right Woos Left*, 2.

109. Ibid., 46. See also David Corn, "X-Men and JFK," *Nation*, January 27, 1992, 80.

110. On Prouty, see Berlet, *Right Woos Left*, 17.

111. Alexander Cockburn, "Why Bother to Conspire against J.F.K.?" *Los Angeles Times*, December 26, 1991.

112. *The Siege at Ruby Ridge*, directed by Roger Young, 1996.

113. C. Moore, *Davidian Massacre*, ix.

114. Danforth, *Interim Report*, i.

115. D. J. Mulloy makes this point about the militias' response to Ruby Ridge and Waco in *American Extremism*, 154.

116. Vidal, *Perpetual War*, 46.

117. Reprinted in ibid., 60, 73.

118. Vidal, *United States*, 874–76, 970, 880–83.

119. Quoted in Vidal, *Perpetual War*, 99.

120. Gore Vidal, "The Meaning of Timothy McVeigh," *Vanity Fair*, September 2001, 352, 411.

121. For an analysis of Kaczynski's ideology, see Lamy, *Millennium Rage*, 139–50.

122. Michel and Herbeck, *American Terrorist*, 398–402, quotes on 400 and 401.

123. Ibid., 399.

124. Knight, *Conspiracy Culture*, 3.

125. See *Wag the Dog* (1997) and *Conspiracy Theory* (1997).

126. Quoted in Delasara, *PopLit*, 8.

127. For analysis of *The X-Files*, see the articles in Lavery, Hague, and Cartwright, *"Deny All Knowledge,"* especially Allison Graham, *"'Are You Now or Have You Ever Been?' Conspiracy Theory and the X-Files"*; Delasara, *PopLit*; Knight, *Conspiracy Culture*, 216–23; Fenster, *Conspiracy Theories*, 132–38.

128. "Redux," *The X-Files*, season five, 1997.

129. Delasara, *PopLit*, 178.

130. Kevin Stevens, "X-Men: Space Cadets Glen Morgan and James Wong Reflect on Their X Tenure," *Sci-Fi Universe*, October 1995.

131. Chanley, "Trust in Government in the Aftermath of 9/11," 472.

CHAPTER 7

1. Breitweiser, *Wake-Up Call*, 137.

2. Ibid., 140. See some of the Jersey Girls discuss this incident in the documentary *9/11: Press for Truth*, directed by Ray Nowosielski, 2006.

3. For attacks on the Jersey Girls, see Dorothy Rabinowitz, "The 9/11 Widows," *Wall Street Journal*, April 14, 2004; "Limbaugh Likened Michael J. Fox to 'Jersey Girls,' " October 24, 2006, available at http://mediamatters.org/items/200610250005, viewed March 20, 2008; A. Coulter, *Godless*, 112, 103.

4. Breitweiser, *Wake-Up Call*, 141.

5. *9/11: Press for Truth*.

6. Hargrove and Stempel, "Anti-Government Anger Spurs 9/11 Conspiracy Belief."

7. Transcript, December 9, 2001, available at http://www.whitehouse.gov/vicepresident/news-speeches/speeches/vp20011209.html, viewed March 20, 2008.

8. Project for a New American Century, "Statement of Principles," June 3, 1997, available at http://www.newamericancentury.org/statementofprinciples.htm, viewed March 20, 2008. On PNAC, see Maria Ryan, "Inventing the 'Axis of Evil': The Myth and Reality of U.S. Intelligence and Policy-Making after 9/11," *Intelligence and National Security* 17, no. 4 (Winter 2002): 55–76.

9. Project for a New American Century, letter to Clinton, January 26, 1998, available at http://www.newamericancentury.org/iraqclintonletter.htm, viewed March 20, 2008.

10. "Rebuilding America's Defenses: Strategy, Forces and Resources for a New Century," report of the Project for the New American Century, September 2000, 51, available at http://www.newamericancentury.org/publicationsreports.htm, viewed March 20, 2008.

11. Nicholas Lemann, "The Iraq Factor: Will the New Bush Team's Old Memories Shape Its Foreign Policy?" *New Yorker*, January 22, 2001.

12. Quoted in Isikoff and Corn, *Hubris*, 74.

13. Isikoff and Corn, *Hubris*, 84.

14. Clarke, *Against All Enemies*, 32.

15. Isikoff and Corn, *Hubris*, 103–4.

16. Paul R. Pillar, "Intelligence, Policy, and the War in Iraq," *Foreign Affairs*, March/April 2006, available at http://www.foreignaffairs.org/20060301faessay85202/paul-r-pillar/intelligence-policy-and-the-war-in-iraq.html, viewed March 20, 2008.

17. Isikoff and Corn, *Hubris*, 140.

18. Quoted in Glenn Kessler and Jim VandeHei, "Misleading Assertions Cover Iraq War and Voting Records," *Washington Post*, October 6, 2004.

19. Transcript of interview with Vice President Dick Cheney on *Meet the Press*, September 8, 2002, available at http://www.mtholyoke.edu/acad/intrel/bush/meet.htm, viewed March 20, 2008.

20. Linda Feldmann, "The Impact of Bush Linking 9/11 and Iraq," *Christian Science Monitor*, March 14, 2003.

21. Virginia A. Chanley, "Trust in Government in the Aftermath of 9/11: Determinants and Consequences," *Political Psychology* 23, no. 3 (2002): 469.

22. Mueller, *War*, 58.

23. Richard Benedetto, "Public Support Slips for Ousting Saddam," *USA Today*, August 23, 2002.

24. Dana Milbank and Claudia Deane, "Hussein Link to 9/11 Lingers in Many Minds," *Washington Post*, September 6, 2003.

25. President Bush's October 7, 2002, address in Cincinnati, available at the American Presidency Project, http://www.presidency.ucsb.edu.

26. *CNN Late Edition with Wolf Blitzer*, transcript of interview with Dick Cheney, March 24, 2002, available at http://transcripts.cnn.com/TRANSCRIPTS/0203/24/le.00.html, viewed March 20, 2008.

27. Quoted in David Barstow, William J. Broad, and Jeff Gerth, "How the White House Embraced Disputed Arms Intelligence," *New York Times*, October 3, 2004.

28. *CNN's Late Edition with Wolf Blitzer*, transcript of interview with Condoleezza Rice, September 8, 2002, available at http://transcripts.cnn.com/TRANSCRIPTS/0209/08/le.00.html, viewed March 20, 2008.

29. Isikoff and Corn, *Hubris*, 35. Bush used the smoking gun–mushroom cloud image in his Address to the Nation on Iraq from Cincinnati, Ohio, on October 7, 2002, available at the American Presidency Project, http://www.presidency.ucsb.edu.

30. "Bush's State of the Union Speech," January 28, 2003, available at the American Presidency Project, http://www.presidency.ucsb.edu.

31. U.S. Secretary of State Colin Powell, address to the U.N. Security Council, February 5, 2003, available at http://www.whitehouse.gov/news/releases/2003/02/20030205–1.html, viewed March 20, 2008.

32. Mohammed ElBaradei quoted in Walter Pincus, "Bush Faced Dwindling Data on Iraq Nuclear Bid," *Washington Post*, July 16, 2003.

33. Hans Blix, statement to the United Nations Security Council, March 7, 2003, available at http://www.un.org/Depts/unmovic/SC7asdelivered.htm, viewed March 20, 2008. For more on the inspections, see Blix, *Disarming Iraq*.

34. Quoted in Rich, *Greatest Story*, 72.

35. In the period from April 14 to 16, 2003, 76 percent of Americans said they approved of Bush's Iraq policy. See http://www.pollingreport.com/iraq2.htm, viewed March 20, 2008.

36. "Bush Makes Historic Speech Aboard Warship," transcript, May 1, 2003, available at http://www.cnn.com/2003/US/05/01/bush.transcript/, viewed March 20, 2008.

37. Ron Suskind, "Faith, Certainty and the Presidency of George W. Bush," *New York Times Magazine*, October 17, 2004. Frank Rich has noted that the official "sounded uncannily like Karl Rove." Rich, *Greatest Story*, 3.

38. "Coleen Rowley's Memo to FBI Director Robert Mueller," *Time*, May 21, 2002; David Johnston, "Pre-Attack Memo Cited Bin Laden," *New York Times*, May 15, 2002. See the FBI Inspector General's report on the Minneapolis and Phoenix cases at http://www.usdoj.gov/oig/special/s0606/chapter1.htm, viewed March 20, 2008.

39. B. Graham with Nussbaum, *Intelligence Matters*, 47.

40. Michael Weisskopf, "Why Didn't the FBI Fully Investigate Moussaoui?" *Time*, May 23, 2002.

41. "What Bush Knew before September 11," *CBS News*, May 17, 2002, available at http://www.cbsnews.com/stories/2002/05/16/terror/main509294.shtml?source=search_story, viewed March 20, 2008.

42. "National Security Advisor Holds Press Briefing," May 16, 2002, available at http://www.whitehouse.gov/news/releases/2002/05/20020516–13.html, viewed March 20, 2008.

43. Associated Press, "FBI Agent Warned about 9/11 Hijacker," September 21, 2002. Moreover, the strategy of crashing a plane into a target building was a staple of fiction from *The Turner Diaries* to Tom Clancy's 1994 *Debt of Honor* to *Lone Gunmen*, a short-lived *X-Files* spin-off early in 2001.

44. "9/11 Chair: Attack Was Preventable," *CBS News*, December 17, 2003, available at http://www.cbsnews.com/stories/2003/12/17/eveningnews/main589137.shtml, viewed March 20, 2008.

45. B. Graham with Nussbaum, *Intelligence Matters*, 163, 166.

46. Ibid., 169.

47. James Risen and David Johnston, "Report on 9/11 Suggests a Role by Saudi Spies," *New York Times*, August 2, 2003.

48. Timothy J. Burger, "9/11 Probe: Aiming High," *Time*, February 3, 2003.

49. John Prados, "'Slow-Walked and Stonewalled': The Administration's Near-Gag Order Assured a Less-than-Satisfactory Outcome to the Congressional Investigation of 9/11," *Bulletin of the Atomic Scientists* 59, no. 2 (March–April 2003), 28–38. See also B. Graham with Nussbaum, *Intelligence Matters*, 137–40.

50. B. Graham with Nussbaum, *Intelligence Matters*, 140.

51. Ibid., 170.

52. U.S. Congress, *Hearings of the Joint Inquiry into Intelligence Community Activities before and after the Terrorist Attacks of September 11, 2001*, September 18, 2002, 1: 40.

53. For a complete list of Breitweiser's fifty-one questions for the committee, see ibid., 37–39.

54. Ibid., 46.

55. B. Graham with Nussbaum, *Intelligence Matters*, 200.

56. Breitweiser, *Wake-Up Call*, 96.

57. Ibid., 108.

58. Michael Isikoff and Mark Hosenball, "Terror Watch: Lingering Questions," *Newsweek*, June 11, 2003.

59. See, for example, Gail Sheehy, "Four 9/11 Moms Battle Bush," *New York Observer*, August 25, 2003.

60. Breitweiser, *Wake-Up Call*, 96.

61. Ibid., 121.

62. A. Coulter, *Godless*, 112, 103.

63. Frank Rich, "As the War Turns," *New York Times*, April 25, 2004.

64. Breitweiser, *Wake-Up Call*, 128.

65. Faludi, *Terror Dream*, 214, 89, 107–14.

66. Jessica Seigel, "*Ms.* Women of the Year: Jersey Girls," *Ms.*, winter 2004.

67. "Lacking Biolabs, Trailers Carried Case for War," *Washington Post*, April 12, 2006.

68. David Kay at Senate hearing, January 28, 2004, transcript, available at http://www.cnn.com/2004/US/01/28/kay.transcript/, viewed March 20, 2008.

69. See Wilson, *Politics of Truth*.

70. Joseph C. Wilson, "What I Didn't Find in Africa," *New York Times*, July 6, 2003.

71. Quoted in Walter Pincus and Richard Leiby, "Retired Envoy: Nuclear Report Ignored," *Washington Post*, July 6, 2003.

72. Transcript of conversation between Nixon and Haldeman on June 14, 1971, available at National Security Archive, http://www.gwu.edu/~nsarchiv/NSAEBB/NSAEBB48/nixon.html, viewed March 20, 2008.

73. Quoted in Suskind, *Price of Loyalty*, 86. Emphasis in original.

74. Clarke, *Against All Enemies*, 232.

75. Ibid., 243.

76. Richard Clarke testimony, in Strasser, *9/11 Investigations*, 175.

77. Paul Pillar, "Intelligence, Policy, and the War in Iraq," *Foreign Affairs*, March/April 2006.

78. *NOW*, PBS, February 6, 2006, transcript, available at http://www.pbs.org/now/transcript/transcriptNOW205_full.html, viewed March 20, 2008.

79. Wilkerson speech to New America Foundation, October 20, 2005, transcript, available at http://www.ft.com/cms/s/c925a686–40f4–11da-b3f9–00000e2511c8.html, viewed March 20, 2008. See also Dana Milbank, "Colonel Finally Saw Whites of Their Eyes," *Washington Post*, October 20, 2005.

80. For analysis of the Downing Street memos, see Danner, *Secret Way*. The quote is on 89, emphasis added. For early reporting on the civil war within the Bush administration over intelligence, see Seymour Hersh, "The Stovepipe," *New Yorker*, October 27, 2003.

81. The Center for Public Integrity later concluded that the president and his aides had "waged a carefully orchestrated campaign of misinformation" about the threat posed by Iraq. See "The War Card: Orchestrated Deception on the Path to War," January 22, 2008, available at http://www.publicintegrity.org/warcard/?source=c0107e3a, viewed March 20, 2008. See also U.S. Senate, Select Committee on Intelligence, *Report on Whether Public Statements Regarding Iraq by U.S. Government Officials Were Substantiated by Intelligence Information*; McClellan, *What Happened*.

82. Walter Pincus and Dana Milbank, "Al Qaeda–Hussein Link Is Dismissed," *Washington Post*, June 17, 2004.

83. Milbank and Deane, "Hussein Link Lingers"; "The Harris Poll: Many Americans Still Believe Hussein Had Links to al Qaeda," *Wall Street Journal Online*, December 29, 2005.

84. "Poll: Less than Half of Americans Think U.S. Can Win in Iraq," cnn.com, March 13, 2007, available at http://www.cnn.com/2007/POLITICS/03/13/iraq.poll/index.html, viewed March 20, 2008. Right before the election of 2004, 47 percent of Americans believed that Bush had lied about the war, but he still won reelection.

85. Duke quoted in Daniel Levitas, "The Radical Right after 9/11," *The Nation*, July 22, 2002; William F. Jasper, "The Action Is in the Reaction," *New American* 18, no. 20, October 7, 2002, available at http://web.archive.org/web/20021009204704/www.thenewamerican.com/tna/2002/10–07–2002/vo18no20_action.htm, viewed March 20, 2008.

86. On Ohio, see Mark Crispin Miller, "None Dare Call It Stolen," *Harper's*, August 2005; Robert F. Kennedy Jr., "Was the 2004 Election Stolen?" *Rolling Stone*, June 1, 2006.

87. Transcript of appearance of Rep. Cynthia McKinney, March 25, 2002, available at http://www.rise4news.net/McKinney.html, viewed March 20, 2008.

88. Curt Maynard, "Pay No Attention to the Soldier Saying 9/11 Is a Lie," http://nationalexpositor.com/News/941.html, viewed May 10, 2008. The phrase "Arabs in caves" is common in 9/11 conspiracy theories.

89. J. Marrs, *Terror Conspiracy*, back cover.

90. For the extraterrestrial theory, see Michael E. Salla, "False Flag Operations, 9-11 and the Exopolitical Perspective," available at www.exopolitics.org; for one of many Zionist MIHOP sites, see "The Israeli Spy Ring," available at http://www.whatreallyhappened.com/spyring.html; for the Illuminati, see http://www.cuttingedge.org/news/n1753.cfm, all viewed March 20, 2008. For the New World Order, see David R. Kimball, "Consolidating Their Power, Tightening Their Grip," flyer in author's possession; for Peak Oil, see Ruppert, *Crossing the Rubicon*.

91. Tarpley, *9/11 Synthetic Terror*, quote from inside back cover.

92. 9/11 Truth Europe, "Who Are We?" available at http://www.911truth.eu/en/index.php?id=3,2,0,0,1,0, viewed March 20, 2008.

93. Meyssan, *9/11*.

94. "About the 9/11 Truth Alliance," available at http://web.archive.org/web/20030809220224/911truth.org/background_info.html, viewed March 20, 2008.

95. Sac Valley 9/11 Truth Pages, http://sac911truth.blogspot.com, viewed March 20, 2008.

96. Andrew Keen, "Web 2.0: The Second Generation of the Internet Has Arrived; It's Worse Than You Think," *Daily Standard*, February 15, 2006, available at http://www.weeklystandard.com/Content/Public/Articles/000/000/006/714fjczq.asp?pg=1, viewed February 23, 2008.

97. Complete 9/11 Timeline Web site, http://complete911timeline.org/, viewed March 20, 2008.

98. See Jebediah Redd, "Suspicious Minds: How a Ragtag Group of Conspiracy Nuts Is Changing Public Perception of 9/11," Radaronline, January 2008, available at http://radaronline.com/from-the-magazine/2008/01/we_are_change_911_conspiracy_theories_alex_jones_luke_rudkow.php, viewed March 20, 2008.

99. Nancy Jo Sales, "Click Here for Conspiracy," *Vanity Fair*, August 2006.

100. *Loose Change 2nd Edition Recut* is available at http://video.google.com/videoplay?docid=7866929448192753501, viewed March 20, 2008.

101. See "Hoax-Promoting Videos," available at http://911review.com/disinfo/videos.html#loosechange, viewed March 20, 2008.

102. See, for example, Jim Hoffman, "*Popular Mechanics'* Deceptive Smear against 9/11 Truth," available at http://www.911review.com/pm/markup/index.html, viewed March 20, 2008.

103. "9/11 Funds Came from Pakistan, Says FBI," *Times of India*, August 1, 2003. For an insightful discussion of the mysteries of 9/11, see Ridgeway, *Five Unanswered Questions about 9/11*.

104. S. Shyam Sunder, the head of the NIST study, quoted in "The Ground Zero Grassy Knoll," *New York*, March 27, 2006.

105. National Institute of Standards and Technology Web site, http://wtc.nist.gov/pubs. For the FEMA study, see http://www.fema.gov/rebuild/mat/wtcstudy.shtm, both viewed March 20, 2008.

106. Dunbar and Reagan, *Debunking 9/11 Myths*; Tarpley, *9/11 Synthetic Terror*, vi.

107. Quoted in Jarrett Murphy, "The Seekers: The Birth and Life of the 9-11 Truth Movement," *Village Voice*, February 21, 2006.

108. Steven E. Jones, "Why Indeed Did the WTC Buildings Collapse?" in Griffin and Scott, *9/11 and American Empire*, 33–61.

109. April 30, 2007, comments on Alex Jones's Web site, http://www.haloscan.com/comments/sonof101/300407freeway/, viewed March 20, 2008.

110. J. Marrs, *Terror Conspiracy*, x.

111. Anna Kasten Nelson, "Operation Northwoods and the Covert War against Cuba, 1961–1963," *Cuban Studies* 32 (2001): 152 n4; United States Assassination Records Review Board, *Final Report*, 41.

112. Memo by General Lansdale, "Meeting with the President, 16 March 1962."

113. For an analysis of Operation Northwoods as a performance, see Tracy C. Davis, "Operation Northwoods: The Pentagon's Scripts for Overthrowing Castro," *Drama Review* 50, no. 1 (Spring 2006): 134–48.

114. Bamford, *Body of Secrets*, 82–91.

115. "The Truth Is Out There" was the headline of a *Harper's* article on Northwoods in July 2001, 21.

116. Ruppert, *Crossing the Rubicon*, 592.

117. For an example of this type of argument, see Griffin, *New Pearl Harbor*.

118. See Jhally and Earp, *Hijacking Catastrophe*; David N. Gibbs, "Pretexts and U.S. Foreign Policy: The War on Terrorism in Historical Perspective," *New Political Science* 26, no. 3 (September 2004): 293–321.

119. *The View*, March 29, 2007.

120. Hargrove and Stempel, "Anti-Government Anger Spurs 9/11 Conspiracy Belief."

121. Sales, "Click Here for Conspiracy."

122. Breitweiser on *Hardball with Chris Matthews*, August 11, 2005, transcript, available at http://www.msnbc.msn.com/id/8925092/, viewed March 20, 2008; Breitweiser, *Wake-Up Call*, 259–64.

123. *9/11: Press for Truth*. See also Seymour M. Hersh, "The Getaway," *New Yorker*, January 28, 2002.

124. Quoted in Shenon, *Commission*, 162. On the politics of the commission, see also Kitts, *Presidential Commissions*, chapter 6.

125. Quoted in Shenon, *Commission*, 99.

126. Stephen Push, quoted in P. Thompson, *Terror Timeline*, 525.

127. Zelikow with Rice, *Germany Unified and Europe Transformed*.

128. Shenon, *Commission*, 43.

129. Ibid., 85, 107–11, 130–34, 145, 321–23, quote on 107. Zelikow says the phone calls were unrelated to commission business, and several staff members have publicly defended his integrity.

130. Breitweiser, *Wake-Up Call*, 146, 148.

131. For a list of Bush's statements connecting Iraq and al Qaeda, see M. Moore, *Dude*, 54–55. For specific examples from Bush's speeches, see "Remarks in Denver, Colorado," October 28, 2002, and "Remarks in Dallas, Texas," November 4, 2002, available at the American Presidency Project, http://www.presidency.ucsb.edu.

132. Breitweiser, *Wake-Up Call*, 79.

CONCLUSION

1. Alan Feuer, "500 Conspiracy Buffs Meet to Seek Truth of 9/11," *New York Times*, June 5, 2006.

2. Morales and Van Auken, quoted in Mark Jacobson, "The Ground Zero Grassy Knoll," *New York*, March 27, 2006.

3. Quoted in Kelin, *Praise from a Future Generation*, 438.

4. Michael Rivero's WhatReallyHappened.Com, http://www.whatreallyhappened .com/McCollum/, accessed March 14, 2008.

5. For an amusing discussion of this trend, see Matt Taibbi, "The Low Post: I, Left Gatekeeper," *Rolling Stone*, September 26, 2006, available at http://www.rollingstone

.com/politics/story/11818067/the_low_post_the_hopeless_stupidity_of_911_conspiracies, accessed March 20, 2008.

6. See ibid.; David Corn, "The September 11 X-Files," Capital Games blog for *The Nation*, May 30, 2002, available at http://www.thenation.com/blogs/capitalgames?bid=3& pid=66, accessed March 20, 2008.

7. Jon Carroll, *San Francisco Chronicle*, March 31, 2006.

8. "Exclusive: Help Us Examine the Lost JFK Files," *Dallas Morning News*, February 22, 2008, available at http://www.dallasnews.com/sharedcontent/dws/dn/latestnews/stories/ 022208dnmetjfkdocs.15b53191, accessed March 8, 2008.

9. Letter to the editor, available at http://www.dallasnews.com/perl/common/ surveys/vote_now.pl, accessed March 8, 2008.

10. Dewey, *Later Works*, 325.

11. Richard Nixon, remarks on departure from the White House, August 9, 1974, available at the American Presidency Project, http://www.presidency.ucsb.edu.

12. "Warren Commission Will Ask Mrs. Oswald to Identify Rifle Used in the Kennedy Assassination," *New York Times*, February 5, 1964.

13. For an excellent analysis of this phenomenon, see Thomas C. Ellington, "Won't Get Fooled Again: The Paranoid Style in the National Security State," *Government and Opposition* 38, no. 4 (Autumn 2003): 436–55.

Bibliography

Books and Essays

Albright, Joseph, and Marcia Kunstel. *Bombshell: The Secret Story of America's Unknown Atomic Spy Conspiracy*. New York: Times Books, 1997.

Alpers, Benjamin L. *Dictators, Democracy, and American Public Culture: Envisioning the Totalitarian Enemy, 1920s–1950s*. Chapel Hill: University of North Carolina Press, 2003.

Alterman, Eric. *Sound and Fury: The Washington Punditocracy and the Collapse of American Politics*. New York: HarperCollins, 1992.

———. *When Presidents Lie: A History of Official Deception and Its Consequences*. New York: Penguin, 2004.

Ambrose, Stephen E. *Nixon: The Education of a Politician, 1913–1962*. New York: Simon & Schuster, 1987.

American Psychiatric Association. *Diagnostic and Statistical Manual of Mental Disorders*, 3rd ed., revised. Washington, D.C.: American Psychiatric Association, 1987.

Anderson, John Thomas. "Senator Burton K. Wheeler and United States Foreign Relations." Ph.D. diss., University of Virginia, 1982.

Andrew, Christopher, and Oleg Gordievsky. *KGB: The Inside Story of Its Foreign Operations from Lenin to Gorbachev*. New York: HarperCollins, 1990.

Andrew, Christopher, and Vasili Mitrokhin. *The Sword and the Shield: The Mitrokhin Archive and the Secret History of the KGB*. New York: Basic Books, 1999.

Ashby, LeRoy, and Rod Gramer. *Fighting the Odds: The Life of Senator Frank Church*. Pullman: Washington State University Press, 1994.

Baldwin, Neil. *Henry Ford and the Jews: The Mass Production of Hate*. New York: Public Affairs, 2003.

Bamford, James. *Body of Secrets: Anatomy of the Ultra-Secret National Security Agency from the Cold War through the Dawn of a New Century.* New York: Doubleday, 2001.

———. *A Pretext for War: 9/11, Iraq, and the Abuse of America's Intelligence Agencies.* New York: Doubleday, 2004.

Barkun, Michael. *A Culture of Conspiracy: Apocalyptic Visions in Contemporary America.* Berkeley: University of California Press, 2003.

Barnes, Harry Elmer. *In Quest of Truth and Justice.* New York: Arno Press, 1972.

———, ed. *Perpetual War for Perpetual Peace.* Caldwell, Idaho: Caxton Printers, 1953.

Barthes, Roland. *Image, Music, Text.* Trans. Stephen Heath. London: Fontana, 1977.

Bartlett, Bruce. *Cover-Up: The Politics of Pearl Harbor, 1941–1946.* New York: Arlington House, 1978.

Beard, Charles A. *The Devil Theory of War.* New York: Vanguard, 1936.

———. *President Roosevelt and the Coming of the War, 1941.* New Haven: Yale University Press, 1948.

Beard, Charles A., and Mary R. Beard. *The Rise of American Civilization.* 1927. Reprint, New York: Macmillan, 1946.

Belin, David. *Final Disclosure: The Full Truth about the Assassination of President Kennedy.* New York: Scribner's, 1988.

Bennett, David H. *The Party of Fear: From Nativist Movements to the New Right in American History.* Chapel Hill: University of North Carolina Press, 1988.

Bennett, Linda L. M., and Stephen Earl Bennett. *Living with Leviathan: Americans Coming to Terms with Big Government.* Lawrence: University Press of Kansas, 1990.

Bentley, Elizabeth. *Out of Bondage: The Story of Elizabeth Bentley.* New York: Devin-Adair, 1951.

Berg, A. Scott. *Lindbergh.* New York: Putnam, 1998.

Berle, Adolf. *Navigating the Rapids, 1918–1971.* Ed. Beatrice Bishop Berle and Travis Beal Jacobs. New York: Harcourt Brace Jovanovich, 1973.

Berlet, Chip. *Right Woos Left: Populist Party, LaRouchian, and Other Neo-Fascist Overtures to Progressives, and Why They Must Be Rejected.* Cambridge, Mass.: Political Research Associates, 1992.

Berlet, Chip, and Matthew N. Lyons. *Right-Wing Populism in America: Too Close for Comfort.* New York: Guilford Press, 2000.

Berlitz, Charles, and William L. Moore. *The Roswell Incident.* New York: Grosset and Dunlap, 1980.

Blakey, George T. *Historians on the Homefront: American Propagandists for the Great War.* Lexington: University Press of Kentucky, 1970.

Blix, Hans. *Disarming Iraq.* New York: Pantheon, 2004.

Borjesson, Kristina, ed. *Into the Buzzsaw: Leading Journalists Expose the Myth of a Free Press.* Amherst, N.Y.: Prometheus Books, 2002.

Bourne, Randolph. *The Radical Will: Selected Writings, 1911–1918.* New York: Urizen Books, 1977.

Boyer, Paul S. *When Time Shall Be No More: Prophecy Belief in Modern American Culture.* Cambridge, Mass: Belknap Press, 1992.

Breitweiser, Kristen. *Wake-Up Call: The Political Education of a 9/11 Widow.* New York: Warner Books, 2006.

Brener, Milton. *The Garrison Case: A Study in the Abuse of Power.* New York: Clarkson Potter, 1969.

Brinkley, Alan. *Voices of Protest: Huey Long, Father Coughlin, and the Great Depression.* New York: Vintage, 1983.

Buckley, William F., and Brent Bozell. *McCarthy and His Enemies: The Record and Its Meaning.* Chicago: Regnery, 1954.

Budiansky, Stephen. *Battle of Wits: The Complete Story of Codebreaking in World War II.* New York: Free Press, 2000.

Bugliosi, Vincent. *Reclaiming History: The Assassination of President John F. Kennedy.* New York: Norton, 2007.

Burk, Kathleen. *Britain, America, and the Sinews of War, 1914–1918.* Boston: G. Allen & Unwin, 1985.

Burnham, James. *The Web of Subversion: Underground Networks in the United States Government.* New York: John Day, 1954.

Carlson, John Roy. *Under Cover.* New York: Dutton, 1943.

Chafee, Zechariah, Jr. *Free Speech in the United States.* Cambridge, Mass.: Harvard University Press, 1941.

Chambers, Whittaker. *Witness.* Washington, D.C.: Regnery, 1952.

Charles, Douglas M. *J. Edgar Hoover and the Anti-Interventionists: FBI Political Surveillance and the Rise of the Domestic Security State, 1939–1945.* Columbus: Ohio State University Press, 2007.

Chernow, Ron. *The House of Morgan: An American Banking Dynasty and the Rise of Modern Finance.* New York: Atlantic Monthly Press, 1990.

———. *The Warburgs: The Twentieth-Century Odyssey of a Remarkable Jewish Family.* New York: Random House, 1993.

Clarke, Richard A. *Against All Enemies: Inside America's War on Terror.* New York: Free Press, 2004.

Clemens, Diane Shaver. *Yalta.* New York: Oxford University Press, 1970.

Cockburn, Alexander, and Jeffrey St. Clair. *Whiteout: The CIA, Drugs, and the Press.* London: Verso, 1998.

Cohen, Robert. *When the Old Left Was Young: Student Radicals and America's First Mass Student Movement, 1929–1941.* New York: Oxford University Press, 1993.

Cohen, Warren I. *The American Revisionists: The Lessons of Intervention in World War I.* Chicago: University of Chicago Press, 1967.

Cole, David. *No Equal Justice: Race and Class in the American Criminal Justice System.* New York: New Press, 1999.

Cole, Wayne S. *America First: The Battle against Intervention, 1940–1941.* Madison: University of Wisconsin Press, 1953.

———. *Charles A. Lindbergh and the Battle against American Intervention in World War II.* New York: Harcourt Brace Jovanovich, 1974.

———. *Roosevelt and the Isolationists: 1932–45.* Lincoln: University of Nebraska Press, 1983.

—————. *Senator Gerald P. Nye and American Foreign Relations*. Minneapolis: University of Minnesota Press, 1962.

Colodny, Len, and Robert Gettlin. *Silent Coup: The Removal of a President*. New York: St. Martin's Press, 1991.

Connally, Tom, as told to Alfred Steinberg. *My Name Is Tom Connally*. New York: Thomas Y. Crowell, 1954.

Cooper, John Milton, Jr. *The Warrior and the Priest: Woodrow Wilson and Theodore Roosevelt*. Cambridge, Mass.: Belknap Press, 1983.

Cooper, John Milton, Jr., and Charles E. Neu, eds. *The Wilson Era: Essays in Honor of Arthur S. Link*. Arlington Heights, Ill.: Harlan Davidson, 1991.

Cooper, Milton William. *Behold a Pale Horse*. Sedona, Ariz.: Light Technology Publishing, 1991.

Costello, John. *Days of Infamy: MacArthur, Roosevelt, Churchill—The Shocking Truth Revealed*. New York: Pocket, 1994.

Coulter, Ann. *Godless: The Church of Liberalism*. New York: Crown Forum, 2006.

Coulter, Matthew Ware. *The Senate Munitions Inquiry of the 1930s: Beyond the Merchants of Death*. Westport, Conn.: Greenwood, 1997.

Craig, R. Bruce. *Treasonable Doubt: The Harry Dexter White Spy Case*. Lawrence: University Press of Kansas, 2004.

Cuordileone, K. A. *Manhood and American Political Culture in the Cold War*. New York: Routledge, 2005.

Dallek, Robert. *Franklin D. Roosevelt and American Foreign Policy, 1932–1945*. New York: Oxford University Press, 1979.

Danner, Mark. *The Secret Way to War*. New York: New York Review of Books, 2006.

Davis, David Brion. *The Fear of Conspiracy: Images of Un-American Subversion from the Revolution to the Present*. Ithaca, N.Y.: Cornell University Press, 1971.

—————. *The Slave Power Conspiracy and the Paranoid Style*. Baton Rouge: Louisiana State University Press, 1969.

Davison, Jean. *Oswald's Game*. New York: Norton, 1983.

Dean, John. *Blind Ambition*. New York: Simon & Schuster, 1976.

Dean, Robert D. *Imperial Brotherhood: Gender and the Making of Cold War Foreign Policy*. Amherst: University of Massachusetts Press, 2001.

Delasara, Jan. *PopLit, PopCult and "The X-Files": A Critical Exploration*. Jefferson, N.C.: McFarland, 2000.

deToledano, Ralph. *Seeds of Treason: The True Story of the Hiss-Chambers Tragedy*. 1950. Reprint, Boston: Western Islands, 1965.

Detzer, Dorothy. *Appointment on the Hill*. New York: Henry Holt, 1948.

Devlin, Patrick. *Too Proud to Fight: Woodrow Wilson's Neutrality*. New York: Oxford University Press, 1974.

Dewey, John. *The Later Works: 1925–1953*. Ed. Jo Ann Boydston. Carbondale: Southern Illinois University Press, 1984.

Diamond, Sara. *Roads to Dominion: Right-Wing Movements and Political Power in the United States*. New York: Guilford Press, 1995.

Didion, Joan. *The White Album*. New York: Simon & Schuster, 1979.

Dinnerstein, Leonard. *Antisemitism in America*. New York: Oxford University Press, 1994.

———, ed. *Antisemitism in the United States*. New York: Holt, Rinehart, and Winston, 1971.

Doenecke, Justus. *Not to the Swift: The Old Isolationists in the Cold War Era*. Cranbury, N.J.: Associated University Presses, 1979.

———. *Storm on the Horizon: The Challenge to American Intervention, 1939–1941*. Lanham, Md.: Rowman & Littlefield, 2000.

Doherty, Thomas. *Cold War, Cool Medium: Television, McCarthyism, and American Culture*. New York: Columbia University Press, 2003.

Donovan, Hedley. *Roosevelt to Reagan: A Reporter's Encounters with Nine Presidents*. New York: Harper & Row, 1985.

Donovan, Robert J. *Conflict and Crisis: The Presidency of Harry S Truman, 1945–1948*. New York: Norton, 1977.

Dower, John. *War without Mercy: Race and Power in the Pacific War*. New York: Pantheon, 1986.

Draper, Theodore. *A Very Thin Line: The Iran-Contra Affairs*. New York: Hill and Wang, 1991.

Dunbar, David, and Brad Reagan. *Debunking 9/11 Myths: Why Conspiracy Theories Can't Stand Up to the Facts—An In-Depth Investigation by* Popular Mechanics. New York: Hearst Books, 2006.

Ellsberg, Daniel. *Secrets: A Memoir of Vietnam and the Pentagon Papers*. New York: Viking, 2002.

Emery, Fred. *Watergate: The Corruption and Fall of Richard Nixon*. London: Jonathan Cape, 1994.

Engelbrecht, H. C., and F. C. Hanighen. *Merchants of Death: A Study of the International Armament Industry*. New York: Dodd, Mead, 1934.

Epstein, Edward Jay. *The Assassination Chronicles*. New York: Carroll & Graf, 1992.

———. *Inquest: The Warren Commission and the Establishment of Truth*. New York: Viking, 1966.

Faludi, Susan. *The Terror Dream: Fear and Fantasy in Post-9/11 America*. New York: Metropolitan Books, 2007.

Feklisov, Alexander. *The Man behind the Rosenbergs*. New York: Enigma Books, 2001.

Fenster, Mark. *Conspiracy Theories: Secrecy and Power in American Culture*. Minneapolis: University of Minnesota Press, 1999.

Fetzer, James H., ed. *Assassination Science: Experts Speak Out on the Death of JFK*. Chicago: Catfeet Press, 1998.

Fish, Hamilton. *Memoir of an American Patriot*. Washington, D.C.: Regnery, 1991.

Flynn, John T. *As We Go Marching*. New York: Doubleday, 1944.

———. *The Lattimore Story*. New York: Devin-Adair, 1953.

———. *The Roosevelt Myth*. New York: Devin-Adair, 1948.

———. *The Smear Terror*. New York: John T. Flynn, 1947.

———. *The Truth about Pearl Harbor*. New York: John T. Flynn, 1944.

———. *While You Slept: Our Tragedy in Asia and Who Made It*. New York: Devin-Adair, 1951.

Forbes, John Douglas. *J. P. Morgan, Jr., 1867–1943*. Charlottesville: University Press of Virginia, 1981.

Fried, Albert. *FDR and His Enemies*. New York: St. Martin's Press, 1999.

Fried, Richard M. *Nightmare in Red: The McCarthy Era in Perspective*. New York: Oxford University Press, 1990.

Friedman, Stanton T. *Top Secret/Majic: Operation Majestic-12 and the United States Government's UFO Cover-Up*. New York: Marlowe, 1996.

Frost, David. *"I Gave Them a Sword": Behind the Scenes of the Nixon Interviews*. New York: Macmillan, 1978.

Gaddis, John Lewis. *We Now Know: Rethinking Cold War History*. Oxford: Oxford University Press, 1998.

Gallup, George. *The Gallup Poll: Public Opinion, 1935–1971*. Volume 1. New York: Random House, 1972.

Garrow, David. *The FBI and Martin Luther King, Jr*. New York: Penguin Books, 1981.

Garson, Barbara. *MacBird!* New York: Grove, 1967.

Gentry, Curt. *J. Edgar Hoover: The Man and the Secrets*. New York: Norton, 1991.

Gerber, David A., ed. *Anti-Semitism in American History*. Urbana: University of Illinois Press, 1986.

Gibson, James. *Warrior Dreams: Paramilitary Culture in Post-Vietnam America*. New York: Hill and Wang, 1994.

Goddard, Arthur, ed. *Harry Elmer Barnes: Learned Crusader*. Colorado Springs, Colo.: Ralph Myles, 1968.

Goldberg, Robert Alan. *Enemies Within: The Culture of Conspiracy in Modern America*. New Haven: Yale University Press, 2001.

Goodman, Walter. *The Committee: The Extraordinary Career of the House Committee on Un-American Activities*. New York: Farrar, Straus & Giroux, 1968.

Goodwin, Doris Kearns. *No Ordinary Time: Franklin and Eleanor Roosevelt: The Home Front in World War II*. New York: Touchstone, 1995.

Graham, Bob, with Jeff Nussbaum. *Intelligence Matters: The CIA, the FBI, Saudi Arabia, and the Failure of America's War on Terror*. New York: Random House, 2004.

Graham, Otis. *An Encore for Reform: The Old Progressives and the New Deal*. New York: Oxford University Press, 1967.

Graumann, Carl F., and Serge Moscovici, eds. *Changing Conceptions of Conspiracy*. New York: Springer Verlag, 1987.

Greenbaum, Fred. *Men against Myths: The Progressive Response*. Westport, Conn.: Praeger, 2000.

Greenberg, David. *Nixon's Shadow: The History of an Image*. New York: Norton, 2003.

Griffin, David Ray. *The New Pearl Harbor: Disturbing Questions about the Bush Administration and 9/11*. Northampton, Mass.: Olive Branch Press, 2004.

———. *The 9/11 Commission Report: Omissions and Distortions*. Northampton, Mass.: Olive Branch Press, 2005.

Griffin, David Ray, and Peter Dale Scott. *9/11 and American Empire: Intellectuals Speak Out*. Northampton, Mass.: Olive Branch Press, 2007.

Griffith, Robert. *The Politics of Fear: Joseph R. McCarthy and the Senate.* Amherst: University of Massachusetts Press, 1987.

Gruber, Carol S. *Mars and Minerva: World War I and the Uses of Higher Learning in America.* Baton Rouge: Louisiana State University Press, 1975.

Hagedorn, Ann. *Savage Peace: Hope and Fear in America, 1919.* New York: Simon & Schuster, 2007.

Hager, Thomas. *Force of Nature: The Life of Linus Pauling.* New York: Simon & Schuster, 1995.

Haines, Lynn, and Dora B. Haines. *The Lindberghs.* New York: Vanguard, 1931.

Hall, John R., with Philip D. Schuyler and Sylvaine Trinh. *Apocalypse Observed: Religious Movements and Violence in North America, Europe, and Japan.* London: Routledge, 2000.

Hamm, Mark S. *Apocalypse in Oklahoma: Waco and Ruby Ridge Revenged.* Boston: Northeastern University Press, 1997.

Hart, John. *The Presidential Branch: From Washington to Clinton.* 1987. Reprint, Chatham, N.J.: Chatham House Publishers, 1995.

Haynes, John Earl. *Red Scare or Red Menace? American Communism and Anticommunism in the Cold War Era.* Chicago: Ivan R. Dee, 1996.

Haynes, John Earl, and Harvey Klehr. *In Denial: Historians, Communism, and Espionage.* San Francisco: Encounter Books, 2003.

———. *Venona: Decoding Soviet Espionage in America.* New Haven: Yale University Press, 1999.

Heinrichs, Waldo. *Threshold of War: Franklin D. Roosevelt and American Entry into World War II.* New York: Oxford University Press, 1988.

Hekma, Gert, Harry Oosterhuis, and James Steakley, eds. *Gay Men and the Sexual History of the Political Left.* New York: Harrington Park Press, 1995.

Herken, Gregg. *Brotherhood of the Bomb.* New York: Henry Holt, 2002.

Herman, Arthur. *Joseph McCarthy: Reexamining the Life and Legacy of America's Most Hated Senator.* New York: Free Press, 2000.

Hersh, Seymour M. *Chain of Command: The Road from 9/11 to Abu Ghraib.* New York: HarperCollins, 2004.

———. *The Dark Side of Camelot.* Boston: Little, Brown, 1997.

Herzstein, Robert Edward. *Roosevelt and Hitler: Prelude to War.* New York: Paragon, 1989.

Higgs, Robert. *Crisis and Leviathan: Critical Episodes in the Growth of American Government.* New York: Oxford University Press, 1987.

Higham, John. *Strangers in the Land: Patterns of American Nativism, 1860–1925.* 1955. Reprint, New Brunswick, N.J.: Rutgers University Press, 1994.

Hinckle, Warren, and William Turner. *Deadly Secrets: The CIA-Mafia War against Castro and the Assassination of JFK.* New York: Thunder's Mouth Press, 1992.

Hodgson, Godfrey. *Woodrow Wilson's Right Hand: The Life of Colonel Edward M. House.* New Haven: Yale University Press, 2006.

Hofstadter, Richard. *The Paranoid Style in American Politics and Other Essays.* 1964. Reprint, Cambridge, Mass.: Harvard University Press, 1996.

Holland, Max. *The Kennedy Assassination Tapes.* New York: Knopf, 2004.

Holloway, David. *Stalin and the Bomb: The Soviet Union and Atomic Energy, 1939–1956*. New Haven: Yale University Press, 1994.

Hoover, J. Edgar. *Masters of Deceit*. New York: Henry Holt, 1958.

———. *A Study of Communism*. New York: Holt, Rinehart, and Winston, 1962.

Hosty, James P., Jr., with Thomas Hosty. *Assignment Oswald*. New York: Arcade Publishing, 1996.

Hougan, James. *Secret Agenda: Watergate, Deep Throat, and the CIA*. New York: Random House, 1984.

House, Edward Mandell. *Philip Dru: Administrator. A Story of Tomorrow*. New York: B. W. Huebsch, 1912.

Hubbell, Webb. *Friends in High Places: Our Journey from Little Rock to Washington, D.C.* New York: William Morrow, 1997.

Hunter, Edward. *Brain-Washing in Red China*. New York: Edward Hunter, 1953.

Isikoff, Michael, and David Corn. *Hubris: The Inside Story of Spin, Scandal, and the Selling of the Iraq War*. New York: Crown, 2006.

Jameson, Fredric. "Cognitive Mapping." In *Marxism and the Interpretation of Culture*, ed. Lawrence Grossberg and Cary Nelson, 347–57. Urbana: University of Illinois Press, 1988.

Jeffreys-Jones, Rhodri. *Changing Differences: Women and the Shaping of American Foreign Policy, 1917–1994*. New Brunswick, N.J.: Rutgers University Press, 1995.

Jenkins, Philip. *Decade of Nightmares: The End of the Sixties and the Making of Eighties America*. New York: Oxford University Press, 2006.

Jhally, Sut, and Jeremy Earp, eds. *Hijacking Catastrophe: 9/11, Fear, and the Selling of American Empire*. Northampton, Mass.: Olive Branch Press, 2004.

Johnson, David K. *The Lavender Scare: The Cold War Persecution of Gays and Lesbians in the Federal Government*. Chicago: University of Chicago Press, 2004.

Johnson, Loch, ed. *Handbook of Intelligence Studies*. London: Routledge, 2007.

———. *A Season of Inquiry: Congress and Intelligence*. Chicago: Dorsey Press, 1988.

Jonas, Manfred. *Isolationism in America: 1935–1941*. Ithaca, N.Y.: Cornell University Press, 1966.

Jones, James H. *Bad Blood: The Tuskegee Syphilis Experiment*. 1981. Reprint, New York: Free Press, 1993.

Judson, Horace Freeland. *The Eighth Day of Creation: The Makers of the Revolution in Biology*. New York: Simon & Schuster, 1979.

Kahn, Albert E., and Michael Sayers. *Sabotage! The Secret War against America*. New York: Lev Gleason Publications, 1944.

Kahn, David. *The Codebreakers: The Story of Secret Writing*. 1967. Reprint, New York: Scribner, 1996.

Kazin, Michael. *The Populist Persuasion: An American History*. New York: Basic Books, 1995.

Kelin, John. *Praise from a Future Generation: The Assassination of John F. Kennedy and the First Generation Critics of the Warren Report*. San Antonio, Tex.: Wings Press, 2007.

Kempton, Murray. *Part of Our Time: Some Ruins and Monuments of the Thirties*. New York: Simon & Schuster, 1955.

Kennedy, David. *Freedom from Fear: The American People in Depression and War, 1929–1945.* New York: Oxford University Press, 1999.

———. *Over Here: The First World War and American Society.* New York: Oxford University Press, 1980.

Kimball, Jeffrey. *Nixon's Vietnam War.* Lawrence: University Press of Kansas, 1998.

Kimball, Warren F. *The Juggler: Franklin Roosevelt as Wartime Statesman.* Princeton, N.J.: Princeton University Press, 1991.

Kimmel, Husband E. *Admiral Kimmel's Story.* Chicago: Regnery, 1955.

Kin, David George. *The Plot against America: Senator Wheeler and the Forces behind Him.* Missoula, Mont.: John E. Kennedy Publishers, 1946.

Kirkham, James F., Sheldon G. Levy, and William J. Crotty. *Assassination and Political Violence: A Report to the National Commission on the Causes and Prevention of Violence.* Vol. 8. Washington, D.C.: U.S. Government Printing Office, 1969.

Kirkwood, James. *American Grotesque: An Account of the Clay Shaw–Jim Garrison Affair in the City of New Orleans.* New York: Simon & Schuster, 1970.

Kitts, Kenneth. *Presidential Commissions and National Security: The Politics of Damage Control.* Boulder, Colo.: Lynne Rienner Publishers, 2006.

Knight, Peter. *Conspiracy Culture: From the Kennedy Assassination to the X-Files.* London: Routledge, 2000.

———. *Conspiracy Nation: The Politics of Paranoia in Postwar America.* New York: New York University Press, 2002.

Koistinen, Paul A. C. *The Military-Industrial Complex: A Historical Perspective.* New York: Praeger, 1980.

Kornbluh, Peter, and Malcolm Byrne, eds. *The Iran-Contra Scandal: The Declassified History.* New York: New Press, 1993.

Kubek, Anthony. *Communism at Pearl Harbor: How the Communists Helped to Bring on Pearl Harbor and Open Up Asia to Communism.* Dallas: Teacher Publishing Company, undated.

———. *How the Far East Was Lost: American Policy and the Creation of Communist China, 1941–1949.* Chicago: Regnery, 1963.

Kutler, Stanley I. *Abuse of Power: The New Nixon Tapes.* New York: Free Press, 1997.

———. *The American Inquisition: Justice and Injustice in the Cold War.* New York: Hill and Wang, 1982.

———. *The Wars of Watergate: The Last Crisis of Richard Nixon.* New York: Knopf, 1990.

Lafeber, Walter. *The American Age: United States Foreign Policy at Home and Abroad since 1750.* New York: Norton, 1989.

Lambert, Patricia. *False Witness: The Real Story of Jim Garrison's Investigation and Oliver Stone's Film* JFK. New York: M. Evans, 1998.

Lamont, Edward M. *Ambassador from Wall Street: The Story of Thomas W. Lamont, J. P. Morgan's Chief Executive.* Lanham, Md.: Madison Books, 1994.

Lamphere, Robert J., with Tom Shachtman. *The FBI-KGB War: A Special Agent's Story.* New York: Random House, 1986.

Lamy, Philip. *Millennium Rage: Survivalists, White Supremacists, and the Doomsday Prophecy*. New York: Plenum Press, 1996.

Lane, Mark. *Rush to Judgment*. New York: Holt, Rinehart & Winston, 1966.

Larson, Bruce L. *Lindbergh of Minnesota: A Political Biography*. New York: Harcourt Brace Jovanovich, 1971.

Lasch, Christopher. *The New Radicalism in America*. New York: Norton, 1965.

Lattimore, Owen. *Ordeal by Slander*. Boston: Little, Brown, 1950.

Lavery, David, Angela Hague, and Marla Cartwright, eds. *"Deny All Knowledge": Reading "The X-Files."* Syracuse, N.Y.: Syracuse University Press, 1996.

Leigh, Michael. *Mobilizing Consent: Public Opinion and American Foreign Policy, 1937–1947*. Westport, Conn.: Greenwood, 1976.

Leuchtenberg, William. *The Perils of Prosperity, 1914–32*. 1958. Reprint, Chicago: University of Chicago Press, 1993.

Levine, Isaac Don. *Eyewitness to History: Memoirs and Reflections of a Foreign Correspondent for Half a Century*. New York: Hawthorn, 1973.

Lewis, Richard Warren, and Lawrence Schiller. *The Scavengers and Critics of the Warren Report*. New York: Delacorte Press, 1967.

Lifton, David. *Best Evidence: Disguise and Deception in the Assassination of John F. Kennedy*. New York: Macmillan, 1980.

Lindbergh, Charles A. *Banking and Currency and the Money Trust*. Washington, D.C.: National Capital Press, 1913.

———. *Why Your Country Is at War and What Happens to You after the War, and Related Subjects*. Washington, D.C.: National Capital Press, 1917.

Link, Arthur S. *Wilson: Campaigns for Progressivism and Peace, 1916–1917*. Princeton, N.J.: Princeton University Press, 1965.

———. *Wilson: The Struggle for Neutrality: 1914–1915*. Princeton, N.J.: Princeton University Press, 1960.

Lipset, Seymour Martin, and Earl Raab. *The Politics of Unreason: Right-Wing Extremism in America, 1790–1977*. Chicago: University of Chicago Press, 1978.

Lipset, Seymour Martin, and William Schneider. *The Confidence Gap: Business, Labor, and Government in the Public Mind*. Baltimore: Johns Hopkins University Press, 1983.

Lipstadt, Deborah E. *Denying the Holocaust: The Growing Assault on Truth and Memory*. New York: Free Press, 1993.

Lowitt, Richard. *George W. Norris: The Persistence of a Progressive, 1913–1933*. Urbana: University of Illinois Press, 1971.

Lowi, Theodore J. *The End of Liberalism: The Second Republic of the United States*. New York: Norton, 1979.

———. *The Personal President: Power Invested, Promise Unfulfilled*. Ithaca, N.Y.: Cornell University Press, 1985.

Lubin, David M. *Shooting Kennedy: JFK and the Culture of Images*. Berkeley: University of California Press, 2003.

Lukas, J. Anthony. *Nightmare: The Underside of the Nixon Years*. New York: Penguin, 1988.

Lusane, Clarence. *Pipe Dream Blues: Racism and the War on Drugs*. Boston: South End Press, 1991.

Macdonald, Andrew. *The Turner Diaries*. 1978. Reprint, New York: Barricade Books, 1996.

MacDonnell, Francis. *Insidious Foes: The Axis Fifth Column and the American Home Front*. New York: Oxford University Press, 1995.

Mailer, Norman. *Oswald's Tale: An American Mystery*. New York: Random House, 1995.

Manchester, William. *The Death of a President, November 20–November 25, 1963*. New York: Harper & Row, 1967.

Marks, John. *The Search for the "Manchurian Candidate": The CIA and Mind Control*. New York: Times Books, 1979.

Marrs, Jim. *The Terror Conspiracy: Deception, 9/11, and the Loss of Liberty*. New York: Disinformation, 2006.

Marrs, Texe. *Dark Majesty: The Secret Brotherhood and the Magic of a Thousand Points of Light*. Austin, Tex.: Living Truth Publishers, 1992.

May, Ernest R., ed. *Knowing One's Enemies: Intelligence Assessment before the Two World Wars*. Princeton, N.J.: Princeton University Press, 1984.

May, Gary. *China Scapegoat: The Diplomatic Ordeal of John Carter Vincent*. Washington, D.C.: New Republic Books, 1979.

McAndrew, James. *The Roswell Report: Case Closed*. Washington, D.C.: Headquarters, U.S. Air Force, 1994.

McCarthy, Joseph R. *America's Retreat from Victory: The Story of George Catlett Marshall*. 1951. Reprint, Boston: Western Islands, 1965.

McClellan, Scott. *What Happened: Inside the Bush White House and Washington's Culture of Deception*. New York: PublicAffairs, 2008.

McGerr, Michael. *A Fierce Discontent: The Rise and Fall of the Progressive Movement in America, 1870–1920*. New York: Free Press, 2003.

McKnight, Gerald D. *Breach of Trust: How the Warren Commission Failed the Nation and Why*. Lawrence: University Press of Kansas, 2005.

McMillan, Priscilla Johnson. *Marina and Lee*. New York: Harper & Row, 1977.

Meagher, Sylvia. *Accessories after the Fact: The Warren Commission, the Authorities, and the Report*. Indianapolis: Bobbs-Merrill, 1967.

———. *Subject Index to the Warren Report and Hearings and Exhibits*. New York: Scarecrow Press, 1966.

Melley, Timothy. *Empire of Conspiracy: The Culture of Paranoia in Postwar America*. Ithaca, N.Y.: Cornell University Press, 2000.

Melosi, Martin V. *The Shadow of Pearl Harbor: Political Controversy over the Surprise Attack, 1941–1946*. College Station: Texas A&M University Press, 1977.

Meyssan, Thierry. *9/11: The Big Lie*. London: Carnot Publishing, 2002.

Michel, Lou, and Dan Herbeck. *American Terrorist: Timothy McVeigh and the Oklahoma City Bombing*. New York: Regan Books, 2001.

Mintz, Frank Paul. *Revisionism and the Origins of Pearl Harbor*. Lanham, Md.: University Press of America, 1985.

Moore, Carol. *The Davidian Massacre: Disturbing Questions about Waco Which Must Be Answered*. Franklin, Tenn.: Legacy Communications and Gun Owners Foundation, 1995.

Moore, Michael. *Dude, Where's My Country?* New York: Warner Books, 2003.

Morgenstern, George. *Pearl Harbor: The Story of the Secret War*. New York: Devin-Adair, 1947.

Morone, James A. *The Democratic Wish: Popular Participation and the Limits of American Government*. New Haven: Yale University Press, 1998.

Moser, John. *Right Turn: John T. Flynn and the Transformation of American Liberalism*. New York: New York University Press, 2005.

Moyers, Bill. *The Secret Government: The Constitution in Crisis*. Cabin John, Md.: Seven Locks Press, 1988.

Moynihan, Daniel Patrick. *Secrecy: The American Experience*. New Haven: Yale University Press, 1998.

Mueller, John E. *War, Presidents, and Public Opinion*. New York: Wiley, 1973.

Mullins, Eustace. *The Federal Reserve Conspiracy*. Union, N.J.: Common Sense, 1954.

Mulloy, D. J. *American Extremism: History, Politics, and the Militia Movement*. London: Routledge, 2004.

Murphy, Paul L. *World War I and the Origin of Civil Liberties in the United States*. New York: Norton, 1979.

Nixon, Richard M. *RN: The Memoirs of Richard Nixon*. New York: Grosset & Dunlap, 1978.

———. *Six Crises*. Garden City, N.Y.: Doubleday, 1962.

Noonan, Peggy. *What I Saw at the Revolution: A Political Life in the Reagan Era*. New York: Random House, 1990.

Novick, Peter. *That Noble Dream: The "Objectivity Question" and the American Historical Profession*. Cambridge, England: Cambridge University Press, 1988.

Nye, Joseph S., Jr., Philip D. Zelikow, and David C. King. *Why People Don't Trust Government*. Cambridge, Mass.: Harvard University Press, 1997.

Oglesby, Carl. *The Yankee and Cowboy War: Conspiracies from Dallas to Watergate*. Kansas City, Mo.: Sheed Andrews and McMeel, 1976.

Olmsted, Kathryn S. *Challenging the Secret Government: The Post-Watergate Investigations of the CIA and FBI*. Chapel Hill: University of North Carolina Press, 1996.

———. *Red Spy Queen: A Biography of Elizabeth Bentley*. Chapel Hill: University of North Carolina Press, 2002.

O'Reilly, Kenneth. *Hoover and the Un-Americans: The FBI, HUAC, and the Red Menace*. Philadelphia: Temple University Press, 1983.

O'Rourke, Kevin H., and Jeffrey G. Williamson. *Globalization and History: The Evolution of a Nineteenth-Century Atlantic Economy*. Cambridge, Mass.: MIT Press, 1999.

Oshinsky, David M. *A Conspiracy So Immense: The World of Joe McCarthy*. New York: Free Press, 1983.

Parish, Jane, and Martin Parker. *The Age of Anxiety: Conspiracy Theory and the Human Sciences*. Oxford: Blackwell, 2001.

Paterson, Thomas G. *Contesting Castro: The United States and the Triumph of the Cuban Revolution*. New York: Oxford University Press, 1994.

Patterson, James T. *Congressional Conservatism and the New Deal: The Growth of the Conservative Coalition in Congress, 1933–1939*. Lexington: University of Kentucky Press, 1967.

———. *Mr. Republican: A Biography of Robert A. Taft*. Boston: Houghton Mifflin, 1972.

Paxson, Frederic L., Edward S. Corwin, and Samuel B. Harding. *War Cyclopedia: A Handbook for Reader Reference on the Great War*. Washington, D.C.: U.S. Government Printing Office, 1918.

Pearson, Drew. *Diaries: 1949–1959*. New York: Holt, Rinehart and Winston, 1974.

Peebles, Curtis. *Watch the Skies: A Chronicle of the Flying Saucer Myth*. Washington, D.C.: Smithsonian Institution Press, 1994.

Peterson, H. C., and Gilbert C. Fite. *Opponents of War, 1917–1918*. Madison: University of Wisconsin Press, 1957.

Phelan, James. *Scandals, Scamps, and Scoundrels: The Casebook of an Investigative Reporter*. New York: Random House, 1982.

Pipes, Daniel. *Conspiracy: How the Paranoid Style Flourishes and Where It Comes From*. New York: Free Press, 1997.

Polenberg, Richard. *Reorganizing Roosevelt's Government: The Controversy over Executive Reorganization, 1936–1939*. Cambridge, Mass.: Harvard University Press, 1966.

Posner, Gerald. *Case Closed: Lee Harvey Oswald and the Assassination of JFK*. New York: Random House, 1993.

Prange, Gordon. *At Dawn We Slept: The Untold Story of Pearl Harbor*. New York: Penguin, 1981.

Preston, William, Jr. *Aliens and Dissenters: Federal Suppression of Radicals, 1903–1933*. Urbana: University of Illinois, 1963.

Quinley, Harold E., and Charles Y. Glock. *Anti-Semitism in America*. New York: Free Press, 1979.

Radosh, Ronald. *Prophets on the Right: Profiles of Conservative Critics of American Globalism*. New York: Simon & Schuster, 1975.

Radosh, Ronald, and Joyce Milton. *The Rosenberg File*. New York: Holt, Rinehart, and Winston, 1983.

Ranelagh, John. *The Agency: The Rise and Decline of the CIA*. London: Weidenfeld and Nicolson, 1986.

Rauchway, Eric. *Murdering McKinley: The Making of Theodore Roosevelt's America*. New York: Hill and Wang, 2003.

Reeves, Richard. *President Kennedy: Profile of Power*. New York: Simon & Schuster, 1993.

Reinarman, Craig, and Harry G. Levine, eds. *Crack in America: Demon Drugs and Social Justice*. Berkeley: University of California Press, 1997.

Ribuffo, Leo P. *The Old Christian Right: The Protestant Far Right from the Great Depression to the Cold War*. Philadelphia: Temple University Press, 1983.

Rich, Frank. *The Greatest Story Ever Sold: The Decline and Fall of Truth from 9/11 to Katrina*. New York: Penguin, 2006.

Ridgeway, James. *The Five Unanswered Questions about 9/11: What the 9/11 Commission Report Failed to Tell Us*. New York: Seven Stories Press, 2005.

Riebling, Mark. *Wedge: The Secret War between the FBI and CIA*. New York: Knopf, 1994.

Risen, James. *State of War: The Secret History of the CIA and the Bush Administration*. New York: Free Press, 2006.

Roberts, Charles. *The Truth about the Assassination*. New York: Grosset & Dunlap, 1967.

Roberts, Priscilla. "A Conflict of Loyalties: Kuhn, Loeb and Company and the First World War, 1914–1917." In *Studies in the American Jewish Experience*, vol. 2, eds. Jacob R. Marcus and Abraham J. Peck, 6–32. Lanham, Md.: University Press of America, 1984.

Roberts, Sam. *The Brother: The Untold Story of Atomic Spy David Greenglass and How He Sent His Sister, Ethel Rosenberg, to the Electric Chair*. New York: Random House, 2001.

Robin, Corey. *Fear: The History of a Political Idea*. New York: Oxford University Press, 2004.

Robins, Robert S., and Jerrold M. Post. *Political Paranoia: The Psychopolitics of Hatred*. New Haven: Yale University Press, 1997.

Rogin, Michael Paul. *Ronald Reagan, the Movie, and Other Episodes in Political Demonology*. Berkeley: University of California Press, 1987.

Rollins, Richard. *I Find Treason: The Story of an American Anti-Nazi Agent*. New York: William Morrow, 1941.

Romerstein, Herbert, and Eric Breindel. *The Venona Secrets: Exposing Soviet Espionage and America's Traitors*. New York: Regnery, 2001.

Roosevelt, Eleanor. *This I Remember*. New York: Harper & Brothers, 1949.

Roosevelt, Elliott, ed. *The Roosevelt Letters: Being the Personal Correspondence of Franklin Delano Roosevelt*, vol. 3 (1928–1945). London: George G. Harrap, 1952.

Rosenberg, Emily. *A Date Which Will Live: Pearl Harbor in American Memory*. Durham, N.C.: Duke University Press, 2003.

Rovere, Richard H. *Senator Joe McCarthy*. New York: Harper & Row, 1959.

Rozell, Mark J. *The Press and the Ford Presidency*. Ann Arbor: University of Michigan Press, 1992.

Rudgers, David F. *Creating the Secret State: The Origins of the Central Intelligence Agency, 1943–1947*. Lawrence: University Press of Kansas, 2000.

Ruppert, Michael C. *Crossing the Rubicon: The Decline of the American Empire at the End of the Age of Oil*. Gabriola Island, Canada: New Society Publishers, 2004.

Russo, Gus. *Live by the Sword: The Secret War against Castro and the Death of JFK*. Baltimore: Bancroft Press, 1998.

Ryan, Michael, and Douglas Kellner. *Camera Politica: The Politics and Ideology of Contemporary Film*. Bloomington: Indiana University Press, 1988.

Ryley, Thomas W. *A Little Group of Willful Men: A Study of Congressional-Presidential Authority*. Port Washington, N.Y.: National University Publications, 1975.

Salisbury, Harrison. *A Journey for Our Times: A Memoir*. New York: Harper & Row, 1983.

Savage, Charlie. *Takeover: The Return of the Imperial Presidency and the Subversion of American Democracy*. New York: Little, Brown, 2007.

Schaller, Michael. *Reckoning with Reagan: America and Its President in the 1980s.* New York: Oxford University Press, 1992.

Schecter, Jerrold, and Leona Schecter. *Sacred Secrets: How Soviet Intelligence Operations Changed American History.* Washington, D.C.: Brassey's, 2002.

Schell, Jonathan. *The Time of Illusion.* New York: Vintage, 1976.

Schlesinger, Arthur M., Jr. *The Imperial Presidency.* Boston: Houghton-Mifflin, 1989.

Schoonmaker, Nancy, and Doris Fielding Reid, eds. *We Testify.* New York: Smith and Durrell, 1941.

Schou, Nick. *Kill the Messenger: How the CIA's Crack-Cocaine Controversy Destroyed Journalist Gary Webb.* New York: Nation Books, 2006.

Schrecker, Ellen, ed. *Cold War Triumphalism: The Misuse of History after the Fall of Communism.* New York: New Press, 2004.

———. *Many Are the Crimes: McCarthyism in America.* Princeton, N.J.: Princeton University Press, 1998.

Schudson, Michael. *Watergate in American Memory: How We Remember, Forget, and Reconstruct the Past.* New York: Basic Books, 1992.

Schwartz, Delmore. *The Ego Is Always at the Wheel: Bagatelles.* Ed. Robert Phillips. New York: New Directions, 1986.

Seldes, George. *Iron, Blood and Profits: An Exposure of the World-Wide Munitions Racket.* New York: Harper, 1934.

Seymour, Charles, ed. *The Intimate Papers of Colonel House.* Vol. 1. Boston, 1926.

Shenon, Philip. *The Commission: The Uncensored History of the 9/11 Investigation.* New York: Twelve, 2008.

Shils, Edward A. *The Torment of Secrecy: The Background and Consequences of American Security Policies.* Glencoe, Ill.: Free Press, 1956.

Showalter, Elaine. *Hystories: Hysterical Epidemics and Modern Culture.* New York: Columbia University Press, 1997.

Sibley, Katherine A. S. *Red Spies in America: Stolen Secrets and the Dawn of the Cold War.* Lawrence: University Press of Kansas, 2004.

Simon, Art. *Dangerous Knowledge: The Kennedy Assassination in Art and Film.* Philadelphia: Temple University Press, 1996.

Skidelsky, Robert. *John Maynard Keynes*, Vol. 3: *Fighting for Britain, 1937–1946.* London: Macmillan, 2000.

Smist, Frank. *Congress Oversees the United States Intelligence Community, 1947–1989.* Knoxville: University of Tennessee Press, 1990.

Smith, Geoffrey S. *To Save a Nation: American "Extremism," the New Deal, and the Coming of World War II.* 1973. Revised, Chicago: Ivan R. Dee, 1992.

Smith, Richard Norton. *Thomas E. Dewey and His Times.* New York: Simon & Schuster, 1982.

Smith, Robert C., and Richard Seltzer. *Contemporary Controversies and the American Racial Divide.* Lanham, Md.: Rowman & Littlefield, 2000.

Stenehjem, Michele Flynn. *An American First: John T. Flynn and the America First Committee.* New Rochelle, N.Y.: Arlington House, 1976.

Stern, Kenneth S. *A Force upon the Plain: The American Militia Movement and the Politics of Hate*. New York: Simon & Schuster, 1996.

Stinnett, Robert. *Day of Deceit: The Truth about FDR and Pearl Harbor*. New York: Free Press, 1999.

Strasser, Steven, ed. *The 9/11 Investigations*. New York: Public Affairs, 2004.

Strout, Lawrence N. *Covering McCarthyism: How the* Christian Science Monitor *Handled Joseph R. McCarthy, 1950–1954*. Westport, Conn.: Greenwood, 1999.

Sullivan, William C., with Bill Brown. *The Bureau: My Thirty Years in Hoover's FBI*. New York: Norton, 1979.

Summers, Anthony. *Not in Your Lifetime*. New York: Marlowe, 1998.

Summers, Anthony, with Robbyn Swan. *The Arrogance of Power: The Secret World of Richard Nixon*. New York: Viking, 2000.

Suskind, Ron. *The Price of Loyalty: George W. Bush, the White House, and the Education of Paul O'Neill*. New York: Simon & Schuster, 2004.

Talbot, David. *Brothers: The Hidden History of the Kennedy Years*. New York: Free Press, 2007.

Tanenhaus, Sam. *Whittaker Chambers*. New York: Random House, 1997.

Tansill, Charles. *Back Door to War: The Roosevelt Foreign Policy, 1933–1941*. Chicago: Regnery, 1952.

Tarpley, Webster Griffin. *9/11 Synthetic Terror: Made in USA*. Joshua Tree, Calif.: Progressive Press, 2006.

Teixeira, Ruy A., and Joel Rogers. *America's Forgotten Majority: Why the White Working Class Still Matters*. New York: Basic Books, 2001.

Theobald, Robert A. *The Final Secret of Pearl Harbor: The Washington Contribution to the Japanese Attack*. New York: Devin-Adair, 1954.

Theoharis, Athan G. *The Boss: J. Edgar Hoover and the Great American Inquisition*. Philadelphia: Temple University Press, 1988.

———. *The Yalta Myths: An Issue in U.S. Politics, 1945–1955*. Columbia: University of Missouri Press, 1970.

Thomas, Evan. *Robert Kennedy: His Life*. New York: Simon & Schuster, 2000.

Thompson, Josiah. *Six Seconds in Dallas: A Microstudy of the Kennedy Assassination*. New York: Bernard Geis Associates, 1967.

Thompson, Paul. *The Terror Timeline: Year by Year, Day by Day, Minute by Minute. A Comprehensive Chronicle of the Road to 9/11—and America's Response*. New York: Regan Books, 2004.

Todd, Lewis Paul. *Wartime Relations of the Federal Government and the Public Schools, 1917–1918*. 1945. Reprint, New York: Arno Press and the New York Times, 1971.

Toland, John. *Infamy: Pearl Harbor and Its Aftermath*. New York: Doubleday, 1982.

Trohan, Walter. *Political Animals: Memoirs of a Sentimental Cynic*. Garden City, N.Y.: Doubleday, 1975.

Troy, Thomas F. *Donovan and the CIA: A History of the Establishment of the Central Intelligence Agency*. Washington, D.C.: Center for the Study of Intelligence, 1981.

Turner, John Kenneth. *Shall It Be Again?* New York: B. W. Huebsch, 1922.

Turner, Patricia A. *I Heard It through the Grapevine: Rumor in African-American Culture.* Berkeley: University of California Press, 1993.

Turner, Stansfield. *Secrecy and Democracy: The CIA in Transition.* Boston: Houghton Mifflin, 1985.

Vankin, Jonathan. *Conspiracies, Cover-Ups and Crimes.* Lilburn, Ga.: IllumiNet Press, 1996.

Vidal, Gore. *Perpetual War for Perpetual Peace: How We Got to Be So Hated.* New York: Thunder's Mouth Press/Nation Books, 2002.

———. *United States: Essays, 1952–1992.* New York: Random House, 1993.

Walsh, Lawrence E. *Firewall: The Iran-Contra Conspiracy and Cover-Up.* New York: Norton, 1997.

———. *Iran-Contra: The Final Report.* New York: Times Books, 1994.

Wang, Jessica. *American Science in an Age of Anxiety: Scientists, Anticommunism, and the Cold War.* Chapel Hill: University of North Carolina Press, 1999.

Webb, Gary. *Dark Alliance: The CIA, the Contras, and the Crack Cocaine Explosion.* New York: Seven Stories Press, 1998.

Weinstein, Allen. *Perjury: The Hiss-Chambers Case.* 1978. Reprint, New York: Random House, 1997.

Weinstein, Allen, and Alexander Vassiliev. *The Haunted Wood: Soviet Espionage in America—The Stalin Era.* New York: Random House, 1999.

Weinstein, Edwin. *Woodrow Wilson: A Medical and Psychological Biography.* Princeton, N.J.: Princeton University Press, 1981.

Weinstein, Harvey M. *Psychiatry and the CIA: Victims of Mind Control.* Washington, D.C.: American Psychiatric Press, 1990.

Welsome, Eileen. *The Plutonium Files: America's Secret Medical Experiments in the Cold War.* New York: Dial Press, 1999.

Wheeler, Burton K., with Paul F. Healy. *Yankee from the West.* Garden City, N.Y.: Doubleday, 1962.

White, G. Edward. *Alger Hiss's Looking-Glass Wars: The Covert Life of a Soviet Spy.* New York: Oxford University Press, 2004.

White, Hayden. *The Content of the Form: Narrative Discourse and Historical Representation.* Baltimore: Johns Hopkins University Press, 1987.

White, Stephen. *Should We Now Believe the Warren Report?* New York: Macmillan, 1968.

Whitehead, Don. *The FBI Story: A Report to the People.* New York: Random House, 1956.

Wilford, Timothy. *Pearl Harbor Redefined.* Lanham, Md.: University Press of America, 2001.

Wilson, Joseph. *The Politics of Truth: A Diplomat's Memoir.* New York: Carroll and Graf, 2005.

Wiltz, John E. *In Search of Peace: The Senate Munitions Inquiry, 1934–36.* Baton Rouge: Louisiana State University Press, 1963.

Wofford, Harris. *Of Kennedys and Kings: Making Sense of the Sixties.* New York: Farrar, Straus & Giroux, 1980.

Wohlstetter, Roberta. *Pearl Harbor: Warning and Decision.* Stanford: Stanford University Press, 1962.

Woodward, Bob. *State of Denial: Bush at War, Part III.* New York: Simon & Schuster, 2006.

————. *Veil: The Secret Wars of the CIA.* New York: Pocket Books, 1988.

Work, Clemens P. *Darkest before Dawn: Sedition and Free Speech in the American West.* Albuquerque: University of New Mexico Press, 2005.

Wrone, David R. ed. *The Freedom of Information Act and Political Assassinations.* Vol. 1. Stevens Point, Wisc.: David R. Wrone, 1978.

————. *The Zapruder Film: Reframing JFK's Assassination.* Lawrence: University Press of Kansas, 2003.

Ybarra, Michael J. *Washington Gone Crazy: Senator Pat McCarran and the Great American Communist Hunt.* Hanover, N.H.: Steerforth Press, 2004.

Zelikow, Philip D., with Condoleezza Rice. *Germany Unified and Europe Transformed: A Study in Statecraft.* Cambridge, Mass.: Harvard University Press, 1995.

Zelizer, Barbie. *Covering the Body: The Kennedy Assassination, the Media, and the Shaping of Collective Memory.* Chicago: University of Chicago Press, 1992.

Ziegler, Charles A., Benson Saler, and Charles B. Moore. *UFO Crash at Roswell: The Genesis of a Modern Myth.* Washington, D.C.: Smithsonian Institution Press, 1997.

Zumwalt, Elmo R., Jr. *On Watch: A Memoir.* New York: Quadrangle/New York Times, 1976.

Government Documents

HEARINGS

President's Commission on the Assassination of President Kennedy. *Hearings before the President's Commission on the Assassination of President Kennedy.* Washington, D.C.: U.S. Government Printing Office, 1964.

U.S. Congress, House Select Committee to Investigate Covert Arms Transactions with Iran and Senate Select Committee on Secret Military Assistance to Iran and the Nicaraguan Opposition. 100th Cong., 1st sess. *Iran-Contra Investigation.* Washington, D.C.: U.S. Government Printing Office, 1988.

————. *Taking the Stand: The Testimony of Lieutenant Colonel Oliver L. North.* New York: Pocket Books, 1987.

U.S. Congress, Joint Committee on the Investigation of the Pearl Harbor Attack. *Hearings before the Joint Committee on the Investigation of the Pearl Harbor Attack.* 39 volumes. 79th Cong., 1st sess. Washington, D.C.: U.S. Government Printing Office, 1946.

U.S. House, Committee on Un-American Activities. *Hearings Regarding Communist Espionage in the United States Government.* 80th Cong., 2d sess. Washington, D.C.: U.S. Government Printing Office, 1948.

U.S. House, Select Committee on Assassinations. *Hearings.* 95th Cong., 2d sess. Washingt
D.C.: U.S. Government Printing Office, 1979.

U.S. House, Subcommittee on Civil and Constitutional Rights of the Committee on t
Judiciary. *Circumstances Surrounding Destruction of the Lee Harvey Oswald Not
Hearings before the Subcommittee on Civil and Constitutional Rights of the Com
mittee on the Judiciary, House of Representatives, on FBI Oversight,* 94th Cong.,
1st and 2d sess., serial 2, pt. 3. Washington, D.C.: U.S. Government Printing Office,
1976.

U.S. Congress, Senate Select Committee on Intelligence and the Permanent Select Committee on Intelligence, House of Representatives. *Joint Inquiry into Intelligence
Community Activities before and after the Terrorist Attacks of September 11, 2001.*
107th Cong., 2d sess. Washington, D.C.: U.S. Government Printing Office, 2004.

U.S. Senate, Foreign Relations Committee. *Treaty of Peace with Germany.* 66th Cong.,
1st sess., August 19, 1919. Washington, D.C.: U.S. Government Printing Office, 1919.

U.S. Senate, Select Committee on Intelligence and the Subcommittee on Health and
Scientific Research of the Committee on Human Resources. *Joint hearings on
Project MKULTRA, the CIA's Program of Research in Behavioral Modification.*
95th Cong., 1st sess., August 3, 1977. Washington, D.C.: U.S. Government Printing
Office, 1977.

U.S. Senate, Select Committee to Study Governmental Operations with Respect to Intel-
ligence Activities. *Hearings, 1975: Unauthorized Storage of Toxic Agents* (vol. 1);
Huston Plan (vol. 2); *Internal Revenue Service* (vol. 3); *Mail Opening* (vol. 4); *The
National Security Agency and Fourth Amendment Rights* (vol. 5); *Federal Bureau of
Investigation* (vol. 6); *Covert Action* (vol. 7). 94th Cong., 1st sess. Washington, D.C.:
U.S. Government Printing Office, 1975.

U.S. Senate, Special Committee Investigating the Munitions Industry. *Hearings.* 40 parts.
74th Cong., 1st sess., 1935. Washington, D.C.: U.S. Government Printing Office.

REPORTS

Commission on CIA Activities within the United States. *Report to the President by the
Commission on CIA Activities within the United States.* Washington, D.C.: U.S. Government Printing Office, 1975.

Danforth, John C. *Interim Report to the Deputy Attorney General Concerning the 1993
Confrontation at the Mt. Carmel Complex, Waco, Texas.* July 21, 2000.

Inouye, Daniel K., and Lee H. Hamilton, chairs. *Report of the Congressional Committees
Investigating the Iran-Contra Affair.* Abridged ed. New York: Times Books, 1988.

National Commission on Terrorist Attacks Upon the United States. *The 9/11 Report.* New
York: St. Martin's, 2004.

President's Commission on the Assassination of President Kennedy. *The Warren Report:
The Report of the President's Commission on the Assassination of President John
F. Kennedy.* Washington, D.C.: U.S. Government Printing Office, 1964.

United States Assassination Records Review Board. *Final Report of the Assassination Records Review Board.* Washington, D.C.: U.S. Government Printing Office, 1998.

U.S. Congress, Joint Committee on the Investigation of the Pearl Harbor Attack. *Report of the Joint Committee on the Investigation of the Pearl Harbor Attack.* 79th Cong., 2d sess. Washington, D.C.: U.S. Government Printing Office, 1946.

U.S. Congress, Senate Select Committee on Intelligence and the Permanent Select Committee on Intelligence, House of Representatives. *Report of the Joint Inquiry into Intelligence Community Activities before and after the Terrorist Attacks of September 11, 2001.* 107th Cong., 2d sess. Washington, D.C.: U.S. Government Printing Office, 2004.

U.S. House, Select Committee on Assassinations. *The Final Assassinations Report: Report of the Select Committee on Assassinations.* New York: Bantam, 1979.

U.S. House, Select Committee on Intelligence. *CIA: The Pike Report.* Nottingham, England: Spokesman Books, 1977.

U.S. Senate, Committee on Foreign Relations, Subcommittee on Terrorism, Narcotics, and International Operations. *Drugs, Law Enforcement, and Foreign Policy: A Report.* 100th Cong., 2d sess. Washington, D.C.: U.S. Government Printing Office, 1989.

U.S. Senate, Select Committee on Intelligence. *Report on Whether Public Statements Regarding Iraq by U.S. Government Officials Were Substantiated by Intelligence Information.* 110th Cong., 2d sess. Washington, D.C.: U.S. Government Printing Office, 2008.

U.S. Senate, Select Committee to Study Governmental Operations with Respect to Intelligence Activities. 94th Cong., 1st sess., 1975. *Alleged Assassination Plots Involving Foreign Leaders.* Washington, D.C.: U.S. Government Printing Office, 1975.

U.S. Senate, Select Committee to Study Governmental Operations with Respect to Intelligence Activities. 94th Cong., 2d sess., 1976 (six books). *Final Reports: Foreign and Military Intelligence* (book 1); *Intelligence Activities and the Rights of Americans* (book 2); *Supplementary Detailed Staff Reports on Intelligence Activities and the Rights of Americans* (book 3); *Supplementary Detailed Staff Reports on Foreign and Military Intelligence* (book 4); *The Investigation of the Assassination of President John F. Kennedy: Performance of the Intelligence Agencies* (book 5); *Supplementary Reports on Intelligence Activities* (book 6). Washington, D.C.: U.S. Government Printing Office, 1976.

U.S. Senate, Special Committee Investigating the Munitions Industry. *Preliminary Report on Naval Shipbuilding.* 74th Cong., 1st sess., 1935. Washington, D.C.: U.S. Government Printing Office.

———. *Preliminary Report on Wartime Taxation and Price Control.* 1935.

———. *Report on Activities and Sales of Munitions Companies.* 1936.

———. *Report on Existing Legislation.* 1936.

———. *Report on Government Manufacture of Munitions.* 1936.

———. *Report on War Department Bills.* 1936.

———. *Supplemental Report on the Adequacy of Existing Legislation.* 1936.

Manuscript Collections

Boise State University, Boise, Idaho
    Frank Church Papers
Federal Bureau of Investigation, Washington, D.C.
    Elizabeth Bentley Files
    Hiss-Chambers Files
    Nathan Gregory Silvermaster Files
Gerald R. Ford Library, Ann Arbor, Michigan
    Richard Cheney Files
Hoover Institution, Stanford, California
    America First Committee Files
    Robert Theobald Papers
    Lawrence Dennis Papers
Library of Congress, Washington, D.C.
    Robert A. Taft Papers
National Archives, College Park, Maryland
    JFK Collection
National Archives, Washington, D.C.
    Records of the Special Committee Investigating the Munitions Industry
    Records of the Joint Committee on the Pearl Harbor Attack
    Records of the House Committee on Un-American Activities
Oregon State University, Corvallis
    Linus Pauling Papers
University of California, Davis
    Extremist literature collection, Special Collections
University of Oregon, Eugene
    John T. Flynn Papers
University of Wyoming, Laramie
    Harry Elmer Barnes Papers
    Husband E. Kimmel Papers
Weisberg Archive of the Beneficial-Hodson Library at Hood College, Frederick, Maryland
    Sylvia Meagher Papers

Index

9/11 commission, 60, 214, 216, 219–20, 229–31
9/11 Truth Alliance, 223
9/11 Truth Movement, 222, 224–25, 233, 235

Able Danger, 230
Abrams, Jacob, 1, 18
Acheson, Dean, 91, 97, 99–101, 103–5
Addison's disease, 129
Adelman, Kenneth, 208
Afghanistan, 1, 207, 222
African Americans
    conspiracy theories and, 186–87 (*see also* Tuskegee syphilis experiment)
    theories about spread of crack cocaine, 187–92
Against All Enemies, 219
Al Qaeda, 205, 207–10, 220–21, 230–31
Ali, Muhammad, 153
All Quiet on the Western Front, 29
Allen, Woody, 136
America First Committee, 50, 69, 71–72
American Civil Liberties Union, 70
American Justice Federation, 197

American Legion, 30–31
American militia movement, 195–96
American University address, 133–34
Andrews, Dean, 139
Anticommunist conspiracy theories
    9/11 and, 221
    end of cold war and, 195
    first Red Scare, 19
    Iran-contra and, 178
    Kennedy assassination and, 116, 123, 142, 148
    mind control, 174–75
    Pearl Harbor and, 72–73
    second Red Scare, 92–109, 112
    See also Castro, Fidel: assassination plots against; Operation Northwoods; Soviet espionage
Anti-Semitism
    in anticommunist theories, 103–4
    in far-right theories, 193, 199–200
    in Nixon administration, 149–50, 155
    in Pearl Harbor theories, 52–53, 69–71, 73
    in Populism, 17
    in World War I theories, 36

Area 51, 197, 199
Army-McCarthy Hearings, 106
Aryan Nations, 193
As We Go Marching, 61–62
Assassination Inquiry Committee, 144
Assassination Review Board, 226–27
Atta, Mohammed, 207, 209
Avery, Dylan, 224, 226

Baker, Howard, 222
Baldwin, Roger, 70
Bamford, James, 227
Barber, Steve, 170
Barkley, Alben, 75
Barnes, Harry Elmer, 224
    and opposition to World War II, 47–49, 51
    and Pearl Harbor theories, 60–63, 66, 70, 74, 79
    and World War I revisionism, 22–23, 27–28,
        30, 39 (*see also* World War I)
Barton, Bruce, 63
Batista, Fulgencio, 123
Bausman, Frederick, 23
Bay of Pigs, 113, 124–25, 155–57
Beard, Charles, 21, 39, 41, 51, 79
Bentley, Elizabeth, 88–96, 99
Berlet, Chip, 200
Berlitz, Charles, 184
Bernstein, Carl, 189
Bertrand, Clay. *See* Shaw, Clay
Bin Laden, Osama, 9, 205–7, 211–12, 219–22
Birkhead, L. M., 71
Bissell, Richard, 124
Blair, Tony, 220
Blix, Hans, 210
Bluebird. *See* MKULTRA
Blum, Jack, 188
Body of Secrets, 227
Boggs, Hale, 118
Bolsheviks, 85, 89, 95, 116, 137
Bone, Homer T., 41
Borah, William, 39, 80
Brady Law, 196
Branch Davidians, 196–97, 200–201

Breitweiser, Kristen, 205–6, 212–16, 229, 231
Breitweiser, Ron, 214
Bremer, Arthur, 156
Brewster, Owen, 77, 79
Bryan, William Jennings, 16, 35
Buck, Pearl S., 55
Buckley, William F., 106
Budenz, Louis, 83
Bureau of Alcohol, Tobacco, and Firearms,
    195–98
Bureau of Investigation, 14. *See also* Federal
    Bureau of Investigation
Bureau of Land Management, 198
Bush, George H. W., 183, 194
Bush, George W.
    and 9/11 commission, 205–6, 213
    conspiracy theories about, 1, 5, 221–22,
        225–31, 235, 236–38
    conspiracy theories of, 9, 208–10, 234
    and control of 9/11 narrative, 211, 215,
        220–21
    and domestic surveillance, 163, 228, 239
    intelligence failure on 9/11, 211–15
    and weapons of mass destruction, 208–10,
        216–20

Cameron, Ewen, 177
Campbell, Judith, 125
Cantor Fitzgerald, 215
Carlson, John Roy, 72
Carroll, Jon, 237
Carter, Chris, 7, 202
Carter, Jimmy, 163, 176, 178
Carter, John Franklin, 69
Casazza, Patty, 215
Casey, William 179, 181
Castellano, Lillian, 111–12
Castro, Fidel
    assassination plots against, 113, 119, 123–26,
        134, 147, 162, 165–66, 168, 234–35
    and Kennedy assassination theories, 113,
        116–18, 142, 147, 168–69, 227
    plot to blame for terrorist attack, 2, 227

Catholics, conspiracy theories about, 4, 14

Central Intelligence Agency, 5, 92, 122, 179
 in Bush administration, 209, 212, 217–19,
  225–26, 229
 and congressional investigations after
  Watergate, 162–64
 conspiracy theories about, 113, 140–42,
  145–46, 165–66, 168, 177–78, 186
 in Cuba, 122–23, 125–26, 155
 and drugs, 8, 175–77, 186–92
 and Iran-contra, 179, 181
 and Kennedy assassination theories, 113,
  118–20, 122, 124, 127, 137, 140–42,
  145–46, 168
 in Nixon administration, 153, 156–59
 See also Operation CHAOS

Chamberlain, John, 75, 78

Chambers, Whittaker, 86, 88, 92, 96–97, 100, 110

Checkers speech, 151

Cheney, Dick
 conspiracy theories about, 9, 204, 217, 220,
  222, 228
 conspiracy theories of, 207–11, 236
 views on executive power, 160, 182,
  213, 228

Christian right, 194

Christiansen, Richard, 143

Church, Frank, 6, 160–61, 163–64, 166, 169,
  171, 224

Church Committee, 162–63, 166, 176, 184, 199,
  213, 228, 239

Churchill, Winston, 50, 64

CIA. See Central Intelligence Agency

Citizens Commission to Investigate the FBI, 153

Clark, Bennett, 31, 37–40, 69

Clark, Champ, 31

Clarke, Richard, 208–9, 219

Cleland, Max, 230

Clinton, Bill, 173–74, 196, 198, 208

Clinton, Hillary, 202

Cockburn, Alexander, 147, 200

cold war, 104, 182–83, 195, 203, 227. See also
 anticommunist conspiracy theories

Colson, Charles, 156, 158, 165–66

Committee to Investigate Assassinations, 132

Committee to Re-elect the President, 157

Communist International, 105

Communist Party, 88, 99, 101, 108–9

COINTELPRO, 10, 107–8, 154, 161, 163, 191

Condon, Richard, 175

Connally, John, 127–30, 137

Connally, Nellie, 127, 130

Connally, Tom, 39, 58

Conspiracy theories
 believers of, 11–12, 166–68, 236–37
 history of, 2, 6
 theories about, 2, 5–8, 233–34
 See also entries for individual conspiracy
  theories

Contras, 178–79, 182, 188–89, 191

Cook, Fred, 132

Cooper, John, 118

Cooper, Milton William, 173, 194,
  199–200, 203

Coughlin, Charles, 54

Coulter, Ann, 216

Creel, George, 18

Crick, Francis, 84

Cuordileone, K. A., 105

Currie, Lauchlin, 90

Czolgosz, Leon, 116

Danforth, John C., 196

Dark Alliance, 189–91

Davies, Joseph, 109

Davis, David Brion, 3

Davis, Hope Hale, 88

Dealey Plaza, 114, 134, 144, 156, 167, 169–70

Dealey Plaza Irregulars, 170, 235

Debs, Eugene V., 19

Decker, Bill, 170

Department of Defense, 109, 149, 195, 217, 228

Department of Justice, 4, 69–70, 84, 116–17,
  127, 153, 168. See also Bureau of
  Investigation; Federal Bureau of
  Investigation; Hoover, J. Edgar

Department of State, 100, 104–5, 108, 132, 149, 182, 195

Derounian, Avedis, 72

Detzer, Dorothy, 29–30, 32

Deutch, John, 190

Dewey, John, 71, 238

Dewey, Thomas, 63, 65–67, 93, 185

Diem, Ngo Dinh, 155

Dies, Martin, 72, 80

Donner, Frank, 68

Donovan, William, 122

Downing Street memos, 220

Draper, Theodore, 181

Du Pont, Pierre, 28, 31–33, 41

Duelfer, Charles, 217

Duke, David, 221

Dulles, Allen, 118, 126–27, 130

Early, Steve, 68

Eglin Air Force Base, 2

Ehrlichman, John, 157

Eisenhower, Dwight, 103, 106, 113, 123–24, 134, 147, 152, 185

Ellsberg, Daniel, 149–50, 154–57, 159, 166, 218

Enemies List, 152, 158

Engelbrecht, Helmuth, 30, 32

Enterprise, 179, 183, 185

Epstein, Edward, 136, 140, 144

Espionage Act, 4, 14, 18

Fair Play for Cuba, 115

Faludi, Susan, 216

Faulk, John Henry, 132

Fay, Sidney, 22

Federal Aviation Administration, 226

Federal Bureau of Investigation, 5, 84
    dramatized on television and in film, 202–3
    growth and secrecy of, 8, 67–69, 81, 107–8, 152, 161–63, 165–66, 168, 195
    investigating communists, 85–89, 91–94, 100, 102–3, 106–9
    investigating far-right groups, 193, 195–96

Kennedy assassination, 111–12, 114, 118–22, 127–29, 132, 137, 139
    role in Bush administration, 209, 211–12, 214, 226, 229
    role in Nixon administration, 152–54, 157–59
    See also Bureau of Investigation; COINTELPRO; Hoover, J. Edgar

Federal Emergency Management Administration, 195, 225–26

Federal Reserve Board, 36–37

Fensterwald, Bud, 132

Ferguson, Homer, 75–76, 79, 101–2

Field, Maggie, 111–12, 135, 137

Fish, Hamilton, 47

Flying disks, 183–84, 202, 222

Flynn, John T., 224
    and anticommunism, 73, 95, 103–4, 106–7
    and hatred of Franklin Roosevelt, 47–49, 51, 53, 55
    and Nye Committee, 32
    and Pearl Harbor theories, 60–65, 69–77, 79–81

Ford, Gerald, 6, 118, 177, 213, 228
    and post-Watergate investigations, 158–60, 171

Ford, Henry, 31

Foreign Intelligence Surveillance Act (FISA), 163, 228, 239

Forrestal, James, 73

Fortune, 30

Fourteen Points Speech, 18

Frazier, Joe, 153

Freedom of Information Act, 7, 147, 176, 228

Friends of Democracy, 71

Frost, David, 164

Fuchs, Klaus, 87–88, 99–100

Fulbright, William, 154, 159

Gaddis, John, 104

Gallery, 170

Gallup poll, 159, 166

Garrison, Jim, 11, 138–46, 167, 169, 224, 235

Garson, Barbara, 142–43

George, Walter, 40

Geraldo, 168

Giancana, Sam, 124–25, 162, 165

Glass, Carter, 40

Glenn, John, 2

Globalization, 15

Gold, Harry, 85, 87, 99

Goldman, Emma, 116

Graham, Bob, 212–14, 225

Graham Committee, 212–14

Grattan, C. Hartley, 23, 27

Great Depression, 28–29, 34, 46, 88

Greenglass, David, 87–88, 99

Gregory, Thomas W., 20, 54

Grey, Edward, 27

Griffin, Burt, 126

Griffith, Robert, 101

Groden, Robert, 168

Gulf of Tonkin, 132

Gulf War (1991), 210, 217

Gun control laws, 199. *See also*
    Brady Law

Haldeman, Bob, 149, 154–55, 160,
    168, 218

Hall, Theodore, 87

Hamilton, Lee, 230

Hanighen, Frank C., 30

Hasselbeck, Elisabeth, 229

Helms, Richard, 113, 125, 146

Hersh, Seymour, 159–61

Hezbollah, 180

History Commons, 223

Hiss, Alger
    accused of espionage, 96–100, 102–4, 134
    and Nixon, 97, 149, 151, 155, 165
    and Nye Committee, 32
    and Soviet espionage, 86, 90

Hofstadter, Richard, 3, 10–11, 233, 236

Holland, Max, 140, 146–47

Hollywood, 70–71, 235. *See also* Motion
    pictures, conspiracy theories; Television,
    used to distribute conspiracy theories

Holmes, Oliver Wendell, 19

Holsinger, Joseph, 177

Homosexuality, used by conspiracy theorists,
    105, 108, 139–40, 199–200

Honegger, Barbara, 12

Hoover, Herbert, 55

Hoover, J. Edgar, 4
    anticommunist crusades, 19, 81, 84, 89,
        91–94, 102, 107–9
    in Church Committee investigation,
        162–63, 166
    Kennedy assassination, 113–14, 116, 119–22,
        125, 137, 148
    in Nixon administration, 152, 154
    in Roosevelt administration, 67–69
    See also COINTELPRO; Federal Bureau of
        Investigation

Hopkins, Harry, 57–58

Hosty, James, 120, 166

House, Edward, 24–27, 42–43. *See also*
    World War I

House Intelligence Committee, 164

House Select Committee on Assassinations,
    169–70

House Un-American Activities Committee,
    94–97

Hubbell, Webster, 173–74, 198–99, 235

Hull, Cordell, 56

Hull Ultimatum, 56

Humes, James, 128–29

Humphrey, Hubert, 157

Hunt, E. Howard, 150, 156, 163, 168, 201

Hussein, Saddam, 207–11, 220, 228, 231

Huston, Tom Charles, 152

Huston Plan, 152, 159

I Find Treason, 71

Idiot's Delight, 33

Illuminati, 4, 28, 222

Income tax, 199

Inouye, Daniel, 179

Inquest, 136

Internal Revenue Service, 153

International Monetary Fund, 92, 97, 103

Internet
  used to distribute conspiracy theories, 1, 7,
    189–90, 196, 221–25, 227, 235, 237–38
  YouTube, 224
Iran-contra scandal, 178–83, 185, 188, 191, 193,
    199–200, 202–3, 228
Iraq
  and 9/11 conspiracy theories, 1, 8, 207–9,
    220–22, 228, 236
  alleged weapons of mass destruction, 210–11,
    217–20

Jackson, Jesse, 190
Jefferson, Thomas, 198
Jenkins, Walter, 114, 122
Jersey Girls, 205–6, 214–17, 229–30, 235
Jews, 3, 155, 193. *See also* Anti-Semitism
JFK, 146, 200, 227, 235
John Birch Society, 192, 221
Johnson, David K., 105
Johnson, Hiram, 49–50
Johnson, Hugh, 52
Johnson, Lyndon, 125, 132, 147
  conspiracy theories about, 140, 142, 236–37
  conspiracy theories of, 113, 117, 126
  Nixon's attempts to discredit, 152, 157
  and Warren Commission, 116–19, 130, 148
Joint Chiefs of Staff, 153. *See also* Department
    of Defense
Jonas, Manfred, 53
Jones, Steven E., 226

Kaczynski, Theodore, 201–2
Kahn, Albert E., 71
Kai-shek, Chiang, 55
Kaplan, John, 143
Katzenbach, Nicholas, 117–18
Katzenbach memo, 117–18
Kay, David, 217
Kean, Tom, 230
Kelly, Michael, 193
Kennedy, David, 47
Kennedy, Jacqueline, 117, 127–28

Kennedy, John F., 109, 163
  assassination of, 111, 114, 118–19, 121–27,
    145–46, 162
  conspiracy theories about assassination of, 5,
    7, 112–18, 124–45, 166–69, 173, 185, 189,
    200–201, 222, 224–25, 236–37, 239
  effects of assassination and theories on
    American people, 145–48, 200, 203, 226,
    229, 235
  Nixon's attempts to discredit, 152, 157
Kennedy, Robert, 113, 117, 125–28, 130,
    144–45, 148, 162, 167, 177
Kennedy, Ted, 156–57
Kent, Tyler, 64
Kerry, John, 188, 216
Kerry Committee, 188
KGB, 91, 93, 98, 140, 146. *See also*
    Soviet espionage
Khomeini, Ayatollah Ruhollah, 179–80, 183
Khrushchev, Nikita, 118
Kimmel, Husband E., 57, 62–63, 73–74,
    76–77, 79
King Jr., Martin Luther, 145, 162, 165–67, 169, 234
Kissinger, Henry, 149, 153, 155, 205–6
Knight, Peter, 202
Korean War, 102, 175
Koresh, David, 196
Kornbluh, Peter, 191
Krock, Arthur, 40
Ku Klux Klan, 161, 221
Kuhn-Loeb firm, 36

Lamont, Thomas, 16, 34, 36–38
Lamphere, Robert, 100
Lane, Mark, 136, 140, 167
Lansing, Robert, 35–36, 39, 42
LaRouche, Lyndon, 200
Lasch, Christopher, 146–47
Lattimore, Owen, 102, 109
L'Effroyable Imposture, 222
Lemann, Nicholas, 208
Lend-Lease, 51, 54, 87
Lenin, V. I., 22, 85

Lennon, John, 177
Lewis, Anthony, 159
Libby, I. Lewis, 207, 218
"Liberal media," 149–50
Liberty League, 31
Liddy, G. Gordon, 157
Lifton, David, 136, 144
LIHOP ("let it happen on purpose")
    theorists, 221–22, 229
Lincoln, Abraham, 198
Lindbergh Jr., Charles A.
    and anti-interventionism, 20–21, 45,
        51–53, 69
    anti-Semitism of, 53, 73
    and hatred of Roosevelt, 48, 64
Lindbergh Sr., Charles A.
    and anti-interventionism, 20–21
    books smashed, 13–14, 234
    conspiracy theories of, 13–14, 23, 38, 141
Little, Frank, 20–21
Lodge Jr., Henry Cabot, 50
Long, Huey, 139
Long, Russell, 139
Loose Change, 1–2, 224–26, 229
LSD, 175–77, 234
Luce, Clare Boothe, 45
Luce, Henry, 55
Lusitania, 16

MacArthur, Douglas, 57
MacBird! 142–43
MacLeish, Rod, 165
Mafia
    and anti-Castro plots, 5, 113, 116,
        123–24, 234
    and Kennedy assassination conspiracy
        theories, 147, 170
Magdoff, Harry, 98
"Magic," 57–58, 60, 65–67, 74, 185
"Magic bullet," 128–30, 169
Maheu, Robert, 124
Mailer, Norman, 135
Mann, Thomas, 71

Marcus, Raymond, 134, 142
Marks, John, 176
Marrs, Jim, 222, 226–27
Marrs, Texe, 194
Marshall, George, 57–58, 66, 76, 103, 185
Marshall, Thomas, 21
Masons, 3
Martin, Shirley, 111, 131, 133
May, Alan Nunn, 89
McAdoo, William, 35–37
McCain, John, 213
McCarthy, Joseph, 6, 12, 84, 138, 144, 155, 195
    anticommunist conspiracy theories of,
        100–109
    detrimental effects of, 123–24, 131–32,
        140–141, 167
McCarthyism, 105, 108, 131
McCloy, John, 91, 118
McCone, John, 113
McCormick, Robert, 75
McFarlane, Robert, 179–80
McGovern, George, 156
McKinley, William, 116
McKinney, Cynthia, 221–22
McManus, Bob, 206
McNamara, Robert, 1, 132, 227
McVeigh, Timothy, 197–99, 201–2, 208
Meagher, Sylvia
    index to Warren Report, 111–12, 135
    and Jim Garrison, 139, 143
    organizes Kennedy skeptics, 131–37, 235
    victim of McCarthyism, 108, 131
"Merchants of death" conspiracy theories. See
    World War I
Meyssan, Thierry, 222
MIHOP ("made it happen on purpose")
    theorists, 221–22, 229
Miller, Adolph, 36
Millis, Walter, 29
Mind control, 174–75, 177–78, 186. See also
    Central Intelligence Agency
Mindszenty, Cardinal, 175
Mitchell, John, 150

Mitchell, William, 77

MKULTRA, 175–76, 234. *See also* Central Intelligence Agency; Mind control

Mobsters. *See* Mafia

Moore, Michael, 11

Moore, William L., 184

Morales, Frank, 235

Morgan, Glen, 204

Morgan, House of, 15–16, 24, 34–38, 42, 61. *See also* World War I

Morgan Jr., John Pierpont, 34–37, 41, 43

Morgenstern, George, 79

Mormons, 3

Motion pictures, and conspiracy theories, 202, 223, 230. *See also JFK*

Moussaoui, Zacarias, 212, 214

Moyers, Bill, 199

Moynihan, Daniel Patrick, 182

Mueller, Robert, 229

Mulder, Fox, 202–3, 227

Murrow, Edward R., 106

Muskie, Ed, 157

Mylroie, Laurie, 208

National Academy of Sciences, 170

National Archives, 112, 129, 226

National Association for the Advancement of Colored People, 190

National Institute of Standards and Technology, 226

National Labor Relations Act, 47

National Security Archive, 227

National Security Council, 123, 153, 179, 213, 229. *See also* Rice, Condoleezza

Nativism, 3. *See also* Anti-Semitism; Catholics, conspiracy theories about

Nelson, Steve, 87

Neumann, William, 61

Neutrality Acts of 1935 and 1936, 42, 48

New Deal, 46–47, 67, 70

alleged Communist influence in, 80, 94–98, 107, 109

See also Roosevelt, Franklin

New Left, 142, 167

New York Times, 149, 151–52, 154, 159–60, 170, 176, 183, 191, 218, 233

Nixon, Richard, 115, 174

paranoia of, 9, 149–55, 163–65, 218, 238–39

role in investigating communists, 94, 97, 99, 101, 108

use of government to punish enemies and obstruct justice, 5, 156–58, 167–68

Noonan, Peggy, 179

Norris, George, 17, 23, 33, 51

North, Oliver, 179–83, 199

Novak, Robert, 218

Nye, Gerald, 31–32, 37, 39–43, 45, 48, 50, 69–70, 107

Nye Committee, 31–42, 51, 85, 94

O'Donnell, Kenneth, 128

O'Donnell, Rosie, 229

Oglesby, Carl, 167

Oklahoma City bombing. *See* McVeigh, Timothy

Olson, Frank, 175–76

O'Neill, Paul, 219

Operation CHAOS, 152, 159, 161. *See also* Central Intelligence Agency

Operation Majestic, 12, 185, 222

Operation Midnight Climax, 176–77. *See also* Central Intelligence Agency; LSD; Mind control

Operation Mongoose, 124, 161. *See also* Castro, Fidel; Central Intelligence Agency

Operation Northwoods, 2, 227, 234–35

Operation Staunch, 180

Order, the, 193

Orwell, George, 116

Oswald, Lee Harvey

background of, 113–17

and FBI, 119–22, 166

Johnson administration's conviction that he was lone gunman, 118–19, 128

and Kennedy assassination researchers, 111, 131, 134–35, 139, 141, 145–46, 169 possible motive, 126, 147–48

Oswald, Marina, 115–16, 120

Oval Office tapes, 149, 154, 158, 182

Pacifists. *See* Detzer, Dorothy; Women's
    International League for Peace and
    Freedom

Page, Walter Hines, 24–25, 27–28, 42. *See also*
    World War I

Palmer, A. Mitchell, 13, 53, 81

Parker, Gilbert, 24

Parkland Hospital, 128

Patriot Movement, 193–94

Pauling, Linus, 83–84, 108–9, 119, 132–34

Pearl Harbor attack, 56–59, 185, 238
    and 9/11, 208, 228
    and alleged communist plot, 95, 104
    conspiracy theories about, 5, 7, 45–46, 61–67,
        74–75, 79–81, 147, 155, 218, 221, 235
    official investigations of, 60, 63, 73–74,
        75–79, 130

Pecora, Ferdinand, 35

Pentagon Papers, 149, 154, 159

Pentagon terrorist attack. *See* September 11
    terrorist attacks

People's Party, 17, 23, 31, 33, 36, 38

Philby, Kim, 90–91, 93

Pierce, William, 198, 201–2

Pike, Otis, 164–65, 171

Pike Committee, 164

Pillar, Paul, 209, 219–20

Plumbers, 150, 153, 157, 159

Poindexter, John, 180, 228

Pope, James, 40

Populists. *See* People's Party

Posse Comitatus, 192

Powell, Colin, 210–11, 220

Presidential Medal of Freedom, 229

Project for a New American Century,
    207–8, 228

Prouty, Fletcher, 200

Public opinion polls, 48, 209, 211, 220, 229. *See
    also* Gallup poll

Pumpkin Papers, 97–98

Radio, used to distribute conspiracy theories,
    54, 71, 103, 189–90, 192, 221–22

Rangel, Charles B., 163

Rankin, John, 94

Rauschenbush, Stephen, 31–32, 36, 38, 42–43

Rauschenbusch, Walter, 31

Ray, James Earl, 145, 166, 169

Reagan, Ronald, 12, 177–83, 200

Red Scare, post–World War II, 84–85, 109. *See
    also* Anticommunist conspiracy theories

Reno, Janet, 196

Reorganization Act, 48

Reserve Index, 119

Rice, Condoleezza, 210, 212, 229–30

Roberts, Charles, 137

Roberts, Owen, 60, 118

Roberts Commission, 60, 73

Rockefeller, Nelson, 160

Rockefeller Commission, 60, 160, 175–76

Rollins, Richard, 71

Roosevelt, Eleanor, 48

Roosevelt, Franklin, 6, 73–74
    alleged communist influence on, 84–86, 90,
        95–98, 104
    growth of government powers, 68–70, 80–81,
        107, 118, 142, 238
    New Deal Programs, 46–48, 80
    Nixon's attempts to discredit, 150, 157
    role in Pearl Harbor conspiracy theories, 45,
        61–67, 74–78, 80–81, 218, 221, 236 (*see
        also* Pearl Harbor attack)
    role in World War I investigation, 29, 31,
        41–43
    support for Allies in World War II, 49–56,
        59, 63, 73

Roosevelt, Theodore, 15

Rosenberg, Emily, 59

Rosenberg, Ethel, 88, 134

Rosenberg, Julius, 88, 99, 102, 134

Rosselli, Johnny, 124

Roswell incident, 183–85, 203

Rove, Karl, 218, 230

Rowe, Korey, 229

Ruby, Jack, 11, 120

Ruby Ridge siege, 195–96, 200, 203

Rumsfeld, Donald, 154, 160, 207, 218, 220

Rush to Judgment, 136

Russell, Richard, 118–19, 130

Russian Revolution, 6, 137

Ryan, Leo, 177

Sabotage! The Secret War against America, 71

Safford, Laurance, 76–77

Safire, William, 165

Salandria, Vincent, 133–34

Salinger, J. D., 177

San Jose Mercury News, 188–91

Saudi Arabia, 213, 225, 229

Sayers, Michael, 71

Schorr, Daniel, 159

Schwartz, Delmore, 10

Schweiker, Richard, 168, 177

Scully, Dana, 202–3, 227

Second Amendment, 195, 197

Secret Brotherhood, 194

Security Index, 119, 121

Sedition Act of 1918, 14, 18. *See also*
    Espionage Act

Seldes, George, 30

Senate Munitions Inquiry, 28

September 11 terrorist attacks
    alternative conspiracy theories about, 1, 5, 9,
        11, 221–31, 236, 238
    intelligence failure to predict, 211–14
    official conspiracy theories about, 9, 207–11,
        236, 238
    official investigations of, 205–6, 211–16, 219,
        229–31
    See also 9/11 commission

Sevareid, Eric, 29

Shanklin, Gordon, 120

Shaw, Clay, 139–41, 145–46

Sheen, Charlie, 229

Shenon, Philip, 230

Sherwood, Robert, 33

Shipstead, Henrik, 64

Short, Dewey, 77

Short, Walter, 57–58, 62, 73–74, 76

Sidey, Hugh, 159

Simpson, O. J., 202

Single-bullet theory. *See* "Magic bullet"

Sirhan, Sirhan, 144, 177

Skull & Bones, 194

Smith, George H. E., 63, 78

Somoza, Anastasio, 178

Soviet espionage, 84–93, 97–100, 147, 204

Springsteen, Bruce, 215

Stalin, Joseph, 51, 73, 85–87, 89, 104

Star Wars, 198

Stimson, Henry, 56, 73

Stokes, Louis, 181

Stone, Harlan Fiske, 67

Stone, Oliver, 7, 146, 200, 224, 226–27, 235

Students for a Democratic Society, 167

Suskind, Ron, 211, 225–26

Taft, Robert, 53

Tague, James, 121

Taliban, 207

Tansill, Charles, 61, 79

Television, used to distribute conspiracy
    theories, 106, 168, 173–74, 200, 202–4,
    207, 229

Tenet, George, 229

Theobald, Robert, 79

Thomas, J. Parnell, 94–95

Thompson, Paul, 223, 225, 227

Three Days of the Condor, 168

Trafficante, Santo, 124

Trillin, Calvin, 135

Trochmann, John, 195

Truman, Harry, 6, 157, 175, 183
    creation of CIA, 122–23
    and domestic anticommunism, 91–93, 95,
        97–99, 101–2, 105
    Pearl Harbor investigation, 74–75, 78

Tumulty, Joseph, 40

Turner, Stansfield, 163, 176

Turner Diaries, 197–98, 201

Tuskegee syphilis experiment, 186–87, 191, 203

Tydings, Millard, 102

Unabomber, 201

Unidentified Flying Objects. *See* Flying disks

United Nations, 97, 103, 109, 115, 196, 210, 217, 220

United States federal government
  conspiracy theories promoted by, 9–10, 234, 239–40 (*see also* Bush, George W.; Iran-contra scandal; Johnson, Lyndon; Kennedy, John F.; World War I; World War II)
  distrust of, 1–3, 173–74, 234, 238–39 (*see also* Iran-contra scandal; September 11 terrorist attacks; Vietnam War; Watergate)
  growth of, 4, 8–9, 14, 18, 235–36
  investigations of conspiracy theories by, 6–8, 169–70 (*see also* Church Committee; Graham Committee; Kerry Committee; Nye Committee; Pike Committee; Warren Commission)

U.S. v. McWilliams, 69

USA Patriot Act, 228

U.S.S. Abraham Lincoln, 211

Van Auken, Lorie, 206, 235, 239

Velde, Harold, 99

Venona, 91–92

Vidal, Gore, 201–2

Vietnam War, 179
  distrust generated by, 80, 132–33, 161, 184, 186
  and Kennedy assassination theories, 140, 142–43, 144–45, 167
  and Nixon, 149, 151, 155

Villard, Oswald Garrison, 26–27

Waco siege, 196–97, 200–201, 203

Waits, Tom, 215

Walker, Edwin A., 115, 141–42

Wall Street. *See* World War I: financial interests in

Wallace, DeWitt, 73

Wallace, George, 156–57, 201

Wallace, Henry, 91, 109

Walsh, David I., 59

Warburg, Paul, 36–37

Warren, Earl, 115, 118, 130, 133, 142–44, 148, 239

Warren Commission, 60
  critics of, 131–47, 166–69, 173
  investigation, 118–30

Warren Report. *See* Warren Commission

"Warrenologists," 131

Washington Post, 154

Watergate scandal, 156–60, 178, 182, 222
  distrust caused by, 80, 165–68, 170–71, 184–85, 191, 202–3

Waters, Maxine, 190

Watson, James, 84

Waugh, Evelyn, 106

Weaver, Randy, 195, 200–201

Weaver, Samuel, 195, 200–201

Weaver, Vicki, 195, 200–201

Webb, Gary, 188–93, 199, 235

Weisberg, Harold, 108, 131, 137, 140

Wheeler, Burton K., 69
  anticommunism of, 103, 107
  opposition to vigilantism, 20–21
  suspicion of FDR, 47, 51–55, 64, 72, 81

White, Harry Dexter, 86, 88, 90, 92, 96, 98, 100, 102–4

White, Jack E., 190

Wicker, Tom, 170

Wilkerson, Lawrence, 220

Willkie, Wendell, 53

Wilson, Joseph, 217–18

Wilson, Valerie Plame, 217–18

Wilson, Woodrow, 83, 95
  accused of lying, 39–41, 238
  and intervention in World War I, 15–17, 238
  rhetoric about World War I, 6, 18–19, 21–23, 40–41, 42, 234

Wilson, Woodrow (*continued*)

in World War I conspiracy theories, 25–28,
  33–35, 201
See also World War I
Wolfowitz, Paul, 207–8, 219
Women's International League for Peace and
  Freedom, 29–30
Wood, Robert E., 49, 61, 66
Woodruff, Roy, 59
Woodward, Bob, 189
World Bank, 92
World Health Organization, 108
World Trade Center, 7, 225–26, 229
World Trade Center bombing (1993), 208
World Trade Center Towers. *See* September 11
  terrorist attacks
World War I
  conspiracy theories about
    German Americans in, 20
  conspiracy theories about U.S. entry into,
    7, 13–14, 25, 181, 234 (*see also* Nye
    Committee)
  conspiracy theories set forth by Wilson
    administration, 18–19, 21–22, 234, 239
debate over U.S. entry into, 5, 17
financial interests in, 15–16, 23–24
  (*see also* Morgan, House of;
  Nye Committee)
turning point in growth of government, 4, 15
vigilantism, 20–21
World War II
  debate over U.S. entry into, 5, 61–63, 66
  See also Pearl Harbor attack; Roosevelt,
    Franklin

X-Files, The, 7, 173–74, 202–4, 227

Yalta Conference, 97–98, 104
Young Communist League, 88
Zaharoff, Basil, 32
Zapruder, Abraham, 127
Zapruder film, 127–28, 130–31, 135, 138, 145,
  168, 224
Zedong, Mao, 99
Zelikow, Philip, 230–31
Ziegler, Charles, 184
Zimmermann, Alfred, 16
Zumwalt, Elmo, 153